Kindergartens and Cultures

Kindergartens and Cultures

The Global Diffusion

of an Idea

Edited by Roberta Wollons

Yale University Press

New Haven and London

Published with assistance from the foundation established in memory of William McKean Brown.

Printed in the United States of America.

Library of Congress Cataloging-in-Publication Data
Kindergartens and cultures : the global diffusion of an idea / edited by Roberta Wollons.
        p.   cm.
Includes bibliographical references and index.
ISBN 0-300-07788-2 (cloth : alk. paper)
1. Kindergarten—History—Cross-cultural studies.   I. Wollons, Roberta, Lyn, 1947–
LB1199.K58   2000
372.21′8′09—dc21   99-059627

A catalogue record for this book is available from the British Library.
The paper in this book meets the guidelines for permanence and durability
of the Committee on Production Guidelines for Book Longevity
of the Council on Library Resources.

10 9 8 7 6 5 4 3 2 1

Contents

Acknowledgments

I thank all the contributors for their patience and generosity in the making of this book. Each chapter represents new work, written in response to the question of how the kindergarten was transmitted across national, language, and cultural boundaries, and how that idea was then evaluated and recast by the recipients. The contributors all understood the challenge of looking at the local level to understand global trends, and together demonstrated that theories of diffusion that privilege the originator of ideas while rendering the recipient invisible are at best incomplete. It has been my pleasure to work with these authors, each of whom adds a new perspective and interpretation to the study of education, culture, and the processes of change.

I also thank friends and colleagues who encouraged the project and offered thoughtful criticism along the way: Farid Alatas, Philip Altbach, Arjun Appadurai, Judy Babbitts, Doris Friedensohn, Sonya Michel, and Lynn Stoner. To them I offer thanks and appreciation for their insightful reading and discussions as I was formulating the central ideas of the book. Any errors or flaws that appear in the book, however, are my responsibility.

Support for the book came from the National Endowment for the Humanities and Indiana University Faculty Fellowships and Grants-in-Aid of Research.

Finally, I thank the editorial and production team at Yale University Press, Gladys Topkis, who first saw the potential of the idea, Richard Miller, who has been patient and supportive through the process, and Nancy Moore Brochin, whose editorial skill has much improved the quality of the book.

Introduction

On the International Diffusion, Politics, and Transformation of the Kindergarten

Roberta Wollons

Upon independence from colonial rule in 1945, the Vietnamese government borrowed a model of the post-Tsarist kindergarten from Russia as a proper beginning to a new education system. Anxious to socialize children into a secular nationalistic identity, government educators ignored the French colonial missionary kindergarten models readily available in Hanoi. Rather, preferring a socialist model, Vietnamese educators coopted and recontextualized the Russian version, which had itself been transformed from the original German, founded on Christian moral lessons and the values of liberal individualism.

Drawing on this and other examples, this book is a study of the diffusion and transformation of the kindergarten around the turn of the twentieth century, concentrating most centrally on the immense power of local cultures to respond to and reformulate borrowed ideas. The eleven case studies represent western and nonwestern national histories, various religious traditions, and a range of political systems from democratic to authoritarian, all of which, for diverse reasons, embraced the kindergarten as a desirable educational form. The chapters are organized around three central themes: methods and routes of diffusion by which the kindergarten idea spread around the world; the function of the kindergarten in various political settings as an agent in the formation of national identity; and the cultural transformations that had to occur at the classroom level for parents to comfortably send their children to school.

Whether as a part of large compulsory schooling systems or as small private enterprises, the kindergarten is a politicized institution, directly linked to the goals of the state in the formation of national identity, citizenship, and moral values.[1] However, to parents at the turn of the twentieth century, the kindergarten was identified with modern practices, scientific child-rearing, and a direct connection to emerging global trends.[2] In addition to its primary educational purpose, the kindergarten was a vehicle for socializing others, whether used by middle-class Americans to uplift the children of recent immigrants, by the communist Vietnamese to create a new nationalism, or by pre-independence Israelis to teach Hebrew and prepare children for communal kibbutz life. The dual functions of the kindergarten, to educate and to socialize, present rich texts for analysis, and more so when overlaid with the complexities inherent in cross-cultural transactions.

The kindergarten is a diasporic institution, global in its identification, and, as these chapters show, local in its execution. For our purposes, *kindergarten* is narrowly defined as the institution originating in Germany in the mid-nineteenth century, based on Friedrich Froebel's theory of child development. It began as a specific system of instruction, brought out of Germany by trained teachers who believed in and taught the original codified system. By focusing on this one relatively clear set of principles and educational methods, therefore, it is possible to demonstrate how the kindergarten was altered through the processes of diffusion, recontextualization, and conventionalization. The special example of the kindergarten, with its popularity and wide dissemination, provides an ideal opportunity to show, case by case, how one idea was diffused globally, separated from its original context, and transformed in each setting by local needs.

The kindergarten movement began in Germany with Friedrich Froebel (1782–1852), an educator and visionary figure in the study of early childhood development.[3] Rejecting religious beliefs about the inherent sinfulness of children, Froebel declared that children were essentially good, that a child's will should not be broken but shaped. He divided the process of early education between birth and age six into discrete stages of physical and mental development. For each stage, he devised special exercises, materials, "gifts," and "occupations," which consisted of objects and games carefully designed to teach specific skills and moral lessons.[4] Suspecting that parents were not capable of giving the child the necessary education and discipline, but believing also that the child was not ready for school, he sought an institutional alternative suited to the "wealth, abundance, and vigor of the inner and outer life" of childhood. His solution was the kindergarten, or "child's garden," where the child could be with peers, outside family restraints, yet in a protected environment.

During Froebel's lifetime his ideas were known and respected among the educated middle class, but these ideas did not find sympathy among Prussian government officials. By 1851 Froebel was identified as a nationalist, and kindergartens were banned as revolutionary, as an arm of the socialist movement. Froebel marshaled some resistance to the edict but failed to have it rescinded. He died a year later, frustrated and unaware of the impact his ideas would have over the next several decades, particularly in the United States, where, he had been convinced, the kindergarten would find fertile ground. In the years following the German revolution of 1848 until the 1870s, educators familiar with Froebel's ideas traveled to Britain and the United States and the countries of western Europe, where the kindergarten remained a small movement dominated by an intellectual coterie of Froebel's German disciples.

Within a relatively short period in the latter decades of the nineteenth century, the kindergarten spread with astounding rapidity around the world. By World War I, the kindergarten was a standard feature of education systems in both modern and developing nations throughout Asia, Africa, and the west. The questions raised by this phenomenon are central to current multiple discourses regarding the influences of western culture on national identity globally: has western-style education been a form of imperialism or colonialism; what is the importance of education in the creation of citizenship and national identity; what are the processes of cultural borrowing by which ideas are diffused and transformed, and, most centrally, how do we understand the hybridized result? Although western structures such as the kindergarten have flowed freely from west to east and north to south, the accompanying presumed ideologies of individualism, Christianity, and democracy have not necessarily accompanied these institutions, as the case studies in the following chapters show. On the contrary, these examples reveal the power of local culture, politics, and nationalism to separate the kindergarten from its original context. In each case, local educators transformed, or recontextualized, the kindergarten. Simultaneously, the kindergarten itself drew the local, particularistic ways of thinking into contact with international organizations, movements, and ideas. Moreover, these cases also suggest that the kindergarten did not always flow from the west to other nations—that it was also borrowed among nonwestern nations, disconnected entirely from its origins in the west.

Cultural borrowing is both common and complex. Peoples have always borrowed from one another, creating fusions of art, music, religion, and more over time. The processes of *educational* diffusion among nations are also histories of borrowing. In 1978, Philip Altbach and Gail Kelly proposed applying the concept of colonialism as a frame within which to understand education not only in colonial and post-colonial nations, but also in nations with internal populations living in a colonized state.[5] Post-colonial theorists have expanded this idea, looking to complex political, social, and psychological responses associated with the penetration of "foreign" ideas into a culture.[6] Arjun Appadurai, for example, has suggested that ideas introduced into new societies become quickly indigenized and brought into the service of state ideologies and counter ideologies, creating a local version suited to that context.[7] Signe Howell expands on these ideas by looking not only at the flow of ideas "from the west to the rest," but the flow back again from nonwestern to western cultures, especially in the areas of art, music, and religious practices.[8] She, too, suggests that the infusion of new ideas into a culture may in fact create a heterogeneity of ideas at the local level, rather than creating the homogeneity of culture globally. Recently, the post-colonial theorist Homi Bhabha suggested that "Hybrid products are results of a long history of confrontations between unequal cultures and forces, in which the stronger culture struggles to control, remake, or eliminate the subordinate partner. But even in the case of extremely imbalanced encounters, subordinates have frequently managed to divert the cultural elements they were forced to adopt and have rearranged them for their own sly purposes within a new ensemble."[9] Through the single example of the kindergarten we can see the processes and consequences of cultural borrowing whether from the west, from neighbors, or from cultural relatives. Indeed, as Norman Brosterman observed, "by the time popularity made the kindergarten an essential part of education and daily life, it resembled Froebel's model in outward appearance only."[10]

The way in which the kindergarten was brought to a nation determined its character and purpose. There are two facets to the acquisition of the kindergarten, and it is clear that the one, the form of its introduction, influenced the second, the process of its adoption. Each chapter in this book discusses how the kindergarten was introduced to a particular country, and then focuses primarily on the latter history, the processes, or recontextualization involved in its adoption.

The forms of introduction fall into distinct, and frequently overlapping, categories. Initially, kindergartens were established by the original students and followers of Froebel, who fled after 1848 to North America, Britain, and western Europe, where they founded their own kindergartens and teacher training schools. By the early 1870s and into the 1880s, the first Froebelian kindergartens had taken root in the United States and western Europe.

The primary form of diffusion was through direct acquisition. Broadly, acquisitions can be described by their distance from the original: primary, secondary, and tertiary. Primary acquisitions were those closest to Froebel's original teaching, for example, those adopted by American educators from the few German disciples who came to the United States in the 1850s, and those adopted in Palestine through teachers educated at the Pestalozzi-Froebel Haus in Berlin.

Secondary acquisitions were those models taken from kindergartens that had gone through a process of transformation. As an illustration, Australian educators enthusiastically imported the Americanized (not the British) kindergarten as their model. Similarly, in their own eclectic style, members of the Japanese government traveled to the United States in 1871, where they were introduced to the kindergarten by Susan Blow and Nicolas Butler Murray in St. Louis, and later hired a German woman to direct the first kindergarten training school in Tokyo in 1875. From kindergarten training schools in the United States, France, and Britain, new teachers included Protestant and Catholic missionaries who would bring the kindergarten to Asia, Africa, and Latin America, either attached to colonial governments or as agents of independent Christian missionary agencies.

Tertiary acquisitions were those taken from models twice removed from the original. In China the kindergarten was borrowed directly from Japan rather than from the west. The Chinese were glad to adopt the Japanese version, which they saw as already adapted to a Confucian social order. As the Japanese kindergarten teachers had created curriculum that reinforced Confucian values, it was easier to adopt the Japanese model than to attempt translating western texts and institutions. In another case, where China had adopted a culturally "Asianized" kindergarten model from Japan for reasons of culture and language, the communist Vietnamese borrowed the post-Tsarist model from Russia for political reasons, ignoring the French colonial model in their midst.

Whether in missionary and colonial settings or as a welcomed acquisition, clearly the sub-text of the kindergarten curriculum was not only to nurture and enhance the natural stages of child development, but also to influence core national values and family practices. In Japan, for example, some kindergartens were under the auspices of missionary institutions whose goals were the religious conversion of children and their parents. Others were handled by the education arm of the government, which adopted the kindergarten to aid in the consolidation of a national identity while providing the most "modern" education available to Japanese children. In the Japanese instance, therefore, different forms of the kindergartens coexisted among educators with opposing agendas.

In Turkey, however, the missionary schools were severely limited by a ban on the teaching of Christianity among the Muslim population. Despite the efforts of missionaries, kindergartens were not especially effective as a means of achieving religious conversions. In Muslim Turkey, Buddhist China, and Buddhist/Shinto Japan, the kindergarten was welcomed at the same time that Christianity was banned. And, in secularized Soviet Russia and Vietnam, the kindergarten directors replaced morality of religion with morality of the state.

Once the kindergarten was acquired, it was incorporated into the larger national education system, imbued with unavoidable political meaning. In some instances, as in the case of Vietnam under French rule, missionary kindergartens were identified with colonial regimes and therefore tainted in the eyes of indigenous parents. As part of the nationalization process, newly emerging governments ignored missionary or colonial kindergarten predecessors when establishing their own schools. Thus whether in Vietnam (under post-colonial communism) or Turkey (under a post-Ottoman republic) the ever flexible kindergarten was reintroduced and popularized as an education innovation under the control of the new national regimes.

As the kindergarten became institutionalized around the globe, it took on the values and cultural symbols of those in control of education. The history of the kindergarten is not only a story of the adoption of an innovation in the field of education and pedagogy. It also exposes relationships of unequal power and authority. While colonial settings are obviously examples of unequal power, kindergarten case studies allow us to observe the socialization of one class, one gender, one ethnic group, or one political faction over another inside national boundaries.[11] In the United States, for example, after their introduction to the kindergarten by a small group of German kindergarten advocates, American kindergarten teachers reorganized the institution. Children were taught in English and learned American patriotism and folk tales. Froebel's games and occupations, disdained by American educators as being too rigid, were modified to encourage the development of individuality rather than emphasizing skills in memorization and other perceived symbols of conformity. Gradually, the American kindergarten developed along two tracks: the first was geared to middle-class children whose parents believed in the value of an educational head start; the second was aimed at the children of immigrants and the poor, who (the middle class educators and reformers believed) needed to be Americanized and controlled.

The United States was not unique in regarding the kindergarten as the site of contested cultural, religious, and political goals. In Poland the kindergarten was used subversively by parents to protect and transmit Polish language and culture during the period of partition and foreign rule. In Asia, the kindergarten was used by missionaries in Japan and China to convert to Christianity and thereby "improve" the indigenous people. In Australia, a turn of the century fear of white depopulation added the dimension of race, resulting in policies which denied aboriginal or African children access to education.

It is clear that while the kindergarten appeared rapidly in nation after nation, the transformations required to facilitate such diffusion illustrate that the thing adopted is not always the same as the thing exported. Borrowing nations did not assume a passive mimicry of the foreign institution, nor did they accommodate themselves to the foreign kindergarten. Rather, all borrowing nations exerted powerful cultural and political agency over borrowed ideas, and, as Homi Bhabha pointed out, rearranged them for their own sly purposes and ultimately were transformed themselves in the process.

In the west, the history of the kindergarten has been included in the larger histories of women's social activism and professionalization in education and the social sciences. The history of western women's involvement in the kindergarten movement was closely linked with what Sonya Michel and Seth Koven have called the politics of maternalism.[12] In northern and western Europe, North America, and Australia, women were the main promoters of the kindergarten and the leading contributors to kindergarten theory. They trained kindergarten teachers and were in charge of promoting the kindergarten to public schools and social service agencies as a critical element in the development of the modern child and thereby, via the child, of a modern educated citizenry. Through a legitimized maternal interest in childhood and education, women entered into social and political activism and came to occupy a newly gendered public space, especially in the field of education. Women from the western nations communicated through an international network of newsletters, journals and magazines, and international conferences. Ideas concerning kindergarten education were shared, debated, and modified as the concept of the modern child was re-

fined. Promoting the kindergarten brought western women into the world of
the politics of education at the state and local levels, and into the politics of the
welfare state. Women leaders projected the benefits of the kindergarten not only
onto the children of the middle class, but also onto the children of the working
class and the poor.

In nonwestern countries, however, the role of women was not necessarily
linked with the rise of social welfare. In Japan, for example, education remained
largely in the hands of male leaders in politics and education who were forging
a new welfare state and national identity in the aftermath of opening to the world
in the late nineteenth century. Similarly, in China education was the domain of
a centralized government which chose to include the kindergarten without
changing the position or status of women in society. In the controlled settings
of post-Tsarist Russia, Vietnam, and Japan, womanhood was linked to loyalty
to the state and liberation for the purposes of work, not for individual advancement. These examples support Koven and Michel, who propose that there was
an inverse relationship between the strength of women's political participation
and the strength of the state governments. Indeed, in strong authoritarian governments, the kindergarten was adopted without the activism of women, and
without benefit to women's advancement.

Missionary women universally had special status, existing in two cultures simultaneously: that of their national origin, and that of their adopted missionary field. In late nineteenth century America, women who were educated and
trained for missionary work were clearly both causal agents and beneficiaries of
the spread of the kindergarten. Missionary women who carried the kindergarten
idea to "foreign" places often became leaders and institution builders abroad in
ways that would have been extraordinary or impossible had they remained in
the United States, Britain, or France. In this period the numbers of single women
missionaries abroad became greater than the number of married women missionaries. The foreign mission became a vehicle for an educated, elite corps of
women to create an education system for women and children that was comparable not only to indigenous systems but also to those being built by male missionaries in the same settings, and also to those at home. In Japan, for example,
Kobe College, run by women missionaries, was equal in status to the men's missionary institution, Doshisha University, to the Japanese-run Tokyo Women's
College, and to the model for most women's colleges in the United States, Mt.
Holyoke.

At the same time that American (and other western) missionaries were advancing their religious and educational goals, including an image of woman-

hood based on a western model, they were also confronting the indigenous women with whom they worked and whose children they were educating. The close interactions between individuals from differing traditions described in this book are also documented in such works as Nupur Chaudhuri and Margaret Strobel's *Western Women and Imperialism: Complicity and Resistance.*[13] It is in the missionaries' daily modification of values, traditions, and cultural symbols that one can observe the process of "contextualizing" the kindergarten in a new place. Unlike other proponents of the kindergarten, missionaries became cultural hybrids, influencing and being influenced by the cultures of their adopted fields of service.

The experiences of missionary women in foreign fields are currently understudied, and further research will no doubt lead to greater insights about these reciprocal processes. For example, factors influencing the missionary experience include whether or not a missionary was attached to a colonial government or was an independent agent of the church, whether her mission was educational, medical, or evangelical. It would be important to know if she was bilingual, her class, and her attitude toward the culture of her missionary residence—all factors influencing the degree to which a recontextualized institution could emerge.

Perhaps not surprisingly, as a function of language and the traditions of activism, the international organizations of the kindergarten movement were located in the west. The Froebel Institute in Chicago, along with other American and British centers, trained the kindergarten leaders, who in turn trained others in western and nonwestern settings. Linked through journals and newsletters, the international movement, composed predominantly of women, refined and debated the details of Froebelian pedagogy and practice and kept in touch with the work of kindergartners "abroad."[14] Froebel's *Mother Play* and other texts were translated and disseminated widely, linking the diasporic kindergartens to the movement's theoretical origins. Among American missionaries who found the kindergarten to be a useful tool for evangelism in Japan, China, and Turkey, many remained connected to the western educationists through regular communication and travel.

In Japan, kindergarten leader and missionary Annie L. Howe organized the missionary kindergartens into a national association, which she then affiliated with the English-speaking International Kindergarten Union. Howe traveled from Japan to Chicago in the 1890s to study at the Froebel Institute, bringing back to missionary educators in Japan the newest ideas and theories concerning kindergarten education. Although she was committed to fostering international exchange between Japanese and western educators, it would take a generation to accomplish the rapprochement. In the meantime, she forged the connection between the local, particularistic missionary kindergarten as it was manifest in Japan, and the larger international discourse in which the kindergarten educators in Japan participated from their own perspective.

In summary, the kindergarten spread from the west, producing a complex global discourse on the child, education, psychology, and a newly evolving science of child rearing and child development. In this respect, nations that adopted the kindergarten, even those distancing themselves politically from the west, were linked to a global community of modern pedagogy. On the other hand, despite the kindergarten's western origin, in each instance the kindergarten became a local institution. As seen in the Japan example, western educators did not regularly participate in an ongoing discourse with local educators in Asia, Africa, or Eastern Europe. International communication in these settings was sustained through networks of missionaries, which did not always include the indigenous educators of their countries, and language was often a barrier to international participation. In the end, the kindergarten took on an identity and function of its own in each national setting, unevenly connected to the rest of the world by a belief in the kindergarten idea, and always conventionalized as a comfortable neighborhood school.

The authors of the following chapters were asked to explain how and when the kindergarten arrived in the countries of their study. They were also asked to provide the preconditions for the arrival of the kindergarten: the existing education system, the role of women and children in the society, political and social attitudes toward citizenship and national identity. What role, they were asked, did the kindergarten play in the minds of political leaders, educators, and parents? Finally and most important, what had to change for the kindergarten to become an accepted part of the educational landscape of the country? What emerges from the chapters is the enormous complexity attendant upon the diffusion of the kindergarten, exposing the multiple tensions and accommodations involved with the spread of a single, widely familiar institution.

The chapters have been organized roughly by how the kindergarten idea flowed around the world. The first chapter, Ann Taylor Allen's study of Germany, is a natural starting point. It is the place that the kindergarten began as an idea and which produced its first disciples. Allen creates a context for events in Germany, and for the entire book, by asking, "How was the miniature world of the kindergarten connected to the larger world of politics?" Making a connection between the kindergarten and women's emancipation from the home and the professionalization of women's educational work, Allen draws the direct connection between the kindergarten and the political goals of the state. Her important comparisons between attitudes toward the kindergarten in East and West Germany show clearly the relationships between politics, society, and the home. In East Germany more kindergartens were available to all classes of women, and at least in principle the equality of women in the workplace was encouraged. In West Germany, however, a deeper public/private division existed, assigning women to the private world of child rearing, resulting in the slow growth of public kindergartens until unification.

The second chapter is Barbara Beatty's study of the Americanization of the kindergarten. Before the kindergarten could flourish in the United States, it had to lose its German identification, and the characteristics Americans would identify as German romanticism. The kindergarten materials were translated into English, songs and games were changed, and what Americans perceived as a German rigidity in the structure of the day and the organization of the games was softened to permit a greater degree of individualism both for the children and the teachers. Beatty then shows how the kindergarten, once fully adopted by the middle class, was used as an instrument to Americanize and socialize poor and immigrant children.

The third chapter, Kevin Brehony's study of the English kindergarten, points out the function of class and social need in the development of the kindergarten. In England, with its tradition of infant and nursery schools already in place, Brehony presents the complex reasons for the failure of the kindergarten to take hold in great numbers, and to develop a distinctive identity as different from other forms of preschool educational programs. Nevertheless, Britain is central to the diffusion of the kindergarten, which arrived in the wake of the 1848 German revolution through Froebel's own advocates: Marie Boelte, Bertha Ronge, and Madame von Marenholtz-Bülow, who became Froebel's chief translators outside of Germany. Brehony links the British Froebel Society to turn of the century progressivism and reform, set in the vibrant atmosphere of competing early childhood education innovations sweeping western Europe and the United States.

Australia, a part of the British Empire, was more successful than Britain in its adoption of the kindergarten. Margaret Clyde's fourth chapter shows how the kindergarten developed in the various states of Australia in vastly different ways. Australia is an unusual example of public/private cooperation, rather than competition. Instead of looking to the United Kingdom, Australian educators borrowed a version that had already been transformed by American kindergartners, reflecting the success of the kindergarten in the United States, and its weakness in the United Kingdom. They borrowed a "child-saving" model, with middle-class teachers uplifting the urban poor. As Clyde explores the developments in the various states of Australia, the reader witnesses enormous variety at the local level based on historical circumstances. Tasmania, for example, which began as one of the penal colonies, created philanthropic kindergartens for the benefit of the poor. Elsewhere, class and ethnic tensions led to policies that could be characterized as interior colonization of aboriginal people, resulting in exclusions and limited access.

In the fifth chapter, I focus on Japan, the first of the nonwestern case studies. The kindergarten arrived early in Japan, the first one established as an import by the new Meiji government in 1875 and then via missionaries throughout the 1880s. Although the kindergarten became contested ground between the government and the missionaries when the government banned Christianity in the 1890s, Japanese educators respected the child development and education goals of the kindergarten idea. The Japanese government kindergartens developed moral lessons based on a Confucian model of family loyalty, respect for elders, and ultimately for the emperor. These lessons, of course, contrasted with the missionary agenda, which promoted Christian virtues and encouraged individualism rather than group and national loyalties. Wanting the pedagogy without the Christianity, Japanese educators developed their own system of kindergarten education in both the public and private spheres (including Buddhist and Shinto kindergartens), teaching Japanese rather than western values.

Limin Bai's study of China, Chapter 6, follows the chapter on Japan because the Chinese kindergarten was borrowed directly from Japan rather than from the west. The Chinese were glad to adopt the Japanese version, which they saw as already adapted to a Confucian social order. With purpose and intention, therefore, the Chinese adopted an "orientalized" version of the institution. Although there were missionaries in China at the time, they made little impact regarding the introduction of the kindergarten. As the Japanese kindergarten already taught Confucian civil behavior, it was easier and more comfortable for the Chinese to adopt the Japanese model than to turn to the western Christian missionaries in their midst.

By the 1880s, the kindergarten had spread throughout Europe, to France, Belgium, Austria, Sweden, and points east. On the eastern European front, the kindergarten in partitioned Poland was used subversively for the protection of

Polish culture and language, and as a form of resistance against the occupying governments. In the seventh chapter, Bogna Lorence-Kot and Adam Winiarz describe Poland as a nation with a long history of innovation in education. The kindergarten, however, was met with some hostility as it represented Germany and the German attempts at "depolonization" under Poland's partition. Prussian Poland banned the kindergarten for the same reasons it banned the kindergarten in Germany: it appeared to foster ideas of equality and individualism in children. Within Russian-controlled Poland, however, unencumbered by any historical association, the kindergarten was treated with indifference, allowing Polish educators a vehicle for passing along Polish culture to the children.

Continuing east, Russian educators also found the German kindergarten too disciplined, replacing the German with Russian folk tales and songs. The kindergarten was largely ignored by the Tsarist regimes, explained by Lisa Kirschenbaum in the eighth chapter as a fortuitous neglect which later became the rationale for Bolshevik support. The Bolsheviks were unconcerned about putting the kindergarten—untainted by prior support by the aristocracy—to use as an agent of socialization.

The ninth chapter, by Thaveeporn Vasavakul, explores Vietnam, where the kindergarten was borrowed directly from Russia. The chapter not only provides insight into post-Tsarist Russia but points out that the kindergarten in Vietnam came from more than one source. It was brought by the French missionaries during French occupation, and then redefined and restructured during the wars for independence and used widely as a tool of socialization by Ho Chi Minh. Under Ho Chi Minh the kindergarten was defined as a mass movement, not as an education advantage for the elite. Through the kindergarten, children were taught to love their government, to love their family and country, and above all to be loyal to Ho Chi Minh. As in East Germany, nationalization of the kindergarten meant the liberation of women workers, and conformity to the socialist ethic, including the ideas of collective space, family, nationalism, patriotism, and work. Family language used in the kindergartens personalized the relationships between nation, state, and the children, defining their leader as "Uncle."

The tenth chapter provides a Muslim example of the kindergarten in the Ottoman Empire and Turkey. Ben Fortna characterizes the Turks as using education as the primary means of inculcating national identity, loyalty, and exerting political control over the population. Their hope was that through the education of the children, nation building had a chance of succeeding over local or ethnic divisions. In the Ottoman Empire, the Turkification of the kindergarten was achieved through the use of one language, and through the regulation of religious stories and moral lessons. In nonwestern countries, the incursion of Christian missionaries played an important role in the establishment of government kindergartens. In almost every non-Christian case (Turkey, Japan, China) Christianity was ultimately banned. This allowed the governments to embrace the universally recognized "modern" ideas of early child development without accepting the divisive underlying western pressure or Christian moral lessons of the missionaries.

The book concludes with Shoshana Sitton's study of Israeli kindergartens, which links the kindergarten directly to the formation of the new Zionist national identity. She identifies the kindergarten as a revolutionary institution which replaced the traditional religious school for boys, the *heder,* thereby opening up early education to girls and simultaneously opening the teaching profession to women. Moreover, the new kindergarten was recontextualized along the lines of secular Zionism: the new "Settlement" was to be based on Jewish history and culture and unified by the Hebrew language. Therefore, when the first kindergarten opened in 1899, the added task of the teachers, many of them immigrants who had studied kindergarten education in Germany, was to instruct Jewish children in the Hebrew language, along with holidays, festivals, and ceremonies newly created to commemorate, and embed, the Settlement of Palestine.

The case studies in this book present a convincing body of evidence that deepens our understanding of how ideas are diffused globally, of the function of education in creating national identity, and ultimately of the complex processes of cultural hybridization. As we suspected when we began this compilation, these studies clearly demonstrate the immense power of local culture to respond to and reformulate borrowed ideas. Additionally, the international diffusion of the kindergarten at the turn of the twentieth century speaks to the widespread elevation of early childhood as an important and distinct stage of life, with its age-related developmental possibilities. Regardless of the cultural or political context in which the kindergarten was set, there emerged at the turn of the century a universal faith in scientific child rearing and a desire for modern ideas pertaining to education through which every government and every kindergarten parent felt they were doing their best for the future of the children and the nation.

NOTES

1. This idea is best summarized by Martin Carnoy, "Education and the State: From Adam Smith to Perestroika," in Robert F. Arnove et al., eds., *Emergent Issues in Education* (New York: SUNY Press, 1992), chap. 9.

2. For a concise general history of the educational ideas of the kindergarten, see Elizabeth Dale Ross, *The Kindergarten Crusade: The Establishment of Preschool Education in the United States.* (Athens, Ohio: Ohio University Press, 1976).

3. For standard works of kindergarten history, see: Norman Brosterman, *Inventing Kindergarten* (New York: Harry N. Abrams, 1997); Barbara Beatty, *Preschool Education in America* (New Haven and London: Yale University Press, 1995); Michael Shapiro, *The Child's Garden: The Kindergarten Movement from Froebel to Dewey* (University Park, Pa.: Pennsylvania State University Press, 1983); Elizabeth Ross, *The Kindergarten Crusade: The Establishment of Preschool Education in the United States* (Athens, Ohio: Ohio University Press, 1976); Nina Vanderwalker, *The Kindergarten in American Education* (New York: Arno Press, 1971; orig. 1908); and *The Kindergarten Centennial, 1837–1937: A Brief Historical Outline of Early Childhood Education* prepared by the Kindergarten Centennial Committee, Edna Dean Baker, chairman, issued by The Association for Childhood Education, 1937.

4. See Bosterman for a concise, skillful elaboration of Froebel's "gifts" and "occupations."

5. Philip Altbach and Gail P. Kelly, *Education and Colonialism* (New York: Longman, 1978), introduction. Altbach and Kelly analyzed educational conflict in systems of "classical colonialism" such as occurred in India; "internal colonialism," as in the case of Native Americans or women in the United States; and "neocolonialism," including an analysis of the distribution of knowledge in the Third World and the implications of a flow of information and technology from north to south and from west to east.

6. The new "post-colonial discourse" literature begins with Frantz Fanon's liberationist *The Wretched of the Earth* (1967), followed by Edward Said's *Orientalism,* published in 1978. Said followed his own call for further research with *Culture and Imperialism* (1993). Recent scholars have drawn from the theories of psychoanalysis (Homi Bhabha), post-modernism (Gayatri Chakravorty Spivak), feminism (Chandra Mohanty), and Marxism (Aijaz Ahmad), and others to add complexity to this direction of inquiry and analysis.

7. Arjun Appadurai, "Disjuncture and Difference in the Global Cultural Economy," in Patrick Williams and Laura Chrisman, *Cultural Discourse and Post-Colonial Theory, A Reader,* p. 328.

8. Signe Howell, "Whose knowledge and whose power? A New perspective on cultural diffusion," in Richard Fardon, ed., *Counterworks: Managing the Diversity of Knowledge* (London: Routledge, 1995).

9. From Smadar Lavie and Ted Swedenburg, eds. *Displacement, Diaspora, and Geographies of Identity* (Durham, N.C.: Duke University Press, 1996), p. 9.

10. Norman Brosterman, *Inventing Kindergarten* (New York: Abrams, 1997), p. 99.

11. Philip Altbach and Gail P. Kelly, *Education and Colonialism* (New York: Longman, 1978).

12. Seth Koven and Sonya Michel, eds., *Mothers of a New World: Maternalist Politics and the Origins of Welfare States* (New York: Routledge, 1993).

13. Nupur Chaudhuri and Margaret Strobel, eds. *Western Women and Imperialism: Complicity and Resistance* (Bloomington, Ind.: Indiana University Press, 1992).

14. *The Kindergarten-Primary Magazine,* vol. 20, September 1907–June 1908 (New York: The Kindergarten Magazine Company, 1907–1908), and throughout the series.

Chapter 1 Children Between Public and Private Worlds: The Kindergarten and Public Policy in Germany, 1840–Present

Ann Taylor Allen

The history of the kindergarten, its origins, and its international dispersion present us with a paradox. Although the kindergarten originated in Germany and was a distinctively German institution, it found much less acceptance in the land of its origin than in many of the countries to which it was exported. The kindergarten's inventor, Friedrich Froebel, was steeped in German philosophical and pedagogical traditions. The kindergarten's development was affected by German political developments, education systems, and religious and feminist movements. But the kindergarten was more representative of the potential than the actual development of German civilization. Because it was closely associated with liberal, democratic, and socialist movements, it shared the fate of these movements: suppression after the revolutions of 1848, marginalization under the German Empire, defeat in the Weimar years, forced "coordination" under National Socialism, co-optation under the German Democratic Republic, and imperfect realization in the early years of the Federal Republic. Thus, compared with its widespread influence in other countries where it was incorporated into public school systems, the development of the kindergarten in Germany has been limited. This chapter links the development of the German kindergarten to broader trends in politics, education, and culture (Allen 1988; Erning 1987a).

How was the miniature world of the kindergarten connected to the larger world of politics? Throughout this period, debates on early-childhood education called into question the public/private boundaries that defined political as well as family life. The small child occupied a contested zone between the public and private spheres. Although early nineteenth century culture had consigned child rearing decisively to a private world presided over by the mother, it also, at the same time, recognized it as a vital public concern, crucial to the preservation of social order and the rearing of a new generation of citizens. Conservatives generally sought to preserve the authority of the family over children; liberals often sought to mitigate this familial authority through alternative values taught in educational institutions. The kindergarten also had important implications for the status of women, for not only did it provide one of the earliest female professional opportunities, but also it potentially freed mothers of small children for public activities. Thus the status of both children and women was and still is a central issue in the development of the kindergarten.

Although eventually internationally accepted, the kindergarten was initially shaped by a specifically German environment—the school systems and preschool institutions of the German states. Most of these had established systems of compulsory elementary education by the middle decades of the eighteenth century, much earlier than most other Western countries. Public elementary schools, though under state supervision, were financed by communities and by tuition paid by parents. Attendance increased over time: in Prussia (the largest German state) about 78 percent of all children attended elementary school in 1848, and 85 percent by 1864. Local school systems provided a substantial role for churches, which often helped to pay teachers' salaries and shaped curriculum; the role of church and state in education was a contentious issue throughout this period. Parents, who often resented compulsory education for depriving them of their children's labor, encouraged their children to complete the required years of schooling as soon as possible by sending them to school at an early age. Most state school systems attempted to counteract this tendency, which they considered detrimental to education standards, by setting a minimum age for school entrance at usually six and sometimes seven years (Friedrich 1987, 123–152). In order to prevent competition from privately run pre-school institutions, school authorities forbade these to teach school subjects. Thus German early-childhood educators (unlike their counterparts in the British infant schools, who taught reading and numbers) were forced by law to develop non-academic approaches to education; the kindergarten was one such approach (Erning 1987a, 28).

The kindergarten developed within a broad spectrum of private, primarily religiously affiliated institutions. The first German early-childhood institution was founded in 1802 by Princess Pauline of Detmold in Detmold (Mörsberger 1978, vol. 1, 199). These centers (or *Bewahranstalten,* as they were usually called) were specifically designed to remedy the social crisis caused by the employment of women among the poor. The founders insisted that their institutions were not intended to substitute for familial care, which remained the God-given norm for child rearing, but merely to compensate for what they perceived as the highly inadequate care received by lower-class children. These institutions were intended only for the children of lower-class working mothers or of other absent parents; middle-class children did not attend them. Their teachers (like almost all German elementary-school teachers at this time) were male. Their programs were devoted to the inculcation of Bible passages and religious values; their pedagogy was based firmly on theories of original sin; and their purpose was to prevent social disorder by teaching respect for religious and secular authority (Allen 1986; Erning 1987a; Heinsohn 1974; Hoffmann 1971).

The Froebel kindergarten presented a very different vision of the child's nature and of the goals of early-childhood education. The basis of kindergarten pedagogy was in the work of Rousseau, who had denied theories of original sin by asserting the child's potential for growth and development and had insisted that education must be responsive to this process. Rousseau's Swiss disciple, Johann Heinrich Pestalozzi, both developed and revised his master's theories. Pestalozzi's pedagogy used the child's own experience, rather than the traditional religiously based curriculum, as the basis of learning. Insisting that the learning process begins in the first days of life, Pestalozzi glorified mothers as the first and best teachers. Rousseau, while assigning the nourishment and custodial care of infants to mothers, had allotted teaching, even of small children, to males. In contrast, Pestalozzi redefined teaching as a female task arising naturally out of a specifically female gift for nurture. Therefore, he set up an institute to train female governesses and teachers at his school at Yverdon (Allen 1991, 22–28; Silber 1973, 37–52).[1] For Pestalozzi, the mother-child bond formed the basis not just for learning, but also for the development of the feelings of loyalty and altruism upon which all organized social life depended (Allen 1991, 22–28). Pestalozzi's pedagogy, which became immensely influential among progressive educators throughout the nineteenth century, provided an important justification for the extension of women's motherly role from the private into the public sphere.

Friedrich Froebel, born in 1782 in the tiny community of Oberweissbach in the central German province of Thuringia, came to early-childhood education in the course of a turbulent career that included philosophical and scientific studies at the University of Jena, military service in the wars of liberation from the Napoleonic Empire in 1811–12, work as a forester, and the founding of a boys' school and institute for teachers in the Thuringian town of Keilhau. After the defeat of Napoleon, nationalist hopes for a unified German state had been defeated; most of the German states remained under some form of absolute rule. Like many German nationalists of his time, Froebel combined aspirations to national unity and to liberal reform. He saw education as a means to that end, and became a disciple of Pestalozzi (Allen 1991, 35–40; Downs 1978).

Froebelian pedagogy was also inspired by the ideas of the Idealist philosophical school that then dominated German intellectual life. The German Idealist philosophers defined the dichotomy between the self and the not-self, the individual and the collective, as the fundamental ethical problem. They asserted that this dichotomy could be overcome only by the willed commitment of the individual to the welfare of the people or nation. In his well-known *Speeches to the German Nation,* the philosopher Fichte urged Pestalozzian pedagogy as a means to such national cohesion. Froebel's teacher, the philosopher Schelling, imagined nature as a great whole animated by a Divine spirit in which all individual beings achieved unity (Mandelbaum 1971, 163–218). Froebel's approach to education combined Pestalozzian pedagogy with these Idealist ethical concepts, aiming to promote both cognitive and ethical development. Like Pestalozzi, he glorified mother-love as the basis for both kinds of learning. Froebel's most famous and widely translated book, *Mother and Nursery Songs (Mutter-und–Koselieder),* was a series of songs accompanied by simple games designed to stimulate the infant's sense perceptions from the first few months of life (Froebel 1883). For somewhat older children, he developed a set of toys, which he called "gifts," designed to teach the relationship of the whole to the parts: blocks, sticks, and cylinders that could be put together to form patterns, and a ball representing wholeness. Froebel rejected the elaborate playthings of his era and created these simple toys (which, of course, are found in kindergartens to this day) to build the child's capacity for abstract thought (Erning 1987a, 36–41).

Although initially Froebel intended these methods to be used by mothers in the home, he was critical of familial child rearing, which he claimed was too often carried on by ignorant nursemaids, and encouraged only traditional religiosity and narrow self-interest (Froebel 1840; Allen 1991, 31–38). In 1840 Froebel called for the founding of a model German kindergarten; although this plan was not realized, institutions using Froebel's methods were founded starting in 1843 (Erning 1987a, 38). These methods differed from those of existing child-care institutions. The Froebel kindergarten based its pedagogical approach on a theory of childish innocence rather than original sin, and its religious orientation was highly unorthodox, sometimes verging on pantheism. It was designed for all classes, not simply for the poor, and it promoted rationality rather than religious obedience (Allen 1982, 1985; Prelinger 1987, 88–94). The kindergarten rejected the rote memorization practiced in the Bewahranstalten in favor of a curriculum based on supervised play with the "gifts." This curriculum based on play—eventually the most internationally influential aspect of kindergarten pedagogy—arose in the context of specifically German prohibitions against academic learning in pre-school institutions.

Froebel first tried to sell his new concept in education to men: to fathers and to a male-dominated teaching profession. But when they failed to respond he turned to women, advocating the new method of education as a means to the elevation of women's status and the broadening of their sphere of action. "It is a characteristic of our time," he declared solemnly, "to rescue the female sex from its hitherto passive and instinctive role and to raise it to the same level as the male sex" (Goldschmidt 1895, 5). The means to this end was not the assumption of male professional roles but the development of a distinctively female capacity to which he gave the name "spiritual motherhood." This concept, though biologically based, did not imply any modern theory of biological determinism; indeed, the scientific theories to which Froebel and his contemporaries subscribed linked physical to spiritual evolution (Mandelbaum 1971, 163–218). Froebel specifically argued against the idea that child rearing could be left to instinct and asserted instead that it was a highly complex task requiring training. The kindergarten was by no means the first early-childhood institution to employ women teachers—indeed, in Germany a Protestant order of deaconesses headed by Theodor Fliedner had set up a training program for women in the 1830s—but it was the first to link early-childhood education explicitly to doctrines of female emancipation and professionalism (Prelinger 1986; Allen 1986).

Although from the beginning the kindergarten was supported by some prestigious male educators, including the influential Adolf Diesterweg, it owed its survival and development largely to women. Female intellectuals in Germany in the early nineteenth century had sympathized with many of the political aspirations of the French Revolution of 1789 but deplored its destructive excesses,

asserting the gradual process of education as a more constructive means to social progress. Early movements for women's rights found many of their adherents among middle- or upper-class women who affirmed the value of female
nurturing roles but rebelled against the narrowness of the domestic environment
(Prelinger 1987, 55–79; Allen 1991, 41–57). Both their own experiences of child
rearing and their work for charities benefiting children had shown these women
the relationship between the private realm of the home and the public world of
politics and economic life.

Among the first reform initiatives in which German women played an important role was the dissenting religious movement which began in 1844, when
Catholic priest Johannes Ronge criticized the authoritarian organization and su-
perstitious religiosity of his Church and urged a more rational, humane, and
progressive faith. Similar movements, whose members were known as the *Licht-
freunde*, grew up in Protestant churches. Eventually, both Catholic and Protestant dissenters forsook their original religious allegiance to found their own, ec-
umenical "Free Congregations" (*freie Gemeinden*). These movements rejected
traditional Christian conceptions of women's roles and supported women's participation in congregational governance, the reform of laws and customs regarding marriage and divorce, and new forms of child rearing (Prelinger 1987;
Paletschek 1990). Emancipation, dissenting women believed, was not the imitation of men but the fulfillment of women's distinctive mission to rear and educate a new generation, "to cultivate the seeds of the divine spirit in the next
generation, and to struggle against everything that stands in the way of its development" (Anon. 1846, quoted in Paletschek 1990, 159). This vision of a
widened maternal role demanded not only access for women to public life but
the infusion of the public sphere with the familial spirit of love, harmony, and
cooperation (Paletschek 1990, 161). Women of the dissenting movements, who
included prominent author Malwida von Meysenbug and social activist Louise
Otto, supported Froebelian pedagogy as the means to this exalted end (Allen
1991, 49, 70, 75–76; Prelinger 1987, 106–110; Gerhard 1979, 189).

Dissenting religious groups supported and participated actively in the revolutionary events of 1848. In that year, popular uprisings in response both to economic hardships and to the news of a revolution in Paris inspired many German
rulers, including the King of Prussia, to promise reform: press censorship was
lifted; elections went forward for an all-German representative assembly
charged with creating a unified German state; reform ministries were appointed
and new constitutions drafted. Froebelian pedagogy experienced an upsurge of
popularity. The women's organizations which had organized to support the dis-

senting congregations founded kindergartens in several cities, including Breslau, Hamburg, Nordhausen, Nuremberg, and Schweinfurt (Paletschek 1990, 213–215, Prelinger 1987, 55–105). In accordance with their founders' egalitarian beliefs, these kindergartens admitted children of all classes. Although tuition was charged, subsidies for poorer children were provided by the women's organizations (Paletschek 1990, 215). Unlike the traditional early-childhood institutions, kindergartens admitted children of all religions and taught religious tolerance rather than orthodoxy. Louise Otto, founder of the first feminist newspaper, the Frauen-Zeitung, praised the kindergarten for providing an opportunity for single, middle-class women to earn a living through dignified, professional work (Allen 1991, 73–77; Prelinger 1987, 106–110; Gerhard 1979, 132–133). Kindergarten teaching was indeed among the first and most important professional opportunities open to German women, for in the German-speaking world public elementary-school teaching, in many countries already a feminized occupation, was vigorously defended as a male preserve (Allen 1986; Albisetti 1994).

Friedrich Froebel was propelled from his obscure and eccentric existence into prominence by the new popularity of the kindergarten. In 1848 a meeting of male teachers at the Thuringian town of Rudolstadt petitioned the Frankfurt Assembly, then debating the constitution for a newly unified Germany, to include the kindergarten in a new system of public education (Allen 1982; Hoffmann 1971, 97). During the revolutionary period, Froebel gained some new disciples, the most important of whom were his niece, Henriette Breymann, and the Baroness Bertha von Marenholtz-Bülow. Breymann, a young girl who rebelled against the conventional behavior enforced by her pastor father, discovered in the kindergarten training institute founded by her uncle the fulfilling mission that she had craved, "to bring to the broader community a quality which until now has been completely lacking—the spirit of motherhood in all its forms" (Lyschinska 1922, vol. 2, 86; Allen 1991, 56). Marenholtz-Bülow, an aristocrat who had recently left an unhappy marriage, likewise became convinced that the kindergarten movement offered both a solution to class conflict and a more responsible and active role for women (Bülow-Wendhausen 1901, vol. 1, 226; Allen 1991, 82). Thus Froebel's pedagogy increasingly provided a rationale for a challenge to the public/private boundaries that restricted the lives not only of children, but of women as well.

In 1848 a Hamburg women's organization associated with that city's dissenting congregations and composed of both Christians and Jews decided to found a post-secondary educational institution, or college, for women. In a culture in which women were barred from higher education, this was indeed a radical experiment. Like many other women reformers of their era, the Hamburg women asserted that the goal of women's education must be to develop women's maternal gifts, then regarded as the basis of public and professional activities (Prelinger 1987, 95–99). As directors of the school, they appointed a nephew of Friedrich Froebel, Karl Froebel, along with his wife, Johanna Küstner, a trained kindergarten teacher.

This couple, influenced by French utopian socialism as well as by German religious dissent, linked the new education theories with revolutionary aspirations to social justice, the emancipation of women, and the ethical regeneration of society (Allen 1991, 66–72; Prelinger 1987, 125–137; Kleinau 1990). The Hamburg College for the Female Sex opened in 1850. Malwida von Meysenbug, later a prominent author, was among the first students. She rejoiced that the school would "make possible the economic independence of women through her development into a being complete in herself and capable of growing in her own way" (Meysenbug 1922, vol. 1, 186; Allen 1991, 68). The curriculum, though not equivalent to university studies, went far beyond the limitations of conventional female education to include natural sciences, philosophy, history, geography, and mathematics, among many other fields (Paletschek 1990, 218–219; Kleinau 1990). Work in a Froebel kindergarten provided professional training. The school's vision of female emancipation was far too radical for Friedrich Froebel himself, who approved neither of his nephew's socialist principles nor of the ambitious and intellectual curriculum. The faculty included controversial scholars and activists who criticized both religious and political orthodoxy (Prelinger 1987, 132–137; Kleinau 1990). At the height of its two-year development, the school had about 100 students, some supported by scholarships provided by women's organizations (Paletschek 1990, 219).

Both the Hamburg College and the Froebel kindergarten shared in the defeat and suppression of the revolutionary movements of 1848. The optimism of 1848 had been unfounded; the weakness of the liberal and democratic forces to which the kindergarten founders, among others, belonged, and the continued strength of conservative forms of authority, soon doomed the revolution to failure. Revolutionary and liberal reform movements were crushed by police measures, among the first of which were prohibitions of Froebel kindergartens in Prussia (the largest of the German states) in 1851, followed by similar measures in most other states (Prelinger 1987, 161–165; Allen 1991, 82). The founders of the Hamburg College responded to the political climate by closing their institution in 1852. The Prussian decree included both the kindergarten and the

Hamburg College in its denunciation of the "Froebelian socialist system, which aims to convert young people to atheism" (Dekret vom 7.8.51, quoted in Paletschek 216). In response to the objection that Friedrich Froebel had been confused with his nephew Karl, the Prussian authorities again denounced kindergarten pedagogy as "a system that bases education on a highly erroneous theory that rejects Christianity" (Dekret vom 7.8.51, quoted by Paletschek 1990, 216). The kindergarten prohibition was, in fact, the first of a series of measures, culminating in the Stiehl Regulatives of 1854, designed to suppress progressive education movements and to restore religious control over education (Herrlitz 1993, 30–58). Kindergartens were closed, some forcibly. "The kindergarten teachers of this period went through a martyrdom that was fully equivalent to the suffering of the many men who were persecuted for their beliefs," wrote feminist Louise Otto, whose own newspaper was also forced by renewed censorship to cease publication (Otto-Peters 1866, 99).

The suppression of the kindergarten in the German lands immediately triggered its export to the many Western countries where it subsequently took root. Many men and women involved in the revolutionary movements were forced into exile. These exiles included Bertha Ronge, who, as Bertha Meyer, had been an active supporter of the Hamburg College. After her divorce and marriage to the leader of the dissenting religious movements, Johannes Ronge, she moved with him to England. Her sister Margarethe moved with her husband Karl Schurz to Wisconsin (Allen 1994). Both set up kindergartens in their adopted countries, initially serving chiefly the children of German immigrants (Shapiro 1983, 29–36; Lawrence 1961, 34–95). Meanwhile the energetic Baroness von Marenholtz-Bülow, grieving the death in 1852 of her revered teacher Friedrich Froebel and frustrated by the ban on kindergarten work in Germany, undertook extensive travels throughout Western Europe to spread the kindergarten idea (Bülow-Wendhausen 1901, vol. 1, 206–240; Allen 1991, 28–27). In the United States, the cause of the kindergarten was taken up by the Boston educator and reformer Elizabeth Peabody, who was a friend of Margarethe Schurz and who in 1867 traveled to Germany to meet Marenholtz and persuaded several trained German kindergarten teachers to return with her to the United States (Allen 1988; Peabody 1984, 351–393). Likewise, in Britain, the kindergarten cause was supported by the pioneer educator and social reformer Emily Shirreff (Ellsworth 1979, 231–258; Allen 1994).

Under the leadership of these and many other progressive educators, especially women, the kindergarten gained in popularity among middle-class parents in both Britain and the United States. Kindergarten methods were also increasingly used in day-care centers for the children of the poor, which in each country were supported by charitable organizations (Davis 1967, 44–47). The prestige accorded to German philosophy and German education in the English-speaking world during the period from 1870 to 1914 reinforced the popularity of the kindergarten (Allen 1994). Similarly, in cultures hostile to Germany such as France, the kindergarten idea, though supported by some education reformers, had much less success during the same period (Luc 1993).

In its land of origin, the Froebel kindergarten seemed for a while to be on its way to acceptance. In 1860, the political climate in Prussia and the other German states became more liberal. Marenholtz, returned from her travels, used her influence at the Prussian court to bring about the repeal of the ban on the Froebel kindergarten (Allen 1991, 86). Despite the aspirations of the first kindergarten founders to transcend class barriers, Froebel kindergarten classes had hitherto served chiefly middle-class children whose parents could afford to pay tuition, for the religiously oriented charitable societies that supported day care for the poor were still hostile to the Froebel methods. In 1863, Marenholtz founded in Berlin an organization known as the Society for Popular Education, which opened seven kindergartens for tuition-paying pupils and then used the funds thus raised to found free kindergartens, or *Volkskindergärten*, for the children of the urban poor (Allen 1991, 86).

Marenholtz developed a rationale for such kindergartens suitable to the industrializing age. The kindergarten, she asserted, must not only train the children of workers in the manual dexterity required by their future occupations, but must "prepare them for the duties of citizenship, at whatever rank of society they may be" (Marenholtz-Bülow 1864, 30). Compared with the approach of the religious day-care centers, this emphasis on skills and citizenship was progressive. But Marenholtz nonetheless rejected the utopian vision of the kindergarten founders of 1848 of a kindergarten open to children of all classes. Upper- and middle-class parents, she argued, would not accept such companionship for their children; and working-class children could not keep up with their more privileged age-mates. Therefore she recommended two types of kindergartens: all-day free kindergartens serving children of working mothers (usually poor), and tuition-supported classes which met for three or four hours and served children of non-working mothers (usually middle- or upper-class) (Marenholtz-Bülow 1864, 60–65). During the 1860s free kindergartens were founded in several German cities; for example, a women's group in Breslau founded twelve between 1861 and 1873 (Allen 1982).

Marenholtz called upon the women of the upper and middle class to provide teachers and administrators for both sorts of kindergarten and thus to assume their "true office in the great social household, namely as the educator of the human family" (Marenholtz-Bülow 1855, 3). This view of the female mission combined altruism with practicality, for the 1860s brought a new concern for the many unmarried, middle-class women who desperately needed professional opportunities (Otto-Peters 1890, 3–13; Bussemer 1985, 169–185). The theoretical complexity of Froebelian pedagogy conferred professional status on its practitioners. Kindergarten training institutes were among the earliest professional schools for women. Johanna Goldschmidt, who had been among the supporters of the Hamburg College during its brief existence, set up the Froebel Seminar in Hamburg in 1860; Marenholtz founded a training institute in Dresden in 1873; and by 1877 twenty kindergarten training seminars had been founded in various cities. The first national German feminist organization, the General German Women's Association (Allgemeiner deutscher Frauenverein), founded in 1865 by Otto-Peters, supported kindergarten training as a means to their most important goal, the provision of economic opportunities (Allen 1991, 97–99; Otto-Peters 1895).

The unification of the German Empire in 1871 brought educational modernization. In Prussia, Minister of Culture Adalbert Falk superintended the gradual introduction of graded instructions into previously one-room schools, reduced class sizes, and revised curricula; in 1888, tuition payments in elementary schools were abolished (Herrlitz 1993, 108–109). In this atmosphere of liberalization and reform, kindergarten advocates also hoped for recognition. In 1874, the various local Froebel societies combined to create a central German Froebel Society, which in 1876 sent a petition to the Prussian Ministry of Culture requesting the addition of kindergarten classes to public school systems. In 1876, Falk responded that, although community school systems were free to add pre-school classes, his ministry favored no specific system "because we have so little evidence of the advantages and disadvantages of any system" (quoted in Allen 1986, 443). In fact, probably because of continuing Church opposition, few public school systems added kindergarten classes.

Thus during the Imperial period the kindergarten continued to develop as a private institution, supported by the dedicated work of various organizations. Although many proprietors and directors of kindergartens were men, teaching and teacher training were maintained jealously as female preserves (Allen 1991, 105–110; Hoffmann 1971, 42–43).

The most famous and influential of all teacher-training institutes was founded by Froebel's niece Henriette Breymann (who, after her marriage to lawyer Karl Schrader, called herself Schrader-Breymann). Schrader-Breymann, who since 1853 had headed girls' schools in her native Braunschweig, moved with her new husband to Berlin in 1872, where two years later she founded a free kindergarten and a kindergarten teacher-training program. These programs, greatly expanded, provided the basis for an institute known as the Pestalozzi-Froebel House, which with the financial support of the Schraders and their many influential friends acquired its first permanent building in 1881 (Lyschinska 1922, vol 2, 1–5; Allen 1991, 111–121). The Pestalozzi-Froebel House soon acquired other divisions, such as after-school centers and school-lunch programs for schoolchildren, a school of domestic arts run by the later prominent activist Hedwig Heyl, a fresh-air camp for inner-city children, and many others (Schrader-Breymann 1890; Allen 1991, 111–134). In some ways, it resembled the settlement houses that developed at the same time in England and the United States.

Schrader-Breymann urged her kindergarten trainees to understand children in the context of the urban society in which they lived. Though continuing to admire Friedrich Froebel, she almost entirely abandoned the Froebel games, which she claimed were too abstract and philosophical, and replaced them with exercises designed to acquaint children with the natural environment, the adult world, and the skills of everyday life. Because she regarded the estrangement of the city child from nature as highly unnatural, she insisted that even urban kindergartens should include a garden in order to teach children where their daily food came from; one of her exercises for kindergarten children involved the cooking of pea soup (Schrader-Breymann 1890)! Schrader-Breymann's pedagogy had international influence, for educators from other European countries and the United States visited and studied at the Pestalozzi-Froebel House. Though some of these foreign observers, such as American kindergarten teacher Elizabeth Harrison, who visited in 1889, were at first rather shocked by Schrader-Breymann's revision of Froebel (Harrison 1930, 120–122), others had a more positive opinion. American psychologist G. Stanley Hall called the institution "the finest kindergarten installation in the world" (Hall 1911, vol. 1, 16–17). Indeed, the transition from Froebel games to more practically oriented forms of learning which occurred in kindergartens throughout the Western world around 1900 (in the United States, under the leadership of Hall and John Dewey) owed much to the influence of the Pestalozzi-Froebel House.

The development of the kindergarten during the period of the German Empire (1871–1918) occurred in the context of a general expansion of social services designed to preserve social stability by mitigating the worst effects of urban poverty. Much official concern was focused on lower-class children, who because of what local authorities regarded as gravely inadequate familial nurture were constantly in danger of neglect or seduction into criminal activity (Steinmetz 1993, 189–191). Increasingly, urban policy makers encouraged Free Kindergartens, which they had hitherto regarded with benign neglect, as a positive influence on the rearing of these children. Most kindergartens remained in private hands, but some received increasing subsidies from municipal welfare departments (including that of Munich, which assumed full responsibility for that city's free kindergartens in 1907) (Allen 1986, 445).

At the turn of the twentieth century, the campaigns of female activists for state recognition of the Froebel kindergarten and its training program appealed to this new concern for child welfare. Some of these campaigns brought results. In 1908, courses and practica in kindergarten teaching were added to the curricula of some public girls' secondary schools, and in 1911, a government-administered accreditation examination for kindergarten teachers was introduced. The Pestalozzi-Froebel House played an influential role in the creation of new curricula and also provided the first setting for women's courses in the new field of social work (Sachsse 1985, 147; Allen 1991, 206). By 1914, the Froebel methods were taught in most kindergarten training seminars and had found acceptance even in religiously sponsored kindergartens (Erning 1987a, 62). The kindergarten teaching profession had also become completely feminized.

Nevertheless, the integration of kindergarten classes into public school systems, advocated during this period chiefly by female activists, continued to meet with resistance. In 1898 the central organization of the German women's movement, the Bund deutscher Frauenvereine, then under the co-directorship of kindergarten founder Henriette Goldschmidt, submitted a petition to all the German states, advocating the addition of two compulsory pre-school classes, taught by the Froebel method, to public elementary schools (Goldschmidt 1901). The petition was rejected by the state authorities and by the annual national convention of teachers in 1899; a speaker at that meeting, Otto Beetz, denounced the kindergarten as an interference with the right of the family to control early education (Beetz 1900; Allen 1991, 130–131). Churches, both Catholic and Protestant, also protected their control over child-care institutions by opposing kindergartens, which were usually non-confessional. Churches also justified their opposition by defending the authority of home and family over the rearing of small children, recommending pre-school education only for children whose homes were non-existent or inadequate (Allen 1986; Reyer 1987b). The fact that the demand for public-school kindergartens, like many traditionally liberal causes, was taken up in the 1890s by socialist women's organizations in order to facilitate the work of women outside the home hardened the opposition of political and religious conservatives (Allen 1988).

Therefore the Froebel kindergartens continued to be a minority of all preschool institutions. In 1912, 59 percent of all pre-school institutions were administered by religious organizations (primarily for poor children); only 22 percent by private organizations including the Froebel societies; and only about 6 percent by cities or communities (Reyer 1987a, 32).

Such attitudes were not universal to Western culture, but distinctively German. The cultures in Britain and America were far more hospitable to the kindergarten's basic aim—the integration of public and private spheres for both women and children—than was its native Germany. Because the teaching profession in both countries was largely female, the expansion of women's professional roles in the schools was not a problem; on the contrary, British and American teachers often actively advocated the addition of kindergarten classes. Because infant-school classes had traditionally been part of many British elementary schools, the advisability of educating young children outside the home was much less disputed in Britain than in Germany, where only a tiny fraction of pre-school children attended any institution (Whitbread 1978, 42–25; Allen 1994). Because American school systems increasingly took on the task of integrating the children of immigrants into American culture—an institutional mission that had no counterpart in Germany—school entry at an early and impressionable age seemed to reinforce rather than threaten social stability. Far from regarding the familial sphere as a sacred zone of privacy, American school authorities mistrusted it as a hotbed of foreign influences from which immigrants' children should be removed as soon as possible (Allen 1988). Because in Britain and the United States the kindergarten was not associated with revolutionary movements, it was less threatening to the churches; indeed, liberal churches and religious organizations actively sponsored kindergartens (Allen 1988).

For all these (and many other) reasons, school systems in English-speaking countries proved receptive to the kindergarten. In the United States, St. Louis school superintendent William Torrey Harris created public-school kindergartens in 1877; many other American school boards soon followed his example (Troen 1975, 99–113). American school kindergartens were commonly in session for only a few hours each day, although many settlement houses and private charities sponsored all-day kindergartens (Davis 1967, 44–47).

In Britain, the National Education Code of 1882, which expanded the newly founded state school system, recommended the use of Froebelian methods in all infant-school classes, and by the 1880s many local school boards required infant-school mistresses to learn kindergarten techniques. Though practical obstacles to the use of the methods in overcrowded classes remained formidable, in principle the kindergarten method was accepted in British state schools by 1890 (Allen 1994; Whitbread 1978, 42–53; Lawrence 1961, 55–60).

In Germany as elsewhere, the period of the First World War saw increasing public and private concern for, and intervention in, many aspects of child welfare. Expanded child-care services were justified not only by the increased employment of mothers replacing absent men in the labor market, but also by a new concern for the value of the next generation as military casualties raised the fear of depopulation. In 1915, representatives of child-welfare organizations met to form a "German Committee on Child Welfare." In 1917 the work of women's organizations was centralized under a "National Committee for Wartime Women's Work" (Erning 1987a, 64–65), under the sponsorship of the War Office. Despite the reservations of the director of the Pestalozzi-Froebel House, Lili Droescher, who complained that it was "unnatural, that these young ones . . . cannot grow up in the family," the first "War Kindergarten," staffed by teachers trained at her institution, opened in Berlin in 1914 (Droescher 1917, 4–5). The rapid establishment of new kindergartens and the overcrowding of existing ones soon led to uncomfortable and dangerous conditions. In 1917 the division of the War Office responsible for women's work issued a national set of directives and guidelines for all early-childhood institutions (Erning 1987a, 67). As in so many areas, wartime legislation set a precedent for peacetime. Federal and state governments had now explicitly included early-childhood education among the social-welfare measures for which the state was responsible.

The German defeat in the First World War led to the overthrow of the monarchy and the establishment of a democratic system, known as the Weimar Republic. During the first years of the Republic, socialist educators attempted to enact reforms such as the abolition of private schools, the requirement that all children attend a common primary school, and the secularization of elementary education. Although some of these attempts, such as the creation of a common primary school, were successful, others, such as secularization, were blocked by conservatives.

This opposition of socialist and conservative educators also shaped the debate on the status of the kindergarten. In 1919, a national school conference (Reichsschulkonferenz) met in response to the mandate of the new Weimar Constitution to create new national guidelines for school systems. In attendance were representatives of teachers' organizations, education ministries, and private child-welfare associations (Die Reichsschulkonferenz 1921). A committee appointed to discuss the future of the kindergarten was divided. A minority, composed chiefly of socialists, recommended that kindergartens be made available (though not compulsory) for all children and that they be transferred from private to public ownership by the state and communal governments which also controlled school systems. But the majority, made up largely of representatives of private organizations, insisted that the expansion of public kindergartens would violate the principle that "the right and duty of raising children of pre-school age belongs basically to the family" (Die Reichsschulkonferenz 1921, 692; Erning 1987a, 71). This majority opinion asserted that only in cases "where those entrusted with child-rearing are permanently prevented from carrying out their duty, so that the moral, physical, or intellectual development of the child is endangered" (Die Reichsschulkonferenz 1921, 692), were public kindergartens appropriate.

The kindergarten thus remained attached to welfare, rather than to public education systems. In 1922, the "National Youth Welfare Law" placed responsibility for regulation and financial support of social services to children and young people in the hands of the federal government. However, the law provided for public intervention only when private institutions were inadequate. The economic crisis precipitated by the inflation of 1920–1924 reduced the available governmental funding, although some private kindergartens were rescued from bankruptcy by state and local funding (Erning 1987b, 88–89). New federal regulations required the hiring of trained personnel and the maintenance of adequate facilities. But neither the structure nor the capacity of early-childhood institutions changed greatly during the Weimar years; the number of kindergartens was about the same as during the pre-war period (7,259 in 1910, and 7,282 in 1930); the number of places had declined from 558,610 to 421,955); and most were still provided by private organizations (Erning 1987c, 32–33). Like many reform projects during the Weimar years, the expansion of kindergartens was limited both by financial crises and by the persistence of conservative attitudes.

Nonetheless, the 1920s brought important developments in kindergarten pedagogy. By 1920 Froebel methods, sometimes in the revised form developed by the Pestalozzi-Froebel House, had become standard in almost all pre-school institutions. The Italian physician and educator Maria Montessori, who had become known when some of her works were translated into German in 1913, challenged the effectiveness of these now traditional methods. Montessori based her method on biological theories that attributed child development more to heredity than to pedagogical intervention. She rejected the Froebel games as romantic and pre-scientific. Instead, she provided scientifically designed play materials through which the individual child, following an inner drive toward intellectual growth, could develop perceptual, manual, and cognitive skills (Hecker and Muchow 1927). Froebelians charged that Montessori's method was too cognitive and individualistic to teach children the social skills necessary to become productive citizens. In 1927, two kindergarten teachers at the Pestalozzi-Froebel House who had visited Montessori's institute in Rome set up an experimental classroom offering both Montessoriean and Froebelian play materials (Hecker and Muchow 1927, 1–43).

Another influence on the kindergarten pedagogy of the Weimar years came from Freudian psychoanalysis. Freudian pedagogues criticized traditional kindergarten discipline for its repression of children's sexual and aggressive drives, and called for deeper insight into the psychological roots of children's behavior (Wolffheim 1930). In general, however, such trends were confined to a minority of kindergarten classes; most continued to use Froebel methods, though in modified form (Klattenhoff 1987, 168–180).

In 1933, the National Socialist Party under the leadership of Adolf Hitler assumed power in Germany and sought to bring all aspects of life, including both school and family, under the control of the state. Like most private organizations, the German Froebel Society was soon placed under new leadership; in 1934 its president, Lili Droescher, was replaced by Nazi educator Hans Volkelt, and kindergarten teachers (formerly independently organized in the Professional Organization of Kindergarten Teachers, Day-Care and Youth Workers) were incorporated into the National Socialist Teachers' Organization (Nationalsozialistischer Lehrerbund) (Volkelt 1934). Government policy called for the abolition of the private organizations that sponsored the kindergartens and their integration into a central governmental agency, the National Socialist Welfare Association (Nationalsozialistischer Wohlfahrtsverband). Thus the National Socialist government affirmed the existing concept of the kindergarten as a welfare, as opposed to educational, institution. However, due to the decentralized organization of the kindergartens, the process of "coordination" (or *Gleichschaltung*) was gradual. The Froebel Society was forced to dissolve itself in 1938 (Schwarz 1938). Most privately sponsored kindergartens were abolished by 1941, but a few were able to survive (Erning 1987a, 77–82; Grossmann 1994, 71–73).

The National Socialist pedagogues who now prescribed guidelines for

kindergarten education scornfully rejected the principle of free individual development upon which both the Froebel and Montessori systems were based.
Kindergarten pedagogy, wrote Nazi theorists, had encouraged softness, sensitivity, and intellectual precocity; by contrast, the National Socialist state aimed
to "raise a hardened generation—strong, reliable, obedient and decent" (Benzing 1941, 7). Although continuing to employ women as kindergarten teachers,
National Socialist educators found Froebel's ideal of "spiritual motherhood"
sentimental and effeminate, and called instead for a masculine pedagogy encouraging physical fitness and military toughness. Outdoor activities and competitive sports, even for the smallest children, replaced the Froebel games. These
prescriptions applied alike to boys and girls; girls, however, were in addition encouraged to play with dolls and domestic objects. "The boy will be a German
soldier," wrote educator Richard Benzing, "and the girl a German mother" (Benzing 1941, 39). To what extent such political guidelines influenced the routine of
the typical kindergarten cannot, of course, be ascertained. During the war, photographs and accounts indicate that military play was emphasized in at least
some kindergartens. "The boys are building an artillery emplacement with the
teacher," recounted one teacher in 1940. "They are bombarding a nearby village.
Some houses have already been destroyed" (Kammann 1940, 189). Girls participated in these activities by cutting out make-believe "ration cards."

Because of the demand for women's work, the number of kindergartens was
increased from 7,282 in 1930 to 9,814 in 1940, and further expanded in wartime
(Erning 1987c, 34). However, in striking contrast to contemporary communist
forms of totalitarianism, the Nazi regime never officially favored universal
public pre-school or day-care institutions as a means to indoctrination, but always encouraged maternal care in the private sphere as the ideal form of child
rearing.

In the post-war period, Germany was divided into two states, each faced with
the task of rebuilding both the physical environment and the theoretical basis
of their social-welfare and educational systems. Both states included kindergartens in this project of reconstruction, within very different ideological frame-
works.

In West Germany, the development of the kindergarten during the post-war
years, from 1945 to 1970, was shaped by a more general trend toward the restoration of the educational systems and theories of the Weimar Republic (Herrlitz
1993, 159–161). The kindergarten, too, was returned to the patterns set during
the Weimar period. As much as possible, kindergartens were returned to the organizations that had owned them in the 1920s, and those set up by the National

Socialist government were largely dissolved. Kindergarten educators affirmed the heritage of Froebel and of other figures in the German progressive peda- gogical tradition as achievements of the liberal Germany now resurrected from the ruins of National Socialism (Erning 1987a, 85–90). The West German state oriented its social policy toward single-income families, discouraging the em- ployment of women (Grossmann 1994, 86). The confessional organizations that ran most kindergartens still specifically rejected the idea of the kindergarten as a phase in the education of all children. A Protestant organization stated in 1962 that the family "should not be relieved of its primary responsibility" by such a system (Soziographisches Institut 1962, quoted in Erning 1987c, 38). Although the number of kindergartens and of kindergarten places increased during the first years of the Federal Republic (from 8,648 kindergartens in 1950 to 14,113 in 1965), their growth did not keep pace with that of the population. For example, the state of Bavaria offered 33 kindergarten places per 100 pre-school-age chil- dren in 1955, but only 32 in 1965 (Erning 1987c, 27). In 1957, a Federal commis- sion recommended the establishment of public-school kindergarten classes, but only for children with special problems (Grossmann 1994, 84).

For liberal critics, the state of the German kindergarten was an important in- dicator of the general conservatism of West German society. In a widely read book, the liberal sociologist Ralf Dahrendorf attributed his compatriots' insis- tence on the rights of the family, as shown through their resistance to public kindergartens, to the persistence of an authoritarian and patriarchal culture. Ar- guing that the early exposure of the child to the wider, public world of the school helped to build the habit of political participation and social responsibility, he called for public-school kindergartens as a means to strengthen German democ- racy (Dahrendorf 1967, 285–314).

The 1960s brought to West Germany a new concern with education reform. A central aim of the reformers was to promote upward mobility and equal op- portunity in a system which hitherto had done more to preserve than to chal- lenge class inequality. Education reform served both practical and idealistic ends; equal opportunity was not only democratic, but also useful in the creation of a skilled labor force for an ever more complex industrial economy. West Ger- many's deficit in pre-school education compared to that in other countries was now seen as a competitive disadvantage (Erning 1987a, 107–110). In addition, the growing percentage of mothers in the labor force created pressure to expand kindergarten education.

Meanwhile, the left-wing student movement of the 1960s had responded to the lack of pre-school institutions by creating their own, called *Kinderläden* (kid shops, so called because they were often located in storefronts). The first of these was opened in Berlin in 1968, by feminist students who demanded organized child care to support the emancipation of women. The founders of the Kinderläden created an anti-authoritarian approach to child rearing that was partly inspired by the psychoanalytic pedagogy of the 1920s. Parents, including fathers, participated actively in the administration and daily activities of these institutions (Grossmann 1994, 88–96; Berger 1990, 85–86).

A policy statement issued by a federal commission in 1970, the Structural Plan for the German Educational System, specifically called into question the adequacy of the family as the exclusive agent of socialization for small children, and recommended the incorporation of the kindergarten into elementary education systems (Erning 1987a, 106; Grossmann 1994, 86). Although implementation was left to the states, which control education systems, the federal government financed many pilot and experimental programs. By 1981 kindergarten places had been created for 78 percent of West German children (Erning 1987c, 38). Though no longer based on Froebelian methods, curricula continued to affirm the founder's basic conception of the kindergarten as a preparation for social life: "children should be taught to solve problems cooperatively and to understand, deal with, or tolerate social conflict," read an official policy statement (Deutscher Bildungsrat 1973, quoted in Erning 1987a, 111). However, this momentum of reforms was slowed by the economic recession of the 1970s, and kindergartens were never fully incorporated into public education (Erning 1987a, 115). Indeed, the majority of kindergartens are still in the hands of church or private associations (though regulated by the states), and public kindergartens are still supervised by child-welfare systems, not by school systems (Erning 1987a, 114–115).

In striking contrast to West Germany, the communist state formed in East Germany, the German Democratic Republic, immediately created a system of public kindergartens for both practical and ideological reasons. The East German regime considered itself the heir to socialist traditions of educational thought, among which was the advocacy of public pre-school education both in order to meet the material needs of the children of working mothers and to introduce the new generation to socialist ideology. The East German School Law of 1946 included the kindergarten in the educational system as a "pre-school institution," which aimed to prepare children for school. The aim of making kindergarten education compulsory, strongly advocated by communist educators, was abandoned for the time being because of the enormous costs involved (Barow-Bernstorff et al. 1974, 423–428).

The expansion of kindergarten education was impressive. According to statistics released by the government, by 1962 one half of all East German children of the appropriate age groups attended a kindergarten (Barow-Bernstorff et al. 1974, 453); by 1988 the number had risen to 81 percent (Ferree 1993). Clearly, the much higher priority given by the East German government than by the West German government to kindergarten education indicated important differences in social policy. Chief among these was the official attitude toward the employment of women, which was discouraged in West Germany but encouraged by the East German system. By 1962, 70 percent of all East German women of working age were employed, many in professional occupations (Barow-Bernstorff et al. 453); by 1988, approximately 91 percent were employed (as compared to about 50 percent in West Germany) (Frevert 1988, 333). Eastern policies toward pre-school education, however, still shared the basic view, derived from tradition, of the kindergarten as a service for the children of working mothers or of otherwise unavailable parents. In East Germany, the few private kindergarten classes that had served the children of non-working mothers for limited hours were condemned as remnants of the bourgeois past and were closed (Barow-Bernstorff et al. 1974, 440). Kindergarten admission policies gave priority to children of working mothers, and school hours were adjusted to suit such mothers' needs (Barow-Bernstorff et al. 1974, 445).

However, the East German kindergarten also served an important educational purpose. In the words adopted by the yearly meeting of kindergarten educators in 1948, "new Germany needs new people and their formation begins in the kindergarten" (quoted in Barow-Bernstorff et al. 1974, 428). The goals adopted by the East German kindergarten bore a superficial resemblance to those of Friedrich Froebel and of the progressive education tradition, which had emphasized the teaching of practical skills and social responsibility. "From earliest childhood," declared the head of the pre-school department of the Ministry of Education in 1967, "the younger generation . . . must be prepared for their role as creators of the socialist society" (Oschmann 1967, 16). But East German educators denigrated the emphasis of Froebel and especially Montessori on individual spontaneity, creativity, and imagination. On the contrary, teachers were required to inculcate a Stalinist ideology which valued order above initiative, and the state above the individual. They defined the aim of the kindergarten as the "many-sided creation of the socialist personality" (Oschmann 1967, 19; see also Barow-Bernstorff et al. 1974, 434). Thus the expansion of public kindergarten education in East Germany co-opted rather than fulfilled Froebel's vision of the kindergarten and its educational mission.

The unification of Germany in 1991 and the coordination of the Eastern and Western education and social-welfare systems have resulted in the substantial reduction of the once-extensive East German kindergarten system. Unlike West German kindergartens, which were financed by private organizations, tuition payments, communities, or states, East German kindergartens received federal as well as state subsidies. The removal of the federal subsidies and the increased financial pressure on the states has necessitated tuition charges that many families cannot afford. Demand for kindergarten places has also been affected by high unemployment, particularly of women, who have experienced severe disadvantages in the transition to a capitalist economy (Ferree 1993). Many East German feminists charge that the reduction in kindergarten places, which has become a prominent political issue, is part of a general plan by the conservative Christian Democratic Party (now the ruling party in Germany) to deprive women of their public role in economic and political life and to return both them and their children to the private sphere, now under the domination of a male breadwinner.

Thus from its beginnings until the present day, the German kindergarten has been at the center of political debates concerning the relationship of family and state, and between public and private spheres. In all Western societies during the era under discussion, the status of both women and children has been defined through public/private boundaries. Feminist movements from their beginnings have therefore challenged these boundaries, asserting both the right of women to enter the public sphere and the relevance of family structure to political and economic life. The kindergarten movement was such a challenge, which called for both the entrance of women into public, or professional, roles and the infusion of familial, or motherly, values into the previously male-dominated domain of education. The fact that the kindergarten was less successful in the land of its origin than in many other countries is probably attributable to a distinctively German insistence on the separate functions of family and school.[2] Whereas education authorities in other countries readily accepted pre-school education as a desirable supplement to familial child rearing, for most of Germany's history it was accepted by the educational establishment only as a substitute for, and specifically designated as inferior to, an absent or unfit mother. Not until recently—since the war in East Germany and since the 1970s in West Germany—has the kindergarten been taken seriously as an educational institution. Now, with the unification of Germany, its development is linked more strongly than ever to the status of women. Now as in the past, the miniature world of the kindergarten is shaped by the wider world of politics.

NOTES

1. I refer throughout this chapter to my own articles and book. These contain references to the many primary sources on which my own research is based. They are too numerous to cite here.
2. This thesis is proposed in Ralf Dahrendorf, *Society and Democracy in Germany* (English edition), New York, Norton, 1967, 285–314, and elaborated by Ann T. Allen, "Let Us Live for Our Children: Kindergarten Movements in Germany and the United States, 1840–1914," *History of Education Quarterly* 28 (Spring 1988): 23–48.

WORKS CITED

Albisetti, James C. 1994. "Deutsche Lehrerinnen des 19. Jahrhunderts im internationalen Vergleich." In Juliane Jacobi, ed., *Frauen zwischen Familie und Schule: Professionalisierungsstrategien bürgerlicher Frauen im internationalen Vergleich*. Frankfurt: Böhlau.

Allen, Ann Taylor. 1982. "Spiritual Motherhood: German Feminists and the Kindergarten Movement, 1848–1911." *History of Education Quarterly* 22 (Fall 1982): 319–340.

———. 1986. "Gardens of Children, Gardens of God: Kindergartens and Day-Care Centers in Nineteenth-Century Germany." *Journal of Social History* 19 (Spring 1986): 433–450.

———. 1988. "Let us Live for our Children: Kindergarten Movements in Germany and the United States." *History of Education Quarterly* 28 (Spring 1988): 405–436.

———. 1991. *Feminism and Motherhood in Germany, 1800–1914*. New Brunswick, N.J.: Rutgers University Press.

———. 1994. "Öffentliche und private Mutterschaft: Die internationale Kindergartenbewegung 1840–1914." In Juliane Jacobi, ed., *Frauen zwischen Familie und Schule: Professionalisierungsstrategien bürgerlicher Frauen im internationalen Vergleich*. Frankfurt: Böhlau.

Barow-Bernstorff, Edith, Karl-Heinz Günther, Margot Krecker, Heinz Schiffenhauer, eds. 1974. *BeitrΣge zur Geschichte der Vorschulerziehung*. Berlin: Vold aun Wissen.

Beetz, K. O. 1900. *Kindergartenzwang! Ein Weck- und Mahnruf an Deutschlands Eltern und Lehrer*. Wiesbaden: Emil Behrend.

Benzing, R. 1941. *Grundlagen der körperlichen und geistigen Erziehung des Kleinkindes im nationalsozialistischen Kindergarten*. Berlin: Zentralverlag der NSDAP.

Berger, Manfred. 1990. *150 Jahre Kindergarten: Ein Brief an Friedrich Froebel, Mit Zahlreichen Dokumenten aus der Geschichte des Kindergartens*. Frankfurt: Brandes und Apsel.

Bülow-Wendhausen, Bertha von. 1901. *The Life of the Baroness von Marenholtz-Bülow*. 2 vols. New York.

Bussemer, Herrad-Ulrike. 1985. *Frauenemanzipation und Bildungsbürgertum: Sozialgeschichte der Frauenbewegung in der Reichsgründerzeit*. Weinheim: Beltz.

Dahrendorf, Ralf. 1967. *Society and Democracy in Germany*. (English edition) New York: Norton.

Davis, Allen F., 1967. *Spearheads for Reform: The Social Settlements and the Progressive Movement, 1890–1914*. New York: Oxford University Press.

Die Reichsschulkonferenz 1920. Ihre Vorgeschichte und Vorbereitung und ihre Verhandlungen. 1921. Leipzig: Quelle und Meyer.

Downs, Robert B., 1978. *Friedrich Froebel.* Boston: Twayne.

Droescher, Lili, 1917. *Die Erziehungsaufgaben der Volkskindergärten im Kriege.* Leipzig: G.B. Teubner.

Ellsworth, Edward W. 1979. *Liberators of the Female Mind: The Shirreff Sisters, Educational Reform, and the Women's Movement.* Westport, Conn.: Greenwood Press.

Erning, Günter. 1987a. *Geschichte des Kindergartens,* 3 vols., ed. Günter Erning, Karl Neumann, and Jürgen Reyer. Vol. 1: *Entstehung und Entwicklung der öffentlichen Kleinkindererziehung in Deutschland von den Anfängen bis zur Gegenwart.* Freiburg im Breisgau: Lambertus.

———. 1987b. "Entwicklung und Formen der Finanzierung und Kostentragung öffentlicher Kleinkindererziehung." In Günter Erning, Karl Neumann, and Jürgen Reyer, eds., *Geschichte des Kindergartens,* 3 vols. Vol. 2: *Institutionelle Aspekte, systematische Perspektiven, Entiwicklungserläufe,* pp. 82–95. Freiburg im Breisgau: Lambertus.

———. 1987c. "Quantitative Entwicklung der Angebote öffentlicher Kleinkinder-erziehung." In Günter Erning, Karl Neumann, and Jürgen Reyer, eds., *Geschichte des Kin-dergartens,* 3 vols. Vol. 2: *Institutionelle Aspekte, systematische Perspektiven, Entwicklungs-verläufe,* pp. 29–40. Freiburg im Breisgau: Lambertus.

Ferree, Myra Marx. 1993. "The Rise and Fall of 'Mommy Politics': Feminism and Unification in (East) Germany." *Feminist Studies* 19 (Spring, 1993): 89–115.

Frevert, Ute. 1989. *Women in History: From Bourgeois Emancipation to Sexual Liberation.* Translated by Stuart McKinnon-Evans. Oxford: Berg.

Friedrich, Gerd. 1987. "Das niedere Schulwesen," vol. 3, pp. 123–152, in *Handbuch der deutschen Bildungsgeschichte,* 6 vols. München: C.H. Beck.

Froebel, Friedrich. 1840. *Entwurf eines Planes zur Begründung und Ausführung eines Kinder-gartens.* Leipzig: Brandstetter.

———. 1886. *Mothers' Songs, Games, and Stories: Froebel's Mutter- und Koselieder.* London: W. Rice.

Gerhard, Ute, Elisabeth Hannover-Druck, and Romina Schmitter, eds. 1979. *Dem Reich der Freiheit werb'ich Bürgerinnen: Die Frauen-Zeitung von Louise Otto.* Frankfurt: Suhrkamp.

Goldschmidt, Henriette. 1896. *Bertha von Marenholtz-Bülow: Ihr Leben und Wirken im Dienste der Erziehungslehre Friedrich Froebels.* Hamburg: Verlagsanstalt AG.

———. 1901. *Ist der Kindergaren eine Erziehungs- oder Zwangsanstalt?* Wiesbaden: Emil Behrend.

Grossmann, Wilma. 1994. *KinderGarten: Eine historisch-systematische Einführung in seine Entwicklung und Pädagogik.* 2 Auflage. Weinheim: Beltz.

Hall, G. Stanley. 1911. "The Pedagogy of the Kindergarten." Vol. 1 in *Educational Problems,* 2 vols. New York: Appleton-Century-Crofts.

Harrison, Elizabeth. 1930. *Sketches Along Life's Road,* ed. Carolyn Sherwin Bailey. Boston: Stratford Co.

Hecker, Hilde, and Martha Muchow. 1927. *Friedrich Froebel und Maria Montessori.* Leipzig: Quelle und Meyer.

Heinsohn, Gunnar. 1974. *Vorschulerziehung in der bürgerlichen Gesellschaft: Geschichte, Funk-tion, Aktuelle Lage.* Frankfurt: Fischer.

Herrlitz, Hans-Georg Wulf Hopf, Hartmut Titze. 1993. *Deutsche Schulgeschichte von 1800 bis zur Gegenwart: Eine Einführung.* München: Juventa.

Hoffmann, Erika. 1971. *Vorschulerziehung in Deutschland: Historische Entwicklung im Abriss.* Witten: Luther Verlag.

Klattenhoff, Klaus. 1987. "Pädagogische Aufgaben und Ziele in der Geschichte der öffentlichen Kleinkindererziehung." Vol. 2 in Günter Erning, Karl Neumann, and Jürgen Reyer, eds., *Geschichte des Kindergartens*, 3 vols. Freiburg im Breisgau: Lambertus.

Kleinau, Elke. 1990. "Die 'Hochschule für das weibliche Geschlecht' und ihre Auswirkungen auf die Entwicklung des höheren Mädchenschulwesens in Hamburg." *Zeitschrift für Pädagogik* 36 (1990): 121–126.

Kammann, Erna. 1940. "Unsere Kinder erleben den Krieg." *Kindergarten* 81 (July/Aug. 1940): 188–189.

Lawrence, Esther, ed. 1961. *Friedrich Froebel and English Education.* London: University of London Press.

Luc, Jean-Noel. 1993. "Salle d'asile contre jardin d'enfants: Les vicissitudes de la methode Froebel en France, 1855–1887." *Pedagogica Historia* 29 (1993): 433–458.

Lyschinska, Mary. 1922. *Henriette Schrader-Breymann: Ihr Leben aus Briefen und Tagebüchern zusammengestellt und erläutert.* Berlin and Leipzig: Walter de Gruyter.

Mandelbaum, Maurice. 1971. *History, Man and Reason: A Study in Nineteenth-Century Thought.* Baltimore: Johns Hopkins University Press.

Marenholtz-Bülow, Bertha von. 1855. *Women's Educational Mission: Being an Explanation of Froebel's System of Infant Gardens.* London: Darton.

———. 1864. *Die Arbeit und die neue Erziehung nach Froebels Methode.* Berlin: Commissions-Verlag.

Meysenbug, Malwida von. 1922. *Memoiren einer Idealistin.* Vol. 2 in Berta Schleicher, ed., *Malwida von Meysenbugs gesammelte Werke*, 5 vols. Stuttgart.

Mörsberger, Heribert, ed. 1978. *Der Kindergarten*, 3 vols. Freiburg: Herder.

Oschmann, I. 1967. "Der Stand der Vorschulerziehung in der DDR und ihre perspektivische Entwicklung." In *Die Gestaltung des Lebens im Kindergarten: Protokoll des IV Internationalen Seminars der Vorschulerziehung, September 1967 in der Deutschen Demokratischen Republik.* Berlin: Volk und Wissen, pp. 15–33.

Otto-Peters, Louise. 1866. *Das Recht der Frauen auf Erwerb: Blicke auf das Frauenleben der Gegenwart.* Hamburg: Hoffmann und Campe.

———. 1890. *Das erste Vierteljahrhundert des Allgemeinen deutschen Frauenvereins gegründet am 18. Oktober 1865 in Leipzig.* Leipzig: M. Schäefer.

Paletschek, Sylvia. 1990. *Frauen und Dissens: Frauen im Deutschkatholizismus und in den freireligiösen Gemeinden, 1841–1852.* Göttingen: Vandenhoeck und Rupprecht.

Peabody, Elizabeth. 1984. *Letters of Elizabeth Peabody, American Renaissance Woman*, ed. Bruce Ronda. Middletown, Conn.: Wesleyan University Press.

Prelinger, Catherine N. 1986. "The Nineteenth-Century Deaconessate in Germany: The Efficacy of a Family Model." In *German Women in the Eighteenth and Nineteenth Centuries: A Social and Literary History*, eds. Ruth-Ellen Joeres and Mary Jo Maynes. Bloomington: Indiana University Press.

———. 1987. *Charity, Challenge and Chane: Religious Dimensions of the Mid-Nineteenth-Century Women's Movement in Germany.* New York: Greenwood Press.

Reyer, Jürgen. 1987a. "Entwicklung der Trägerstruktur im der öffentlichen Kleinkindererziehung." In Günter Erning, Karl Neumann, and Jügen Reyer, eds., *Geschichte des Kindergartens,* 3 vols. Vol. 2: *Institutionelle Aspekte, systematische Perspectiven, Entwicklungserläufe,* pp. 40–66. Freiburg im Breisgau: Lambertus.

———. 1987b. "Kindheit zwischen privat-familiärer Lebenswelt und öffentlich veranstalteter Kleinkindeererziehung." In Günter Erning, Karl Neumann, and Jürgen Reyer, eds., *Geschichte des Kindergartens,* 3 vols. Vol. 2: *Institutionelle Aspekte, systematische Perspectiven, Entwicklungserläufe,* pp. 232–284. Freiburg im Breisgau: Lambertus.

Sachsse, Christoph. 1985. *Mütterlichkeit als Beruf: Sozialarbeit, Sozialreform und Frauenbewegung, 1871–1929.* Frankfurt: Suhrkamp.

Schrader-Breymann, Henriette. 1890. *Der Volkskindergarten im Pestalozzi-Froebel-Haus.* Berlin.

Schwarz, Ella. 1939. "Weshalb Auflösung des Deutschen Fröbel-Verbandes." *Kindergarten* 79 (1938): 204–206.

Shapiro, Michael Steven. 1983. *Child's Garden: The Kindergarten Movement from Froebel to Dewey.* University Park: Pennsylvania State University Press.

Silber, Kate. 1973. *Pestalozzi, The Man and His Work.* London: Routledge.

Steinmetz, George. 1993. *Regulating the Social: The Welfare State and Local Politics in Imperial Germany.* Princeton: Princeton University Press.

Troen, Selwyn K. 1975. *The Public and the Schools: Shaping the St. Louis Public Schools System.* Columbus: University of Missouri Press.

Volkelt, Hans. 1934. "Unser Weg 1934." *Kindergarten* 75 (Jan. 1934): 1–5.

Whitbread, Nanette. 1972. *The Evolution of the Infant-Nursery School: A History of Infant and Nursery Education in Britain, 1800–1970.* London: Routledge.

Wolffheim, Nelly. 1930. *Psycholanalyse und Kindergarten.* Wien: Verlag der Zeitschrift für psycholanalytische Pädagogik.

Chapter 2 "The Letter Killeth": Americanization and Multicultural Education in Kindergartens in the United States, 1856–1920

Barbara Beatty

Anna Bryan's speech to the National Education Association in 1890 marked a critical juncture in the American kindergarten movement. Bryan realized that if American kindergarten teachers did not stop following German kindergarten methods to the letter, they would kill the spirit of the kindergarten—along with all hope for its universalization in the United States. During the 1860s and 1870s when the kindergarten was introduced to the United States, most German-American and American kindergarten educators replicated Friedrich Froebel's methods as carefully and faithfully as possible. This slavish imitation of Froebelian pedagogy served the kindergarten movement well initially. The kindergarten needed to distinguish itself from older, unsuccessful preschool models, and establish methods clearly different from educational practices for older children. But the "Germanness" of the kindergarten soon became problematic in the United States.

In the 1880s and 1890s, during the second phase of the kindergarten movement, the Froebelian kindergarten was Americanized and promoted as a private preschool and charity. No longer an institution for the preservation of German culture or a purely German pedagogical importation, the American kindergarten was transformed by the conditions of city life and by science. Most American kindergartens allowed for considerable cultural and religious diversity, within a rubric of unity and ethnic harmony. The internationalism and universalism of Froebel's kindergarten ideology fit well with American needs to socialize young children from different backgrounds to coexist and cooperate peaceably and voluntarily. Rather than requiring immigrant children to relinquish all their ethnic differences, urban kindergarten teachers added information about the backgrounds of immigrant children to existing kindergarten curricula albeit in a somewhat superficial manner. This incorporation of cultural differences was one of the first examples of explicit multicultural education in the United States.

During the third phase of the American kindergarten movement, from the 1890s through the end of World War I, kindergartens were adopted in public schools throughout the country. Americanizing immigrant children was one of the main rationales for public kindergartens. But many public kindergarten teachers continued to use multicultural curricula and to visit the homes of immigrant families, and immigrants attended kindergarten mothers' meetings. The American kindergarten was permanently changed by these cross-cultural encounters. Americanization and multiculturalism proved to be relatively compatible, except when the United States was at war with other countries.

The Americanization of the kindergarten reveals much about the complex interrelationship of pedagogical practice, nationalism, and cultural identity. Kindergarten teachers attempted to inculcate children with the social habits and public values of the dominant American culture. At the same time, teachers mediated the domains of the home and the school, and were influenced by the cultures of the immigrant children and families with whom they worked. How was the German kindergarten Americanized? How did the Americanized kindergarten serve as an agent of Americanization? How was the American kindergarten changed by the multicultural children it was Americanizing?

INTRODUCTION OF THE GERMAN
KINDERGARTEN TO THE UNITED STATES

Froebel, who conceived of the kindergarten as a universal preschool method, hoped it would be established in America in particular. The kindergarten was introduced to the United States in the mid-1850s by Germans fleeing from the failure of the revolution of 1848. These liberal "freethinkers" brought German ideas on education to the Midwest and other areas where they settled. Conducted in German, these early kindergartens were intended to preserve German language and culture and to promote Froebelian pedagogy, which had been banned in Germany for its association with liberalism.[1]

The first kindergarten in the United States was founded in 1856 in Watertown, Wisconsin, by Margarethe Meyer Schurz. Margarethe Meyer was born in 1832 in Hamburg. Her wealthy, politically liberal Jewish family supported many educational and cultural causes. She was educated in kindergarten methods by Froebel, who was apparently very impressed by her as a student. In 1852, Meyer moved to London to aid her ailing sister, Bertha Meyer Ronge, who was married to the radical German Catholic religious dissident Johann Ronge. The Ronges had started the first kindergarten in England, in which Margarethe taught. Johann Ronge introduced her to Carl Schurz, a university-educated Christian freethinker who had been exiled from Germany for his involvement with the revolution. Margarethe Meyer and Carl Schurz were married in 1852 and emigrated to the United States, where they eventually settled in Wisconsin.[2]

In fall 1856, Margarethe Schurz started a small home kindergarten for her three-year-old daughter, Agathe. Six children, including four of Agathe's cousins and another little boy, attended Schurz's private, German-speaking kindergarten, which she soon moved to her relatives' house in downtown Watertown. Schurz taught in the kindergarten only briefly, as her husband's advancing career as a general in the Union Army and prominent Republican politician caused the family to move frequently. Her relatives maintained the program in Watertown for a number of years.

Records show that at least nine or ten other German-speaking kindergartens existed in the United States in the late 1850s, 1860s, and early 1870s. Another of Froebel's students, Caroline Louise Frankenburg, began a private kindergarten in Columbus, Ohio, in 1858. Many early kindergartens were founded in connection with the bilingual German-American academies that opened in cities such as Louisville, New York, Detroit, and Milwaukee. Adolph Douai began a kindergarten in 1861 as part of the German-American academy he directed in Newark, New Jersey. Another kindergarten opened in a similar school in Hoboken at about the same time, and in 1865 William N. Hailmann added a kindergarten to the German-American academy he directed in Louisville, Kentucky. Presentations on the kindergarten were made at conventions of the German-American Teachers Union held in Cincinnati, Ohio, in 1871 and in Hoboken, New Jersey, in 1872.[3]

The kindergarten did not remain a German institution for long. Shortly af-

ter its introduction to the United States, upper- and middle-class Americans became interested in the kindergarten as an educational method for their own children. In the 1860s and 1870s, private, English-speaking kindergartens, most of
which were taught by German kindergarten teachers, were begun in major
American cities. Criticism of these German kindergartens soon arose, however.
Some American parents complained about Froebelian rigidity, "Germanness,"
and lack of early reading instruction. The source of some of these concerns can
be seen in well-known kindergarten guides such as Edward Wiebe's *The Paradise of Childhood,* published in Springfield, Massachusetts, in 1869 by game and
education supply manufacturer Milton Bradley, and Maria Kraus-Boelte's and
John Kraus's two-volume *Kindergarten Guide,* published in New York City in
1877 by Ernst Steiger, the other main supplier of kindergarten materials. The
distinguishing feature of these guides, other than their length and specificity,
was their insistence on orderliness and absolute fidelity to Froebelianism. As
Wiebe stated, everything in a kindergarten must be done "with a great deal of
precision" as "order and regularity in all the performances" were "of utmost
importance."[4]

The failure of some of the first kindergartens run by Germans for American
children demonstrates that some American parents may have been sensitive to
potential conflict between American and German cultural and educational values. Both of the kindergartens started in New York and Boston in the mid-1860s
by Matilda Kriege, a protegee of Baroness Marenholtz, one of Germany's leading kindergarten trainers, were unsuccessful. Some American parents objected
to Kriege's insistence on using German songs, games, and folk stories. Kriege
herself suggested that American parents' desire to have their children taught to
read at an early age was the main source of difficulty. German-American kindergarten educator William N. Hailmann also criticized American parents' demands for premature academic work.[5]

But the emphasis on following Froebel's directions carefully and faithfully
also helped the kindergarten when it was introduced in the United States. A previous European preschool importation, the infant school, had been rejected by
Americans in the 1830s as too school-like for young children. Strict adherence
to Froebelianism distinguished the kindergarten from the newly established
"common school," the public primary schools which were started in American
cities beginning in the early 1800s. As American kindergarten advocate Elizabeth Peabody emphasized, the kindergarten was "not the old-fashioned infant
school," nor was it a "public primary school," but a very different kind of institution, "a garden of children."[6]

A few influential American educators were aware of the kindergarten very early on and began promoting it enthusiastically. Henry Barnard reported in an 1856 article in his *American Journal of Education* on an exhibit of Bertha Meyer Ronge's kindergarten work he had seen at the International Exhibit of Educational Systems and Materials in London in 1854. Articles on the kindergarten attracted the attention of Elizabeth Peabody, who may also have heard about the kindergarten from Margarethe Meyer Schurz. Much enthused, Peabody opened the first English-speaking kindergarten in the United States in Boston in 1860.

Most American kindergarten advocates had only a superficial understanding of Froebel's methods, however. Peabody wrote her first *Kindergarten Guide* after having read only portions of Froebel's *Education of Man,* and little or none of his kindergarten pedagogics. Published in 1863, the guide included academic exercises tacked on to Froebel's methods. She disavowed this academicism after she met with German-trained Froebelians in Germany in the 1870s, and began focusing on play-based learning. The differences between Peabody's first guide and her second guide, published in 1877, were also indicative of the shift from Calvinist to Romantic modes of education—a shift which had evolved further in Germany than in America. As Ann Taylor Allen shows, German kindergarten teachers such as Henrietta Schrader-Breyman had begun liberalizing Froebelian methods a decade or two before Americans did.

The fight over Anna Coe's "American Kindergarten" exhibit at the Centennial Exposition in Philadelphia in 1876 provides further evidence of the tensions in America between play-based and academic instruction. Realizing that many American parents still wanted their four- and five-year-olds to be instructed in academic skills, Coe designed and advertised a so-called American Kindergarten which did just this. Elizabeth Peabody was horrified at this challenge to Froebelian dogma, though she had recommended similar methods in her own first kindergarten guide. Coe's kindergarten attracted much attention at the Centennial. In response, Peabody condemned Coe in the pages of *The Kindergarten Messenger,* and published lists of approved, "genuine" kindergartens. For some time, Peabody was able to enforce relatively strict adherence to Froebelianism. St. Louis kindergarten advocate Susan Blow hung on even longer and enlisted the aid of powerful St. Louis school superintendent William Torrey Harris in the Froebelian cause. But neither Elizabeth Peabody nor Susan Blow was capable of making American kindergarten teachers stick to traditional German Froebelian methods after charity kindergartens began serving the children of the poor.[7]

AMERICANIZING THE KINDERGARTEN

By the 1880s, Froebelianism was firmly established in the United States as a preschool model for the young children of the upper classes. Most American cities had private kindergartens, and a kindergarten supply industry started. Americans began opening more private kindergartens and training schools. Well-to-do American mothers joined kindergarten clubs and enrolled in training classes, and many home kindergartens were begun.[8]

In the 1880s and 1890s, charity, or "free," kindergartens in large cities began modifying Froebel's German kindergarten pedagogy to meet the needs of poor and immigrant children and families. As the social welfare functions of the kindergarten became more salient, educators at charity kindergartens began adding new activities based on the experiences of urban children. These educators also adopted scientific ideas about children's development and modernized Froebel's methods to be more in accord with new psychological data.

American kindergarten teachers both resisted and accepted urbanization and science. Nostalgic for rural, small-town life, they thought city children needed to be taken on field trips to the country and taught in classrooms that simulated natural environments. At the same time, urban kindergarten teachers began to see the city and human social environments as a source of curricular innovation. Progressive Era concerns about poverty and family pathology and the Froebelian concept of the kindergarten as a bridge between home and school coalesced. Teachers at charity kindergartens visited the homes of their students and ran classes for mothers. In the process, kindergarten teachers learned about what was happening to their pupils outside of school, and began incorporating this information into their teaching. As these teachers shifted their focus from stylized songs and games about flowers, birds, and farm animals to more informal play activities involving interactions among family members and everyday experiences, kindergarten curricula began to concentrate on American children's real lives, rather than on German folklore and artificial naturalism.

This new emphasis was first apparent in the work of Alice Putnam. Born in Chicago in 1841, Putnam became interested in the kindergarten when her children were young. After studying with Maria Kraus-Boelte and Susan Blow, she became a kindergarten trainer. Putnam worked with other Progressive reformers in the Chicago area, including Jane Addams, John Dewey, and Francis W. Parker. She taught kindergarten training classes at Hull House, the University of Chicago, and Cook County Normal School. In 1880, Putnam was instrumental in founding the Chicago Free Kindergarten Association and the Chicago

Froebel Association, where numerous American kindergarten teachers were trained. Known for her practical, non-dogmatic approach to the kindergarten and her child-centered methods, Putnam influenced many younger kindergarten teachers, including Anna Bryan, whom she trained, and Annie Howe, who brought kindergartens to Japan.

It was Anna Bryan, the director of the Louisville Free Kindergarten Association, who began the process of Americanizing the kindergarten. Born in Louisville in 1858, Bryan studied kindergarten methods in a program sponsored by the Chicago Free Kindergarten Association. In 1887, she was invited back to Louisville by the Union Gospel Mission to start a kindergarten for indigent children. After convincing the church group that a more broad-based, free kindergarten association was needed, she worked intensively in Louisville until the winter of 1893. During the six years Bryan was in Louisville, her kindergarten methods became very well known. From all accounts, she was an unusually alert and intellectually original thinker, and a lively, magnetic teacher. According to her assistant Patty Smith Hill, Bryan encouraged her pupils, both children and adults, to exercise "liberty of thought." The result, as Hill put it, was "a deliberate though unaggressive break with the traditional practice of that time."[9]

Bryan's break with traditional German Froebelianism grew out of her experiences working with poor families and children. A description of the Louisville Free Kindergarten and Anna Bryan's methods by Cora L. Stockham documents the ill effects of alcoholism, abuse, and poverty on many of the children. To counter the "degradation and absolute hatred for work" in "the environments from which these children came" Bryan developed a curriculum that would reach the children directly and capture their interest. Bryan realized, Stockham said, that the children "knew more about their homes (such as they were) than anything else." Consequently, Bryan designed activities based on the children's everyday lives and substituted these activities for Froebelian themes. Instead of following the Froebelian "occupations"—patterned play activities based on traditional German folk occupations such as weaving or stitching abstract patterns on paper cards—the children stitched dishes, tables, stoves, beds, and other things they had seen at home. Instead of using Froebel's "gifts"—sequenced educational materials such as wooden cubes and rods used for making complicated, prescribed geometric patterns—the children used Froebel's materials to construct everyday objects. Instead of playing Froebel's prescribed German games, such as "Fish in the Brook" and "Hare in the Hollow," the children in Anna Bryan's kindergarten pretended they were clocks or fireboxes and acted out skits in which they did real-life activities such as mailing a letter.[10]

This seemingly innocuous substitution of themes from children's daily, urban lives for Froebel's artificial naturalism was the key step in the Americanization of the kindergarten. Some saw Bryan's work as a dangerous watering down of the purity and symbolic sophistication of Froebelian methods. In the highly dogmatic world of the kindergarten movement, where any variation from Froebel caused consternation and criticism, Bryan's innovations attracted immediate attention. Bryan influenced John Dewey, whose "subprimary department" at the University of Chicago was much like Bryan's pragmatic kindergarten. German-American kindergarten leader William M. Hailmann and Progressive educational reformer Francis Wayland Parker came to Louisville to visit Bryan's "reconstructed" kindergarten. Approving of what they saw, they encouraged Bryan to write up her results and present them to the National Education Association.[11]

In her address to the N.E.A. meeting in St. Paul, Minnesota, in 1890, Bryan said the kindergarten was "stagnating" because of overly rigid adherence to the "letter" rather than "the spirit" of Froebelian methods. Teachers needed to keep their minds "free, creative, . . . never losing sight of the child's immediate inward condition and needs, never becoming so fascinated by the tools as to study them more than the child." Children, Bryan said, needed to be "both orderly and creative," but the Froebelian kindergarten stressed only the former. Bryan made an important distinction between "dictation play" and "free play." Dictation play, the copying of patterns or following instructions to games, could help "timid children, or those with few resources and small invention, unused to working out ideas," and "erratic children." Although poor children in free kindergartens were often "literal-minded" and "unimaginative," Bryan thought that it was exactly for this reason that they needed more time for open-ended free play.[12]

The other force for modernization of the American kindergarten movement and challenge to German Froebelianism came from the new field of psychology. G. Stanley Hall's child study movement, a precursor of modern developmental psychology, influenced many kindergarten teachers. Child study was a populist form of applied psychology in which teachers helped researchers collect data on young children's knowledge, predilections, fears, habits, and so on, using surveys conducted in classrooms. Hall initially supported the kindergarten, gave speeches at kindergarten conferences, and enlisted kindergarten teachers in his research. He became increasingly worried, however, as his work on the progression of large to small muscle development suggested that Froebel's emphasis on the manipulation of small objects and intricate handwork could cause fatigue and nervous problems in young children.

Many kindergarten teachers learned about child study at institutes at Clark University, in Worcester, Massachusetts, where Hall was president. At Hall's summer sessions in the mid-1890s, kindergarten teachers studied children's development and learned psychological ideas that led some of them to modify their Froebelian teaching methods. The roster of kindergarten leaders who attended either the 1894 or 1896 session of the Clark University Summer School shows the extent of Hall's influence. Anna Bryan and her assistant Patty Smith Hill attended, as did Kate Douglas Wiggin and Nora Archibald Smith from San Francisco, Alice Putman from Chicago, and Lucy Wheelock from Boston. All well-known kindergarten trainers, these women then went on to teach new, scientifically based kindergarten ideas and methods to other kindergarten teachers. Their trainees in turn worked in kindergartens and training schools in other parts of the United States and in other countries. The international kindergarten movement was thus introduced to child study and the concept of adapting curriculum to children's development.[13]

Beginning with the innovations of Anna Bryan and other educators in urban charity kindergartens in the 1880s, and the introduction of G. Stanley Hall's child study ideas in the 1890s, the American kindergarten movement turned away from German Froebelianism toward more progressive, science-based pedagogy. By 1900, G. Stanley Hall's student Frederic Burk, who was superintendent of the Santa Barbara, California, public schools, was offering kindergarten children the choice of playing with Froebelian materials, or balls, swings, beanbags, and other toys. Not surprisingly, the children chose the toys. Burk's Free Play Kindergarten pulled the movement even further from Froebelianism.[14] Patty Smith Hill, who in 1904 was invited to teach kindergarten methods at Teachers College at Columbia University, developed new, larger wooden unit blocks, which in a different form would become the staple of modern kindergarten and nursery school supplies.

This shift away from Froebelianism helped the kindergarten withstand the criticisms of Progressives and psychologists like John Dewey, who considered Froebelianism artificial, rigid, and unscientific. But there was also resistance to science and modernization. Some kindergarten teachers used child study more as a mantra than as a guide to classroom practice. Although Lucy Wheelock changed some of her teaching methods because of Hall's warnings about nervous strain, she had stopped using some of Froebel's materials earlier based on her own pedagogical judgment. Elizabeth Harrison, author of the popular kindergarten book for mothers, *A Study of Child Nature from the Kindergarten Standpoint* (1890), recommended that mothers base their childrearing practices on science, but in fact wrote primarily about character education. Some kindergarten teachers resisted Bryan's realism, insisting that classical, pure Froebelianism was what poor city children most needed. This ambivalence was particularly apparent in the writings of Kate Douglas Wiggin, the founder of the Silver Street Kindergarten program in a San Francisco slum. Wiggin was the author of both *The Story of Patsy* (1882), about a crippled street urchin who dies in his kindergarten teacher's arms, and *Rebecca of Sunnybrook Farm* (1904), the best-selling idyll of countrified childhood.[15]

But despite this ambivalence about science and urbanization, Froebelian methods were gradually Americanized and modernized, paving the way for widespread public and public school acceptance.

AMERICANIZATION AND
MULTICULTURAL EDUCATION

In the third phase of the American kindergarten movement, the Americanized kindergarten, which had been brought to the United States by immigrants, was reconceived as a means to Americanize immigrants. The promotion of the kindergarten as an antidote to problems caused by immigration was a key factor in its successful institution in the public schools. Huge increases in immigration and in immigrant birthrates sparked concerns about ethnic disunity. Americans were worried that immigrant parents were not socializing their children in American mores. There were complaints of immigrant children running wild on city streets, committing petty crimes, and threatening public safety. Kindergartens, classes for kindergarten mothers, and home visits were seen as vehicles for reaching immigrant families, and for preventing crime and other social problems.

Because many charity kindergartens were subsumed whole into public systems, their methods and curricula set the tone for public kindergartens. Urban kindergarten teachers around the turn of the twentieth century responded to the presence of immigrant children in their classes by creating an Americanistic multicultural curriculum which introduced diversity in a controlled way. Kindergarten children were exposed to other cultures through songs, games, and stories from many countries. They were also implicitly taught that all differences could be harmonized. This uniquely American form of multiculturalism was most common in kindergartens in the western part of the United States. Kate Douglas Wiggin's Silver Street Kindergarten included children from many different national and ethnic backgrounds. The reports of the San Francisco

Kindergarten Society, which sponsored the Silver Street Kindergarten, document Wiggin's multicultural methods. The Society's Eighth Annual Report in 1889, for instance, reported proudly on its "cosmopolitan regiment" of children with "curly yellow hair and rosy cheeks . . . swarthy faces and blue-black curls . . . wooly little pows and thick lips . . . the fire and passion of the Southern races and the self-poise and serenity of Northern nations."[16] Meanwhile, children in the Crocker Kindergarten in San Francisco learned about "How little Pen-Se raised Silk-worms."[17] The tone of these reports was uniformly glowing and positive. Any tensions among immigrant groups and between foreign and native cultures were glossed over. In American kindergartens at the turn of the century, multiculturalism was made cute.

Subtler political messages were embedded in this new Americanistic multiculturalism. The kindergarten, Wiggin stated, had the potential to do two things: bring about a radical unification of the races in America and at the same time teach American values. What "an opportunity for amalgamation of races and for laying the foundation of American citizenship" there was in a kindergarten which contained "Pat," "Topsy," "Abraham and Isaac," "Gretchen and Hans," "Christina," and "Duncan," the Eighth Annual Report trilled. The curricula of some kindergarten training schools in California during this period were also overtly multicultural and assimilationist. Members of the California Kindergarten Study Club studied the educational systems of "China, Japan, India, Persia, and the people of Israel and Egypt," and learned about how children from different backgrounds could play together in harmony. Although biased, stereotyping, and simplistic, these programs were among the first examples of overt multicultural education in the United States.[18]

Religious diversity was also characteristic of the American kindergarten movement. Protestant churches supported kindergartens for poor, immigrant, African-American, and Latino children. Congregationalists in particular sponsored charity kindergartens and became involved in kindergarten missionary work in Asia, Africa, and elsewhere, as this volume attests. Lucy Wheelock helped organize a free kindergarten for African-American children at Hope Chapel, under the auspices of Boston's Old South Church. Presbyterian missionaries sponsored "plaza kindergartens" for Latino children in New Mexico. Jewish support for kindergartens was strong as well, although not among Orthodox Jewish communities. Felix Adler, the founder of the Ethical Culture Society and a leader of Reform Judaism, was an influential kindergarten advocate.[19]

Charity kindergartens promoted non-sectarian universalism rather than espousing a specific religious affiliation. In fact, the religious toleration of kindergarten educators was such that some teachers in charity kindergartens were accused of godlessness. The San Francisco Kindergarten Society, organization of which was spurred in part by a visit from Felix Adler, encouraged kindergarten teachers to "respect the religious beliefs of all parents" and to "give no specific instruction on topics unsuited to the mind of the child," such as "creed, doctrine, or dogma." Responding to criticism of being "godless," the society's 1881 Annual Report stated that the kindergarten dealt with the "development of the best humanity," and implied that to criticize the kindergarten was to be a "narrow bigot, and ignorant babbler, or a purely vicious assailant."[20] Although some of this criticism may have been due to the association of the kindergarten with the well-known agnosticism of Robert Ingersoll, whose sister Sarah B. Cooper was a kindergarten leader in San Francisco, most charity kindergarten do seem to have been interested in teaching general moral and spiritual values, rather than proselytizing.

As with multiculturalism, this religious toleration was somewhat superficial, however. The kindergarten was probably perceived by some religious groups as a front for a secular humanistic form of pan-Judeo Protestantism. That the kindergarten was not initially as accepted by all religious groups is suggested by differences in the numbers of Jewish and Catholic school kindergartens. Records of the Bureau of Jewish Education, for instance, indicate that in the Boston area almost all private Jewish day schools had kindergartens from their inception or added them very early on. The office of the Superintendent of Catholic Schools of the Archdiocese of Boston documents that few Catholic private or parochial schools had kindergartens until as late as the 1970s or 1980s. These differences may have been due in part to financial factors and lack of space in Catholic schools. But orthodox and fundamentalist groups of any religion were less supportive of kindergartens because of the kindergarten's non-traditional pedagogical methods and association with liberal religious ideas.[21]

After the turn of the twentieth century, when immigration rates were seen as posing more of a threat to the foundations of American society, some kindergarten teachers began forcing Americanization more directly. This shift can be seen in descriptions of the New York Kindergarten Association, in which Americanization rather than multiculturalism was emphasized as a goal. In 1907, New York kindergarten supporter James Bruce argued that public kindergartens were important because they could capture immigrant children while they were young and "still plastic" so that they could be "so swayed and molded as to grow up Americans, to absorb by natural processes, by normal unconscious assimilation, the tone and tendencies of our social and political structure" and "can breathe in the American spirit."[22]

In 1918, when the United States was at war with Germany, this "natural" and "unconscious assimilation" became coercive. A U.S. Bureau of Education kindergarten pamphlet recommended using mothers' visits and classes as a means of neutralizing the "danger" of the "new electoral power" these women's husbands wielded, and to teach immigrant women to change their foreign dietary and other habits.[23] But only a year later when the war with Germany was over, another U.S. Bureau of Education pamphlet questioned whether it was in the American spirit to "'rob' the immigrant of . . . language, customs, racial traditions, religious beliefs," and suggested using kindergarten mothers' meetings for "receiving . . . foreign customs of dress, food, music" so that there could be an "exchange of ideas . . . as well the opening wedge for the tactful introduction of approved American customs."[24]

It is difficult to ascertain how many kindergarten teachers actually followed any of these recommendations about using kindergarten and mothers' classes for Americanization. Certainly the "songs and flag drills" and "elementary patriotic exercises" that New York kindergarten advocate James Bruce thought would cause children to "breathe in the American spirit" occurred, but these took place in other grade-level classes as well, before, during, and after World War I. Kindergarten teachers' frequent, direct contacts with families made their potential role in the Americanization process more prominent than that of other teachers. But coercive Americanization seems to have been a phenomenon of the xenophobic war years rather than an underlying characteristic of the kindergarten itself. After World War I, most kindergarten teachers returned to the more indirect kind of Americanistic multiculturalism that blended curricular materials and activities from foreign cultures with an introduction to American life.

CONCLUSION

Like most successful educational reforms, the kindergarten succeeded in the United States because it could be many things to many different people. It attracted an initial group of loyal followers who supported kindergartens as a means of preserving German cultural identity in a new, polyglot culture. But some of the characteristics that served the kindergarten well during its introductory phase later became obstacles. The kindergarten encountered resistance because of its "Germanness," because of Froebelian pedagogical rigidity, because it did not provide reading instruction, and because its pre-scientific methods did not fit the emerging canons of developmentalist psychology. Filled with immigrants from around the world and with poor children whose educational needs demanded new teaching approaches, the city was the crucible in which the kindergarten's modern multicultural identity was forged. Ironically, the same factors that Americanized the kindergarten also created support for its use as a means of Americanization. The kindergarten was used as an explicit Americanizing agent during periods of perceived national emergency. Usually, however, American kindergartens combined multiculturalism and Americanization in a "cute," noncoercive fashion.

The cuteness of kindergarten multiculturalism belies its more serious functions and meaning. Children in the Progressive Era were growing up in an America that was rapidly becoming multicultural and modern. The kindergarten connected private family life, where children were raised in the traditions of their particular culture, and the public world of the school, where children were taught American values. The kindergarten was where these disparate cultures first came into contact on a daily basis and where assimilation and pluralism blended in the curriculum. The kindergarten embodied the contradictions of multiculturalism and modernization. Kindergarten teachers' nostalgic recreation of country life reflected the resistance to urbanization and other social dislocations characteristic of the Progressive Era. At the same time, kindergarten teachers saw science as a solution for human problems, and advocated modern, scientific approaches to childrearing and education. The American kindergarten thus both resisted and embraced modernization and multiculturalism. It was able to attract a broad base of popular support by recreating rural naturalism and incorporating urbanism. It was able to meet the demands of different groups by melding and maintaining diversity in a nation that has managed to survive by constantly recalibrating the precarious balance between national, cultural, and individual identity.

NOTES

1. On Froebel's hopes for kindergartens in America and the kindergarten movement in Germany, see Michael Steven Shapiro, *Child's Garden: The Kindergarten Movement from Froebel to Dewey* (University Park, N.J.: Pennsylvania State University Press, 1983), and Ann Taylor Allen, *Feminism and Motherhood in Germany, 1800–1914* (New Brunswick, N.J.: Rutgers University Press, 1991).
2. Biographical sources on Margarethe Meyer Schurz include Joseph Schafer, ed., *Intimate Letters of Carl Schurz, 1841–1869* (Madison: State Historical Society of Wisconsin, 1928);

Hannah Werwath Swart, *Margarethe Meyer Schurz: A Biography* (Watertown, Wis.: Watertown Historical Society, 1967); Jonathan Messerli, "Margarethe Meyer Schurz," in Edward T. James and Janet Wilson James, eds., *Notable American Women 3* (Cambridge: Harvard University Press, Belknap, 1971): 242–43; Sy Quam, *First Kindergarten in the United States* (Watertown, Wis.: Watertown Historical Society, 1988); and Barbara Beatty, "Margarethe Meyer Schurz," in John A. Garraty, ed., *American National Biography* (New York: Oxford University Press, 1999) vol. 19, 449–50.

3. On German-American kindergartens, see Elizabeth Jenkins, "Froebel's Disciples in America," *American-German Review 3* (March 1937): 15–18; Edward W. Hocker, "The First American Kindergarten Teacher," *American-German Review* 8 (February 1942): 9–10; Nina C. Vanderwalker, *The Kindergarten in American Education* (New York: Macmillan, 1908), 12–14; and John Kraus, "The Kindergarten (Its Use and Abuse) in America," in National Education Association, *Addresses and Proceedings, 1877* (Salem, Ohio: Office of the National Teacher, 1877), 198.

4. Edward Wiebe, *The Paradise of Childhood* (Springfield, Mass.: Milton Bradley), 95.

5. Matilda H. Kriege, *The Child, Its Nature and Relations: and Elucidation of Froebel's Principles of Education* (New York: E. Steiger, 1872), 145. For more on the Kriege, Hailmann, and German-American kindergartens, see Barbara Beatty, *Preschool Education in America: The Culture of Young Children from the Colonial Era to the Present* (New Haven and London: Yale University Press, 1995), 53–57.

6. For more on Peabody, see Ruth M. Baylor, *Elizabeth Palmer Peabody: Kindergarten Pioneer* (Philadelphia: University of Pennsylvania Press, 1965); Hersha S. Fisher, "Elizabeth Peabody: Her Family and Its Influence" (qualifying paper, Harvard Graduate School of Education, 1978); idem, "The Education of Elizabeth Peabody" (Ed.D. Diss., Harvard Graduate School of Education, 1980); and Bruce A. Ronda, ed., introduction to *Letters of Elizabeth Palmer Peabody: American Renaissance Women* (Middletown, Conn.: Wesleyan University Press, 1984).

7. For more on Coe's American kindergarten and Peabody's criticisms, see Barbara Beatty, "Preschool Advocacy and Teaching as an Occupation for Women in Nineteenth-Century Boston" (Ed.D. Diss., Harvard Graduate School of Education, 1981), 83–89, and Shapiro, *Child's Garden*.

8. For more on Blow and Harris, see Beatty, *Preschool Education in America*, 64–67; Selwyn K. Troen, *The Public and the Schools: Shaping the St. Louis System, 1838–1920* (Columbia: University of Missouri Press, 1975), 99–115; and Shapiro, *Child's Garden*, 46–50.

9. Patty Smith Hill, "Anna E. Bryan," in International Kindergarten Union Committee of Nineteen, *Pioneers of the Kindergarten in America* (New York: Century), 226. For more on Bryan, see Beatty, *Preschool Education in America*, 81–83; M. Charlotte Jammer, "Anna E. Bryan," in Edward T. James and Janet Wilson James, eds., *Notable American Women* (Cambridge: Harvard University Press, Belknap, 1971), vol. 1: 263–64; Eva B. Whitmore and Alice Temple, "Anna E. Bryan in Memoriam," Finnie M. Burton and Patty S. Hill, "The Work of Anna E. Bryan in Louisville, KY," and Alice Putnam, Anne Allen, and Bertha Payne, "In Memoriam—A.E.B.," *Kindergarten Magazine,* 8 (April 1901), 433–441; and Barbara Beatty, "Anna E. Bryan," in John A. Garraty, ed., *American National Biography* (New York: Oxford University Press, 1999) vol. 3, 805–6.

10. Cora L. Stockham, "A Glimpse of the Louisville Kindergartens," *Kindergarten Magazine* (April 1890), 383, 385.

11. Anna E. Bryan, "The Letter Killeth," *Journal of Proceedings and Addresses* (National Education Association), 575–577, 579.

12. For an opposing view on Bryan see Norman Brosterman, *Inventing Kindergarten* (New York: H.N. Abrams, 1997).

13. Summer School records, boxes 1 and 2, Clark University Archives, Worcester, Massachusetts. "Clark University Summer School," *Kindergarten Magazine* 12 (September 1899): 22. On Hall and child study, see Beatty, *Preschool Education in America,* 73–80; Dorothy G. Ross, *G. Stanley Hall: The Psychologist as Prophet* (Chicago: University of Chicago Press, 1972); and Sheldon H. White, "Child Study at Clark University: 1894–1904," *Journal of the History of the Behavioral Sciences* 26 (April 1990): 131–50.

14. Frederick and Caroline Frear Burk, *A Study of the Kindergarten Problem* (San Francisco: Whitaker and Ray, 1899); Beatty, *Preschool Education in America,* 85–86.

15. For more on Wheelock, Harrison, and Wiggin, see Beatty, *Preschool Education in America.*

16. Silver Street Kindergarten Society, *Annual Statement of the Silver Street Kindergarten Society for the Year Ending December 31st, 1889* (San Francisco, Calif.: C.A. Murdock and Co., Printers, 1889), 8. Bancroft Library, University of California at Berkeley, Berkeley, California.

17. Silver Street Kindergarten Society, *Annual Statement of the Silver Street Kindergarten Society for the Year Ending December 31st, 1891* (San Francisco, Calif.: C.A. Murdock and Co., Printers, 1891), 11. Bancroft Library, University of California at Berkeley, Berkeley, California.

18. Silver Street Kindergarten Society, 1889, 8; California Kindergarten Study Club, "First Paper. Subject: History of Education," 1889. Bancroft Library, University of California at Berkeley, Berkeley, California. On Wiggin and Silver Street, see Beatty, *Preschool Education in America,* 94–97; Kate Douglas Wiggin, *My Garden of Memory* (Boston: Houghton Mifflin, 1923); Nora Archibald Smith, *Kate Douglas Wiggin as Her Sister Knew Her* (Boston: Houghton Mifflin, 1925); Lois Rather, *Miss Kate: Kate Douglas Wiggin in San Francisco* (Oakland, Calif.: Rather, 1980); and Doyce B. Nunis, Jr., "Kate Douglas Wiggin," in Edward T. James and Janet Wilson James, eds., *Notable American Women,* 605–7.

19. Susan M. Yohn, "An Education in the Validity of Pluralism: the Meeting Between Presbyterian Mission Teachers and Hispanic Catholics in New Mexico, 1870–1912," paper presented at the Annual Meeting of the Organization of American Historians, Washington, D.C., March 25, 1990, and personal correspondence with author, April 10, 1990. On Felix Adler's kindergarten advocacy, see Shapiro, *Child's Garden.*

20. San Francisco Public Kindergarten Society, *Report for the Three Years Ending September 1st, 1881* (San Francisco, Calif.: C.A. Murdock and Co., Printers), 1881, pp. 6–7. Bancroft Library, University of California at Berkeley, Berkeley, California.

21. Dr. Daniel J. Margolis, Bureau of Jewish Education, Boston; Leora Isaacs, director of research and education, Jewish Education Service of North America, New York; Sister Judith Ward, S.N.D., regional director for elementary schools, Department of Education,

Archdiocese of Boston, Dorchester, Mass.; Patricia Cronin, Catholic Charities, Somerville, Mass. On Catholic resistance to Protestantism in public schools, see Diane Ravitch, *The Great School Wars* (New York: Basic Books, 1974).

22. James M. Bruce, "New York Kindergarten Association," *Kindergarten Magazine and Pedagogical Digest* 29 (1907), 576.

23. *U.S. Bureau of Education Kindergarten Circular No. 3* (Washington, D.C.: Government Printing Office, 1918), 3.

24. S. E. Weber, "The Kindergarten as an Americanizer," *U.S. Bureau of Education Kindergarten Circular No. 5* (Washington, D.C.: Government Printing Office, 1919), 2, 4.

Chapter 3 The Kindergarten

in England, 1851–1918

Kevin J. Brehony

INTRODUCTION

Comparatively little has been written to date about the history of the
Froebel movement and the kindergarten in England.[1] This may simply be indicative of the latter's marginal status relative to the "infant
school," the main institution established during the nineteenth century for the education of young children by figures like Owen, Wilder-
spin, and Stow. On the other hand, the marginality of the kindergarten
might arise from the fact that it was promoted principally by women
and that, as a result, it has suffered, in E. P. Thompson's memorable
phrase, from "the enormous condescension of history."[2] Whatever the
reasons for this neglect by historians, in the standard account of the
Froebel movement in England, it is claimed that, "the British Isles
proved suitable soil" for its growth.[3] In this chapter it is argued that
this claim is only partly accurate, as the introduction of the kindergarten into England was a failure to the extent that it did not supplant
existing forms of schooling for young children and that it was not
widely adopted by these forms.[4] The kindergarten's greatest impact was
upon the discourse of early education and the theories supplied dur-

ing training to the teachers of young children. Despite the challenge to it posed by Montessori at the beginning of the twentieth century, this discourse is still heavily inflected with Froebelian notions. A necessary but by no means sufficient condition of the achievement of this hegemonic position was the state's constitution of universal schooling for children in their early years.

Which History? What Periodization?

Although infant schools catering to children between the ages of two and seven were established in England from the 1820s onward, it was not until the 1870s—with the arrival of universal elementary schooling, consequent upon the 1870 Education Act—that the state assumed responsibility for the schooling of young children. The act set five as the minimum age of attendance, after which age the local school boards and the voluntary schools could compel attendance. But large numbers of children between two and five years old attended elementary schools until the beginning of the twentieth century. Regarding the curriculum of these schools, play in general was a feature of the infant school founded by Owen, but by the mid-nineteenth century, these schools had become places where, in contrast to the kindergarten, "children learned to read, write and count, and above all to sit still."[5]

Other differences notwithstanding, the practice of accepting very young children made the English elementary school system rather different from those in the rest of Europe and the United States. It also had considerable effects upon the reception accorded to the kindergarten in England; as the Froebelians could not hope to supplant the infant schools and departments with the kindergarten, their only viable strategy was to try to reform or supplement them.

Hence, the history of the kindergarten in England may be subject to a three-fold periodization based upon its relation to the growth of the state elementary school system. An initial period lasting from 1851 to 1870 was characterized by the establishment of privately owned and organized kindergartens catering to the middle classes, and by some success in getting the kindergarten adopted in girls' high schools and some training colleges. This was followed by a period from 1870 to 1901 when, following the Education Act of 1870, the elementary school and the code that regulated it were the principal focus of Froebelian efforts to get the state system to adopt the kindergarten. The final period lasted from 1901 until 1918 when, after educators experienced limited success in securing the support of the state, attention turned to the free kindergartens, which were founded outside the state system.

These are somewhat arbitrary divisions, as each of the institutions chosen to typify a period had its own temporal rhythms. These rhythms were articulated, in turn, with the history of the training of kindergarten teachers and the history of secondary schooling for girls, and also with internal pedagogic transformations that took place within the Froebel movement in England during the period. The transformations fall into three general phases. The first may be termed the "orthodox," and consisted mainly of a literal reading of Froebel's practice.[6] The second period, beginning in the late 1880s, resulted from a reading that produced a different inflection to Froebel's work so that it came to be seen as, almost exclusively, a form of manual training. The third period began in the late 1890s when those who may be termed "revisionist" Froebelians inspired by G. Stanley Hall and John Dewey began to abandon the apparatus, the gifts, and occupations and their mystical legitimation; by so doing, in Weber's sense, they rationalized the kindergarten.[7] The principal outcome of this move was the creation of conditions that enabled the transformation of the kindergarten from a specifically middle-class institution to one thought particularly appropriate for the education of the poorest sections of the working classes. This transition constitutes yet another history, one intimately connected to the professionalizing project of the middle-class women who constituted the Froebel, and later the Montessori, movements in England. Consideration of all these histories is beyond the scope of this chapter, with its focus on the relation between the local and the global. This consideration would necessitate a historical account that is best framed by a periodization centered on institutional forms but which also refers to the transformations in Froebelian pedagogy.

Introduction of the Kindergarten to England

The kindergarten arrived in England in 1851 in the wake of the failed revolutions of 1848 and the migration of many liberals from Germany and other parts of Europe to England. Among these were Johannes and Bertha Ronge, who established the first kindergarten in London at Hampstead in 1851. This school was poorly supported, and in 1854 it was moved to 32 Tavistock Place, St Pancras, and was conducted by Madame Ronge, who had been a student of Froebel, with Maria Boelte as her assistant.[8] The kindergarten attracted the attention of social critics and members of oppositional or alternative cultures. The famous English novelist Charles Dickens was a frequent visitor, and the brother of Sir Rowland Hill, the founder of the penny post, sent his children there.[9]

In 1854 the Society of Arts held an International Exposition and Congress in London. Specimens of pupils' work were sent; Madame von Marenholtz-Bülow, Froebel's chief interpreter, sent an exhibit of kindergarten material; and Bertha

Ronge lectured on its use. An inspector of schools for one of the voluntary school societies, the Rev. Muirhead Mitchell, saw the exhibit, was interested by it, and subsequently visited the Tavistock Place school, thereby granting the kindergarten its first official recognition. Another visitor to the Congress who was impressed by what he saw was Dr. Henry Barnard from the United States. On his return, he wrote enthusiastically about the kindergarten, and these writings led to the kindergarten's introduction to the United States.

In 1855 the Ronges published their highly successful manual *A Practical Guide to the English Kindergarten.*[10] In the preface to the 1858 edition, the Ronges claimed that they knew of about thirty schools in England that were implementing the kindergarten.[11] Many of these privately funded schools were linked through key figures in the early diffusion of Froebelian practices who trained in the earliest centers in London and Manchester, then moved from one town to another opening new schools or teaching in existing ones. It is, of course, difficult to predict the fate of the kindergarten had it remained solely in the private sector. In the education market, it was merely another brass plate competing with many others, albeit one with a certain social cachet and attractive to wealthy parents who were outside the hegemonic culture of the Tory party, the Church of England, and the landed capital bloc. Such people—Jews, Unitarians, and others outside the mainstream—were discriminated against by the hegemonic bloc because they were held to be culturally inferior. In addition, within the private sector, the integrity of the kindergarten was constantly threatened, as anyone could open a school and call it a kindergarten. The desire to distinguish schools that conformed to Froebel's vision of the kindergarten from those that simply called themselves kindergartens was one of the motives that led to the founding in London of the Froebel Society.

The Establishment of the Froebel Society

First-wave feminists,[12] who included campaigners for women's work, for girls' secondary education, and the professionalization of middle-class or secondary school teaching, were all prominently represented in 1874 when a decision to establish a Kindergarten Association in London was taken at the house of Miss Doreck, a German kindergarten educator.[13] Among those involved were German kindergarten educators Eleonore Heerwart and Madame Michaelis, and the leaders of the Women's Education Union, Maria Grey, Emily Shirreff, and Mary Gurney. Joseph Payne, of the College of Preceptors and England's first professor of education, was invited to join, as were the heads of the major girls' secondary schools such as Miss Buss (North London Collegiate School), Miss Beale

(Cheltenham Ladies' College), Miss Jones (Notting Hill High School for Girls), and Miss Neligan (Croydon High School for Girls).[14] Joseph Payne, who joined the first Committee of the Froebel Society, was also the chair of the central committee of the Women's Education Union and the first of several men to play a prominent role in the leadership of the Froebel Society.

That the struggle for women to receive a secondary and higher education and the Froebel movement became inseparable is further demonstrated by the network of social and family connections of Caroline Garrison Bishop (1846–1929), who played a prominent part in the early Froebel Society. Like so many other leading Froebelians, Caroline Bishop came from a Unitarian family that supported progressive causes. She was given her middle name as a sign of her father's allegiance to the cause of anti-slavery.[15] Bishop had been a pupil at the Tavistock Place kindergarten when it was run by Bertha Ronge's successor, Mina Praetorius.[16] Caroline Bishop's step-cousin, Adelaide Manning, became the Froebel Society's first secretary, and Adelaide's mother was the first mistress of the women's college at Hitchin.[17] In 1870, Manning's step-mother was succeeded as mistress of the women's college by Emily Shirreff, who, on the death of Doreck in 1875, became president of the Froebel Society.

It was originally intended that the London Froebel Society should be an association of trained and experienced kindergarten teachers or persons well versed in the principles of Froebel's system, which was to become a center for their diffusion among the general public.[18] This association was found to be too exclusive, so membership was made open to all who supported the objectives of the society and who would pay the annual subscription of five shillings. In 1875 the society adopted as its full title "The Fröbel Society for the Promotion of the Kindergarten System," and lectures on the kindergarten commenced for its members. The society's early activities were not solely to promote the kindergarten. A scheme for the training and certification of children's nurses was soon discussed, and within a year an examination committee was planning the examination and certification of students.[19]

To the objective of disseminating Froebelian ideas and practices another function of the society was added in 1876: the award of a certificate to successful candidates. The purposes of the Froebel Society in its early phase were summed up by Maria Grey when she said, "the strength of the Froebel Society should be chiefly concentrated on the examination of students, the inspection and registration of kindergartens and the diffusion of information."[20] Thus, the Froebel Society's activities were orientated toward the transmission of the official interpretation of the kindergarten and its defense through the inspection and registration of kindergartens. While these acts of codification and certification can be seen as being very closely involved in moves toward the professionalization of middle-class women teachers, they also served to create an air of exclusivity which became an obstacle to the kindergarten's spread.

Despite these pressures, which gave the kindergarten movement in England a somewhat introverted character, countervailing tendencies were at work. From the beginning, for example, the English Froebel Society was conscious of being situated within an international movement. As might have been expected, contacts with German kindergarten educators, including Frau Luise Froebel, were frequent. Soon after the society was established, Eleonore Heerwart read a letter to the committee from Elizabeth Peabody in the United States outlining the spread of kindergartens there. In the following year Miss Lord read a paper on the kindergartens she had visited in Italy and Germany, which included the one founded by Julie Salis Schwabe in Naples and which was later to be the model for the Froebel Educational Institute in London.[21] At the center of the world economy, London was a world-city[22] and thus ideally placed to act as a nexus for international cultural movements such as that associated with the kindergarten. This position, which enabled the English Froebelians to be open to the ideas and practices of other sections of the international Froebel movement, continued throughout the period, and it made available to them a constant source of pedagogic regeneration.

Public or Private?

Prior to 1870, the elementary school system was run, under state regulation, by voluntary societies differentiated by religious affiliation. As well as schools, the societies ran training colleges in which elementary school teachers were trained. It was through the adoption of the kindergarten by one of these societies that the Froebelians in England were first able to break out of the private school sector to which they had been confined in their earliest years. The first semi-public institution to adopt the kindergarten was the Home and Colonial Society. Founded by a group of evangelical Protestants in 1836, the society was concerned principally with encouraging the growth of infant schooling. By the 1840s, its pedagogical theories had lost the stridently evangelical flavor which they had initially possessed, and they were now drawn mainly from the ideas and practices of the Rev. Charles Mayo (1792–1846) and his sister, Elizabeth (1793–1865). These two were followers of Pestalozzi, and it was primarily through their work that the society adopted Pestalozzian principles and the object lesson, that most ubiquitous of nineteenth-century elementary school methods.

In the 1850s the society had two practice schools in London. One was for students who intended to work in inspected schools, and the other was for governesses, private school teachers, and teachers intending to become missionaries overseas. In 1857, Professor Heinrich Hoffman, a pupil of Froebel, took charge of the kindergarten training of the private student teachers and lectured to the infant school student teachers. The result was that some kindergarten activities were grafted on to the Pestalozzian pedagogy reproduced by the Home and Colonial Society. When the Froebel Society began its own examinations in 1876, the Home and Colonial Society presented private student teachers for them. By the 1880s, all student teachers at the college received some training in the kindergarten.

The Kindergarten and the British and Foreign Society's Colleges

The British and Foreign School Society's college for women at Stockwell was another semi-public institution to adopt the kindergarten. At Stockwell, all the students taught in the four practicing schools, one of which was a kindergarten, whether or not they intended to teach infants.[23] Following the departure of Eleonore Heerwart, lectures on the kindergarten were given by Lydia Manley, the Mistress of Method, as part of the course on school management.[24] In 1884, the British and Foreign School Society opened another college at Saffron Walden for women who wished to teach infants.

Together with the Home and Colonial college, the colleges of the British and Foreign Society may be viewed as having formed a wing of the Froebel movement closest to the education of the working classes in the public elementary schools. Their students were mainly from the respectable layer of the working class, and the kindergarten was given an inflection which made it more suited to the conditions existing in working-class infant schools (such as the large numbers of pupils) than the version of the kindergarten transmitted in the private sector. As nearly all the students from the college at Saffron Walden went on to teach in state-provided School Board schools, lectures on kindergarten methods and principles were said to have been given, "with a special view to their application to the work of elementary schools." Two hours per week there were devoted to lectures and notes on the kindergarten, and an additional hour each week was devoted to "illustrative kindergarten hand work."[25] Although Saffron Walden was a college monitored by the state's inspectors, it was the closest in approach to an institution which was regulated by the Froebel movement's own certificating body, the National Froebel Union (NFU), which was founded in 1888.

THE PUBLIC ELEMENTARY SCHOOLS AND THE
ADAPTATION OF KINDERGARTEN CURRICULUM

The second period in the history of the kindergarten in England began after the Education Act of 1870, which sparked a rush by the newly established school boards to build schools and "fill in the gaps" left by reliance on the voluntary system. The denominational voluntary societies and the (popularly elected) school boards entered into an intense, and sometimes bitter, competition, spurred by the "religious question," to provide schools. In the larger cities, Liberals, Nonconformists, feminists, and even socialists were able to get themselves elected to the school boards and thereby break the hegemony of the established church and its Tory party and landed capital allies. Among the ranks of the Liberals and Nonconformists, referred to in London as the Progressives, were many educational modernizers prepared to support innovation in pedagogy and curriculum. Women of this political and religious complexion were particularly prominent in supporting local initiatives of this nature, including support for the introduction of kindergarten practices into the state schools.[26]

Successes in certain localities notwithstanding, those who attempted to get the kindergarten adopted by the public elementary schools confronted many powerful obstacles. Of these, perhaps the most intractable was the existence of the elementary school code. Introduced in 1862, the Revised Code established the "payment by results" system that lasted, for the most part, until the end of the twentieth century. Under this system, schools received grants that depended largely on the performance of their pupils on an annual examination conducted by Her Majesty's Inspectors (HMI). Inevitably, this system—combined with very large classes which were far in excess of the twenty-five pupils to each teacher recommended by the Froebelians—forced teachers to adopt methods of rote learning. Under the Code of 1871, the Standard 1 examination was to be taken at the age of seven. Thus an infant school or department was created that was free from the annual examination, and, consequently, there was some space for innovation. Nevertheless, that space was highly circumscribed by the downward pressure to ensure that pupils could take and pass the Standard 1.

The Mundella Deputation

One of the first attempts the Froebel movement made, in the 1880s, to secure implementation of the kindergarten system in the elementary schools occurred when the Froebel Society sent a deputation to the vice-president of the Committee of Council on Education, Anthony J. Mundella (1825–1897). Politically,

Mundella was a Radical. A Member of Parliament (MP) from 1868 to 1897, his "whole career was devoted to strengthening the alliance between the Liberal party and organized labour."[27] He was a Nottingham hosiery manufacturer with a branch in Germany at Chemnitz. During the course of his visits, Mundella became familiar with German technical education and the Herbartian system of teaching, which his friend and business associate Henry Felkin (and Felkin's wife) brought to the attention of English educators.[28] Mundella's involvement in the politics of education through support for technical education and the Nonconformist cause made him a typical "industrial trainer"[29] and educational modernizer.

Many hoped for reform in education when, in 1880 following Gladstone's famous Midlothian campaign, the Liberals took office and Mundella was appointed as vice-president of the Committee of Council on Education. Most unionized teachers were hoping for the possible reform, if not the outright abolition, of the system of payment by results. The executive of the National Union of Elementary Teachers (NUET) met with Mundella and the Education Department's *de jure* head, Lord Spencer, in December 1881. The NUET delegation asked for changes in the code which would have given teachers more freedom from prescription. The proposed changes would also have removed some of the pressure on teachers to obtain grant money based on their calculated percentage of students who passed the standardized examination.

When the code appeared in 1882, however, few of the teachers' demands had been met. A prominent member of the NUET delegation felt that it was Patric Cumin, an official at the Education Department, and not Mundella who had the most power to determine the contents of the code and that he was not disposed to allow the code to be subjected to major revision.[30] Given that the NUET, the most powerful of the teachers' organizations, had achieved little, it was unlikely that any other organization whose demands depended on the abolition of payment by results would be successful either.

Within the Froebel movement, the initiative to approach Mundella came from William H. Herford of the Manchester Kindergarten Association, who wrote to the Froebel Society in 1880 requesting its cooperation.[31] The purpose of the deputation, in Herford's view, was nothing less than to ask for the "introduction of Froebel's system into the Government Elementary schools." The Committee of the Froebel Society agreed to join the deputation, and Rosamond Davenport Hill, a Progressive member of the London School Board, promised the support of some of her fellow board members. At a meeting called to discuss tactics prior to the deputation, the discussion focused mainly upon the demands of the Manchester Kindergarten Association. Among these was the often re-peated request that the present Teachers' Certificate not be required for teach-ers in the kindergarten but that training in kindergarten college should be recognized as sufficient instead. This, if conceded, would amount to state recog-nition of the Froebel Certificate. Fearing the inspection of kindergartens by un-sympathetic inspectors, those at the meeting also resolved to ask that kinder-gartens be inspected by other than the "ordinary Inspectors."[32]

In July 1881, the Froebel Society and the Manchester Kindergarten Associa-tion, together with representatives from a number of kindergarten colleges and the London School Board, formed a deputation of sixteen strong, six of whom were women, which was received by Mundella. Its purpose, as formulated by Alfred Bourne, was to "urge that Her Majesty's Inspectors be directed to allow as teaching suitable to the age of the children under seven, that which is known as kindergarten training, and to employ in the examination of the infants in any properly constituted kindergarten, a method of ascertaining results approved by capable exponents of the system."[33] This audacious demand amounted to a vir-tual takeover bid of state-regulated infant schooling.

It is, therefore, not surprising that this demand was rejected. Mundella coun-seled patience, and he drew attention to the conflicts over cost that the London School Board had become involved in. He told the delegation that "the ratepay-ers resisted what they considered as mere 'fads'"; and that, "it was rather a dan-gerous thing to be thought to be an educationalist . . . a creature with a wild theory which had produced no good results."[34] Atheoreticism and even out-right hostility toward theories was a prominent characteristic of English educa-tors even after the 1890s when the subject of education began to enter the uni-versities.

Mundella, however, was not entirely unsympathetic to the Froebel move-ment. He was, after all, a vice-president of the denominational British and For-eign School Society, which ran the Stockwell Training College. Moreover, the Secretary of the British and Foreign School Society, Alfred Bourne (1832–1908), was a prominent member of the Froebel Society and had accompanied Emily Shirreff on the deputation. At the end of their meeting Mundella assured the deputation that if anything could be done to "encourage the system" and give it "some kind of official recognition" he would do what he could. In later years, Mundella, while chairing an annual meeting of the Froebel Society, declared himself to be "an out-and-out Froebelian."[35] Even if the possibility that he was merely attempting to ingratiate himself with his audience is discounted, there was little that a vice-president alone could do to satisfy the demand of the Froebel

Society, however much he was sympathetic to its objects. This was even more the case if, as was highly likely, it would have led to increased expenditure.

Obstacles to the Adoption
of the Kindergarten by the Public
Elementary Schools

The failure of the deputation to secure the changes in the code that the Froebel Society desired provoked a crisis of confidence among its members. It produced a good deal of introspection and the consideration of new strategies. Central to these were analyses of why progress toward the public elementary schools' adoption of the kindergarten was so slow. One of the explanations considered was the kindergarten's foreign origin. Evidence of this concern was a resolution to the 1880 annual general meeting of the Froebel Society. The resolution insisted that "Froebel's system can be adapted to all countries, and forms the true basis of national scientific and elementary education."[36] Nevertheless, Dr. B. W. Richardson, who chaired the meeting, suggested that the name *kindergarten* ought to be anglicized and adapted to what he referred to, unspecifically, as "English tastes." This view of the kindergarten as a foreign importation which would be more acceptable if anglicized was a recurrent theme in Froebelian attempts to analyze their failure to convince the state education system to adopt it. Leading Froebelian Madame Michaelis observed that her experience in different countries had shown her that "Froebel's principles, properly understood, were adapted to the child, no matter what his nationality."[37]

At the next annual general meeting in 1881, Miss Manning, one of the society's founding members, led a discussion on whether the Froebel Society should continue its independent existence or merge with the Education Society.[38] In view of the society's chronic financial problems and failure to attain its main objectives, such a debate was understandable. The society, however, resolved to carry on as an independent organization, and in 1883 the appearance of Circular 228 demonstrated that the state educational bureaucracy could be sympathetic to the kindergarten. This was confirmed later with the release of more circulars that gave qualified recognition to the kindergarten and, as in the case of Circular 322 of 1894, the principles upon which it was based.[39]

Circular 228 set out the conditions which had to be met before infant schools and departments could be awarded a merit grant. The merit grant may be regarded as an attempt by Mundella to raise the quality of infant schooling in line with his reformist education objectives. Under the new conditions for the receipt of a merit grant, a school or department judged as fair by the inspector was entitled to a grant of two shillings for each pupil in average attendance. Schools assessed as good received four shillings, and those held to be excellent were given a grant of six shillings.[40] In order to qualify for the merit grant, schools had to make provision for, among other things, "appropriate and varied occupations." It was explained by the Education Department in Circular 228 that the elementary subjects consisted of reading, writing, and arithmetic and that the third condition for the grant could be met by the provision of "the exercises usually known as those of the Kindergarten." In the view of influential HMI Joshua Fitch, the changes made by Mundella "for the first time" recognized "the importance of the Froebelian system in the infant schools."[41]

However, while some Froebelians welcomed the granting of official, albeit limited, approval to their system by the Education Department many did not. The prominent Froebelian William Herford likened the approval to "the little drops of a sweet tasting fluid which came down from certain trees at various seasons of the year, but which was not a moisture such as the plants underneath enjoyed, or the cultivators of those plants entirely welcomed."[42]

This granting of recognition led to a division among the Froebelians. Some sought the incorporation of elements of the kindergarten into elementary school practice while others, like Herford, wanted nothing less than its wholesale adoption. While members of the Froebel movement debated the best strategy to follow, Mundella's New Code was subjected to a wide-ranging attack under the heading of the "over-pressure controversy."[43] The mounting criticism of the system of payment by results was significant in that it strengthened the position of those Froebelians who rejected the strategy of incorporation. This rejectionist position stood against the liquidation of the opposing or alternative elements in the Froebelian program. Eleonore Heerwart, among others, articulated this position at a conference held in 1883 to discuss the introduction of kindergartens into the elementary schools. Heerwart was unyielding on the Froebelian position that no book learning should take place before the age of seven. Fitch and another HMI responded that this was hopeless, as the Education Department could not be induced to postpone the First Standard examination for a year. Heerwart also argued that certain features of the kindergarten—like the occupations, which were adapted mainly to German rural life—should be revised to fit more closely the different conditions of life in London.[44]

Under attack from those who sought to adapt to "English" conditions were action songs about pre-industrial occupations such as "The Charcoal Burner's Hut," "The Wheelwright," and "The Joiner." This criticism also contained an anti-German aspect, evident in the call of the *Journal of Education* for more "English songs and games." Revisionist Froebelians like Herbert Courthope Bowen (1847–1909) went so far as to suggest that Froebel's songs ought to be dropped in favor of ones which reflected England's physical and social environment. For children, he declared, "actual life and actual nature around them—or which can be placed close to them—are the Froebelian means of education."[45]

Within the Froebel movement there were other, sometimes conflicting, accounts of why the state had failed to adopt the kindergarten. Few Froebelians could understand why the "superior claims" of the kindergarten had not been recognized. Emily Shirreff felt that the problem lay with the lack of appropriately trained teachers.[46] The London School Board had tried to remedy this by appointing a Froebelian Mistress of Method to instruct teachers in the kindergarten. Caroline Bishop was the first to hold the post in 1874; when she resigned, her successor, Mary Lyschinska, was given the title of Superintendent of Method in Infant Schools. Her task was to secure, wherever possible, "the application of kindergarten principles to the teaching of ordinary subjects." In addition, she was required to give "occasional model lessons illustrative of the mode in which this object may be secured."[47]

During her nineteen-year tenure, Lyschinska aroused opposition among many of the teachers to whom she introduced the principles and practices of the kindergarten. Although this hostility was partially a result of her autocratic manner, the primary cause likely stemmed from the fact that the conditions in the schools were unsuitable for the implementation of Lyschinska's ideas.[48] These conditions included the social background and behavior of the pupils. Over this, teachers' leaders like Walter Runciman singled out the London School Board for attack and, by implication, the principles underpinning the Froebelian pedagogy. The board, he wrote, "took for granted that there are no wicked children; the gushers talk of moral suasion; but practical men know that you cannot try moral suasion on a young wretch who has not even an elementary conception of morality, and whose mind cannot assimilate the faintest idea of goodness. You must use the one argument that he understands; you must employ the short, sharp discipline of pain."[49]

Attitudes like these underlay the refusal of many board school heads to employ middle-class, Froebel-trained women on the grounds that they were not capable of maintaining control.[50] But even when the schools were not awash with Runciman's "young wretches," the conditions, as the Froebelian teacher Clara Grant recalled, "tended to crush out any one with refined manners or a soul."[51]

Introduced as a lesson to large classes of often recalcitrant pupils by teachers who understood little of the purposes behind them, the kindergarten exercises were "dreary and mechanical." Grant records how she taught a kindergarten lesson on Wednesday afternoon for half an hour. A favorite time, she observed ironically, for "the development of the spontaneous activity of children and the harmonious development of their powers."[52] Her unease was shared by many Froebelians, and it was clear to them that what had entered the public elementary schools was not the same as what passed for the kindergarten in the private sector. In their analyses of why the kindergarten was not being adopted by the state, explanations emphasizing the unpropitious conditions in the elementary schools far outweighed those that highlighted the "foreign" provenance of the kindergarten. Thus, although it was undoubtedly present, pressure to adapt the kindergarten to English cultural forms was far less than the pressure to adapt it to the culture of the urban elementary school.

Hand and Eye

During the 1880s, the voice of the industrial trainers grew louder in response to heightened perceptions of industrial competition from the United States and Germany; they exhorted educators to pay more attention to scientific, technological, and vocational forms of schooling. Liberal in politics and Nonconformist in religion, the industrial trainers were natural allies of the Froebelians. Some of them even actively promoted the kindergarten, but no one more so than William Mather (1838–1920). Mather, who had received part of his education in Germany, became the chair of the Manchester-based engineering firm of Mather and Platt. In view of his support for the Froebel movement and manual training, it is not insignificant that Mather obtained the European rights to manufacture Thomas Edison's dynamo. Its development assisted Mather's firm in securing the contract, in 1889, for the electrical equipment for the first London Tube. Thus, Mather was not only somewhat unusual among industrialists in prominently supporting technical and manual training ventures but also, significantly, engaged in one of the new industrial sectors which required the application of scientific knowledge.

Some of the leading Froebelians recognized the opportunity the industrial trainers had created with their campaign, and they aligned themselves with it. Emily Shirreff, for example, made explicit her support for this strategy during her address to the annual meeting of the Froebel Society in 1889. The gathering was chaired by Mundella, by then a leader of the industrial trainers' lobbying organization, the National Association for the Promotion of Technical and Scientific Education (NAPTSE). Shirreff declared, "Let the promoters of technical training . . . help us to make Froebel known through the length and breadth of the land and they will have done more than they have yet done to promote their own cause."[53]

Earlier, in 1884 at the International Health Exhibition, Eleonore Heerwart read a paper entitled "The Kindergarten in Relation to the Various Industrial Products of a Country."[54] Heerwart was an orthodox Froebelian whose attitude toward Froebel's gifts and occupations was most dogmatic; for her, they were both simple and "correct." According to her, they were the best possible basis for a technical education. Consequently, Heerwart concluded, "the Kindergarten, viewed in this light, commends itself to the notice of employers in every country." The distance between the kindergarten occupations and the requirements of the "nation's industries" was spanned by the training of hand and eye that naturally followed from performance of kindergarten tasks such as paper-twisting, stick-plaiting, stick-laying, the jointed lath, pea-work, ring- and thread-laying, drawing, and sewing on cards.

The Froebelian emphasis on the importance of work and the dignity of labor predated the emergence of the debates in the 1880s, which were initiated by industrial trainers. These debates focused on the role schools should play for industry and the industrial decline of Britain. In Heerwart's view, the child at an early stage "must be prepared for work" because, as Froebel said, God works and therefore so should we.[55]

Race Recapitulation

Froebelians promoting the kindergarten as a pedagogy that provided manual training used race recapitulation arguments to legitimate their stance. The first English translation of the Baroness Von Marenholtz-Bülow's book *Hand Work and Head Work* had appeared in 1883. In it, the Baroness presented her conception of the relation between the hand and the brain. She drew extensively on the doctrine of race recapitulation, which, as Gould notes, was, "among the most influential ideas of late nineteenth century science."[56] This doctrine held that in its passage from the embryo to adulthood, the human species, or the "race," recapitulates former stages of evolution not only physically but, in some versions, culturally as well. Herbert Spencer claimed that the French sociologist Auguste Comte originated this notion, but Froebel had earlier expressed a similar theory in his *Education of Man.*[57]

Commonly, race recapitulation was used to link notions of childhood, conceived of as an evolving series of hierarchically ordered stages, to the inherently hierarchical concept of "race." Therefore, Heerwart wrote, in the kindergarten a historian regarding children's use of occupations would, "watch the stages of development as history has witnessed those of barbarous tribes, who have afterwards excelled in arts and industries." The implication of this race-based conception was that industrial society was the end point of evolution and that the kindergarten was the best preparation for it.

By 1892, viewing the kindergarten as primarily a system of hand and eye training was so prevalent within the Froebel movement that a journal to promote this orientation, called appropriately *Hand and Eye,* was begun in that year. Later in that year the Council of the Froebel Society was told that *Child Life,* the original journal of the movement, might merge with *Hand and Eye,* and it was accepted that the new magazine be a medium of communication with members.[58] *Hand and Eye* soon eclipsed *Child Life.* The principal function of the new journal was not the promotion of the kindergarten, however, but the popularization among teachers of a system known as Sloyd.

The Sloyd System

In the late 1880s there occurred in England a remarkable surge of interest, among teachers and others connected with schooling, in a system of handwork known as *Slojd,* or, as it was more commonly spelled, *Sloyd.* This fashionable system originated in Sweden, where it had been developed by Otto Salomon (1849–1907). His practice was based on that of Uno Cygnaeus (1810–1888), the organizer and director of the "folk-schools" of Finland. Cygnaeus, in turn, claimed that his ideas and practices, which made handwork the basis of education, were derived from Froebel and Pestalozzi. The derivation of the system, however, is perhaps less important in explaining the popularity of Sloyd among Froebelians than their receptivity to ways of teaching by "things" rather than words.

One of the first accounts of the Sloyd system appeared in 1887, in an article written by Evelyn Chapman and published in the *Journal of Education.*[59] Chapman's article contained a description of a course held at Nääs, where in 1872 Salomon's uncle, a wealthy Gothenburg merchant, had founded a Sloyd "seminary." At Nääs, the system consisted of the production of a graded series of wooden models, including the emblematic spoon, by a number of processes which included carving with the equally emblematic "Sloyd knife."[60] These activities were designed to form the educational core for children aged eleven years and older, who were too old for the kindergarten occupations. Among those who attended the summer course at Nääs was another industrial trainer, Arthur Acland, who became the nominal Minister of Education in the 1890s.

The craze for Sloyd continued into the 1890s and, for a while, threatened not simply to eclipse but to replace the kindergarten. By 1895, however, there were signs that the Sloyd tide was ebbing. Miss Dorothea Beale, the head of Cheltenham Ladies' College, prepared a paper which argued that the Froebel Society "should encourage teachers to adapt methods to changed times and places." She wanted more, "original and definite 'Child Study' on a scientific basis following the lead of the Clarke University in America. There was a branch in Cheltenham in full activity." She thought that the present was a critical time in the history of elementary schools and that "the Froebel Society would fail to grasp the situation and use its opportunities if it merely offered hand and eye occupations." At the meeting at which Miss Beale's paper was discussed, J. J. Findlay, who became John Dewey's most prominent English interpreter, said that he "feared the impression had got abroad that the kindergarten was simply the introduction to Manual Training . . . [and] if Manual Training were to be the only sequel then the methods of the kindergarten could not be developed into a legitimate system." Challenging the hand and eye emphasis, he argued that "the English parent had yet to be shown that our purpose in teaching was to teach the child's heart and elevate his character, not merely to teach his hands and eyes."[61] In 1898 after yet another discussion as to whether or not to dissolve the Froebel Society, a decision was made to break with the concentration on hand and eye training and manual training.

Revisionism and the Free Kindergartens

Child study and the work of John Dewey, both imports from the United States, were instrumental in ending the dominance of the hand and eye emphasis and in paving the way to the third period of the kindergarten in England, which was characterized by the founding of free kindergartens. Toward the end of the nineteenth century following the revival of Socialism in the 1880s, the first signs appeared that the Liberals could no longer actively represent organized labor. As a consequence, a number of Socialists became active in Froebelian circles. The most famous of these was Margaret McMillan. Despite her later criticism of Froebel, McMillan was an active Froebelian for several years, even serving on the committee of the Froebel Society. McMillan was a frequent contributor to a weekly newspaper called the *Christian Commonwealth,* which was recommended to Froebelians in their own journal, *Child Life.* The paper was also recommended to Froebelians by Maria Findlay, who played a major role in fracturing the Froebelian orthodoxy. She, together with others of a new generation of Froebelians, including Grace Owen, had spent some time in the United States and were familiar with the revisionist arguments of Dewey and G. Stanley Hall.

After 1900 Findlay played a central role in the move away from the symbolism and the gifts and occupations which were central to the practice of the first Froebelians and the creation of a revisionist Froebelian pedagogy that put play at its center.[62] Articles like Elsie Murray's "That symmetrical Paper Folding and Symmetrical Work with Gifts Are a Waste of Time for Both Students and Children," began to challenge the orthodoxy.[63] In the syllabus of the National Froebel Union, the gifts and occupations began to receive less emphasis and were replaced by occupations derived from Dewey's reading of race recapitulation theory. As was frequently the case, this transformation had an international dimension. The Americans have already been mentioned, but a key figure in this transition in England, who also influenced G. Stanley Hall, was Henriette Schrader-Breymann.

Henriette Schrader-Breymann
and the Pestalozzi-Froebel House

The formative moment for both the revisionist reading and the Froebelian child-saving ideology was the foundation, in 1881, of the Pestalozzi-Froebel House in Berlin by Froebel's grand-niece, Henriette Schrader-Breymann. The practices developed there flowed, in part, from Schrader-Breymann's critical reading of Froebel and Pestalozzi and from her own sympathies for German liberalism.[64] From the outset, her followers were at odds with literal interpretations of Froebel which stressed the sanctity of the gifts and occupations and the mysticism surrounding them. After having spent some time in 1871 at Keilhau, the site of Froebel's "Educational Institute," Henriette Breymann married Karl Schrader, a railway administrator and Liberal politician. They moved to Berlin in 1874, where Henriette reorganized the "Society for Family and Popular Education." This organization had been set up by the Baroness Von Marenholtz-Bülow to run private kindergartens, which, in turn, subsidized kindergartens and the training of teachers for working-class children. In 1881, the Schrader-Breymanns purchased a house in Berlin for the purpose of running a training seminar. This became the Pestalozzi-Froebel House. There, attempts were made to reproduce the social relations and the educative community which were thought to have existed in the pre-industrial family idealized by Pestalozzi and Froebel. A public kindergarten was begun in addition to a training department, an intermediate class, an elementary class, a manual trade school for children up to the age of fourteen, and a cooking school. The courses included one on infant care, another in domestic work, and evening classes for mothers.

This focus on welfare by the Pestalozzi-Froebel House blurred the boundaries between teaching and social work, thereby making concrete Henriette Schrader-Breymann's view of the most appropriate social role for middle- and upper-class women. This view hinged on her belief that men and women should occupy equal, complementary, but separate spheres and that motherhood, both within the family and within a society which greatly needed the influence of women, was the role best suited to middle- and upper-class women.[65]

Often referred to as "spiritual motherhood" or "social maternalism," this view is commonly regarded as a link to women's acceptance of male domination.[66] In the context of Germany in this period and to a lesser extent that of England, however, spiritual motherhood may be seen as an ideological accompaniment to the entry of middle-class women into employment. At the center of this version of women's mission, as presented by Schrader-Breymann, was the requirement that women should be trained. This was one of the features which distinguished those who had attended the Pestalozzi-Froebel House from other women of similar social backgrounds who were also engaged in forms of social work.

Insofar as Schrader-Breymann organized training for middle- and upper-class women who wished to become teachers, her objectives were little different from the professional goals of many middle-class women of the period. Where she departed from them, however, was in suggesting that such women should "go among the poor" and perform good works. By doing so, they would fulfill the aim of the Pestalozzi-Froebel House, which was, in true settlement movement style, "to forge a natural rapport between rich and poor, between the educated and uneducated classes."[67] In England, following the Pestalozzi-Froebel House practice, this was precisely what the promoters of the free kindergartens tried to do.

The Free Kindergartens

In 1899 the followers of Schrader-Breymann established a "House for Home Life Training" in London modeled on Berlin's Pestalozzi-Froebel House. Known as Sesame House, its chief significance to the Froebel movement and state education lay in its relation to the free kindergarten movement. This role lay in its training program, and at least three free kindergartens were started by its former students. Like the Pestalozzi-Froebel House, Sesame House intended to establish a free kindergarten, that is, a kindergarten for the children of the poor which charged no fees. Accordingly, a kindergarten was opened in 1899 with six children in attendance. By the end of its first year of operation, the kindergarten contained, "forty little ones from houses in the neighbourhood, both poor and well-to-do." In the third report on the work of Sesame House, the claim was made that its "child garden" was "the first of its kind opened in this country for the poor."[68]

This claim to be associated with the poor was also strengthened by an account of an exchange between students at Sesame House and students at Caroline Bishop's Kindergarten Training College in Birmingham. The advantage for the Birmingham students, it was announced, was that they would "gain experience with the poor." However, in the same report, mention was made of a proposal to admit fee paying children to the kindergarten. This was carried and, in 1905, the kindergarten was said to contain a few children of the "well-to-do" plus the children of a policeman, a baker, and a coachman.

As at the Froebel Educational Institute, opened in London in 1895, financial problems proved an insurmountable obstacle in running a free kindergarten at Sesame House. Its location in a middle-class area was also a major drawback in working with the poor, but the failure to meet the intended objectives of the free kindergarten was rationalized by a reference to what were held to be "the beneficial effects gained by all in the mixing of classes" which followed the introduction of fees. Revisionist Elsie Murray, who included a survey of the free kindergartens in her history of the Froebel movement, dismissed the Sesame House kindergarten's claims to be a true free kindergarten on the grounds that it did not "reach the neglected little ones."[69]

Little is known of the free kindergarten established by Mather in Manchester in 1871. The earliest mention in the Froebelian literature of free kindergartens occurred in an article in the *Journal of the Froebel Society* in 1883. The context was a report on the founding of free kindergartens in America. The writer described free kindergartens as being "intended to reach the children of the very poorest classes, and [they] aim at rescuing infants at the very beginning of their life from the influence of sin and misery that surround them."[70] In July of that year the same journal carried a letter from Hannah E. Turner calling on the Froebel Society to set up free kindergartens in England. What is generally recognized as the first free kindergarten in England opened at Woolwich in 1900. For the most part, it owed little to the supporters of Sesame House or the Pestalozzi-Froebel House. Instead, it was formed and supported by a combination of figures involved in the church and the settlement movement. The idealist and mystical strands in Froebel's thought attracted many followers who were interested in questions of a religious nature and the specific problem of how best to teach religion. In addition, some Sunday schools, such as one at the Robert Browning Settlement at Walworth, adopted Froebelian methods.[71] In Birmingham, West Hill Training College was begun by a Canadian child study enthusiast, George Hamilton Archibald, and his Froebel-trained daughter Ethel specifically to train Sunday School teachers in Froebelian methods. The free kindergarten, which was known as the Woolwich Mission Kindergarten, began in a room provided by a Christian Socialist, a vicar, the Rev. Walter Wragge.[72]

The kindergarten, run by Muriel Wragge, was founded by her sister, Adelaide Wragge, a former Bedford Kindergarten Training College student who had founded, and was the principal of, the Blackheath Training College and Kindergarten. The Woolwich Mission Kindergarten, like the previous free kindergartens, soon encountered financial problems. It was closed in 1903 but was reopened in 1905 in the Women's House of the Maurice Hostel Settlement, a Christian Union Settlement in Hoxton, a poor part of London.[73] Altogether, about twelve free kindergartens catering to children between the ages of three and six were opened in England and Scotland between 1900 and 1910. In contrast, according to Adelaide Wragge, there were in New York alone three hundred free kindergartens in 1900. This large difference was due to the fact that in the United States, as in Scotland, children did not attend school until the age of five or six. In England in 1900, 43 percent of all children between the ages of three and five years attended school. By 1910 as a result of state action, reinforced by an adverse report by Froebelian inspectors on school conditions,[74] that proportion had fallen to about 23 percent.[75] Nevertheless, Froebelians were still dissatisfied with the schooling provided for young children and particularly that provided for the "slum child." This latter object of their intervention—deficient in language, the ability to play, and maternal guidance—was introduced to a revised pedagogy in which the gifts and occupations were largely absent. One of the aims of the Greet free kindergarten in Birmingham, for example, was to "give a basis for school instruction by experiences gained in connection with garden and domestic work and the care of pets."[76] As recommended by Dewey, domestic activities also were valued alongside play. The kindergarten had become a civilizing agent for the lowest strata of the working classes.

The crisis of the urban child of the poor was so deep and extensive that voluntary effort alone was insufficient to cope with it. Consequently, those Froebelians who were associated with the free kindergartens did not want a voluntary alternative to the state-run infant schools and departments—they wanted the state to provide kindergartens. Their strategy was one in which the free kindergartens would "serve as object lessons to point the way in which the community's efforts on behalf of the young child of the slums may be directed." The collectivist implications of this position were widely recognized. Professor Oliver Lodge, a prominent spiritual leader, told the Birmingham People's

Kindergarten Association that if he had his way, the free kindergartens would be lavishly supported out of public funds.[77]

From Kindergarten to Nursery School

The free kindergartens were given support from local education authorities after the passage of the 1918 Education Act. At this point they ceased to be called "kindergartens" and became "nursery schools." Fourteen of these existed in 1919, but ten years later the number had risen to only twenty-eight, despite both widespread agreement among educators that they were beneficial and a vigorous campaign in their favor.[78] The failure of nursery schools to thrive in England, a failure which persists to this day, has almost nothing to do with the foreign origin of some ideas and practices that constitute nursery education and almost everything to do with their relative expense and to the patriarchal view that the best place for young children is at home with their mothers.

Murray claims that Madame Michaelis, later president of the Froebel Society and principal of the Froebel Educational Institute, was the first to use the term *nursery school* as an English equivalent of *kindergarten* in 1890.[79] Nevertheless, the term did not become generally accepted until after 1904. In that year, the Froebel Society took part in a conference arranged jointly by the Bradford local education authority, the West Riding County Council. The theme of the conference held at Bradford was consideration of "the need for nursery schools for children from three to five years now attending the Public Elementary Schools." This conference resolved that "the best solution of the difficulty would be to remove all the children under five years of age out of the infant schools and put them into special 'nursery schools,' where the methods and conditions could be specially adapted to their tender age." The term is also associated with Margaret McMillan, who used it for her school. Although the school contained recognizable kindergarten practices, it was derived from other sources as well.[80] This outcome was particularly ironic given that the bulk of the schools recognized as nursery schools after 1918 had begun as free kindergartens.

CONCLUSION

Between 1851 and 1918, significant changes occurred in the ways young children were educated. By the end of this period, the gallery in which large numbers of infants were forced to sit immobilized while teachers gave oral lessons was gradually being replaced by rooms with furniture more suited to the requirements of the growing child. The curriculum had become less reliant on books as handwork and nature study were introduced, and trained teachers gradually became preferable to "motherly girls" when it came to teaching young children. Attribution of these changes to the impact of the kindergarten movement is, however, very difficult. While some of the changes had affinities with what the Froebelians advocated, others corresponded more closely to proposals by Dewey and Montessori. Once the focus on gifts and occupations in the curriculum for young children had been relegated in importance, it was not easy to discern what was distinctive about the Froebelian kindergarten. Froebel's principles such as the fostering of the self-activity of the child were shared by many educators, including Montessori, to whom many Froebelians turned when accounts of her work began to appear in England from 1909 onward.[81] By the first decade of the twentieth century, despite the revisionists, the kindergarten was widely associated with the apparatus of the gifts and occupations and its frequent misuse. It could also be regarded as old fashioned when contrasted with Montessori, who also fetishized her apparatus but had the advantage of being "scientific"—at least, that is what she so often claimed.

The practices of the English infant school were developed pragmatically, and their sources were pluralistic rather than being attributable to only one system. This was true also of the nursery school, that English transmutation of the kindergarten which traversed the path between an institution for the children of middle-class, cultural outsiders and one fitted best to the education of the children of the slums, the poorest layer of the working class. The private sector provision bears this out: in 1952 there were just eleven private schools recognized by the National Froebel Foundation as Froebel Schools.[82] For less fortunate children, other changes took place. From Margaret McMillan, a concern for the health of the child was grafted onto the kindergarten. Furthermore, if in any particular nursery school the teaching of reading was present while the telling of imaginative stories was not, then it was likely that the school owed more to Montessori than to Froebel.

For McMillan and Montessori, the slum child constituted the main focus of their practice. This indicates the centrality of social class to the education of the period, but it also specifically underlines the power of social class to shape educational practice. It was this latter phenomenon and the way it manifested itself in English society and culture, rather than an unsympathetic national culture, that contributed most to the kindergarten's relative failure in England. Furthermore, social class is always articulated to gender divisions. The middle-class women who were unable to enter the public elementary school system but who were committed to their own professionalization came to dominate the teacher training institutions. From that institutional base, they were able to capture and dominate the discourse of early-years education. Despite the attacks upon the child-centered position formerly by the New Right now continued by New Labor, it has proved remarkably resilient despite the frequent absence of the material conditions for its realization. The embeddedness of the child-centered view in early-years education is arguably the main legacy of the kindergarten in England.

NOTES

1. E. R. Murray, *A Story of Infant Schools and Kindergartens* (London: Sir Isaac Pitman, 1912); T. Raymont, *A History of the Education of Young Children* (London: Longmans, Green, 1937); P. Woodham-Smith, "History of the Froebel Movement in England, in E. Lawrence (ed.), *Friedrich Froebel and English Education* (London: University of London Press, 1952), pp. 34–39; J. P. Slight, "The Froebel Movement in England," *National Froebel Foundation Bulletin*, 76 (1952), pp. 2–8; K. J. Brehony, "The Froebel Movement and State Schooling, 1880–1914: A Study in Educational Ideology," The Open University, 1988, Unpublished Ph.D. dissertation; J. Liebschner, *Foundations of Progressive Education* (Cambridge: Lutterworth Press, 1991).

2. E. P. Thompson, *The Making of the English Working Class* (Harmondsworth: Penguin, 1968), p. 13.

3. Woodham-Smith, "History of the Froebel movement in England," pp. 34–94.

4. Which, unlike the impression created by the author quoted, is not synonymous with Great Britain.

5. E. R. Murray and H. Brown Smith, *The Child Under Eight* (London: Edward Arnold, 1920), p. 35.

6. More accurately, that of his interpreters such as the Baroness Bertha von Marenholtz-Bülow, as none of Froebel's work was published in English until 1885.

7. H. H. Gerth and C. Wright Mills (eds.), *From Max Weber* (London: Routledge & Kegan Paul, 1948).

8. After her marriage in the United States, Boelte became Maria Kraus-Boelte. With her husband, she opened the New York Normal Training Kindergarten. Murray, *Story of Infant Schools and Kindergartens*, p. 67. W. A. C. Stewart and W. P. McCann, *The Educational Innovators 1750–1880* (London: Macmillan, 1967), pp. 298–309.

9. J. Ronge and B. Ronge, *A Practical Guide to the English Kindergarten* (London: A. N. Myers, 1865), p. v.

10. The reasons behind the choice of "English" in the title may only be speculated upon. It is clear, however, that the Ronges adapted the kindergarten to their own ideas. In 1885 the Bedford Kindergarten and Training College published the *Bedford Kindergarten Journal*, which was subtitled "A practical journal for English Kindergartens." Again, the reasoning behind the choice of "English" may only be guessed at, but it is likely that behind both usages there lay an intention to domesticate the kindergarten.

11. Ronge and Ronge, *A Practical Guide to the English Kindergarten,* p. vii.

12. For a definition, see S. Walby, "From Private to Public Patriarchy," *Women's Studies International Forum,* 13, 1/2 (1990), pp. 91–104.

13. Froebel Society Minutes, vol. I, 1874.

14. R. Aldrich and P. Gordon, *Dictionary of British Educationists* (London, Woburn Press, 1989), pp. 192–193.

15. William Lloyd Garrison had founded the Anti-Slavery Society.

16. E. Last, *Memoir of Caroline Garrison Bishop* (London: Headley Brothers, 1936), p. 3.

17. In 1873 this became Girton College, Cambridge.

18. B. Webb, "English Teachers and Their Professional Organization," *The New Statesman,* 130 (1915), p. 2.

19. Froebel Society Minutes, vol. I, November 1875.

20. Froebel Society Minutes, January 1878.

21. Froebel Society Minutes, vol. I, 1876.

22. For an explanation, see F. Braudel, *Civilization and Capitalism 15th–18th Century: The Perspective of the World,* vol. 3 (London: Fontana, 1985).

23. PP. *Royal Commission on the Working of the Elementary Education Acts.* "The Evidence of Miss Lydia Manley," vol. 25, 1886, Q. 13,045.

24. PP. *Royal Commission on the Working of the Elementary Education Acts,* vol. 36, 1888, p. 180. Miss Katherine Phillips, who also worked in the Kindergarten Department of Maria Grey, gave "illustrations of the special methods of the kindergarten" at "intervals" throughout the Stockwell course.

25. PP. *Royal Commission on the Working of the Elementary Education Acts,* vol. 36, 1888, p. 161. The college was opened to train teachers of infants in 1884.

26. P. Hollis, *Ladies Elect: Women in English Local Government* (Oxford: Clarendon Press, 1989).

27. E. P. Thompson, *William Morris* (London: Merlin, 1977), p. 206.

28. H. M. Felkin and E. Felkin, *An Introduction to Herbart's Science and Practice of Education* (London: Swan Sonnenschein, 1895); Felkin, "Herbart's Life and System," *Journal of Education,* 14 (January 1892), pp. 25–27; Felkin, "Herbart's Life and System," *Journal of Education,* 14 (February 1892), pp. 78–80.

29. A term applied to those who saw education in terms of future adult work. See R. Williams, *The Long Revolution* (Harmondsworth: Penguin, 1965).

30. G. A. Christian, *English Education from Within* (London: Wallace Gandy, 1922), pp. 44–45.

31. Froebel Society Minutes, vol. II, 1880.

32. Froebel Society Minutes, vol. II, 1880.

33. Froebel Society Minutes, vol. II, 1880.

34. Froebel Society Minutes, vol. II, 1880.

35. *Journal of Education,* 14, p. 168.

36. Froebel Society Minutes, vol. II, 1880.

37. Anonymous,"Froebel Society's Conference on Froebelian Training in Elementary Colleges," *Child Life,* July 1899, p. 166.

38. Froebel Society Minutes, vol. II, 1881.

39. Education Department, Circular 322, "Instruction of Infants." Revised Instructions, Appendix VII, 1893, pp. 51–53. Education Department, Circular 332, "Instruction of Lower Standards in Schools for Older Scholars." Revised Instructions, Appendix VII, 1894, pp. 56–57. Education Department, Circular 369, "Object Teaching," 1895. *Report of the Committee of Council on Education, 1895–96*, p. 530. Education Department, Circular 374, "Suitable Occupations." *Report of the Committee of Council on Education 1896–97*, pp. 576–570.

40. *Report of the Committee of Council on Education 1881–82.*

41. J. G. Fitch, "Teachers and the State," *Journal of Education*, 17 (May 1895), pp. 278–279.

42. International Health Exhibition (ed.), *The Health Exhibition Literature* (London: William Clowes.), p. 145.

43. A. B. Robertson, "Children, Teachers and Society: The Over-Pressure Controversy 1880–1886," *British Journal of Educational Studies*, 20 (1972), pp. 315–323.

44. *Journal of Education*, 5 (July 1883), p. 226.

45. H. C. Bowen, "Hints to Froebel Students." *Journal of Education*, 9 (May 1887), p. 231.

46. E. Shirreff, "Infant Schools and Kindergartens," *Journal of Education*, 9 (April 1887), 187–188.

47. Raymont, *A History of the Education of Young Children*, pp. 239–240.

48. T. Gautrey, *Lux Mihi Laus: School Board Memories* (London, Link House, 1937), p. 114.

49. J. Runciman, *Schools and Scholars* (London: Chatto and Windus, 1887), p. 249.

50. Board of Education, *Reports on Children Under Five Years of Age in Public Elementary Schools by Women Inspectors of the Board of Education* (London, HMSO, 1905).

51. C. E. Grant, *Farthing Bundles* (London: Fern Street Settlement), p. 35.

52. Grant, *Farthing Bundles*, p. 54.

53. *Journal of Education*, 11 (February 1889), p. 92.

54. E. Heerwart, "The Kindergarten in Relation to the Various Industrial Products," in International Health Exhibition (ed.), *The Health Exhibition Literature* (London: William Clowes, 1884), pp. 96–105.

55. Ibid.

56. S. J. Gould, *The Mismeasure of Man* (Harmondsworth: Penguin, 1981), p. 114. The notion is dealt with extensively in Gould, *Ontogeny and Phylogeny* (Cambridge, Mass.: Harvard University Press, 1977).

57. F. Froebel, *The Education of Man* (New York: D. Appleton Century, 1885), pp.18, 40–41, 160, 282–283.

58. Froebel Society Minutes, 1892.

59. E. Chapman, "Slöjd," *Journal of Education*, 9 (February 1887), pp. 71–74.

60. Both the knife and the spoon were described at some length in T. G. Rooper, *School and Home Life* (London: A. Brown and Sons, 1896), pp. 465–479. Rooper was an HMI and supporter of the kindergarten.

61. Froebel Society Minutes, 1895.

62. H. Brown Smith, ed., *Education by Life* (London: George Philip, 1925).

63. E. R. Murray, "That Symmetrical Paper Folding and Symmetrical Work with Gifts Are a Waste of Time for Both Students and Children," *Child Life*, 5 (1903), pp. 14–18.

64. A. T. Allen, "Spiritual Motherhood: German Feminists and the Kindergarten Movement

1848–1911," *History of Education Quarterly,* 22(1982), pp. 319–339; Allen, "'Let Us Live with Our Children': Kindergarten Movements in Germany and the United States, 1840–1914," *History of Education Quarterly,* 28 (1988), pp. 23–48.

65. M. J. Lyschinska, "Froebel, Stanley Hall and Henriette Schrader," *Journal of Education,* 23 (August 1901), pp. 501–503.

66. J. Lewis, *Women in England 1870–1950* (Brighton: Wheatsheaf, 1984).

67. Allen, A. T. "Spiritual Motherhood: German Feminists and the Kindergarten Movement, 1848–1911," *History of Education Quarterly,* vol. 22, no. 3 (1982), p. 331.

68. I. Margesson and A. Jonson, "Report of the First Year's Work at Sesame House," *Child Life,* 2, 8 (1900), pp. 252–254; "Sesame Club. The Third Year's Record of Sesame House," *Child Life,* 5, 17 (1903), pp. 43–44; *Child Life,* 5, 17 (1903), p. 235

69. Murray, *A Story of Infant Schools and Kindergartens.*

70. Anonymous, "Notes and Gleanings," *Journal of the Froebel Society,* 1 (1883), p. 22.

71. *Journal of Education,* 20 (June 1898), p. 353.

72. For information on the Rev. Walter Wragge, see J. Attfield, *With Light of Knowledge* (London: RACS/Journeyman Press, 1981).

73. E. S. Newman, "Mary Adelaide Wragge. In Memoriam," *Child Life,* 9 (1907), 95–97. See also A. Wragge, "A Mission Kindergarten for Woolwich—An Appeal," *Child Life,* 2 (1900), p. 62. M. Wragge, "The Mission Kindergarten in Woolwich," *Child Life,* 2 (1900), pp. 247–248. Anonymous, "Free Kindergartens Woolwich and Edinburgh." *Child Life,* vol. 5 (1903), pp. 84–85.

74. Board of Education, *Reports on Children Under Five Years of Age in Public Elementary Schools by Women Inspectors of the Board of Education* (London: HMSO, 1905).

75. Board of Education, *Report of the Consultative Committee on Infant and Nursery Schools* (London: HMSO, 1933).

76. *Report of the Birmingham People's Kindergarten Association, 1903–1904.*

77. Murray, *A Story of Infant Schools and Kindergartens.*

78. N. Whitbread, *The Evolution of the Nursery-Infant School* (London: Routledge and Kegan Paul, 1972).

79. Murray and Brown Smith, *The Child Under Eight,* p. 1.

80. M. McMillan, *The Life of Rachel McMillan* (London: J. M. Dent, 1927), pp. 73–91.

81. M. G. May, "A New Method in Infant Education," *The Journal of Education,* 31 (September 1909), pp. 645–647.

82. O. B. Priestman, "The Influence of Froebel on the Independent Preparatory Schools of Today," in E. Lawrence (ed.), *Friedrich Froebel and English Education* (London: University of London Press, 1952), p. 125.

REFERENCES

Bruce, James M. (1907). New York Kindergarten Association. *Kindergarten Magazine and Pedagogical Digest* 29, 546–574.

Bryan, Anna E. (1890). The Letter Killeth. *Journal of Proceedings and Addresses* (National Education Association) 573–581.

California Kindergarten Study Club (1889). "First Paper. Subject: History of Education." Bancroft Library, University of California at Berkeley, Berkeley, CA.

Hill, Patty Smith (1924). "Anna E. Bryan," in International Kindergarten Union Committee of Nineteen, *Pioneers of the Kindergarten in America*. New York: Century, 223–230.

Peabody, Elizabeth (1863). *Kindergarten Guide,* in Elizabeth Peabody and Mary Mann, *Moral Culture of Infancy and Kindergarten Guide*. Boston: T.O. H.P. Burnham.

———(1877). "The Festival of Froebel's Birthday." *Kindergarten Messenger* (new series), May–June, 70.

San Francisco Public Kindergarten Society (1881). *Report for the Three Years ending September 1st, 1881*. San Francisco: C.A. Murdock and Co., Printers. Bancroft Library, University of California at Berkeley, Berkeley, CA.

Silver Street Kindergarten Society (1889). *Eighth Annual Report for the Year Ending December 31st, 1889*. San Francisco: C.A. Murdock and Co., Printers. Bancroft Library, University of California at Berkeley, Berkeley, CA.

———(1891). *Annual Statement of the Silver Street Kindergarten Society for the Year Ending December 31st, 1891*. San Francisco: C.A. Murdock and Co., Printers. Bancroft Library, University of California at Berkeley, Berkeley, CA.

Stockham, Cora L. (1890). "A Glimpse of the Louisville Kindergartens." *Kindergarten Magazine,* April, 383–86.

U.S. Bureau of Education (1918). *Kindergarten Circular No. 3*. Washington, D.C.: Government Printing Office.

Weber, S. E. (1919). The kindergarten as an Americanizer. *U.S. Bureau of Education Kindergarten Circular No. 5*. Washington, D.C.: Government Printing Office.

Wiebe, Edward (1869). *The Paradise of Childhood: A Practical Guide to the Kindergarten*. Springfield, MA.

Chapter 4 The Development of

Kindergartens in Australia at the

Turn of the Twentieth Century:

A Response to Social Pressures

and Educational Influences

Margaret Clyde

AUSTRALIA, 1788–1890

Australia at the turn of the twentieth century was in a unique position
in western society. Barely one hundred and ten years since the establishment of the first permanent white settlement, the various states
were in the process of evolving from either convict settlements created
by the British crown or free settlements developed by British agricultural entrepreneurs into one nation undivided. This was to be a federation in which the various disparate states, often still suspicious of the
motives of their colleagues in the other states, were to retain the majority of the power. The human services were to remain the province
of each state, so that in the various states the development of children's
services in general, and kindergartens in particular, was different: in
New South Wales a philanthropic organization assumed the greatest
responsibility; in Victoria various churches worked together to develop
these services; in South Australia the state government provided resources. These differences were a reflection of the origins and development of each colony into a state and finally into a part of a federation.

During the one hundred years of British domination of the continent of Australia there had been no great social pressure such as sudden indus-trialization, no revolutionary ideological movements, no wars or other bellicose experiences apart from minor "troubles" at the gold fields. It was an emerging nation in the Asian section of the world with a particular British and Irish tra-dition. Even the economic depression of the 1890s was not as intensely experi-enced in Australia as it was in the more industrialized nations of western Europe and North America.

In spite of these supposed advantages for the emerging Australian nation, two facts remained undeniably clear: first, the Australian colonies possessed an in-ordinate number of destitute young children whose care did not appear to be the responsibility of anyone; second, this overabundance of uncared-for chil-dren had been apparent since the inception of the first penal colony at Sydney Cove in 1788.

When plans for the first colony in New South Wales were drawn up in Lon-don, no provision had been made for children's services. Rightly or wrongly, it was assumed that parents would provide for their own children. As the first set-tlement contained male and female convicts as well as jailers and their families, this assumption could be questioned. In the first fleet twenty-six children and a number of pregnant women arrived in Australia in January 1788, and by 1800 the number of white children (as opposed to the indigenous population) had risen to seven hundred and twenty-five, including thirty-four orphans (Mellor, 1990:3). This is a considerable increase in a twelve-year period, notwithstanding the fact the British government continued to send convicts to Australia while very few convicts returned home. It is reported that gangs of "neglected, deserted or orphaned children" roamed the settlement at Sydney Cove, to the growing concern of both the governor of the colony and church officials. Following en-treaties from Governor King, both the Anglican and Catholic churches opened orphan schools in Sydney in 1803 as residential schools, thus signifying the first organized children's services in Australia. They were unique in that although they were funded by the government authority, they were operated by the two churches. The children of the military jailers and other officials were not so lucky; there were no organized educational services for them in the new colony.

In 1824 the Rev. Richard Hill established the first infant school at St. James Hall, Castlereagh Street, Sydney. Its task was to take the poor children off the streets, as they were becoming a nuisance to society. There was no organized plan for the educational process to be developed; rather the priorities were to keep the children alive and, at the same time, protect them from the influences and example of the men and women among whom they lived (Harrison, 1985). Resources, finances, and qualified personnel were lacking, while the curriculum consisted of rote learning, the "3 Rs," and religion. In the same year the Department of Public Instruction established infant schools for the care and education of children under the age of six. Several schools were established in Sydney but they were poor, noisy, and overcrowded, with a lack of outdoor space, and the curriculum was described as "inappropriate."

In July 1853, the Society of the Relief of Destitute Children was established. The existence of this voluntary organization indicates an emerging social conscience among the people of Sydney. Shortly after the 1860s, the first government "ragged schools" were established to assist parents by providing a support to the home. During the second half of the nineteenth century, both government and private agencies were active in providing children's services, particularly in the areas of welfare and health; at that time, the Australian colonies had a higher infant mortality rate than that in British cities (Mellor, 1990).

If expediency was the reason for initiating children's services in the neophyte colony, the situation emphasized key issues which have confronted children's services in Australia ever since: whose responsibility is it to provide these services, and what were the rights and responsibilities of the colonial government for those children whose parents failed to care for them? These are the issues that informed public policies in all areas of community services throughout the various states.

In retrospect, it is easy to determine why so many children were destitute, and equally easy to wonder why the British government was not able to foretell that such a situation would arise. From the outset, women sent to the colony as convicts were usually allocated roles as domestic servants, yet many of them had neither the training for such a role nor the skills to assume that role, probably a result of their dissolute lifestyles. In addition, they had no family to support them, so when they lost their domestic jobs they were often forced into prostitution or a series of "liaisons" in order to gain food and shelter. This placed the women in a catch 22 situation: the chances of pregnancy were increased, but at a cost of securing employment or marriage in the future. In addition, existing family relationships were threatened by the loss of a parent and the lack of extended families to assume some of the parenting responsibilities.

Other factors peculiar to nineteenth-century Australia caused family dislocation and neglected children: the gold rushes in the states of New South Wales and Victoria in the 1840s, and in Queensland and Western Australia in the 1880s and 1890s, respectively, and the depression of the 1890s. Many men who joined in the gold rushes abandoned their wives and children, leaving them without adequate means of support. This situation was sometimes exacerbated when an absent husband fathered a second family at his new location. A later factor contributing to the number of uncared-for children, reflecting a broader world situation, was the depression of the 1890s. During periods of economic hardship it was not uncommon for men to travel from one colony to another in search of work. The various state governments contributed to this form of migration by initiating relief through large work projects such as train lines and mining developments. Annual agricultural shifts in burgeoning products such as wheat and wool also led to migration; workers went where jobs were available, irrespective of the sometimes huge distances involved.

For the first one hundred years of the penal colony in New South Wales, the government and the churches endeavored to cope with the demands of education for children of all ages. However, in 1868, the Public Schools Act abolished the dual Denominational Board and the Board of National Education and created a single state system of education. The churches no longer received any assistance toward the education or care of children of any age. Consequently, one avenue of support to parents in need was closed at a time when more support was required. Thus, while a system of compulsory, free, and secular education was provided for all children over the age of five years, preschool-age children lost the opportunity to attend primary schools forever.

Meanwhile the social conscience of the Australian colonists was being reformed by the late-nineteenth-century interpretation of history, namely, that there is a clear obligation on the part of the rich to help the poor. However, this belief was inhibited by the prevailing opinion that poverty per se was the result of some personal failing such as drunkenness, promiscuity, or just plain laziness (Mellor, 1990). Obviously, hard work and independence were valued highly, and poor homes were viewed as being "bad" homes. Combined with the growing perception in England and elsewhere that children were both vulnerable and innocent and in need of protection from physical and moral harm, there was a belief that children must be "saved" from poor (and bad) homes. The child rescue movement, with support from members of the evangelical movement who came to Australia in the 1860s and 1890s from Great Britain, was established. All church denominations became more active in both religious reform and social welfare issues, including children's services. However, the range and extent of services varied from state to state: for instance, in New South Wales the Benevolent Society, a society of volunteers, was most active but relied on government funds for support; Victoria, a non-convict state, relied almost totally on private philanthropy assisted by government grants; Tasmania, which began as a convict settlement, had few private programs in the late 1860s and 1870s, and relied heavily on government initiatives; and South Australia, another non-convict state, had a tradition of government provision of children's services from general revenue, which was unique in Australia.

THE LEGACY OF THE DEPRESSION:
KINDERGARTENS FOR DESTITUTE CHILDREN

The provision of children's services in the various states may have continued in this somewhat ad hoc, patchwork manner had it not been for the depression of the 1890s. While it can be argued that the 1890s depression was worldwide and that it did not affect Australia as badly as some other western countries, it had a profound effect on the system of social values which had underpinned children's services up to that time in the six colonies. In 1890 a crippling maritime strike had left New South Wales, the most populous state, with fifteen thousand men out of work, and had caused the price of necessities such as butter and potatoes to double. The economic recession deepened into a depression as overseas banks foreclosed on loans, and by 1893 banks in all the colonies except those in West Australia had ceased trading. As a result, thousands of previously "well-off" families lost their life savings, homes, businesses, and jobs. Apart from causing untold hardship, the situation made a mockery of the argument made by churches and charities that poor equals bad; thousands of the new poor were not from the traditionally poor inner suburbs. As one writer has pointed out, "Many who had epitomised the old virtues of thrift and hard work had been reduced to poverty. As a result, views about poverty changed. Poverty was being (however haltingly) redefined in terms that placed less emphasis on immorality, fecklessness and drink and more on economic circumstances" (Mellor, 1990:12).

Although the economy of all the colonies had improved by the end of the 1890s, the depression had challenged the traditional values which surround human services, including the relative roles of the human services, and the relative roles of the government and private institutions in the provision of these services. This reappraisal of institutional roles was mirrored by a reappraisal of the role of women in several areas; women assumed an increasingly active role in the organization and provision of human services, including children's services. From the 1890s the universities of Sydney, Melbourne, and Adelaide, the three most populated areas of Australia, permitted women to graduate with degrees in medicine, thus raising the status of women in the community in general while at the same time creating a pool of qualified women. Women became increasingly active in political life through various organizations associated with the suffrage movement (women in South Australia were the first women in the western world to gain the right to vote) and translated this newfound power into community services.

As cultural and social values changed and thus paved the way for change to services for children in the following decade, the blossoming of Australian nationalism of the 1880s and 1890s (which culminated in the federation of Australia in 1901) sparked a growing sense of patriotism and independence. The high proportion of destitute children and infant mortality was perceived as a blow to national pride and a potential threat to the general well-being of a healthy, expanding nation. The scene was set for drastic and dramatic changes to children's services in the first decade of the twentieth century. It is clear that the depression of the 1890s, the gradual but emphatic emancipation of women, and the transmission of Froebel's ideas to the various Australian colonies paved the way for the development of kindergarten in Australia.

THE DEVELOPMENT OF KINDERGARTENS IN
NEW SOUTH WALES: THE ROLE OF THE STATE

From 1880 to 1900, Australia witnessed the birth of the kindergarten. In 1854, M. Mitchell, H.M. Inspector of Schools in England, had been very impressed with a demonstration of Froebel's gifts and occupations and the theories underlying them which he had observed at the annual exhibition of the Society of Art in London. He included a description of the principles and processes in his annual report, which was read by William Wilkins, the inspector of schools for the National Board of Education in Sydney.

The first mention of Froebel's work and the idea of kindergarten in Australia was made by William Wilkins in 1856. In a report to the board, he referred to Froebel's principles as "mingling employment with instruction and combining employment with both" (Walker, 1964:10). While Wilkins can be credited with bringing Froebel's ideas to Australia, it can be argued that he did not understand the tenor of Mitchell's report.

Wilkins's report suggested the Froebel's sole contribution to the education of the young child was the provision of techniques which ensured that children were "reasonably happy" as well as being kept busy. This report was a clear signal that officials of the government schools of the time in the colony of New South Wales had misinterpreted Froebel's principles and in fact were misusing Froebel's gifts and occupation as preparation for technical education skills.

Wilkins sponsored the introduction of "kindergarten methods" in a special Nursery Class, which was established at the Fort Street Model School to serve children aged two to five years. "As the name of Froebel is probably new to the Colonial public" (Walker, 1964:119), Wilkins explained, he would attempt to present the Froebelian principles as he perceived them from his reading of Mitchell's report of 1856. However, Wilkins's perceptions were that kindergarten was a form of training of the senses. "The chief instruments are models and pictures, cubes, wooden bricks, the ball-frame, colours—everything, in short, that appeals to the eye and the other senses" (Walker, 1964:120).

At this time kindergartens were in their infancy in Great Britain, while in the United States no kindergartens had been opened for English-speaking children. In addition, the first publication of an English translation of Froebel's works was still thirty years off, so it is not surprising that William Wilkins, so far from the center of western educational theory, possessed only a superficial knowledge of Froebel's kindergarten.

In 1880, Edward Combes, a New South Wales member of Parliament and engineer, was sent to Great Britain, Europe, and North America to examine lighting, heating, and ventilation of schools. This mission was in keeping with the rapid expansion of public education at that time. During his trip he became convinced that the "school house and surroundings are instruments of education in themselves" (Walker, 1964:125). In addition to the detailed observations pertinent to his project, his report contained an extra section devoted to a new development, the kindergarten system. He had visited kindergartens in France, Austria, Belgium, Sweden, Great Britain, and the United States, so he had firsthand knowledge of the way in which Froebel's principles could be translated into practice and what could be expected of children after they leave the kindergarten, which he saw as a year prior to attending school at the age of six. This would appear to be the first detailed account of the work of Froebel published by an Australian, which also included a statement on the training of kindergarten teachers.

Probably because of his background as an engineer, Combes, like others before him, saw particular value in technical education. At a public gathering in 1882, he confirmed his opinion that the kindergarten system was in reality technical education. While he did acknowledge the value of Froebel's ideas of providing ordered freedom for young children and self-active learning rather than progress in the "3 Rs," the Department of Public Instruction and the press remained unimpressed by Combes's commitment to the kindergarten. For example, the *Sydney Morning Herald* of May 20, 1880, stated "it may be questioned whether in its present form the [Combes] report is worth the trouble it has cost the writer and the expense it has been . . . to the government" (quoted in Walker, 1964:129). Clearly public opinion, as reflected in the media, was skeptical of the new ideas generated by Combes, and saw little value in educating children of preschool age.

The Public Instruction Act had come into force in New South Wales in 1881. It provided a state-controlled system of compulsory, secular education for children aged six to fourteen years and was financed with government funds. It reflected the growing awareness of the need for universal education at a time of progress toward nationhood. However, the practice of sending children younger than six prevailed, especially in rural areas where the presence of the young children was needed to keep the schools open. In 1881, of the 146,106 pupils on the rolls of state schools, 17.3 percent were aged four to six, while a further 2.4 percent were under the age of four. It was clear that more attention needed to be given to the education of these younger children; there were too many to be ignored. As a result of these compelling numbers of young children in the colony, it was clear that the government had to formalize some educational program for children under the age of six.

Also in 1881, the Ministry of Public Instruction employed Amelia Crowley, a recent arrival from Great Britain via New Zealand. She had trained for a short time at the Stockwell Kindergarten College in the United Kingdom, which was operated by the British and Foreign Schools Society. She had been recruited by Christchurch Normal School (New Zealand) to introduce "Froebel's System of Infant Training" (Elliot, 1990). Between 1878 and 1880, she supervised the operations of what appeared to be a most successful kindergarten within the infants' department of a practicing school.

Following her appointment, Crowley attempted to gain public and professional support for Froebel's ideas. In April 1882, she published an article in the *Sydney University Review* in which she protested attempts to introduce Froebel's ideas without an understanding of the underlying principles. She pointed out that the gifts and occupations as developed by Froebel were designed not merely to develop manual dexterity as a precursor to a more advanced technical education. At the same time, she gained the interest and support of influential people in Sydney: members of Parliament, a newspaper editor, judges, ministers of religion, and women in responsible positions were quoted by Crowley as appreciating that kindergarten constituted a "solid system of self education beginning with children of a tender age" (*Sydney Morning Herald*, January 9, 1883, quoted in Walker, 1964:136).

Crowley established the first kindergarten in Crown Street, Surry Hills Public School. The beginnings were not auspicious, as detailed in her article in the *Sydney Morning Herald* of December 29, 1833: "The birthplace (of the kindergarten) in New South Wales was in the little cloak room of the Crown Street Public School, the floor covering serving as seats, to enable the forms to do duty as tables (necessary furniture in lieu of the ordinary desks). Later on this accommodation was replaced by a little building erected purposely, supplied with suitable tables, etc., but whose situation courted the most violent rays of a New South Wales sun, as our steaming faces bore testimony too frequently" (Walker, 1964:132).

In spite of Crowley's careful preparation of the public through newspaper articles and the accumulation of influential persons to support her endeavors, the government school inspectors who visited the school were not impressed with what they saw. They were still looking for evidence of facts memorized and skills mastered, that is, evidence of a traditional formal education system. It should be noted that Crowley's task was not an easy one. About ninety children were enrolled, one-third of whom were described as "very young," she had only pupil-teachers (untrained girls aged fifteen or so) to assist her, and the large school room was divided in two by green curtains so the noise of the older sixty children undertaking the normal junior primary lessons must have proved very distracting.

Crowley's articles in the *Sydney Morning Herald* were sneered at. "[It] is little more than a nursery maintained at the expense of the state," one critic proclaimed (Mellor, 1990:61). The *Sydney Morning Herald*'s article of January 1, 1885, was particularly scathing: "In a country where education must be at the public cost and under public control, the basis must be literary rather than mechanical and the aim must be to teach the rudiments of reading writing and arithmetic . . . we have only a few children on whom the experiment (kindergarten) might be carried out as a work of charity and a still smaller number upon whom it might be attempted as an amusement" (Walker, 1964:145). The *Herald*'s criticism appeared to reflect the opinions of the Department of Public Instruction, which was convinced that although it had given the proponents of the kindergarten system ample opportunity to prove itself, it had not been compatible with the existing mode of public, state-funded education (Elliott, 1990).

Despite comments such as these, the Department of Public Instruction continued to be interested in kindergarten methods, but Froebel's ideas were modified to suit large classes. As a result, kindergarten was often seen as training in physical coordination, which became a lesson on the timetable along with reading, writing, and arithmetic. The value of self-directed activity—one of the principles on which Froebel's work was based—was barely, if ever, mentioned. The Hurlstone Training Institution was opened in 1882 to train elementary school teachers. A British woman, Caroline Mallett, was engaged to serve as "training mistress." She had some knowledge of the kindergarten system and provided all trainees with lectures on the role of Froebel and training in the use of the gifts and occupations. So all graduates of this program for elementary school teachers also possessed a rudimentary knowledge of Froebel's ideas.

In 1884 or 1886, Elizabeth Banks, a kindergarten-trained teacher at the Birmingham (Great Britain) School Board, was appointed to Crown Street school for four hours per week. She worked with the five-year-old children on "kindergarten activities" including drawing, paper-folding, paper-coloring, mat-plaiting, and stick-laying. Unlike Crowley, Banks managed a positive report from the inspectors. At the same time, Banks began lectures to trainee teachers on kindergarten principles. Her interest and enthusiasm was recognized, for in 1888 Banks was appointed to succeed Mallett as kindergarten training mistress at Hurlstone. Her appointment coincided with the centenary jubilee celebrations in Sydney, which included an exhibition of women's industries held "to demonstrate the various branches of work in which the women of the Colony are now engaged and the standard of excellence they have attained" (Walker, 1964:157). One hundred and fifty children from Riley Street Surry Hills Public School gave a demonstration of "kindergarten activities," and several qualified teachers offered lectures on Froebel's principles.

While Froebel's ideas did have some effect in lessening the public school emphasis on rote learning, memorization, and verbal instruction, it must be argued that this modified form of kindergarten was an advance in pedagogy. Although it did not embrace the principle of development through play, it did offer opportunities for children of all ages to build and to draw—as a precursor to the manual education activities programed for the older children.

In 1889, an inspector of the Department of Public Instruction was requested to furnish a report on kindergartens. In this report, a distinction was made between "kindergarten classes," consisting of thirty-two classes using the gifts and occupations as preparation for manual dexterity, and five kindergartens which relied on Froebel's ideas as a basis for their program. This report emphasized the basic misinterpretation of Froebel's gifts and occupations in the state-run schools and the way in which the term *kindergarten* was misrepresented to the public.

However, in spite of these difficulties, in 1894 Chief Inspector Frederick

Bridges showed a new interest in kindergarten methods and advised that all schools were to have "kindergarten exercises" for thirty minutes each day. In light of this decision it is somewhat ironic that Goulburn Superior School was awarded a medal at the 1896 Chicago World Fair for an exhibit of "kindergarten work" (Walker, 1964).

Australian educators of the 1880s were not solely to blame for this misunderstanding of Froebel's principles. The modifications were based on the English pattern, and New South Wales was a colony of Great Britain at the time. An Australian, W. C. Grasby, wrote in 1892: "I did not find one true kindergarten in connection with an English public elementary school. I saw an abundance of so-called 'kindergarten work' but not a kindergarten. In America, both in Canada and USA, I saw many" (Walker, 1964:148). This statement exemplified the way in which Froebel's teachings had burgeoned in the United States through European immigrants' firsthand knowledge of the system, while it had been allowed to languish in the United Kingdom, which lacked teachers with such knowledge.

A 1903 report commissioned by the Department of Public Instruction acknowledged the need for kindergartens as such for young children rather than as a subject on the timetable for all children. The report, written by G. H. Knibbs and J. W. Turner, suggested that the absence of a kindergarten year constituted "a serious defect in any scheme of public instruction." It further suggested that such a class should be largely Froebelian in kind: "The whole of the instruction should be developed through play—self activity should be promoted. The course should not be allowed to become changed and burdened merely with primary work—desultory employment of some or all of the Gifts and Occupations is not a true kindergarten" (Knibbs and Turner, 1903:31). The report went on to recommend full professional training for kindergarten teachers through the establishment of a kindergarten training college and demonstration school. Having made such a strong plea for a "true kindergarten," Knibbs and Turner modified their position by agreeing that "the exact function of kindergartens is one about which absolute agreement does not exist" (Knibbs and Turner, 1903:16).

Clearly, had the dissemination of Froebel's philosophy and principles been left to the state, Australia may never have had a place in the history of the kindergarten. In 1908, one lone voice, Professor Alexander Mackie, introduced a special course for second-year students at the Sydney Teachers' College, entitled "Kindergarten." The New South Wales state government was less than competent in its introduction of the kindergarten. It permitted a poor replication of

Froebel's theory to be implemented, and it failed to protect people such as Amelia Crowley, who understood the system, from the vehemence of the press. The government's posture reflected the belief that education for young children was not a priority, but merely a welfare activity for the children of the poor and/or destitute.

THE DEVELOPMENT OF THE KINDERGARTEN:
THE ROLE OF PRIVATE SCHOOLS

Although the public school system had not assimilated the kindergarten concept in its originally planned form, public interest in New South Wales had been heightened by a number of factors, including the pioneer work of Amelia Crowley, the exhibit of kindergarten activities at the centennial jubilee industrial demonstration, and the introduction of kindergarten methods into the infants schools. The kindergarten's popular appeal was exploited by people with little or no training and probably no knowledge of the system. As a result, many attempts were short-lived, but a nucleus persisted in three private schools: The College for Girls, Wesleyan Ladies' College, and Maybanke, all of which opened kindergartens between 1884 and 1886. The Wesleyan Ladies' College opened the first specially designed kindergarten building in Australia (Walker, 1964). All three schools had trained kindergarten teachers and charged fees; they were not designed to educate or care for children whose parents could not afford private tuition.

One of the major problems was finding suitable lecturers to provide the necessary theory as well as the experience of putting the theory into practice. This had been one of Crowley's major weaknesses; although she was knowledgeable about Froebel's ideas, she found it difficult to implement them with young children.

In 1895 the graduates of the training courses offered by these three schools in conjunction with the kindergarten classes established a Teachers' Association. The association initiated a systematic course known as the Kindergarten Certificate and included lectures on the science of education and the art of teaching, three months of observation and teaching in approved schools, and examinations in theory and practice which involved the preparation of notes and lessons on Froebelian gifts and occupations and a singing game. It is interesting to note that the observations took place in a registered kindergarten which had previously paid half a guinea for this privilege and had satisfied the board as to the amount of space per child, light, ventilation, apparatus, furniture, playground, staff, timetable, and programs (Walker, 1964:181). This process may have been the forerunner of the accreditation process.

In 1897, Harriet Newcomb and Margaret Hodge, trained kindergarten teachers, arrived in the colony from Great Britain. They were employed by the newly formed Teachers' Association to lecture, and in 1900 they opened their own school, "Shirley," in order to demonstrate best practice. Hodge was firm about the importance of excellence in teacher training: "The foundations must be laid by the best workmen. Let us remember that intellectual work, properly graduated, is not distasteful but delightful to the child and that the future fate of the kindergarten system must depend wholly upon the qualifications of the kindergarten lecturers" (quoted in Harrison, 1985:14).

Newcomb and Hodge had an important part to play in the changing pattern of kindergartens in Australia, and the manner in which teachers in training came to better understand Froebel's ideas. Ruth Harrison, a former principal of the Sydney Kindergarten Training College, summed up their work. "They regarded children as personalities to be brought to full function and they held that harmonious personable development came from self activity in as many ways as possible. The emphasis was on learning and not on teaching, on experience and not on second-hand information" (Harrison, 1985:15). This observation exemplified the Froebelian principles, as espoused by other adherents of Froebel.

By 1890 there were thirteen registered kindergarten teachers and two trainers, but this was not the only contribution of the Teachers' Association to the development of kindergartens for several hundred children. It had encouraged both cooperation between the public and private schools as well as an interest from the University of Sydney, which provided support and lecturing expertise to kindergarten training for the following seventy years.

THE DEVELOPMENT OF
KINDERGARTEN UNIONS

The kindergarten movement—in one form or another, in state public schools and several private schools—served an educational function. However, the economic conditions of the colony of the 1890s reflected the world-wide depression; plans for rehousing of the poor and a general slum clearance had been put on hold. Unemployment was widespread, particularly for those in semi-skilled and unskilled positions, and the great suburban housing development had outstripped the city proper. Industrial growth was confined to the inner city, thus aggravating the problem of finding adequate housing. In addition, "larrikin groups" of young troublemakers roamed the streets (larrikins are mischievous young persons). For many women faced with an uncertain economic future any paid employment became a necessity; many were engaged as laundry or cleaning maids, but in jobs such as these there was no provision for the care of their young children.

For some philanthropically minded people there was a strong urge to bring about social reform and to improve the quality of life of the children and their mothers living in poverty in the deprived areas of Sydney. One such person was Margaret Windeyer, an officer of the Public Library of Sydney, and secretary of the National Council of Women. She had returned from a trip to the United States in 1895, impressed by the work of the Golden Gate Kindergarten Association in San Francisco. Her friends and colleagues in Sydney who read the annual report of the Golden Gate Kindergarten identified many similarities between the cities of Sydney and San Francisco. Both had developed slum areas teeming with children, each had no provision for the care of small children, and each saw the work of the kindergarten as the best means of initiating social reform.

These philanthropists interested in bringing about social reform to better the health and welfare of young children were supported by a group striving to bring about educational reform. Supporters of the so-called progressive approach to education perceived the "true" kindergarten approach embodied in Froebel's principles as a means of bringing reform to current educational practices (Harrison, 1985).

Influential educators interested in progressive education included Professor Francis Anderson, professor of philosophy at the University of Sydney, and Peter Board, later to become director of education in the Department of Education. A cry for reform in education might have gone unheeded, but it "was comparatively easy to arouse interest in the conditions of neglected children and the imminent dangers of larrikinism" (Maybanke Anderson in Walker, 1964:189). The philanthropic and educational appeal of establishing a kindergarten movement in Sydney was so strong that philanthropists, university staff, and interested kindergarten personnel formed a Kindergarten Union in New South Wales. Maybanke Anderson, a co-founder of Maybanke College (and wife of Professor Anderson), described the situation as "the policy which made philanthropy go hand in hand with education" (Walker, 1964:189).

Anderson was president of the Womanhood Suffrage League of New South Wales and editor and publisher of a fortnightly paper entitled *Women's Voice*. In addition to all these roles, she was the honorary secretary of the newly formed Kindergarten Union (Walker, 1964). In 1895 she divorced her first husband and turned the family home into a school (Maybanke), which developed a reputation for innovative and successful teaching methods. In July of that year the first meeting of the Kindergarten Union was held. The expressed aims were as follows: "To set forth kindergarten principles. To endeavour to get those principles introduced into every school in New South Wales. To open Free Kindergartens whenever possible in poorer neighbourhoods" (Scott, 1960:16–17). Scott is of the commonly held opinion that the proposed education of the preschool-aged child appears to have had a primarily child-saving purpose and only secondarily an educational goal. There was no intention of working collaboratively with the public school system; rather, kindergartens were to cater to children in their preschool years.

In July 1896, the first free kindergarten was opened at Woolloomooloo, a dockyard area in Sydney. Children up to the age of six were enrolled. From an initial enrollment of thirteen, it expanded very quickly to seventy-six, indicating the urgent need for such a center. For parents who were poor or destitute or unable to care for their children due to work commitment, this kindergarten was a welcome innovation. Mrs. Dane, an Australian kindergarten teacher who had gone to the United States to train, described the site in these terms: "Crowded into these unattractive premises some 75 to 80 unwashed, uncared-for little children, ranging in age from 18 months to 6 years of age—and you will have in brief, a description of the place which in 1896 did duty as the first free kindergarten in Australia" (Harrison, 1985:20). Financial support was meager, but following a series of public meetings and demonstrations of the activities, vice regal patronage was obtained.

In May 1896 the wife of the governor of New South Wales agreed to a meeting of members of the Kindergarten Union at Government House. This provided the first real publicity for the Kindergarten Union, which emphasized the social reform aspects of the movement. Public response varied, and some critics argued that the government should have been providing kindergartens instead of leaving that task to volunteers. However, the state government, due to the financial constraints of the depression, was not able to meet the full social and educational responsibilities of the state. Other criticism was more vitriolic; *The Bulletin* of August 3, 1896, describes the kindergarten movement: "As long as it is under the patronage of the fashionable and the faddists, [the movement] promises to become another excrescence on the educational system of the country. Froebel's idea is to teach by play, but play is healthy and invigorating only when it is free and spontaneous, and the kindergarten 'bossed' by any broken-down governesses who can do the requisite amount of mechanical stuffing with the 'groups' of toys will add another horror to child life in our great cities" (quoted in Walker, 1964:194). This view can only be construed as extremely prejudiced, but it did point to a fundamental weakness in any educational movement forced to rely on public donations for survival and whose education policy is determined by a lay committee. In spite of these often trenchant criticisms, the kindergarten movement in Australia was developed in the tradition of Froebel's ideas as they had been observed in operation in North American kindergartens (Scott, 1960). There was an emphasis on the child's individual development through its participation in social activities. This was the way John Dewey and F. W. Parker had interpreted Froebel's ideas in American kindergartens: "The work was planned in great detail and followed the established pattern of morning greeting, songs and 'news' on the circle, work periods with gifts, handwork, sand tray, etc., talk of 'planned period' music, games and story. There was much teacher direction, the groups were large and the children were expected to sit quietly and listen attentively, although great freedom was allowed in the choice and use of materials . . . the planned program remained the usual pattern until the nineteen thirties" (Walker, 1964:275–277). The child-saving emphasis also affected the curriculum, with cleanliness and good manners featured prominently. The children were bathed each day. "The bathing parties, as they were called, were not necessarily enjoyed by the children or staff, but were essential for the health and wellbeing of all at the centre" (Harrison, 1985:38).

The Kindergarten Union expanded slowly, dependent on philanthropic organizers and voluntary financial donations. By 1908 only nine kindergartens had been established in the poorer ports of Sydney. In one center attached to the Kindergarten Training College, parents paid fees, but in the other eight centers the service was free: "Parents make voluntary cash contributions of a few pence per week and they also give services in helping with the chores of the kindergarten. Through their Mothers' Club they also assist in raising money for the support of the kindergarten" (Cumpston and Heinig, 1945:198).

Mothers' clubs and regular home visits were techniques used by the kindergarten teachers to influence inner city working-class parents to "do better." The press as well as the Kindergarten Union's own magazine was always able to find space for anecdotal evidence of the benefits of kindergarten. The following was written by a Sydney kindergarten teacher in the *Australian Kindergarten Magazine* of April 1911: "once established[,] its influence for good soon became a very real one . . . in connection with this a doctor was heard to say that he always knew at once when he entered a home where children attended kindergarten, there was always a cleaner and brighter atmosphere, and he saw evidence of the effort to have a dainty touch here and there" (Spearritt, 1979:10). It can be argued that such articles were an attempt to not only publicize the work of kindergartens but to garner financial support from like-minded persons.

The Kindergarten Union recognized that in many cases its centers were used by parents as child minders. Despite this recognition, they offered only morning programs until 1915 and did not accept children under three years of age (Spearritt, 1979). This decision appears to have been based on the philosophy that children under the age of three should be nurtured by their mother at home, but after that age (presumably, when they were weaned) they could be expected to spend more time on the streets—hence the need for the kindergarten. The idea that the care of working-class children should not be left solely to their parents gained wide acceptance by the turn of the century, and received support from eminent persons such as Meredith Atkinson, director of tutorial classes at the University of Sydney, who suggested that if "we could open more kindergartens we could almost shut the prisons" (quoted in Spearritt, 1979:12). Initially kindergartens filled a child-minding role at a time when government-initiated child care was nonexistent.

In addition, members of the Kindergarten Union became more vociferous about their educational role, which had largely been ignored because of health and welfare needs of the children. They argued that, unlike state public school kindergartens, their kindergartens were not intended to be seen as an "early edition of school or as a means of seeing that the child will be advanced in intellectual achievements when he goes to school (Pearse, 1963:25). Rather, the child as an individual within a group situation was recognized and responded to.

TEACHER TRAINING IN KINDERGARTENS

From the outset, the Kindergarten Union in New South Wales and the Department of Public Instruction each had its own training system, but the fundamental philosophical differences between the two systems ensured that the two groups became more independent of each other as the Kindergarten Union increased in size and influence. In May 1890, the Kindergarten Training College was opened in Darlinghurst, Sydney, a residential college solely for kindergarten teachers employed by the Kindergarten Union. This was a clear signal that the members of the Kindergarten Union had cut off their programs from government assistance by declining to associate with the kindergarten training already in existence at Hurlstone College. After a long and tedious correspondence with institutions in both Great Britain and the United States the Kindergarten Union selected Bridle Lee Buckey, who trained at Cook County Normal School in Chicago under the direction of Francis W. Parker. Her training ideas obviously reflected her professional background, and she sought to place more emphasis in the course on the development of the child. The child study movement in America, to which Buckey belonged, had emphasized the need to study children firsthand, and to gather factual information about each child through observation rather than undertaking a merely theoretical study of development. Chicago had been the center for much of this child study process. Buckey arrived in Sydney in July 1897, and the first meeting of the Child Study Association was held the following year (Harrison, 1985:112).

In the months that followed, a series of so-called anthropometric measurements were completed on each child in a Kindergarten Union center. Data included the height, weight, head, chest, and limb measurements of each child as well as a survey of his or her ability to see, hear, smell, and taste (Walker, 1964). The Child Study Association promised to provide more exact information on each child than was previously available, and Buckey asserted its importance in order to understand individual differences and their importance.

Buckey also changed the training course considerably. She instituted a regular two-year training course in lieu of the "training classes" previously held three afternoons a week. In addition, she planned and implemented a third, postgraduate year for those who wished to become training directors. Her ideas had developed as a result of her training and experience in the mainland Unites States and Honolulu, and her programs obviously reflected this background. Her explanation for a third year of the course included the following argument: "Each year gives additional insight into Froebel's great principles of education but it is only in the blending of the three years that the harmonious and firm grasp of this method is attained. The three (years) embody a drama in which each experience is necessary to the whole . . . if the first year stands for the practical side of the profession, the second brings the intellectual grasp and the last (third) holds the spiritual element" (Walker, 1964:202). This is a significant change in that for the previous sixty years the training course for primary school teachers was only two years.

The kindergarten course, held initially in the upper room of the Woolloomooloo Kindergarten, consisted of psychology, nature study, technical work involving Froebel's gifts and occupations, program work, Froebel's *Mother Plays*, games and songs, physical culture, drawing, music, as well as history and philosophy of education, which included a study of Froebel's most important works (Walker, 1964).

Buckey made it clear that programs had to value and encourage each child's social development, including freedom and active participation in social contexts. Extra materials were added to each trainee teacher's repertoire, including excursions, sand, clay, nature study, and the development of garden plots and pets. By 1899, the Newtown Kindergarten had an array of pets, including a kookaburra, a porcupine, two canaries, a kitten, and a white rabbit.

Buckey worked in the center at Woolloomooloo in the morning with the children, and she lectured to the students each afternoon. The Kindergarten Union agreed that student teachers should be found to assist Buckey with the morning teaching load in return for afternoon instruction. However, it proved difficult to locate suitable girls to undertake the student teaching role; people did not regard kindergarten work very highly, and "it was said that 'anybody can mind little children'" (Harrison, 1985:25). How little have things changed in a hundred years!

Parents who had children enrolled at Kindergarten Union centers were encouraged to visit the centers; consequently, the trainees' course was extended to include ways of running meetings, lecturing to parents, and explaining and describing children's activities. In 1897, eight students were enrolled in the inaugural two-year course: "The training offered to the girls was unmistakably middle-class. In the late 1890s the syllabus taught by the female American lecturer specially appointed to the College included . . . a monthly assessment system . . . and marking content included neatness, understanding of child nurture, orderliness, punctuality, and intellectual and practical grasp of kindergarten ideas and ideals" (Spearritt, 1979:8).

The early Kindergarten Union–trained teachers were young and inexperienced, and it was clear that they needed support. The lecturers at the college supported them, thus creating a nexus between lecturing staff, teaching staff, and students, a process which continued until at least the 1970s. Teachers were involved also in fundraising efforts as well as teaching. As some of the fundraising contributed to the teachers' meager salaries, most soon became very skillful at soliciting funds.

By the turn of the twentieth century it was recognized that young middle-class women who were not clever enough to pursue a university course but whose parents were prepared to pay the necessary fees were ideal enrollees for the kindergarten course. However, the Sydney Kindergarten Union's annual report of 1905–1907 tried to argue that the course would be useful beyond kindergarten teaching: "It is recognised that whether a woman is to be in her home or is to follow a profession, she will have a broader outlook on life, her sympathies will be deeper and more far-reaching and she will withal be a more useful woman for having had her kindergarten training" (Harrison, 1985:25).

Buckey's contribution to the initial kindergarten training course was monumental. She laid the foundations for a new pattern of kindergarten work, a pattern based on the principles of Froebel but at the same time using a fresh approach to the ideas implemented in the United States. She introduced the notion of personal development to a heavily professionally oriented course by adding music, art, and literature to the training curriculum for the students' own development. When Buckey returned home in 1901, she was replaced by another American, Chicago-trained Frances Newton, whose aim was to "wipe out from the minds of any who are yet ignorant of our aims the idea that a kindergarten is a philanthropy only. It is a first step in a rational system of education and is suited to all ranks in child life" (Walker, 1964:221). These were daring words at a time when the New South Wales government refused to provide a grant to the Kindergarten Union on the grounds that because the kindergarten was free, it was not eligible for a subsidy. However, in 1899, a "gift" of ten pounds from the state government became an annual grant, rising to a more realistic eight hundred and fifty pounds in 1907 (Walker, 1964:205). This "gift" and subsequent gifts acknowledged the influence of the members of the kindergarten movement in areas as diverse as banking, industry, and education.

THE SPREAD OF THE KINDERGARTEN
MOVEMENT IN OTHER STATES

By 1916 every state in Australia had established a Kindergarten Union or Kindergarten Association to develop private kindergartens in areas of need, mainly in industrial areas. The state of Queensland, for example, established a Creche and Kindergarten Association in 1916 so that the organization best reflected that state's particular needs in the area of care for infants and toddlers. The growth was not rapid, as each new Kindergarten Union was relying on charity and philanthropically minded people to establish the organization. In South Australia the Kindergarten Union was initiated by clergymen of various denominations. In Victoria, the establishment of the Free Kindergarten Union (FKU) quickly attracted vice regal patronage as well as the interest and support of administrators of the University of Melbourne, directors of public education, and other "notable personages" (Fry, 1975:1). The first president of the FKU was Mrs. Alfred Deakin, wife of the first prime minister of Australia.

However, the educators in these different states were united in their philosophy, in that the influence of Froebel and Dewey (and, to a lesser extent, Montessori) were obvious in guiding the establishment and development of the kindergarten movement in Australia. This eclectic approach pervaded in all areas of the kindergarten's work, from children's curricula to teacher training.

The growth of the Kindergarten Unions continued to reflect the straitened economic times in the newly federated states of Australia, together with a growing awareness among the church and lay community of the need for society to assume a greater responsibility for young children whose families were perceived to be in need, for whatever reason (Clyde, 1990). This was a direct response to the changed perceptions of the poor as people in need of support, rather than as degenerate "no hopers."

By 1910 there were thirty-two kindergartens in Australia, and separate kindergarten training colleges had been established in Sydney (1895), Adelaide (1907), Brisbane (1911), Perth (1912), and Melbourne (1916). The colleges continued the curriculum introduced by Buckey in Sydney. The emphasis was on students' developing skills in child observation and child development as a basis for program planning, and on the notion that children learn through play, as opposed to verbal instruction.

DEVELOPMENT OF KINDERGARTENS
IN OTHER STATES

In the state of Victoria, the philanthropic and progressive education devotees developed their ideas about kindergarten in parallel fashion, rather than in tandem. However, it must be acknowledged that as early as 1887 the Victorian Education Department had "imported" an English kindergarten-trained teacher to train sub-primary (age undefined) trainee teachers at the department's Model School. Unfortunately, this innovation was cut short by the economic depression of the 1890s, but by this time the concept of kindergarten had found some acceptance among Melbourne's educated middle class, most of whom had church affiliations. In 1902 a Kindergarten Society was formed, known from 1908 on as the Free Kindergarten Union. This society appointed Annie Westmoreland as president. The purpose of the society was to train kindergarten teachers, and Westmoreland was ably suited to this role. In 1899 she had begun a series of Saturday morning classes for trainee teachers and had established her own kindergarten class at a Melbourne private school, Ruylon, as a demonstration site.

By 1901 trained kindergarten teachers were available to conduct kindergartens for the "neglected hungry, ignorant children" living in narrow streets, crowded lanes, and unsanitary houses as a result of the depression (Gardiner, 1982). Carlton Kindergarten was opened by the Baptist Church in 1901, followed by similar kindergartens in 1906—ten established by the Presbyterian and Methodist churches, the Church of Christ, and the Women's Christian Temperance Union, respectively. The Christian missionary motive was the guiding force, and church and lay members of the congregations established and maintained the kindergartens. Collingwood Kindergarten, for instance, established in 1907, was described in the first annual report as "a gracious answer to many prayers" (Gardiner, 1982:5).

The voluntary management committees were known, misleadingly, as "local committees." However, they were not composed of local people but rather of men and women from a "better" community elsewhere who had the time and the income necessary to help alleviate the plight of the desperate and the poor.

For the Christian philanthropists who established the initial kindergartens in Victoria, kindergarten work was perceived as women's work: it was concerned with children and caring, and it had a social theme. It followed also that working in kindergartens was not only an excellent preparation for the "ultimate calling" of marriage but also a thoroughly Christian occupation, either unpaid or paid so little that it was merely "pin money" and therefore it did not diminish the importance of the father—the provider for his womenfolk.

John Smyth, principal of Melbourne Teachers' College, and a keen devotee of Froebel, was anxious to ensure that those women who worked with young children in the state schools had the special training necessary. He wrote, "too long the cry has been that anyone can teach infants (young children). Rather should we say that the most highly trained teachers are needed for them" (Walker, 1964:44).

In 1908, when church groups had established four kindergartens, Smyth appointed Emmeline Pye as mistress of kindergarten method at Melbourne Teachers' College. At the same time, Smyth and Pye met with delegates from the various church groups to set up the Free Kindergarten Union. For several years there appeared to be some cooperation between the voluntary church groups and the government-run teachers' college in the area of teacher training. This afforded the existing kindergartens and those established after 1908 to provide an education program based on fractal principles without subverting their social role.

However, the church members of the FKU became more determined to regain control of the training of kindergarten teachers. In 1916 the FKU established its own training college, the Melbourne Kindergarten Training College, and for the next sixty years kindergarten training moved out of the education sphere. These battles for control of training had long-term effects on the provision of preschool education in Australia, in that kindergartens were denied access to education funding at state and, later, federal levels. In Victoria, for example, kindergartens ultimately linked with the health department, a decision that resulted in Victorian kindergartens assuming a different role from their counterparts in other states.

In South Australia, Lillian de Lissa, who trained under Francis Newton at the Sydney Kindergarten Training College, established the first "real" kindergarten in 1906. Her position regarding the training of kindergarten teachers was similar to that of her Victorian counterparts; she did not want kindergarten training to occur in the government-run training college. She argued that at this institution, students were not encouraged to be independent thinkers, whereas kindergarten students are encouraged "not to obey like dumb-driven cattle, but to think out problems for themselves" (Jones, 1975:141). She went on: "By the transfer [to the control of Education Department] kindergartens would become merely places of instruction like the infant schools, instead of places for the development of character. Kindergartens would be crushed under the department routine and red tape" (Jones, 1975:142) De Lissa became principal of the Adelaide Kindergarten Training College, established in 1907. It can be argued that the kindergarten in South Australia (a state which, although settled by convicts, contained more free settlers than did earlier states) reflected a more educational philosophy for its programs than did, for example, the original kindergartens in New South Wales.

Tasmania, the only non-mainland state of Australia which was established originally as a convict colony, had a history of government-controlled human services—which was unique in Australia. For instance, Ragged Schools were established as early as 1867, and children under five years of age had attended these schools since their inception. Following the economic downturn of the 1890s, government finances became less generous, and the children under five in the community, especially those whose parents had suffered most during the depression, were in great need of support. E. Mainwaring has described the establishment of the first kindergarten in this way: "It was due to the initiative of Mr. and Mrs. Henry Dobson in 1910 that the first Free Kindergarten was established in Hobart (the state capital). Government aid was offered on a pound-for-pound basis and Mr. Dobson undertook to be responsible for two years for the amount required to be subsidised. The site chosen for the kindergarten was the one owned by the Ragged School Committee on Central Street. The Ragged School children were still occupying the building and it was in a small back room, with its tiered seats, that the first kindergarten began (with a Sydney-trained teacher). The pupils were the younger brothers and sisters of the Ragged School children" (Mainwaring, 1977:9). The government-voluntary committee nexus, unique to Tasmania, continues to this day, probably influenced by the fact that Tasmania is the least populated of all the Australian states and many human services initiatives are initiated and continued on a somewhat ad hoc basis.

THE ROLE OF WOMEN IN THE FORMATION
OF KINDERGARTENS IN AUSTRALIA

It would be too easy to argue that the concept of kindergarten per se lent itself to female participation. A more honest observation would be that although Dewey's version of Froebel's ideas about the kindergarten did establish a special role for women, the dominant role of women in the development of the kindergarten movement in Australia at the turn of the twentieth century required further ingredients in order for their achievements to be recognized. At least two additional factors need to be acknowledged. First, during this time Australia was still a pioneer country—not yet a nation, but a slowly unifying group of people who had tamed a virtually undeveloped country and moved toward economic independence in a little over one hundred years. This move from convict settlement to a prosperous country necessitated hard work by all adults, not just the men; the women of Australia were used to working side by side with their menfolk, in participating in decision-making and in sharing the hardships and the rewards. Second, Australia was spawning a number of middle-class, well-educated women who became directly involved in the new movements for social reform. For instance, women graduates of the University of Sydney had founded a University Union for slum dwellers in suburbs adjoining the campus, and they showed an interest in the provision of hospitals for the inner city poor and in kindergartens for deprived and/or "larrikin" children. These were further steps in women's commitment to the provision of human services for the needy (Spearritt, 1979).

H. Jones has suggested that there may have been an element of feminist influence on some of these women. "It is tempting to believe that the feminism of the Chicago Women's Club may have had an effect in Australia. Tonia Bowen, a well known member of that club, may have had an effect on the thinking of (Lillian) de Lissa and others : women with a sense of responsibility for public affairs naturally resent having the door shut in their faces when the work they have initiated and long maintained is taken into the halls of state" (Jones, 1975:214).

Bowen's ideas may have well encapsulated a major reason for the schism which developed in most states between state government bodies and the free kindergarten groups. Philanthropically minded women (and men) of independent financial means initiated and implemented the kindergartens of the poor and needy; the state government, run by men, offered free education for middle- and lower-class children.

A third factor contributing to the successful role of women in Australian kindergartens can be attributed to the spread of secondary education for girls throughout Australia. Following completion of the teacher training course, some middle-class parents encouraged their daughters to take up kindergarten training as both employment and as a preparation for life. The prospectus for the Sydney Kindergarten Training College of 1911–12 confirms this: "For a woman to have reached the age of thirty and have no definite objective in life is conducive to all sorts of bodily and mental ills . . . as a noted educator (unnamed) has said: the kindergarten training is invaluable to all women, regardless of whether or not they continue the profession"(Spearritt, 1979:6).

These women who were suspicious of government control, who believed in the necessity for kindergarten teachers to be trained, and who dominated the kindergarten movement for at least sixty years must not be dismissed. One of the more interesting facts about the kindergarten women is the lack of a "cultural time lag" between the development of Dewey's social meaning with respect to Froebel's philosophy in the Chicago Laboratory School and the time at which such ideas were introduced in Australia. This was due, no doubt, to the importation of American-trained kindergarten educators to Australia, combined with the initiatives taken by their Australian counterparts to travel overseas—all encouraged and supported by the voluntary management groups.

A final thought relating to the role of women in the Australian kindergarten movement: from its inception, the Free Kindergarten movement argued that women's "natural calling"—the care of childhood, as Froebel called it—had to be accompanied by rigorous and extensive training. This emphasis on training, which was never sacrificed to expediency in the kindergarten field, may be our foremothers' major contribution to kindergarten, which has endured until the present day.

CONCLUSION

The kindergarten movement in Australia—although a late starter compared with its counterparts in other European and English-speaking countries—

spawned in the 1990s a nationwide program for children in the year before school. Despite the fact that the importance of the church and voluntary groups has been superseded largely by state government funding and control, the successful beginnings cannot be discounted. Australia is witness to a fortuitous combination of philanthropic endeavor and American expertise which recognized and transposed Froebel's ideas to our shores. It is an example of one of the earlier breakaways from English domination, and we must acknowledge that the kindergarten movement may not have succeeded had we studiously emulated the "Mother Country."

REFERENCES

Clyde, M. (1990) "Historical Content of Early Childhood in Australia." Unpublished paper.

Cumpston, J. and Heinig, C. (1945) *Pre-school Centres in Australia.* Canberra: Commonwealth Department of Health, Canberra.

Elliott, A. S. (1990) "Mrs Amelia Crowley: The First Kindergartener." *Unicorn* Vol. 16(2), pp. 129–132.

Fry, Joan. (1975) "Background to the Development of Pre-School Education in Australia and Some Factors Influencing Its Direction." Paper presented to participants in the E.C. Program. Macquarie University.

Gardiner, L. (1982) *The Free Kindergarten Union of Victoria 1908–1980.* Melbourne: Australian Council for Educational Research (ACER).

Harrison, R. (1985) *Sydney Kindergarten Teachers' College 1897–1981.* Sydney: Sydney Kindergarten Teachers' College.

Jones, H. (1975) "The Acceptable Crusader: Lillian de Lissa and Preschool Education in South Australia," in E. Mellor and S. Murray-Smith (Eds.), *Melbourne Studies in Education.* Melbourne: Melbourne University Press.

Knibbs, G. H., and Turner, J. W. (1903) Interview, *Report of the Commissioners on Certain Parts of Primary Education.* Sydney: NSW GP.

McNulty, B. (1982) "The Rise and Fall of the Children's Services Program 1972–1982." *Australian Journal of Early Childhood,* Vol. 7(2), pp. 4–12.

Mainwaring, E. (1977) "A Kindergarten Is Born: Barclay Kindergarten 1910–1977." Internal publication of Barclay Kindergarten.

Mellor, E. J. (1990) *Stepping Stones: The Development of Early Childhood Service in Australia.* Sydney: Harcourt Brace, Jovanovich.

Pearse, M. (1963) "The Child at the Preschool Level." *Australian Preschool Quarterly,* Vol. 4(1), pp. 8–10, 25.

Scott, P. (1960) "The Influence of Nursery School Experience in the Development of Cultural Values in Preschool Children." Unpublished Ph.D. Thesis, University of Sydney.

Spearritt, P. (1979) "Child Care and Kindergartens in Australia 1890–1975," in P. Langford and P. Sebastian (Eds.), *Early Childhood Education and Care in Australia.* Melbourne: A.C. Press.

Walker, M. L. (1964) "The Development of Kindergartens in Australia." Unpublished M.Ed. Thesis, University of Sydney.

Chapter 5 The Missionary Kindergarten in Japan

Roberta Wollons

The spread and adoption of German educator Friedrich Froebel's kindergarten ideas in Japan occurred early in the history of the international kindergarten movement. The kindergarten was introduced as one among the vast array of Western educational ideas that flowed into Japan from Europe and the United States between 1868 and 1880. The years after 1880, however, were marked by increased governmental efforts to centralize authority, a strong shift in attitude away from Western learning, and government efforts to strengthen its control of education in Japan's movement toward modernization. During the Meiji era (1868–1912), a period of profound transformations in Japan, the conditions that paved the way for kindergartens to become a permanent part of the educational landscape also transformed the kindergarten from a Western to a Japanese institution. Because the kindergarten in Japan began as a deliberately "borrowed" educational institution, the history of the kindergarten is a model case study of the process by which a foreign educational institution became distinctively Japanese.[1]

In the 1870s and 1880s, Japanese kindergartens developed along several distinct lines. Unlike the United States, where the first kindergartens were private, the first Japanese kindergarten was introduced through the government's Ministry of Education shortly after the modern national education system was proclaimed in 1872.[2] A second strand came later, through the private efforts of women educators, primarily Christian missionaries. Still others were founded as private kindergartens, under the auspices of Buddhist and Shinto sects, and as private venture schools. Japan may be the only case where the kinder-gartens were initiated by the government, and competition came later from pri-vate and foreign educators.

The content of all non-Christian kindergartens, whether public or private, came to represent the values of the state, whereas those originating in Christian missionary schools adhered to the original intention of Friedrich Froebel, Chris-tian identity, independence, and an international perspective. Though both the Japanese and Christian kindergartens had many similar features, the character-istics of the Christian kindergartens corresponded more closely to the kinder-garten ideas being generated in the United States and Europe, and were anti-thetical to the consolidation of a Japanese national ideology.

This chapter intends to show how the Japanese government embraced the kindergarten idea, modifying it to suit a newly forming ideology of Japanese modernization while effectively distancing the Japanese from the Christian kin-dergartens. The process of cultural and pedagogical transformation of kinder-gartens in Japan revolves around three major themes: the tension between Chris-tianity and the rise in support for a Japanese morality that became the basis of Japanese kindergarten and elementary education in the late Meiji period;[3] the consolidation and centralization of education by the government that disad-vantaged all private schools; and the commitment of individual leaders to es-tablish standards for kindergarten education.

The history of missionary work in Japan began several years prior to the start of the Meiji Restoration in 1868. In 1854, following the arrival of Commodore Matthew C. Perry, it became known that Japan had negotiated peace treaties with several Western powers, and the Board of Foreign Missions in the United States requested one of its representatives in China to go to Japan. The right of permanent residence for foreigners, however, was not established until 1859. During that year, four ports were declared open to foreign commerce and for-eign residents—Nagasaki, Yokohama, Kobe, and Hakodate—allowing mis-sionaries of three Protestant churches to begin developing roots in Japan. Un-der the principle of "extra-territoriality," foreign residents came under the laws of their respective countries, and were officially isolated in designated locations.[4]

During the period between these first arrivals and 1872, missionaries faced hostility both from the factions opposed to foreign intrusions, particularly among the samurai class, and from the government, which prohibited Christianity among its citizens.[5] This period, however, was also marked by government efforts first to separate Buddhism from Shinto, and then to elevate Shinto to a position of centrality in the new national ideology. The efforts to demote Buddhism had already begun during the late Tokugawa period, prior to the Meiji Restoration, but were strongest in the late 1860s. Within weeks of the formation of the new government in 1868, regulations streamed from the Office of Rites effectively separating Shinto and Buddhist practices, clergy, and property, and excluding Buddhist leaders from policy formation. Symbolically, plans for a new university initiated in the summer of 1870 were crippled by ideological differences among Shinto, Confucian, and Western scholars, but with Buddhist scholars noticeably absent from the debate. Martin Collcutt suggests that some Buddhist leaders, defending their very existence, urged "that Buddhism alone or in concert with Shinto would serve as a bulwark against unwanted Christian intrusion."[6] The government attack on Buddhism was coupled with its strictures against Christianity in a dual effort to gain centralized authority within Japan and to stave off potential threats of further disunity. Missionaries caught in these internal developments found willing students of English and Western culture in greater abundance than students of religion.[7]

According to Herbert Passin, "The opening mood of the new era was strongly utilitarian and Westernizing." In a statement that was to have lasting repercussions, the new Emperor's Charter Oath of 1868 declared that "knowledge was to be sought throughout the world." A school commission was formed that year to supervise the development of a school system, the Japanese Ministry of Education was created in 1871, and schooling for all Japanese children was first proclaimed in the Fundamental Code of Education in 1872. Considered a liberal victory, the Fundamental Code declared, "It is only by building up his character, developing his mind, and cultivating his talents that man may make his way in the world, employ his talents wisely, make his business prosper, and thus attain the goal of life." The code emphasized the individualistic nature and the personal benefits of learning, conspicuously omitting any reference to personal ethics or national goals.[8]

One of the central framers of the new Japanese education system was Tanaka Fujimaro, who became the vice minister of education in 1873. Tanaka visited the United States and Europe in 1871 with the Iwakura Mission, a group that included forty-eight of the new leaders of the Meiji Restoration and fifty-nine students. The Iwakura Mission traveled throughout the United States and Europe for a year and a half, from 1871 to 1873, studying European and American educational, social, political, and economic systems. Upon his return, Tanaka invited David Murray of Rutgers University to Japan as his advisor. Murray remained in Japan until 1878, when Tanaka began to lose support to those with more conservative views in the government. During his period of leadership, from 1871 to 1878, school buildings, textbooks, and teaching styles were largely adapted from the West. However, despite the government mandate for universal education, schools were not built fast enough to accommodate all children, and private schools already in existence, including Christian schools, filled in the gaps at the elementary and secondary levels. Moreover, enforcement of government curricula was weak, and great variation of textbooks and subject matter was tolerated in both public and private schools until the latter part of the 1880s.[9]

Tanaka represented a faction of the new Meiji leadership favoring Western learning.[10] During his travels in the United States, Tanaka had visited with William T. Harris and Susan Blow in St. Louis, and was impressed with the new public kindergarten he observed there. In fact, the public school he visited was the first of its kind in the United States and was considered experimental.

It was not until a model kindergarten was exhibited in the women's pavilion at the Philadelphia Centennial Exposition of 1876, however, that the kindergarten gained its place in American popular culture. As kindergarten historian Michael Shapiro first observed and Barbara Beatty has further demonstrated, the ideas had to be transformed first and adapted to American terrain. For the kindergarten promoters the exposition was an unprecedented opportunity for publicity.[11] The publicity, moreover, extended not only to Americans, but to Japanese educators as well. Tanaka and Murray, who were in the States observing and buying books and furniture for their newly developing schools, visited the exposition, where Japan had mounted an impressive exhibit.[12]

Popular recognition of the kindergarten in America occurred simultaneously with the introduction of kindergartens in Japan. The first private Japanese kindergarten was established in 1875, attached to an elementary school in Kyoto, and the first national kindergarten was established in 1876, attached to the Tokyo Women's Normal School.[13] In the beginning, the few government kindergartens primarily served the nobility.[14] Newly established government and private kindergartens initially adopted the principles of Froebel in their entirety. It is therefore not surprising that the first head teacher at Tokyo Women's Normal School was Clara Matsuno (1853–1941), a German woman who had trained in one of Froebel's kindergarten training schools. A few early private Japanese kindergartens were also formed as entrepreneurial ventures by individuals who either traveled or read literature on early childhood education in Europe. One such founder was a naval officer, Makoto Kondo (1831–86), who visited the world exhibition in Vienna in 1873 and was impressed by the exhibition of kindergartens in foreign countries and by a book on German kindergartens. He published *Kosodate no Maki* ("On Raising Children") in 1875, to introduce Froebelian kindergartens to the general public. Shinzo Seki (1843–79), the first superintendent of the kindergarten attached to Tokyo Women's Normal School, translated a three-volume book on the kindergarten in 1872, and later added *Kindergarten Guide* by American kindergarten educator Elizabeth Peabody as a fourth volume in his translation.[15] Support for the German kindergarten idea, with its emphasis on individual development, was consistent with the principles announced in the preamble to the Fundamental Code of Education of 1872. Thus, the concept of the kindergarten was well established for more than a decade before the arrival of a missionary kindergarten and training school in 1887. It was Christianity rather than the kindergarten that had to await sanction.

The situation for missionaries changed dramatically in 1872. Western powers with whom Japan was attempting to form treaties insisted upon safety and freedom of religious practice for the missionaries. Among the Japanese leadership, extensive contact with the West had by then not only softened fears about Christianity, but in the minds of some, elevated Christianity to the religion of progressive nations. Moreover, in the towns and villages, according to George B. Sansom, "the mass of the people were indifferent, not hostile to Christianity."[16] In addition to the easing of restrictions against Christianity, extraordinary reform measures were taken by the government, including the principle of compulsory schooling.[17] In that year, the number of Protestant missionaries arriving in Japan doubled, bringing the total number to fifty-five. Missionary activity continued to increase thereafter, both in numbers and in groups represented, including Catholics, Baptists, Episcopalians, Methodists, the American Home Mission, and Presbyterians. The missions began their work in Japan by establishing elementary schools, secondary girls' schools, and the pinnacle of Christian education—the Doshisha University in Kyoto, founded by Neeshima Jo, in 1875.[18]

By the end of the 1870s, attitudes toward Western learning began to change. According to Thomas Rohlen, "reaction to the extremes of foreign influence surfaced in the 1880s and 1890s." As the sentiment that Japan needed a unifying ideology grew, the curriculum came to reflect a large chasm between Japanese and Christian purposes. In a government statement of 1881 on early childhood education, the kindergarten was defined solely as a place to supplement home education and to prepare for entrance into elementary school.[19] This marked not only a curricular but also an ideological departure from the Froebelian model. Presaging later laws, the emphasis was on moral education.

Moral education in Japan differs from the Western version, which is premised on the individual's relationship to God and the private relations between individuals, and it is largely entrusted to private institutions. Broadly drawn, Japanese moral education as it developed in the late Meiji era had two ideological bases. The first was Confucianism, and the second a movement called *kokugaku,* or national learning. Unlike the Western emphasis on individual rights in relation to the state, Confucianism, borrowed from China, c. 400 A.D., was (and remains) a universalistic social ethic defining the duties of children to parents, wives to husbands, and families to the state. With the ultimate goal of a well-ordered society, each individual is obliged to undertake responsibilities incumbent upon her or his status.

The second source of moral education, national learning, promoted the uniqueness of Japanese identity. It developed as a reaction to Confucian studies in the late Tokugawa period, and emphasized Japanese history, language, and religion (Shinto). In the 1880s, the combination of these principles was expressed as filial piety, loyalty, and patriotism, placing the emperor as the head of state to whom all Japanese people were "mystically" and morally bound. Moral education, as it appeared in the education laws and rescripts of the period, was forged from a complexity of vying factions intent on forming a stable modern state, with a unified people. Regardless of who was arguing it, as Carol Gluck persuasively shows, moral education was intended to serve the state.[20]

The most influential, and controversial, figure affecting the change in kindergarten education was Mori Arinori (1847–89), minister of education under the first prime minister, Ito Hirobumi (1841–1909). Mori was among the Meiji leadership who had studied in the United States during the period when Western ideas were liberally imported to Japan. He lived in the United States from 1870 to 1873 as the first minister in residence, and was for some time influenced by Swedenborgian Thomas Harris. By the time of Mori's appointment in 1884, however, prevailing national attitudes, including his own, had shifted to a skepticism of Western culture. With his ideas only vaguely understood by people outside the government, various critics came to identify Mori with both the liberal West and conservative nationalism. On the one hand, Mori was accused not only of being too wedded to Western ideas but of being Christian as well; and on the other hand, he was criticized for ushering in nationalism and militarism in the schools. He was assassinated on 11 February 1889 by a young samurai loyal to the emperor, on the day that the first constitution was promulgated. While Mori had felt that Japan must participate in the intellectual life of the West, he also opposed adopting American republicanism in Japan, fearing "the evils resulting from the misuse of freedom."[21] He proposed a two-tier educational system, consisting of discipline and moral education in the elementary schools and academic freedom at the university level. Prime Minister Ito supported Mori's merger of Western learning with a secularized Japanese patriotism. From the time of his appointment in 1884 to his death, Mori set up the modern education system, including the ideas of physical training, morality, discipline, and nationalism as the basis of elementary school education.[22]

A series of education laws issued during the 1880s marked the shift from the importation of Western learning to the development of a national education ideology. The laws not only chronicle the formation of national education policy but link the centrality of teaching the Japanese ethical system in the schools to the fate of Christian education in Japan. In this process, missionary educators were both welcomed for their expertise and marginalized for their foreignness. National education was codified in the Educational Ordinance of 1879, and was revised in 1880. The 1879 version had placed ethics instruction at the end of the list of standard elementary school subjects (reading, writing, arithmetic, geography, and history). The new version, engineered by influential Confucianists, moved ethics to the top of the list. In 1881, the "Guidelines for Elementary School Teachers" evidenced the "same emphasis on promoting imperial loyalty and indigenous morality."[23] Moreover, licensing guidelines for teachers insisted on the appointment of "Confucian scholars" to teach ethics. Under the influence of Mori Arinori, another revision of the Education Ordinance occurred in 1885 and was replaced in 1886. In the 1885 version, Mori formulated his unique ideology that combined patriotism and self-discipline divorced from both the Confucian model of filial piety, and national learning with its implications of returning to a national past.

By 1889, much of the modern system of education was in place. Richard Rubinger argues that although the centralization of education raised standards, minimized class inequities, and broadened access to schooling, it also weakened the private sector. "The centralized bureaucracy of the 1880s inevitably brought with it diminishing possibilities for individual and local influence in the control and practice of education. . . . The private schools were no longer outside the system, but were appendages of it."[24]

Following Mori's death and the adoption of the new constitution in 1889, the Educational Rescript of 1890 was issued, ushering in a period of institutionalized nationalism and governmental-imposed anti-Christianity in the elementary school curriculum. Despite a new constitutional guarantee of freedom of religion, Christianity, which had enjoyed a brief period of "favor among the elites in the seventies and eighties, both as a personal faith and as the religion of 'civilization,' was again under attack," most directly with regard to education.[25] Mori's death allowed room for the more conservative Motoda Eifu (1818–91), the Confucian tutor to the emperor, and Nishimura Shigeki (1828–1902), also an imperial tutor, to influence the direction of education. Motoda had differed with Mori, lamenting the "excesses" of Western education. He favored a return to the national past, Confucian morality, and the centrality of the emperor in the new political system—all points he had been arguing since the appearance of the liberal Education Act of 1872. The final draft of the Rescript listed the purposes of education as loyalty, filial piety, learning, observance of the laws, and service to the state, in that order. Gluck suggests that the Rescript provided a "national text" to defend "native creeds and denounce foreign ways." In a controversy that came to be known as the "Conflict between Religion and Education," aimed at Japanese Christians, it was claimed that because Christianity lacked a nationalistic spirit, "Christianity is fundamentally at odds with the spirit of the Rescript."[26] In the schoolhouses, removed from lofty ideological debates, imperial portraits were hung in every school, and the Rescript was read aloud to the students at all ceremonial occasions.

It was at the peak of these ideological conflicts over the proper Japanese education that Glory (Shoei) Kindergarten was founded in 1889 as a missionary kindergarten, along with a kindergarten teacher-training school. The only other Christian kindergarten had been established in 1886, a full ten years after the first Japanese kindergarten. As there was only one Japanese government teacher-training school in Tokyo, for a short time Glory offered the only alternative for kindergarten teacher training.

The organization to which Glory Kindergarten and the training school were attached was the American Board of Commissioners for Foreign Missions (ABCFM), established in Kobe in 1869. Annie Lyon Howe (1852–1943) came to Japan in 1887 as a Congregational missionary and spent her life introducing Froebel's principles to children and training kindergarten teachers. Sought after for its strong educational pedagogy, Howe's kindergarten attracted both Christian and non-Christian Japanese parents, and the training school became a model used by private Japanese and Christian kindergartens throughout

Japan. Her translations of Froebel's works and her treatises on kindergarten education were widely adopted by the public schools as well and used as training materials in Japanese teacher-training schools. Throughout her forty years in Japan, Howe maintained ties with the kindergarten leaders in Japan and the United States, and with the American progressive educational movement.[27] At the same time, she inevitably became deeply involved with the educational politics and curriculum of the Japanese government kindergartens, as well as with the interdenominational politics that affected the Christian kindergartens.[28]

Howe was thirty-five years old and already an experienced teacher when she arrived in Japan. A graduate of Rockford Female Seminary in Rockford, Illinois, Howe was imbued with the religious and academic standards set by Rockford's forceful president, Anna Peck Sill. She then received training in the new field of kindergarten work at the Chicago Froebel Association in the 1870s, where the American strain of kindergarten education was just taking hold. She began her career teaching in a kindergarten on the north side of Chicago, one of the first to be established in that city.[29]

Howe had joined the Bethany Union Church in Chicago in 1872, where she met Carrie Electa Atkinson, a missionary living in Japan. When Atkinson asked her to start a kindergarten in Japan, she decided to go. She arrived in Kobe in 1887 to find that the women of the Congregationalist Kobe Church had begun plans for the kindergarten. The women included both Japanese and American Christians. There were twenty kindergartens in Kobe by that time, including two Japanese kindergartens associated with government elementary schools and the rest private Japanese schools.[30]

By the time of Howe's arrival, although much of the public hostility toward Christianity had waned, government restrictions against the travel and residency of foreigners again increased. Howe reported on "the government restrictions which of course do not allow much freedom so far as Christianity is concerned." The records of the missionaries are enthusiastic and optimistic, but the numbers of converted Christians remained small.[31] The consolidation of a national ideology undoubtedly militated against popular interest in Christianity. The school nevertheless attracted Japanese mothers, whether Christian or not, for its educational value.

Howe began her work in Japan slowly by studying Japanese, in which she became fluent, and by teaching English at the YMCA.[32] She investigated the government kindergarten methods and materials as best she could, though she did not feel entirely welcome. Shortly after her arrival, she wrote, "The Kindergartens here in Kobe are under the government, and any uninvited instruction on my part would be resented." Nevertheless, she and the Congregationalist women of Kobe continued with their plans for the new school. Howe visited the local kindergartens, comparing their adherence to Froebel's original ideas with her own ideas about the structure and games recommended in Froebel's *Mother Play*. She also had Japanese kindergarten books translated into English in order to know what was being taught in Japanese schools and what the teachers had read. She saw that the Japanese kindergartens had taken the idea of the kindergarten and adapted it to a blend of Japanese educational values for moral and physical training, to the idea that kindergarten was to supplement the work of mothers and prepare for elementary school, and only lastly (and inconsistently), to Froebel's systematic lessons and games.[33] By the late 1880s Japanese moral education was already the emphasis in the kindergarten curriculum.

In 1889, the Kobe church opened a kindergarten and a kindergarten training school, headed by Howe. This was the first—and would become the most prominent—training school within the Christian community.[34] The first kindergarten class enrolled fifty children, who appeared on the first day with grandmothers and nurses to show the children what to do. Howe wrote, "For a short time, a vigorous system of eviction was in progress, and then the doors were mercilessly closed on the inferno out in the hall, where mad grandmothers and wounded hearts mourned together." In two or three days, Howe was able to teach the children on her own. Clearly the Japanese mothers' enthusiasm for kindergarten education overcame their suspicion of Howe's foreign ways. The first kindergarten teacher-training class was limited to twenty Japanese students. Drawing on her training at the Froebel Institute in Chicago, Howe was strict in her interpretation of Froebel, following the text, games, and Western moral lessons in his manual. Moreover, she believed that his teachings were consistent with her own principles of divine rather than state loyalties, and included Bible stories and Christmas celebrations. Later, Howe would compromise by including Japanese national holiday celebrations, hanging a picture of the emperor, and conforming to the Japanese practice of Saturday classes.[35]

In its first year, the training school was already under public scrutiny, as this was the year of Mori's assassination, and the issuance of the new constitution. Moreover, while the forthcoming Imperial Rescript on Education was being drafted for release in 1890, there was extensive public debate and much anticipation in the Christian community over how restrictive the Rescript would be.[36] As described above, the Imperial Rescript clearly set the tone for circumscribing Christian education.

Dissatisfied with the content of the Japanese kindergarten material, Howe began a translation of Froebel's *Mother Play* into Japanese. It was one of her most significant contributions to kindergarten education in Japan, in both Christian and non-Christian sectors. In addition to translating the lessons, she had an artist create woodblock prints of the pictures, redrawn in a Japanese context. Howe reported that she found the Japanese educators were interested in the translation but still distrustful of her, both as a foreigner and as a Christian. "The Japanese look to me for the real guidance, yet so jealous lest a foreigner should have too much authority." Little by little, however, as graduates of the kindergarten moved successfully into the public schools, the reputation of the school as a model of Froebelian instruction spread. Teachers from Osaka, Kyoto, and Tokyo came to visit her school, and in 1891, the public schools in Kyoto invited Howe to instruct their kindergarten teachers. In 1892 the first of her own students from the training school began a kindergarten in Hokkaido. By 1893, Howe had gained a reputation substantial enough that the Kobe government invited Glory Kindergarten to join the Japan exhibition at the Columbia Exposition in Chicago.

American education had been represented in the Philadelphia World Fair of 1876, where Japan had concentrated on its arts rather than its modern institutions. In 1893, however, Japan presented much of its modernized civilization, including its education system, along with traditional aspects of the culture. Neil Harris suggests that it was at this point that Japan chose to introduce itself as a modern cultural equal to the West, to counter the exotic image that resulted from the 1876 event.[37]

In 1893, the same year Howe's kindergarten was represented at the Japan exhibit in Chicago, the anti-Western Education Council in Tokyo proposed that the Japanese take control of all foreign schools. In Kyoto, the government refused permission to open a new Christian kindergarten. Despite such persistent ambivalence toward Christian education within the government and by individuals, Howe and her book were very well received. She was invited to a national Teachers' Association meeting in Kyoto with Japanese teachers, and hosted Japanese visitors to her school regularly. Her chronicle of these years in Japan is replete with reports of talks, lectures, visits to Japanese kindergartens and kindergarten teachers, and visits of Japanese observers to her school. In her first six years of service, the training school graduated twenty-three teachers, five of whom started kindergartens of their own.[38]

Howe returned to the United States on sabbatical in 1895 to study the history of education at the University of Chicago for six months and immerse herself in kindergarten activities in her native country. Significant change occurred in

Japan during her absence, however, and when she went back in 1897, she found that many missionaries had returned home, forced to close their schools by new laws limiting religious instruction. One of Howe's own teachers confronted her with a rejection of Christianity, declaring that "while the Training School is a mission affair, the kindergarten is Japanese." The implication was that the kindergarten should be more aligned with Japanese ideas, and that it should no longer be entirely in Howe's control. Marius Jansen argues that by this time, Japanese teachers had begun to take control of Western teaching methods, modifying the content of curricula to conform to Japanese norms. Stated succinctly by Jansen, "by the 1890s those 'foreign' teachers had for the most part been replaced by their students." Not only had the students learned from the teachers, but more to the point, Japanese teachers were modifying Western curricula perhaps to support the consolidation of a Japanese national curriculum. Government regulations would be directed to kindergartens explicitly in the 1899 Imperial Ordinance on Elementary Education and Infant Training.[39]

Howe found herself in competition for good kindergarten teachers when a Japanese kindergarten training school opened in Kobe, and potential Japanese kindergarten teachers had to choose between the schools. The problems peaked in 1898–99. Discussing local kindergarten teachers' "clubs," Howe remarked, "These clubs in Kyoto and Osaka will not touch Christianity with gloves." The Educational Rescript of 1899, she had learned, would decide who controlled the school—the mission or the government. Before that time, private kindergartens were not directly affected by the government's curricular regulations for elementary education, though they were subjected to the same skepticism of things Western articulated in the 1890 Education Rescript. The seriousness of the situation was apparent in Howe's letters. She believed that the school had to be in her control or she would have to leave. Assuming the worst, she confided her intention to resign, deciding that ten years after her arrival was a good breaking point. If she stayed, she wrote, "As the kindergarten was run with permission from the government, and Christianity was not formally allowed, there might be some time when there could be trouble."[40]

In 1899, the government ended the extra-territoriality rule, allowing free travel and residence of foreigners. Although the government gave more freedom to foreigners in some respects, it also made them subject to Japanese law, adding considerably to the degree of control the government could exercise over specific activities of foreigners.[41]

The Educational Rescript of 1899 provided the philosophical grounds to contain the spread of Christian kindergarten education in Japan. Under the cabinet of 1899, the government prohibited religious instruction in the schools, whether government or private, officially deeming Christianity incompatible with national loyalty. It expanded the instructions for the content of kindergarten education, reinforcing the earlier ideas that the kindergarten was to enable children to become "sound in mind and body, cultural morals, and to help home education."[42] The prohibition of religious instruction in the schools, it should be noted, also disadvantaged Buddhist schools. The prohibition may have been intended less as an anti-religious effort and more as a means to control and centralize the curriculum. The outcome nevertheless decimated Christian education in Japan.

In response, the Tokyo missions had to close their primary schools, creating a problem for the Japanese public schools, which could not accommodate the new students. Doshisha University, long considered the bastion of Christian higher education, succumbed to government regulations by closing its secondary schools and removing Christian subjects from its curriculum. (Although the study of Christianity was not banned in private colleges, all benefits, such as deferment from military service for education, were rescinded.) It was not clear, however, how this rule would affect Glory Kindergarten. The training school was exempt because the regulations applied only to children under the age of fourteen, the last year of compulsory education.

In the end, Howe had to apply for permission to be principal of the training school.[43] Under the Government Rules for the Establishment and Maintenance of Primary Schools and Kindergartens, issued in 1899, a foreigner could be principal of a school if she or he could show sufficient evidence of Japanese language proficiency. After an oral examination in Japanese, Howe was approved to be head of the training school, to be principal, and to be an officially authorized teacher in Japan. Having come to respect Japanese society and to accept the conditions of foreigners in Japan, Howe considered it a triumph, both personally and for progressive education in Japan. After more than a decade of receiving praise for her work in Japan, it is telling that she expressed no private or public resentment toward the new regulations requiring a demonstration of her ability. As it turned out, the banning of religious instruction was to apply explicitly to children over the age of six, which exempted the kindergarten and permitted its continuation.[44]

As a consequence of the ideology symbolized by the 1899 Rescript, an inevitable split arose between the Japanese kindergarten teachers and the Christian teachers. Some Japanese supporters of the Rescript openly rejected the Christian kindergartens, expressing their displeasure that the Christian kindergartens were allowed to continue. Deepening the division was the fact that by this time over thirty separate Protestant denominations were represented in Japan. Many Japanese saw the range of regional and national churches as antithetical to a single national loyalty, and—with the exception of the Catholic church, which was perceived as universalistic—mistrusted the interdenominational divisiveness acted out in Japan as elsewhere. Sansom argues that this situation curtailed the spread of Christianity and created distrust. Howe herself complained about the "lamentable state of things when missionaries could not commune together, nor recognize each other as Christians." Despite her personal efforts, the issues dividing foreign and Japanese kindergarten educators were beyond Howe's control. Faced with governmental enmity and Christian disunity, Howe took the situation as a challenge, declaring, "I am going to establish something out here which will *compel* the recognition and sanction of the most progressive and thoughtful educators both Japanese and foreign."[45] She decided that the best she could do was to unite the various Christian denominations providing kindergartens.

In 1906, Howe organized and presided over the first annual meeting of the Christian Kindergarten Union of Japan. At that time, kindergartens represented a significant proportion of all Christian educational work. Twenty Christian kindergartens, twelve denominations, and various nationalities were represented. The new union included neither private nor public Japanese kindergartens. Moreover, the bylaws stipulated that the annual meetings would be conducted in English, guaranteeing a missionary-only membership.[46] It is not clear from the record whether this action was intended to exclude Japanese kindergarten educators, or whether the Japanese educators themselves were unwilling to associate with the Christian organization. Regardless, the division became institutionalized with the formation of the Kindergarten Union of Japan. Howe was the first president, aligning herself completely with the foreign, Christian kindergartens.[47]

In her presidential address, Howe emphasized the need for unity among the twelve denominations represented and expressed her hope for future integration with the Japanese kindergarten associations as well. Her opening call for forging acquaintance among the members of the new union was an undisguised commentary on the disunity among the Christian denominational schools, compared with what she perceived as the unified Japanese kindergartens. Moreover, Howe directly addressed the chasm that existed between the Christian kindergarten teachers and the Japanese. "They have their associations, their publications, it is folly for us to remain ignorant of it all, when mutual acquaintance might result in mutual respect and mutual assistance." Implying that the Christian kindergarten teachers had limited understanding of Japan, she implored the members of the new Kindergarten Union to know more about the Japanese education system to which the young kindergarten students would be graduating. She further urged the members to take an increasingly international view of kindergarten work, to participate in the International Kindergarten Union, and thereby in the discourse being conducted by kindergarten educators around the world.[48] Howe related her own experience studying at the University of Chicago as essential for the continuing education of teachers.

Howe clearly viewed her goal as the improvement of kindergarten education in Japan, a commitment to raising standards of training for the teachers, and a faithful adherence to Froebel's plan of systematic work. She neither criticized Japanese kindergartens nor remarked on the limitations placed on Christian kindergartens in Japan. Rather, she leveled her criticism directly at the isolationism of the Christian denominational kindergartens themselves.

The curricular changes in Japanese kindergartens that departed from the original Froebelian ideas were complex. Simply redrawing Froebel's pictures of the gifts and games was not sufficient to adapt the Western kindergarten to the Japanese educational system. By the time kindergartens did become a fixture of Japanese children's education, the curriculum had been transformed by Japanese teachers to conform to the most basic elements of Japanese social and political identity, including discipline, respect for parents, and preparation for first grade, in equal measure with ideas about the natural development of the child. In 1906, there were 423 public and private Japanese kindergartens in Japan, attesting to the importance the Japanese placed on preschool education. That the curriculum did not completely coincide with either the original Froebelian model or the Christian model implies that kindergarten teachers in Japan, as in all other countries in which the kindergarten was successfully adopted, modified the content to conform to national educational, political, and cultural norms.[49]

The kindergarten was of minor importance in the early stages of consolidating a national education system, and the Ministry of Education paid scant attention to the kindergarten curriculum until 1899. The relatively late interest by the government puts into perspective the degree to which the prevailing governmental ideology toward the fundamental principles of education *alone* influenced the majority of kindergartens, without direct regulation. Thus, transformed by consensus, the kindergarten idea was embraced by Japanese educators and parents for its educational value, divorced in practice from its Western origins.

For the Christian community, however, kindergartens loomed large on the education horizon. With only twenty-seven kindergartens from all denominations, kindergartens nevertheless represented 42 percent of their efforts in the area of education, making the kindergarten the key not only to spreading Christian teaching to the children but also to gaining access to Japanese homes through the children.[50] Restrictions on Christian education hurt missionary efforts at the elementary and secondary levels, and at Doshisha University, leaving the kindergarten as the central Christian educational enterprise.

The "Taisho Democracy," from 1912 to 1925, proved to be a time of experimentation and progressivism in the elementary schools, and in the kindergartens as well. Many private Japanese kindergartens favored a freer atmosphere, eliminating the structured time segments of the Froebelian model and allowing children more freedom in choosing their own activities. The Montessori method of instruction was introduced in Japan in 1911, as were the ideas of John Dewey, and generally new methods of instruction were welcomed. These changes also opened greater dialog between Christian and Japanese kindergarten educators. By 1914, a rapprochement began between the Japanese and missionary kindergarten educators when an entire convention session was devoted to Japanese kindergartens, conducted in Japanese.[51] In 1916, the Kindergarten Union of Japan was admitted as a full member of the International Kindergarten Union, and by 1917, the bylaw regarding the use of English was repealed.[52] In 1926, an imperial ordinance on kindergarten education, the Kindergarten Act, was passed. Recognizing the variety of kindergarten education being practiced, it guaranteed freedom to individual kindergartens to decide their own curricula. The new act reinforced an era of vibrancy in Japanese early childhood education.

In 1926, Annie Howe was coming to the end of her career and was asked to retire by the ABCFM after forty years of service. She was seventy-four years old. Under financial pressure, the mission wanted to merge the kindergarten and training school with Kobe Women's College, which Howe did not approve. Moreover, the Showa era (1926–89) ushered in a new period of drastic restrictive regulations against foreign teachers.[53] Although the liberal atmosphere of the Japanese kindergartens would persist until 1937, missionary teachers and principals were suddenly again without permits to continue, and Howe was neither asked to nor wanted to continue fighting for the autonomy of her school.

Under Howe, Glory graduated more than 1,400 children from the kindergarten, and 270 students from the training school, all Japanese—though not all

Christian. Fifty-eight of those training school students were in charge of Christian kindergartens, and more were either teaching or in charge of Japanese kindergartens.[54] When she left in 1927, her *Mother Play* translation was in its fourth edition and had become an important text for kindergarten training schools throughout Japan, both foreign and governmental. For a school of its relatively small size, Glory proved to be a prodigious model for kindergarten education standards throughout Japan for many years.

As the Japanese schools were increasingly centralized and based on national moral principles, Howe continued to represent the small, independent Christian presence in Japan. During her years in Japan she received praise for her kindergarten work, largely divorced from Japan's official rejection of Christian education. Annie Howe's departure from Japan was bittersweet. She was lavishly honored by Japanese educators, including teachers she had trained and several generations of kindergarten graduates, while she lost control of her school. She was remembered, however, for the high standards she set and the contributions she made to Japanese education, personally transcending the internecine struggles for a national ideology that characterized the modernization of Japanese education during her years of service.[55] In 1941, the emperor of Japan awarded Howe the rare Blue Ribbon medal, the highest award an individual can receive from the government, for her long and distinguished public service in education.[56] She retired to her brother's home in New York, where she died in 1943.

Internationally, the kindergarten movement was promoted largely by an organized female network of correspondence, publications, and zeal, and existed in similar pedagogical forms in many countries. In Japan, however, the kindergarten was largely controlled by the government, male dominated, and national rather than international in outlook. Moreover, the curriculum was molded to Japan's national civil morality, rather than the "scientific," individualistic principles of early childhood development dominating American and European progressive education. Indeed, before it could flourish, the kindergarten had to go through a process of becoming a Japanese institution, which meant subordinating the Froebelian curriculum to the principles of Japanese national identity. During the period of Japanese national consolidation, curricular support for an ideological connection between children, the emperor, and Japanese society distinguished the Japanese kindergarten from its Western counterparts. In real and symbolic terms, the relationship between Glory Kindergarten and the Japanese kindergartens during the Meiji era dramatized that process.

Although missionary kindergartens were tolerated, private Christian schools

were ultimately marginalized by the enormous government education bureaucracy, to the degree that they did not pose a threat. The Japanese government
could afford to honor Annie L. Howe's pedagogical contribution, disconnected
from its roots in Christianity, American-style individualism, and international
discourse.

NOTES

1. For the purposes of this chapter, I make a distinction between Japanese kindergartens, both
   public and private, and Christian kindergartens controlled by the missions. This does not
   mean, however, that the children or teachers of these schools were exclusively Western or
   Japanese. All kindergarten children were Japanese, as were most of the teachers in the training schools.
2. In the United States, the kindergartens began as private enterprises and only slowly were
   adopted by public schools, on a district-by-district basis.
3. A note on periodization: In an effort to conceptualize the changes that occurred between
   1868 and 1912, some historians of Meiji Era Japan use a decade-by-decade approach. Shunsuke Kamei, for example, refers to the period 1868–77 as "civilization and enlightenment,"
   a time of learning and absorbing Western learning; 1878–87 as a time of "liberty and the
   people's rights," marked by demands for a national assembly and greater popular representation; and the third decade, 1888–97, as a "national rights" period in which Japan had
   gained self-confidence from the experiences of the preceding twenty years and was seeking
   not to adopt Western ways but to form a unified identity and gain greater equality with
   Western nations. This last decade, in his view, was a period of disappointment and disillu-
   sionment with the West, and of consolidating social and political features that were distinctively Japanese (Shunsuke Kamei, "The Sacred Land of Liberty: Images of America in
   Nineteenth Century Japan," in *Mutual Images: Essays in American-Japanese Relations,* ed.
   Akira Iriye [Cambridge, Mass., 1975], 55–72). This study, however, uses a simplified notion of early and late Meiji (1868–80, 1880–1912) to frame the changes in attitude from the
   systematic importation of learning from the West to the formation of distinctive Japanese
   education policies.
4. Kenneth Scott Latourette, *A History of the Expansion of Christianity: The Great Century in
   Northern Africa and Asia, A.D. 1800–A.D. 1914* (New York, 1944), 374, 382; Rev. G. G. Verbeck, "History of Protestant Missions in Japan," Osaka Report of 1883, p. 740, Kobe College Archives, Nishinomiya, Japan; Annie L. Howe, "Excerpts from Annie L. Howe Letters, 1887–1927," Kobe College Archives. Howe's niece, Alice Howe, transcribed this
   collection of Howe's letters from the written to typed pages (hereafter, Howe, "Excerpts").
   Howe wrote in a letter home, "foreigners cannot travel in Japan without a government
   pass—that these passes are only for a limited time and only for health or scientific research."
5. Verbeck, *A History of Protestant Missions,* 753. A Japanese government edict stated that citizens who practiced Christianity would be put to death. However, as with a law that prescribed the same punishment for people who lived abroad and returned to Japan, the edict

was not enforced. Report after report from missionaries in the field testifies to the open hostility from the samurai classes, and to the occasional imprisonment or harassment of the missionaries by government officials. See also G. B. Sansom, *The Western World and Japan: A Study in the Interaction of European and Asiatic Cultures* (New York, 1965), 468–88; and Otis Cary, *A History of Christianity in Japan* (New York, 1909), 2 vols.; Latourette, *The Great Century,* 376.

6. Martin Collcutt, "Buddhism: The Threat of Eradication," in *Japan in Transition from Tokugawa to Meiji,* ed. Marius B. Jansen and Gilbert Rozman (Princeton, N.J., 1986), 143–67, quotation on 154; Sansom, *The Western World and Japan,* 468. See Richard Rubinger, "Education: From One Room to One System," in *Japan in Transition,* ed. Jansen and Rozman, 195–230, for a discussion of the ascendancy of Western learning in the first national university. For further history of Japanese universities, see Ikuo Amano, "Continuity and Change in the Structure of Japanese Higher Education," in *Changes in the Japanese University: A Comparative Perspective,* ed. William K. Cummings, Ikuo Amano, and Kazuyuki Kitamura (New York, 1979), 10–39.

7. The notion that in the early Meiji period missionaries were sought after for their knowledge of the West more often than for religious instruction is supported in Latourette, *The Great Century,* 400; and Sansom, *The Western World and Japan,* 474.

8. Herbert Passin, *Society and Education in Japan* (New York, 1965; reprint, Tokyo, 1982), 63, 210 (for Fundamental Code in English), 67–68 (for a discussion of the influence of Western utilitarian and individualistic ideas on the framers of the code).

9. Upon his return to Japan, Tanaka wrote a fifteen-volume book on his observations, *Rijikootei* (Passin, *Society and Education,* 64). The Iwakura Mission's findings would continue to influence the development of the new government throughout the Meiji period. See Marius B. Jansen, ed., *The Cambridge History of Japan,* vol. 5, *The Nineteenth Century* (Cambridge, England, 1989), 26, 462; and Marius B. Jansen, *Japan and Its World: Two Centuries of Change* (Princeton, N.J., 1980), 51–68. One of the members of the mission was a six-year-old girl, Tsuda Umeko, later founder of Tsuda College for Women (Jansen, ed., *Cambridge History,* 5: 462; Barbara Rose, *Tsuda Umeko and Women's Education in Japan* [New Haven, Conn., 1992], 6–7). Murray was not alone acting in an advisory capacity to the developing educational system in Japan. Tanaka Fujimaro and Mori Arinori corresponded extensively with American educators, including Theodore D. Woolsey, ex-president of Yale. Horace Capron, U.S. Commissioner of Education, and William S. Clark of the Massachusetts Agricultural College, took part in developing what would become Hokkaido University (see Passin, *Society and Education,* 71). For an extensive discussion of the role of private schools during this period, see Richard Rubinger, "Education: From One Room to One School," 195–230.

10. Passin, *Society and Education,* 83.

11. Michael Shapiro, *The Child's Garden: The Kindergarten Movement from Froebel to Dewey* (University Park, Pa., 1983), 21, 70–72. Friedrich Froebel, "The Small Child," in *Friedrich Froebel: A Selection of His Writings,* ed. Irene Lilly (Cambridge, England, 1967), 31–39.

12. It was in 1876 that American kindergartners gained popular support for the movement. American leaders included Susan Blow, Sarah Cooper, Caroline T. Haven, Elizabeth

Palmer Peabody, and Henry Barnard. For biographies, see Vandewalker, *The Kinder-garten in American Education;* and *Notable American Women.* Shapiro, *The Child's Garden,* 26. On the importance of the centennial exposition, see Shapiro, ch. 5; and William Torrey Harris, "Reflections on the Educational Significance of the Centennial Exposition," 27. *Twenty-Second Annual Report of the Saint Louis Board of Education 1876,* 174–79. On Japanese participation, see Passin, *Society and Education,* 71; and Neil Harris, "All The World a Melting Pot? Japan at American Fairs, 1876–1904," in *Mutual Images: Essays in American-Japanese Relations,* ed. Akira Iriye (Cambridge, Mass., 1975), 24–54.

13. The Kyoto school was Yanaike Elementary (Early Childhood Education Association of Japan, ed., *Early Childhood Education and Care in Japan* [Tokyo, 1979], 11). The earliest kindergarten still in existence opened in 1876, attached to Tokyo Women's Normal School. The Kindergarten Training School became Ochanomizu University. See also Tsunekichi Mizuno, *The Kindergarten in Japan* (Boston, 1917), 31.

14. These were members of the Imperial Court, many of whom moved from Kyoto to Tokyo in 1871.

15. *Early Childhood Education and Care in Japan,* 21. Clara Matsuno came to Japan to marry Jun Matsuno in 1876 and was appointed to be the head teacher of the new kindergarten attached to the Tokyo Women's Normal School. Jun Matsuno was an official in the Ministry of Agriculture and Forestry. Makoto Kondo later translated Froebel and the *Kindergarten System of Elementary Education,* by J. Payne, into Japanese and published it in 1879. Seki had been a Buddhist priest and engaged actively in anti-Christian campaigns. Nevertheless, his tomb, built of cylindrical and cone-shaped stones, imitated Froebel's tomb. The kindergarten created strange bedfellows. Fuyu Toyota, a former samurai of the Mita clan, was also a proponent of the kindergarten, but he strongly favored foreign intercourse and was assassinated for his views by a radical opponent.

16. Sansom, *The Western World and Japan,* 469, 471; Carol Gluck, *Japan's Modern Myths: Ideology in the Late Meiji Period* (Princeton, N.J., 1985), 132–35.

17. In 1872 Japan also formally abolished the class system, formulated prefectures to replace domains, revised the land tax system, established the ministries of the army and the navy, and introduced national conscription. Western clothing became compulsory attire for government employees, and Japan changed from the lunar to the solar calendar.

18. For a history of the development and politics surrounding Doshisha University, see American Board of Foreign Missions, "Mission News: Doshisha Supplement, No. 2," vol. 11, no. 3, Kyoto, Japan, April 1899, Kobe College Archives.

19. Thomas Rohlen, *Japan's High Schools* (Berkeley, Calif., 1983), 53. See also Ivan Parker Hall, *Mori Arinori* (Cambridge, Mass., 1973); Hall, "The Confucian Teacher in Tokugawa Japan," in *Confucianism in Action,* ed. David S. Nivison and Arthur F. Wright (Stanford, Calif., 1959); and Japanese Ministry of Education, 1881, *An Outline of Early Childhood Education,* reprinted in English in Passin, *Society and Education,* 210.

20. Gluck, *Japan's Modern Myths,* 103. This brief rendering of moral education in Japan draws on the works of Sansom, *The Western World and Japan,* 482; Gluck, *Japan's Modern Myths;* and Estelle James and Gail Benjamin, *Public Policy and Private Education in Japan* (New York, 1988), 14.

21. Mori continues to be a controversial figure. See Passin, *Society and Education,* 86–90; Ronald S. Anderson, *Education in Japan: A Century of Modern Development* (Washington, D.C., 1975); Ivan Parker Hall, *Mori Arinori* (Cambridge, Mass., 1973); Tetsuya Kobayashi, *Society, Schools, and Progress in Japan* (Oxford, Eng., 1978). In 1867, Mori and a few other Japanese students lived on Harris's experimental farms, The Brother of the New Life, in Amenia and Salem-On-Erie, New York. See Hall, *Mori Arinori;* and Kimura Rikio, *Ibunka Hendekki Sha: Mori Arinori* (Tokyo, 1986). For the ideological turmoil created by the assassination and the constitution's promulgation, see Gluck, *Japan's Modern Myths,* 45, 226. Mori Arinori, *Life and Resources in America* (Washington, D.C., 1871), 298–99, quoted in Shunsuke Kamei, "The Sacred Land of Liberty," 61.

22. Passin, *Society and Education,* 86–91; Gluck, *Japan's Modern Myths,* 123. University education in Mori's view was to be the domain in which individuals could pursue their intellectual interests on a free and liberal basis.

23. Gluck, *Japan's Modern Myths,* 108. The Educational Ordinance of 1879 replaced the first Education Act of 1872.

24. See Richard Rubinger, "Education: From One Room to One System," 195–230, quotation on 230.

25. Educational Rescript of 1890, reprinted in English in Passin, *Society and Education.* Quotation from Gluck, *Japan's Modern Myths,* 132.

26. For a biographical sketch of Motoda Eifu, see Donald H. Shively, "Motoda Eifu: Confucian Lecturer to the Meiji Emperor," in *Confucianism in Action,* eds. Nivison and Wright. See also Passin, *Society and Education;* Sansom, *The Western World and Japan,* 368. For a biographical sketch and explanation of Nishimura Shigeki's Confucian ideology, see Donald H. Shively, "Nishimura Shigeki: A Confucian View of Modernization," in *Changing Japanese Attitudes toward Modernization,* ed. Marius B. Jansen (Princeton, N.J., 1965), 193–241. Passin, *Society and Education;* Gluck, *Japan's Modern Myths,* 121, quotations on 127, 128, 133.

27. The ABCFM founded the Doshisha University in 1875. The ABCFM missionaries were also responsible for the founding of Kobe Women's College. Howe corresponded with G. Stanley Hall and Earl Barnes of Stanford. Howe, "Excerpts," 79.

28. Ibid., 21 and passim.

29. Roberta Wollons, "The Impact of Higher Education on Women: The Case of Rockford College, 1870–1920" (paper delivered at the Mid-West Conference on the History of Women, St. Paul, Minn., October 1977). Howe was already conscious of her position as one of the pioneering generation of educated women and was aware of the options available to her generation of unmarried women. In 1893, she wrote, "It is a blessed age for unmarried women. The ability to earn one's own living and to be of use in the world is a great improvement over those days when the spinster must stay at home, dependent and practically a child until her death" (Howe, "Excerpts," 89). Rev. Clyde McGee, Bethany Union Church, Chicago, Ill., 31 Oct. 1943, Kobe College Archives (from a memorial service upon her death on 25 Oct. 1943 at the age of ninety-one).

30. Howe, "Excerpts," 13.

31. Ibid., 21, 60, 10 (quotation); Verbeck, *History of Protestant Missions in Japan,* 877–78. Ver-

beck reported in 1882 the population of Catholics to be 4,094, and the population of Protestant missionaries to be 347.

32. She was, during her time there, able to give speeches, and read and translate in Japanese. Howe, "Excerpts," 5, 22.

33. Howe, "Excerpts," 6. There were twenty kindergartens already in Osaka (ibid., 13). Friedrich Froebel, *Mother Play* (1847; Boston, 1888); *Early Childhood Education and Care in Japan*, 23. Unlike the curriculum of the elementary school, that of the kindergarten was not strictly prescribed; consequently, private kindergartens varied tremendously according to region, individual founder, and teaching experience.

34. Shoei Tandai exists today as a junior college in Kobe.

35. Howe, "Excerpts," 33, 34, 9, 49, 51. Glory Kindergarten had a two-year waiting list. Mothers enrolled their children two years prior to when their children would be old enough to attend the school.

36. See Gluck for an extended discussion of the ideological debates that preceded the issuance of the 1890 Imperial Rescript on Education. *Japan's Modern Myths*, 115–27.

37. Howe, "Excerpts," 90, 40 (quotation), 44, 75. For a detailed examination of the Japan exhibit at the Columbian Exposition in Chicago, see Neil Harris, "All the World a Melting Pot?," 24–54.

38. Howe, "Excerpts," 92, 100. Annie L. Howe, "Kindergartens in Japan," in *A Chapter of Mission History in Modern Japan, 1869–1895*, ed. James H. Petee, Kobe College Archives. Howe also notes in her journal the predominance of men actively engaged in kindergarten instruction in Japan. The missionary schools were generally run by women, and they usually trained women, but the population of government teachers remained predominantly male throughout this period. This gender difference is unique to Japan; in other countries, the kindergarten movement was dominated by women educators and reformers.

39. Howe, "Kindergarten in Japan"; Howe, "Excerpts," 104–6, 109 (first quotation). Doshisha University, founded by Neeshima Jo as a Christian College, gave up its middle school and its Christian curriculum in 1896 to comply with the new government regulations banning Christian education. This was a major setback within the Christian community, and the model against which Christian educators fought. Marius B. Jansen, *Japan and Its World: Two Centuries of Change* (Princeton, N.J., 1980), 65. Act 196 of the Imperial Ordinance began with the rule, "Infant training should supplement home education by cultivating sound mind and good habits." This vague statement implied social, rather than developmental, training. For a critique of kindergartens, see Tsunekichi Mizuno, *The Kindergarten in Japan: Its Effects upon the Physical, Mental, and Moral Traits of Japanese School Children* (Boston, 1917), 33. He argued that kindergartens were good for intellectual, but not moral, training.

40. Howe, "Excerpts," 111, 112.

41. Rev. D. C. Greene, "General Historic Review of Missionary Work in Japan since 1883: First Paper," 78, Kobe College Archives.

42. Gluck, *Japan's Modern Myths*, 57. Howe, "Excerpts," 117–18. See also Latourette, *The Great Century*; Sansom, *The Western World and Japan*, 482, and "Act of the Content and Facilities of Kindergarten Education," in *Early Childhood Education and Care in Japan*, 11.

43. *Mission News of the ABCFM in Japan* 11 (April 1899), Doshisha Supplement. Howe, "Excerpts," 119.

44. Howe, "Excerpts," 117–22.

45. Ibid., 121, 130, 124; Sansom, *The Western World and Japan,* 481.

46. "The Widening Circles of Christian Kindergarten Work in Japan: 1886– 1919," and *By-Laws of the First Annual Meeting of the Japan Kindergarten Union, 1906,* Kobe College Archives.

47. Nevertheless, in an address to the Froebel Association in Chicago in 1904, Howe spoke with admiration for the Japanese education system, the rapid advancements that Japan had made, and the values asserted in the 1872 Fundamental Code of Education. She went on to praise the Japanese kindergartens for their physical construction, patriotic spirit, and lessons in the appreciation of nature. Casting the best light on Japanese kindergartens, to which she clearly felt connected, Howe minimized the curricular differences between the Christian and Japanese schools and showed intense loyalty to the country in which she had built her career. Annie L. Howe, "The Kindergarten in Japan," Kobe College Archives.

48. Kindergarten Union of Japan, President's Address, Karuizawa, 14 Aug. 1907, Kobe College Archives. Japanese kindergarten teachers were organized into two associations, the Froebel Association of Tokyo and the Kindergarten Association of Kyoto, Osaka, Kobe, and adjacent towns. Annie L. Howe, "The Kindergarten in Japan" (paper presented to the Chicago Froebel Association, 1905), 23. Kindergartens were by that time represented in fourteen Western countries and Japan.

49. Mizuno, *The Kindergarten in Japan,* 39–40.

50. "The Widening Circles of Christian Kindergarten Work, 1886–1919," and "Glory Kindergarten and Training School," pamphlet from the *Annual Report of the Federated Missions in Japan, 1917,* p. 1, Kobe College Archives. The pamphlet author reports, "Our Graduates have access to 1,441 children, and 1,441 homes"; Howe, "Excerpts," 40.

51. Howe, "Excerpts," 147.

52. Early Childhood Education, 17, 29; *History of the Japanese Kindergarten Union, 1941,* Kobe College Archives.

53. The ruling applied to both Christian and government kindergartens.

54. Howe, "Excerpts," 163.

55. In the Early Education Association of Japan pamphlet, *Early Childhood Education and Care in Japan,* published in 1979, Howe is the only foreigner mentioned in connection with the history and development of the kindergarten in Japan.

56. From the perspective of the fiftieth anniversary of the bombing of Pearl Harbor, the irony of this date should be noted, though a detailed analysis is beyond the scope of this chapter.

REFERENCES

Iriye, Akira, (ed.). *Mutual Images: Essays in American-Japanese Relations.* Cambridge, Mass., 1975.

Jansen, Marius B., and Gilbert Rozman (eds.). *Japan in Transition from Tokugawa to Meiji.* Princeton, N.J., 1986.

Latourette, Kenneth Scott. *A History of the Expansion of Christianity: The Great Century in Northern Africa and Asia, A.D. 1800–A.D. 1914.* New York, 1944.

Sansom, G. B. *The Western World and Japan: A Study in the Interaction of European and Asiatic Cultures.* New York, 1965.

Shapiro, Michael. *The Child's Garden: The Kindergarten from Froebel to Dewey.* University Park, Pa., 1983.

Chapter 6 The Chinese Kindergarten Movement, 1903–1927

Limin Bai

Kindergarten was not introduced into China by individuals but accompanied the birth of a new national school system, which was modeled on those of Western countries and Japan. As the modern school system developed, pre-school education was at first neglected and then it entirely imitated that of Japan. Missionary kindergartens were founded in China before the arrival of the Japanese influence, but they did not have much impact on the society before the May Fourth Movement of 1919. It was not until the 1920s that the kindergarten movement entered a new era, when a new generation of education reformers equipped with scientific knowledge and modern education theories endeavored to break away from the blind imitation of both Japanese and Western models. The intellectual efforts to create a new type of kindergarten were marked by the establishment of village kindergartens.

THE ARRIVAL OF THE KINDERGARTEN:
THE JAPANESE MODEL AND THE BIRTH OF A
MODERN EDUCATION SYSTEM,
1903–1911

The arrival of the kindergarten paralleled the late Qing education reform and the birth of modern education, which resulted from the applications of military force by aggressive Western nations and Japan. From the Opium War of 1840–1842 to the first Sino-Japanese War of 1894–1895, China was humiliated and defeated repeatedly, and was forced to open its door to the world. In the meantime, the seeds of modernization were sown. Military threats and invasions awakened some open-minded scholar-officials and brought about the movement of "self-strengthening." Leaders of the first period of the movement—such as Prince Gongi (1833–1898), Zeng Guofan (1811–1872), Zuo Zongtang (1812–1885), and Li Hongzhang (1823–1901)—realized the efficacy of Western arms and urged China to borrow Western weapons and naval technology in order to increase its strength. As a supplement to traditional Chinese education, China established a few modern government schools (such as the Beijing College of Languages) and several modern arsenals and shipyards. The national school system and its curricula remained unchanged, however.

After 1885, in response to increasing demands from the West and Japan and failures in negotiations with foreign powers, the latter-day leaders of the movement, such as Zhang Zhidong (1837–1909), became interested in not only Western arms and technology but Western education as well. Compared to the previous generation of self-strengtheners, Zhang Zhidong and his contemporaries received more information about politics, the economic and social situation, and modern education systems in Western nations and Japan by reading translated works, employing Western advisers, and sending students abroad. Many open-minded intellectuals as well as those officials dealing with "school affairs" advocated borrowing from the West and following Western models of education. Among them, Rong Hong (1828–1912) was the earliest advocate of sending students to study abroad, while others were dedicated to the circulation of information about Western education. For instance, in his *Shengshi weiyan* (Warnings to a prosperous age), Zheng Guanying (1842–1922) presented a chapter on modern school systems in the West and Japan (Jian 1953, 1:45).

In addition to the Chinese intellectual endeavor, missionary activities in education contributed to the delivery of the modern message among the Chinese educated elite. In 1887 Timothy Richard (1845–1919), one of the most outstanding missionary educationists, presented a pamphlet on modern education as carried on in the seven leading nations in the world. The Chinese title of the pamphlet was first *Qiguo xinxue beiyao* (Essential information of modern education in seven countries), then *Xinxue bazhang* (Eight chapters on modern education), which was published as a series of articles in the *Wanguo gongbao* (The globe magazine). In the pamphlet, Richard stressed four methods of education—the historical, the comparative, the general, and the particular (Soothill 1924, 158; Wang 1965, 249–50). He distributed this pamphlet among leading statesmen like Li Hongzhang. Richard's writings on reform and information about politics, education, and technology in the West compelled these statesmen and literati to face the fact that China was the most backward nation at that time.

In 1898, the One Hundred Day Reform constituted the peak of the "self-strengthening" movement. The revolutionary edicts of the reform concerning education issues included: (1) to abolish the civil service examination system; (2) to establish a university for the study of Western science in Beijing; (3) to convert temples to modern schools; (4) to establish a translation board that would translate books on modern subjects into Chinese; and (5) to send young Manchus abroad to study foreign languages. Unfortunately, the 1898 reform failed, and all innovations of the reform except the University in Beijing (Jingshi Daxuetang) were eliminated by the empress dowager and the government. However, the Boxer movement in 1900 forced the government to carry on reform. In 1901, the government determined to reinstate reforms, and education was one of the reforming issues.

Therefore, in 1902 the Director of School Affairs Zhang Baixi drafted an edict, which envisaged a Chinese system with schools at six levels: *mengyangyuan* (a stage prior to junior primary school), *xiaoxue* (junior primary school), *gaodeng xiaoxue* (senior primary school), *zhongxue* (secondary school), and *gaodeng xuetang* (university). The draft combined traditional Chinese principles of education with some information about Western school systems, reflecting a lack of understanding of the nature of modern education. In particular, the Zhang Baixi of the edict did not grasp the nature of kindergarten and confused it with traditional Chinese education for young children.

In the traditional Chinese system, the process of education was divided into only two stages: *xiaoxue* (elementary education) and *daxue* (higher education). Theoretically, students under the age of fifteen were supposed to enroll in the *xiaoxue*; older students entered the *daxue*. There was no concept of pre-school education. The term *mengxue* could vaguely refer either to the entire period of elementary education in general or to education for younger children. *Meng* originally meant a kind of grass, or small and insignificant (Xu 1977, 26). Gradually, it came to mean *ignorant*. The *Book of Changes* said: "[The method of dealing with] the young and ignorant (*meng*) is to nourish what is correct" (SSJZS 1979, 1:20). Here, the "young" (*you*) and "ignorant" (*meng*) were linked. Children under the age of fifteen were called *youtong* or *tongmeng*. According to Xu Shen, *you* meant young and small. Originally, this written character looked like a newborn baby (Xu 1977, 83). *Tong* referred to young slaves or servants (Xu 1977, 58, 260). From an etymological perspective, the terms *youtong* and *mengtong* reflected the ancient Chinese conceptions of childhood, that is, children under fifteen were intellectually ignorant as well as physically weak and small.[1] *Mengxue* or *youxue,* then, relevantly referred to education for children under fifteen. Some schools, particularly those serving children five or six years of age, were called *mengguan.* The term means "to awake ignorant children," who were to begin their course of study with recognition of basic Chinese characters (Liu 1960, 2–3). Yet this kind of institution bore no resemblance to the kindergarten. Rather, it was similar to the first year of primary school.

The term *kindergarten* meant "child garden" in German. Friedrich Froebel (1782–1852) opened the first kindergarten at Keilhau, Germany, in 1837. According to Froebel's theory, kindergarten was an institution where the protective gardenlike atmosphere would guard children between the ages of three and six against the corrupting influence of society and the dangers of nature. Based on this theory, Froebel designed a simple educational apparatus consisting of six "gifts" for learning elementary laws of physical science by experiment, and systematized a series of "occupations" for developing motor dexterity. The fundamental moral lessons, Froebel insisted, should be included in the songs and games of the kindergarten (Shapiro 1983, 19–28; Whitbread 1972, 31–34; Lilley 1967, 68–119).

In particular, two basic principles characterized Froebel's kindergarten. First, only children between three and six years of age would be admitted to the kindergarten. This age-range clearly indicates the aim and function of Froebel's kindergarten: to take its place midway between infancy and childhood, the family and the school, and nature and society. Second, Froebel's kindergarten placed the emphasis on games and play, and the use of toys as educational materials. With a child-centered approach, Froebel designed the kindergarten as a new social institution of education to nourish the child's physical, social, and spiritual development.

By contrast, according to the 1902 edict in China, children were to be enrolled in *mengyangyuan* at six years of age, where they would study for four years and would be taught subjects including self-cultivation, recognition of Chinese characters, the practice of writing characters, the study of Confucian Classics, history, geography, and gymnastics. In the third year, mathematics was added. After graduation from the *mengxue*, children under age fifteen would then enroll in junior primary school for another three years. Except for the subject of recognition of Chinese characters, which was replaced by composition, the curriculum in this junior primary school resembled that of *mengxue* (Yuan 1968, 140). Apparently, *mengyangyuan* was more similar to the junior primary school than to the kindergarten.

Specific knowledge of Froebel's kindergarten was introduced into China through Japanese translations of Western books and the movement to study in Japan. The Japanese victory over China in 1895 was the greatest influence on many intellectuals, who realized that traditional Chinese education and the imperial examination system could not provide training adequate to meet the challenge of the modern technology mastered by the West and Japan. Impressed by Japanese achievements, many young literati determined to go to Japan to discover the secrets behind the Japanese success. Equipped with information about modern education in the West and Japan, as well as the high value of education in Chinese tradition, the Confucian reformers of the time were convinced that Western nations and Japan had increased their strength by means of education. In particular, Meiji Japan held a special place in their minds. They marveled at Japan's success in combining modern technology and traditional ideology, which suggested a pattern that China could follow in its journey toward modernization (Fairbank and Liu 1980, 343–47).

As early as 1898, in his famous pamphlet *Quanxue pian* (Exhortation to learning), Zhang Zhidong pointed out the need to follow the Japanese model in education reform. In his opinion, the customs and conditions of Japan and China were comparable; both countries had similar moral codes and respected Confucianism. These similarities meant that China should also be able to effectively absorb Western learning while preserving traditional learning as its "roots" and "substance." Therefore, Zhang strongly recommended the Japanese model and advocated studying in Japan. He listed particular advantages of studying in Japan. First, he said that Japan was nearby and inexpensive for travel. Second, the Japanese language used the same characters and was therefore more closely allied to Chinese than the language of any European country. More important, Zhang continued, the Japanese had translated much of what was necessary from the West (Zhang 1963, 6:3727). Consequently, not only did he recommend sending students to Japan, but he eagerly advocated learning the Japanese language and translating Japanese books as well. He firmly believed that by learning Japanese, the Chinese could possess themselves of the store of Western knowledge without having to learn Western languages (Zhang 1963, 6:3731).

It is true that the language interaction between Chinese and Japanese, to a certain extent, played an important role in late Qing China's transformation from traditional to modern schools. A large number of Japanese words absorbed into the Chinese lexicon at the end of the nineteenth century were character compounds; of these, some were contained in early Chinese translations of Western works and were then widely accepted in Japan, but most were coined by the Japanese to translate Western terms. Apart from these two categories was vocabulary which was simply derived from classical Chinese and related to traditional Chinese thought (Gao and Liu 1958).

The dynamic of this language interaction was to encourage the Confucian reformers to follow Japan's model rather than those of other Western nations. Because of the imperfections of the 1902 edict, at the beginning of 1903 Rong Qing was appointed to amend it along with Zhang Baixi. At the same time, Zhang Zhidong was called to Beijing for an audience with the empress dowager. Soon after his arrival in Beijing, Zhang Baixi submitted a memorandum to the empress dowager, asking that Zhang Zhidong be assigned to consult with him and Rong Qing to create a new national school system (Chen 1927, 47–48; Ayers 1971, 230–31). Through reading the Japanese works, Zhang realized that *mengyangyuan* (the institute for nourishing younger children) in the 1902 system was not kindergarten but junior primary school. Therefore, the 1903 edict adopted the term *youzhiyuan*, a borrowed Japanese usage, to refer specifically to kindergarten (Shu 1981, 1:195).

The 1903 regulations for *mengyangyuan* copied verbatim the Japanese regulations for kindergartens in 1900. The terms and concepts relating to pre-school education, such as *youzhiyuan* and *baomu* (referring to kindergarten teachers), were all borrowed from the Japanese language (Kuroda 1969, 181–88). These loan terms actually helped the regulation makers to form a theoretical framework within which they could transform Froebel's model and ideas of kindergarten to conform with China's educational ideology and the traditional system. For instance, the term *youzhiyuan* was created by combining two Chinese words: *youzhi* meant "young and ignorant," and *yuan* meant "garden." This newly coined word not only expressed the traditional Chinese understanding of childhood but also translated the meaning of kindergarten—"the garden for young and ignorant children."

Another classic example is the term *baomu,* a Chinese classical compound adopted by modern Japanese to refer to kindergarten teachers. According to the *Liji* (the book of rites), in the Zhou Dynasty (1122 B.C.–255 B.C.) some concubines in the palace were chosen to nurse and teach the sons of emperors. They were employed either as teachers, who were in charge of their education; or as *cimu* (kind mother), who were supposed to take care of their needs; or as *baomu,* whose duty was to nurse them. Later generations broadened the meaning of the term *baomu,* which referred specifically to the women who nursed and looked after other people's children (*Cihai* 1980, 1:347). The use of the term *baomu* to refer to kindergarten teachers reflected the Japanese understanding of the nature of kindergarten: to protect children between three and six years of age and to nourish their physical, social, and spiritual development.[2] In the late Qing education reform, Zhang Zhidong and his colleagues were willing to adopt the kindergarten as part of the modern school system. Nevertheless, the term *baomu* in the 1903 regulations provided these Confucian reformers with a basis on which to modify the nature and form of Froebel's kindergarten in order to comply with traditional Chinese concepts and the then existing institutions.[3] It is evident that the regulation makers were well informed about the nature and system of Froebel's model of kindergarten.

However, because of the problem of female education, Zhang and his associates attempted to create a new institution—*mengyangyuan*—as an alternative to kindergarten. Institutionally, *mengyangyuan* was a subsidiary body of two institutions: *yuyintang* (orphanage) and *jinjietang* (home for respectable and virtuous women). Both institutions were founded by the government and aimed to support orphans and the *jiefu,* widows who were not going to remarry. Zhang and other regulation makers attempted to use these organizations as substitutes for normal (teacher training) schools. In their understanding, with a limited training, kindergarten teachers were similar to traditional Chinese wet-nurses or *baomu,* who typically came from poor families and were uneducated. The regulations claimed that these poor women could be trained in these two institutions and then they would be qualified as kindergarten teachers or that they would be ready for employment in rich families (Shu 1981, 2:381–82). The 1903 regulations of mengyangyuan claimed: "The *mengyangyuan* aims to nurse and teach young children aged between three and seven *sui.* [These children] would be taken care of by baomu, who are graduates from female normal school. . . . There are kindergartens in other countries. The system of our *mengyangyuan* resembles that of kindergarten. . . . Yet in present China, female education should not be advocated, for it would bring about many social and moral problems. Girls' school does not suit China's situation. For this reason, we are not able to establish many kindergartens over the country, [for there are no well-trained *baomu*]. Nevertheless, we can set up regulations for *mengyangyuan* based on the model of the foreign kindergarten" (Shu 1981, 2:381).

The textbooks intended for *baomu* training did not differ from those used for the traditional education for women. These texts included *Xiaojing* (The classic of filial piety), *The Four Books, Lienü zhuan* (Biographies of saintly women), *Nüjie* (Admonitions for women), *Nüxun* (Teachings for women), and *Jiaonü yigui* (Posthumous regulations for daughters). In Chinese tradition, the role of a woman in a family was to serve parents, parents-in-law, and husband, and to raise children. The majority of women did not have the opportunity to learn to read and write. So-called female education centered primarily on the cultivation of women's virtues as presented by these books. This kind of *baomu* training had little in common with the training for kindergarten teachers. Zhang Zhidong and his colleagues acknowledged this difference, but they refused to grant girls the right to a modern education, which they thought would cause the corruption of public morality. In addition, they insisted that pre-school education should be carried out primarily at home in a traditional way (Shu 1981, 2:383). Therefore, pre-school education in the 1903 education system was only in name, because there was no normal school to train kindergarten teachers.

Evidently, China's new school system in its formative stage was an integration of Japanese influence and Chinese tradition. Because China imitated the Japanese model, modern elements presented in the 1903 regulations were inevitably related to Japanese influence. On the other hand, because of conservative attitudes toward traditional Chinese education, the regulation makers tried very hard to preserve traditional ideology.

From this perspective, the second section of the regulations for *mengyangyuan* and family education appeared to reflect a remarkable Chinese understanding of Froebel's kindergarten. The section included three items: (1) the definition of *baoyu* (to protect and to nurse), a term derived from the Japanese language; (2) the methods of teaching and nursing children in *mengyangyuan*; and (3) the number of hours each day children should be in the kindergarten. In its definition of the term *baoyu*, this section correctly acknowledged the aim and function of the kindergarten: to encourage children's physical, intellectual, and moral development. In addition, it apparently accepted Froebel's design for kindergarten, emphasizing games, play, and the use of children's eyes and hands to discover nature and to develop their intelligence (Shu 1981, 2:384–85).

It is doubtful, however, that the regulation makers actually understood much of Froebel's model of the kindergarten; the regulations were merely a copy of the Japanese system. The regulations indicate that as long as new ideas about education did not conflict with traditional Chinese principles, those Confucian reformers were willing to accept them. For instance, under the item that defined the methods of teaching and nursing children, four issues were presented: playing games, singing, speaking, and making handcrafts. The first two issues were addressed apparently in response to the theory represented by Wang Yangming (1472–1528) and, later, other education theorists in the Qing era.[4]

A unique characteristic of Wang Yangming's theory of elementary education was its accommodation of the nature of children: "to love to play and to dislike restriction." Wang Yangming suggested that young pupils would be engaged by a curriculum that included singing. He said that singing was an important means to release children's energy, which they typically "[expressed in] jumping around and shouting," and that it would "free them through rhythm from depression and repression." Wang Yangming also believed that teaching children etiquette not only helped to "make their demeanour dignified" but, more important, contributed to their good health. The practice of "bowing and walking politely" would improve children's "blood circulation." Through the activities of kneeling, rising, and extending and contracting their limbs, children could "strengthen their tendons and bones" (Chan 1963, 183).

To the regulation makers, the purpose of the kindergarten as stated by Wang was similar to that stated by Froebel: to teach children morality through playing and singing. Yet at this stage, they did not know much about Froebel's games, so their regulation focused on songs (Shu 1981, 2:384). The "songs" referred to short poems, which were easy to read and remember, and were often used as a type of teaching manual for young children in traditional Chinese education.[5] The regulation makers thus encouraged the use of singing as a means of teaching, because it had already existed in traditional Chinese education.

In practice, nevertheless, the pioneering kindergartens were not only influenced by the Japanese model but also run by Japanese teachers, as at that time China did not have any qualified kindergarten teachers. At this point, Froebel's kindergarten had been imported to China from Japan, and the imported Japanese "package" included teachers, curricula, teaching materials, and equipment. An example of this wholesale importation was Hubei Youzhiyuan, one of the earliest Chinese kindergartens, which was set up in 1903 by Duan Fang, the viceroy of Hubei Province. After January 1904, when the new school system was announced, Hubei Youzhiyuan became Hubei Mengyangyuan in order to be consistent with the new system. However, under either name, the school was run by three Japanese teachers. The curriculum was also entirely Japanese, including seven items: (1) *xingyi* (manner); (2) *xunhua* (instructions for children); (3) *youzhiyuan yu* (speech in kindergarten); (4) the Japanese language; (5) crafts; (6) singing; and (7) playing (Shu 1981, 2:387).

Furthermore, kindergarten teachers were trained according to Japanese practices. In 1905, twenty female students in Hunan Province were sent to Japan, where they undertook one-year courses in education. Afterward women from other parts of China followed their path and enrolled in teaching training in Japan. Upon graduation, these Japanese-trained teachers returned to China and set up their own normal schools for training kindergarten teachers. One example is the first private normal school, Baomu Chuanxisuo (a Japanese term meaning "the school for training kindergarten teachers"), established in Shanghai in 1907. The school was run by Mrs. Zhu Wuzhe. Mrs. Zhu was assigned to study in Japan by Wu Huaijiu, the manager of Shanghai Wuben Girls' School, founded in 1903. Because the aim of the normal school was to train kindergarten teachers, a kindergarten called Gongli Youzhishe (public kindergarten) was attached to the school (Chen 1927, 4). This example suggests that at that time, girls could receive only a rudimentary education: a few years of elementary school and, later, kindergarten teacher training, as well as practice teaching in the kindergarten.

Another private enterprise, Yanshi Primary Girls' School, developed a similar system. Yan Xiu (1860–1921), a reformer and translator in the late Qing period, founded a family school for girls in 1902. In 1905, the school was named Yanshi Primary Girls School, under which there was one Mengyangyuan and one Baomu Jiangxisuo (this term, like Baomu Chuanxisuo mentioned above, also referred to the school for training kindergarten teachers). In his institute, Yan Xiu employed Japanese teachers, adopted Japanese teaching material, and purchased Japanese equipment (Zhu 1986, 1(B): 909–10).

However, it is not always easy to distinguish Japanese influence on kindergartens from Chinese tradition because of the interaction of the Japanese and Chinese languages and a recognizable shared Confucian past between the two nations. For instance, the 1905 curriculum framework of Hunan Mengyangyuan strongly suggested the degree of the Japanese impact, which was apparently embodied in the use of Japanese terms, such as *xiushenhua* (the theme of moral cultivation), *shuwuhua* (names of various things), *dufang* (reading skill), *shufang* (counting skill), and *huafang* (drawing). Yet, in the curriculum for moral education, the guidelines recommended Chinese stories with good examples of filial piety and the games played by Confucius when he was a child (Shu 1981, 2:

388–91). In the absence of evidence, it is difficult to determine whether these recommendations came from the original Japanese works or were added by the Chinese in the adaptation process.

Thus, in the formative period of a national school system, Chinese kindergartens, both official institutes and private enterprises, entirely imitated the Japanese model. The open-minded intellectuals and the reformers in the late Qing court believed that China could simultaneously revive Confucianism as the moral basis of the nation and adopt Western learning for practical use—if it followed the Japanese model.[6] Therefore, the Japanese influence dominated the 1903 regulations, the administration of kindergartens, and the training of kindergarten teachers. Nevertheless, the fact that the two nations shared a Confucian past enabled China to modify Froebel's model of kindergarten as *mengyangyuan*, a combination of modern elements and Chinese traditional institutions. Furthermore, *mengyangyuan* was not an independent educational entity but only an affiliate of charitable institutions; pre-school education at that time was not yet recognized as necessary to the wider school system.

THE VITAL ELEMENTS: FEMALE EDUCATION, MISSION SCHOOLS, AND DEVELOPMENT OF THE KINDERGARTEN MOVEMENT, 1912–1919

Female education was vital to the development of the kindergarten. The 1903 regulations showed that Zhang Zhidong and his colleagues attempted to limit the education of the female population. They insisted that female education should aim to train women to be proper wives and mothers in accordance with Confucian rites. They appreciated Chinese tradition, which forbade females and males to communicate with each other freely. They also forbade young girls from attending school, reading Western books, and adopting Western customs (which, Zhang and his colleagues believed, would encourage them to choose their husbands themselves and not to respect their parents and husbands to the degree dictated by tradition). In order to avoid this kind of "corruption," the regulation makers stressed strongly that girls ought to be educated at home, either by a private tutor or by their mothers. According to the regulations, girls were to learn basic Chinese characters and counting skills, which served the needs of running a household, as well as sewing skills and other women's duties. The regulations claimed that this kind of knowledge was enough for women, and that they should be forbidden to learn how to write a poem or an article, to participate in anything outside the household, and to discuss anything relating to state affairs (Shu 1981, 2:383).

However, a campaign for female education paralleled the self-strengthening movement in the late nineteenth century. Reformers, such as Liang Qichao, who was well informed of modern education through his working with Timothy Richard and his reading of Japanese works, started campaigning for female education. In his *Bianfa tongyi* (General discussion of reforms), Liang presented a chapter on female education, which he believed was related to China's fate and future: "the basic reason that made our country weak was the factor that women were not educated" (Liang 1941, 38). Two fundamental principles guided the self-strengthening movement, said Liang. One was to correct people's minds, and the other was to gather talented people. In Liang's opinion, these two principles were actually based on elementary education, and mothers usually initiated children's education (Liang 1941, 38). From this perspective, Liang pointed to a significant link between female education and the future of China: "education for women is a vital factor influencing a country which may survive or perish and may become strong or weak" (Liang 1941, 41).

Liang's campaign focused on creating new types of *xianqi liangmu* (model wives and mothers) through modern education. According to the old Chinese saying, "women without abilities have virtues." Thus *xianqi liangmu* usually referred to women without education and professional training. Liang refuted this stale concept and redefined the term *xianqi liangmu*. He argued that if women's virtue was without learning, then the virtuous women must be illiterate; but nobody could prove that illiterate women were more virtuous than literate women. In fact, continued Liang, learning could broaden one's mind and help one earn a living. Women without education often fought each other for very trivial things because they did not know about anything beyond the household and were kept at home like animals and slaves. Consequently, they became a physical burden and spiritual poison for men, because they could not support themselves, and their quarrels spiritually tormented men. Liang concluded that *xianqi* of this kind were really just like poison and men should not be close to them (Liang 1941, 39–40).

More important, Liang maintained, it was impossible for this kind of *xianqi* to become a good mother. Like other Chinese writers, Liang emphasized the role of the mother in a child's early education: "If a mother educates her children properly, her children will easily have a successful life later. Otherwise, it will be difficult for them in the future, if they do not receive a proper education from their mother" (Liang 1941, 40). This was not a new point. Traditional Chinese education theory often stressed the necessity of early education. It was believed that what children learned at an early age would significantly influence their characters and their nature; and a mother usually was the first teacher in a child's life. The new aspect of Liang's elaboration was that he recommended the teaching of modern subjects as part of the curriculum in female education. He believed that this innovation would relate significantly to a modern education for young children. He stated: "If a mother knows the basic principles of education and the methods of educating children, her children before ten will learn the basic knowledge of various subjects and the way of life" (Liang 1941, 40).

Liang criticized the content of traditional Chinese elementary education. Equipped with information on Western education, Liang realized that China did not have pre-school education, and primary schools had not been established. Usually children under ten were looked after by either mothers or nursing maids (if in a wealthy family). Most women did not have an education at all, and the early education they could provide for children, as Liang pointed out, consisted of the trivialities of the household. In other words, what children heard and saw everyday was primarily women fighting over trivial things. Liang then sketched the future of the children who received this kind of early education: "Among them, the best ones may be taught to succeed in the civil service examinations, to have emolument, to inherit family property and to have offspring. . . . When they are grown up, in their minds, there is nothing more important than this kind of event. [Then] thousands of households are concerned about the same thing. Gradually, a trend in the whole society is formed: people seek only private gains and become shameless, stubborn and brutal. . . . In the aspects of knowledge and interests, even Chinese scholars are not able to match with Western children in primary school" (Liang 1941, 40). This backward and ugly picture, in Liang's view, resulted not from different races but from different ways of educating children.

Liang Qichao then used the examples of America and Japan to support his argument. In his view, the strongest country in the West was America, and the newly rising country in the East was Japan. Liang was informed that equal rights of education between men and women were first advocated by America and then accepted by Japan. Like his contemporaries, Liang was especially astonished by Japan's achievement in modernization, and then related it to the Japanese success in education for women (Lian 1941, 43). He noticed that most subjects taught in Japan's female schools resembled those in male schools. In particular, he appreciated modern education that provided both men and women with useful subjects, such as agriculture, trade, medicine, science, and engineering. In

Liang's understanding of an ideal country, men and women should be educated together, and both should be able to have jobs to support themselves. He concluded that the more that female education was flourishing, the stronger a country could be, and such a country could then conquer other countries without the use of military force. In poor countries, female education declined and people had to struggle for survival (Liang 1941, 43). In 1898, the first girls' school founded by the Chinese—Jingzheng Nüshu (Jingzheng girls' school)—was opened in Shanghai. Because of the failure of the reform, this school was closed in 1900.[7] However, other girls' schools—such as Shanghai Aiguo Nüxue (patriotic girls' school), founded by Cai Yuanpei in 1902—were later established.

Following the trend in modern education, in 1903 (before he was assigned to Beijing to complete the new school system) Zhang Zhidong set up the first girls' normal school for training kindergarten teachers in Hubei. The school accepted women between the ages of fifteen and thirty-five. Yet Chinese people were shocked. Female students on their way to school were surrounded by people who were curious about the event. Fights broke out between these onlookers and school security guards. Zhang was very sensitive about this and ordered the closure of the school (Zhang 1963, 3:1917–18). Thus first Chinese school for training kindergarten teachers disappeared immediately.

However, no matter how hard the regulation makers worked to deprive women of a modern education, the number of girls' schools gradually increased. Ironically, not long after the announcement of the regulations, the empress dowager allowed a girls' school to be set up inside the palace. In 1906, she ordered the Department of Education to draft a series of regulations for female education. The following year two regulations—Regulations for Female Primary School and Regulations for Female Normal School—were promulgated. According to these regulations, female students were allowed access to modern subjects, on the one hand; on the other, they had to learn and practice the Confucian ethics. Furthermore, female education was limited to an elementary level: four years for lower primary school and another four years for higher primary school. There was no advanced education for women except for female normal school (Shu 1981, 3:800–818).

Originally, the mission schools were the pioneers in the field of education for women. When the 1842 treaty forced China to open the ports of Guangdong, Xiamen, Fuzhou, Ningbo, and Shanghai to foreign trade, missionaries were free to establish schools in China. In 1844, Miss Aldersey, a member of the Church of England, set up the first school for Chinese girls at Ningbo (Burton 1911, 35). Afterward other girls' schools, a large proportion of which were founded by

American and British societies, were opened. According to Ida Belle Lewis's study, the number of girls in mission schools began to increase in 1877 until 1896. This can be seen from table 1, which presents the growth in the number of girls in Protestant mission schools in China (Lewis 1974, 24).

However, the influence of these girls' mission schools, both in preparing kindergarten teachers and in provoking social demand for female education, was not strong. This is because the aim of the mission education was to train "intelligent Christian wives and mothers anewing the Christians of the next generation" (Chen 1979, 123). Therefore these schools, with other institutions set up by missionaries, remained isolated from the self-strengthening movement and educational reform of the time. It was true that some missionaries, such as Timothy Richard, as well as Young J. Allen of the American Methodist Episcopal Church South (known to the Chinese as Lin Lezhi), endeavored to spread modern information among intellectuals and high-ranking officials. At the same time, the Chinese reformers, such as Liang Qichao, Kang Youwei, and (later) Zhang Zhidong, had contacts with those missionaries. Nevertheless, neither these missionaries nor the reformers, as Jessie G. Lutz points out, were typical representatives of their communities, for the majority of the Chinese intellectual groups and those evangelistic missionaries were antagonistic to each other (Lutz 1971, vii, 10). In particular, the curriculum of these mission schools included the study of Christian morals and doctrine, and the daily reading of the Bible, which conflicted with Chinese intellectual interests. This may account, in part, for why the 1903 regulations did not mention mission education, insisting that China should preserve Confucianism while embracing Western learning.

In addition, it is difficult to assess the role of mission education in the initial stage of the Chinese kindergarten movement, because Chinese writers rarely commented on the subject. It was not until the 1920s that some educators acknowledged the fact that in 1902 six kindergartens had been established by missionaries, and that out of a total of 194 children, 97 were girls (Shu 1927, 4). The information originated from Young J. Allen's *Wudazhou nüsu tongkao* (A general study of women's customs in five continents).[8] Yet the period 1903–1907

Table 1. Number of Girls in Protestant Mission Schools, 1849–1896

Year	1849	1860	1869	1877	1896
Schools	3	12	31	38	308
Students	Fewer than 50	Approximately 196	556	524	6,798

saw the growth of a number of Chinese private municipal and government schools for girls, including kindergarten teacher training schools, which were often modeled after Japanese schools (or were directly under the administration of Japanese teachers) rather than after mission girls' schools.

After the Revolution of 1911, female education and the kindergarten movement appeared to be given a greater impetus. According to the education system as outlined on 3 September 1912, the *mengyangyuan* was no longer attached to orphanages and homes for elderly people but was an educational institution, and girls were encouraged to attend the same schools as boys in the lower elementary grades. Obviously, compared with the 1903 regulations, the 1912 system had made impressive progress—at least, in the following two areas. First, *mengyangyuan* was regarded as an education entity instead of as an affiliated part of charitable institutions. Second, no distinction was made between girls and boys, and girls were allowed to enter not only primary school and normal school for training kindergarten teachers, but also high school. In addition, the 1912 education system required that *mengyangyuan* and primary schools be attached to girls' normal schools, and high school to girls' normal high schools, despite the fact that *mengyangyuan* was still not considered an initial stage in the school-wide system (Shu 1981, 1:223–28).

Under the 1912 system, some girls' mission schools became kindergarten teacher training schools. Suzhou Jinghai and Hangzhou Hongdao, for example, were founded in 1916 and were well known to Chinese educators of the time. Perhaps these establishments can be seen as a positive response to the proposal put forward at the National Missionary Conference in 1913, which stated that mission education should include kindergarten as well as schools for training kindergarten teachers. Furthermore, these mission schools would even accept non-Christian students, in order to provide teachers for Chinese government and private schools as well as kindergartens. The curriculum of mission girls' normal schools typically included three subject areas: English and religious studies; general subjects such as the Chinese language and music; and professional subjects including psychology, school administration, and kindergarten teaching methods (Zhang 1985, 756). However, most mission girls' normal schools accepted a very limited number of students, so the proportion of graduates was naturally very small. For example, Hangzhou Hongdao Girls' Normal School graduated only one student in 1918 and in 1920 (He 1990, 138).

With the development of female education, the number of mission and Chinese kindergartens increased proportionally. According to Chen Hongbi's study (Chen 1927, 5), in Shanghai alone there were twelve kindergartens, half run by missionaries and half by the Chinese (see table 2). Nevertheless, in this period the mission kindergarten pattern did not have much impact on the Chinese kindergarten movement. In other words, Chinese education authorities at that time were still in favor of the Japanese model. In regard to the curriculum and teaching methods in the kindergarten, both the 1912 system and the 1916 detailed regulations simply restated the 1903 regulations, which endorsed the Japanese influence on the kindergarten movement. Pre-school education during this period did not develop significantly, even though statistical reports indicate the spread of the kindergarten.

TRANSFORMATION: THE AMERICAN MODEL AND THE NATIONALIZING OF KINDERGARTENS, 1920–1927

The May Fourth Movement of 1919 highlighted a shift from the Japanese to the Western kindergarten model, which was related to the change in focus of study abroad. As discussed earlier, in the late Qing education reform, Japan was chosen as the best model of modernization for China to follow. This policy resulted in a trend toward study in Japan. However, Japan's aggression towards China curtailed this trend. In 1915, Japan's Twenty-one Demands on China inspired national indignation. In 1919 Japan claimed the former German concessions in Shandong Province, which led to the May Fourth demonstration. Anti-Japanese sentiment reached a peak nationwide. Many students in Japan were also involved in protests, which resulted in the departure of Chinese students from Japanese schools in both 1915 and 1918. In addition, in 1908 the United States decided to return to China a major portion of the $24 million indemnity from the Boxer uprising of 1900 for educational and cultural purposes. This remuneration effectively encouraged the Chinese to change direction in its program of study abroad, and the United States soon became the most important recipient country.

To a certain extent, this change contributed to the formation of a new generation of education reformers, most of whom were "returned students" from

Table 2. Number of Kindergartens in Shanghai, 1918

	Mission Kindergartens	Chinese Kindergartens	Total
Kindergartens	6	6	12
Students	160	279	439
Teachers	13	29	42

the United States. Like the reformers in the late Qing, these reformers believed that a good modern education could save the country and increase China's strength quickly. However, they preferred the American pattern of education to the Japanese model, and propagated the Dewey Experiment, which they believed represented a more advanced and liberal education theory.

Under the influence of the Dewey Experiment, the 1922 regulations acknowledged the connection between education and the construction of a modern and democratic society. On this basis, the regulations required that an education be provided for the masses rather than only for the rich, and advocated *shenhuo jiaoyu* (life education). The regulations also required that education be affordable for the majority of the population. Moreover, the regulations emphasized the individual's development through education, which contrasted with the principles of traditional Chinese education (DZJN 1934, 8).

In regard to kindergartens, Froebel's ideas and Western education theories were introduced into the Chinese school system by this new generation of reformers. Institutionally it was the first time that the kindergarten was recognized as an independent institute and as the first stage of a universal education. The regulations made it very clear that "children under six are admitted to kindergarten" (Chen 1927, 200). More important, Froebel's and Dewey's models of child-centered education received more attention than ever and were put into practice in pre-school education.

The spread of the Dewey Experiment in China was attributed to the activities of Dewey's former Chinese students at Columbia University, who invited Dewey to visit China in 1919 and translated some of his works, such as *How We Think* and later *The Child and the Curriculum*. After Dewey's stay in China, from 1921 to 1927, other American experts in education, such as Paul Monroe, George R. Twiss, William H. McCall, Helen Parkhurst, and William Kilpatrick, either gave lecture tours or conducted research in China. For example, in 1922 McCall and Twiss set up educational tests including intelligence tests to standardize education in China. In the 1920s, Kilpatrick's Project Method and Parkhurst's Dalton Plan were employed in Chinese elementary education (Keenan 1977, 35, 85, 108). These American scholars' activities and theories, as well as the Chinese reformers' promotion, expedited kindergarten curriculum reform and the use of modern teaching methods in pre-school education.

While Western education theories were diffused among Chinese intellectuals, mission kindergartens gradually developed and attracted Chinese intellectual attention. Especially after the May Fourth Movement, the Japanese kindergarten model no longer met Chinese demands for a modern liberal education.

The curriculum in the Japanese kindergarten typically included games, conversation, crafts, singing, the recognition of Chinese characters, arithmetic, drawing, the writing of characters, and so on. However, these subjects were organized into daily programs and were not flexible. In the classroom, usually teachers sat in front of a lectern, and children were forbidden to move or speak freely and had to sit quietly in line (He 1990, 134). This type of curriculum and teaching method clearly ran counter to modern education theories, which emphasized child-centered pre-school education. However, because of the influence of traditional Chinese education, this model was easily accepted by the Chinese in the late Qing education reform. In the 1920s, as Western ideas flooded into China without the Japanese language as a medium, many educators became familiar with the ideas of Pestalozzi, Froebel, Maria Montessori, and Dewey, and realized that the nature of mission kindergartens was closer to Froebel's model than that of the Japanese pattern, even though most mission kindergartens were too religious (Zhang 1985, 392–93). In the meantime, graduates from mission normal schools, who undertook teaching in kindergartens, also contributed to their promotion.

The shift in education reform helped the growth of mission kindergartens. Between 1902 and 1919 the number of mission kindergartens increased from 6 to 139. In 1924, of the 190 kindergartens throughout China, 156 were mission kindergartens. However, Japanese kindergartens—that is, those imitating the Japanese model or operated by Japanese teachers—still existed.[9] According to Zhang Xuemen's study of 30 kindergartens in Jiangsu, Zhejiang, and Zhili (now Beijing) in 1926, out of 30 kindergartens, 5 were Japanese kindergartens, 12 were mission kindergartens, and 13 were run by the Chinese (Shu 1927, 6). These numbers suggest that at the time, the kindergarten in China was a venture in education with foreign labels.

Nevertheless, the new generation of Chinese education reformers launched out into research on early childhood and pre-school education. The majority of these pioneering researchers were graduates from Columbia's Teachers College, such as Tao Xingzhi (1891–1946) and Chen Heqin (1892–1982), and their students and followers, such as Zhang Zonglin (1899–1976). Their research activities and experiments in transformation of kindergartens signalled a new era in the Chinese kindergarten movement.

According to these researchers, the blind imitation of Western and Japanese patterns was one of the deficiencies in the kindergartens of the time. For instance, not only were American or Japanese curricula adopted, but these kindergartens were full of Western or Japanese toys and pictures as well. Instead of celebrating Chinese festivals, these kindergartens celebrated Christmas and other Western or Japanese holidays. Tao Xingzhi sharply criticized this practice: "If you visit today's kindergartens, what you see and hear is all from foreign countries, e.g. teachers play the foreign piano, children sing foreign songs; teachers tell foreign stories and children play with foreign toys. Even desserts are not Chinese style either. Thus Chinese kindergartens become foreign markets, where kindergarten teachers perform the sale of foreign products, and poor children became the victims of foreign products" (Tao 1983, 1:619).

Tao's attack on the superficial borrowing from abroad was a reflection of his generation of educational reformers who determined to establish the kindergartens with authentic Chinese characters. Historically, this determination was associated with the 1924–1925 debate over the remaining "unequal treaties" of the nineteenth century, as well as the movement to "retrieve educational rights" from the privileged missionary schools in China. In reality, the problems of cultural imitation in the kindergarten movement were also obvious: the Japanese model was inconsistent with Froebel's principles, and Chinese children in the mission kindergartens were required to practice Christian doctrines and ceremony every day, which conflicted with Chinese intellectual interests. Therefore, these progressive educationists decided to reform the curriculum in accordance with Froebel's principles. In southern and central China, Chen Heqin, Zhang Zonglin, and their colleagues led the movement, while in Beijing Zhang Xuemen (1891–1973) actively contributed to curriculum development in the Chinese kindergartens.

The first kindergarten established by these pioneering researchers was Nanjing Gulou Kindergarten, managed by Chen Heqin. Chen received his master's degree in education at the Teachers College of Columbia University, where he majored in education and psychology and studied under such eminent scholars as Paul Monroe and William Kilpatrick. In 1919, he was invited to take a position as a professor of education in the Department of Education at Nanjing Higher Normal School, where he conducted research on child psychology and early childhood, as well as teaching.[10] In 1920 his son was born, and Chen observed and analyzed his son's physical and psychological development for 808 days. The findings of the study were delivered in his book *Ertong xinli zhi yanjiu* (The study of children's psychology), which laid the groundwork for the study of child psychology in China. Furthermore, in 1923 he founded Gulou Kindergarten in his own home, where twelve children were enrolled and teaching was undertaken by graduates from Hangzhou Hongdao Normal School and a friend from the American Society. Later Zhang Zonglin was assigned as Chen's research assistant by the Department of Education of Nanjing Higher Normal School. With the help of other researchers, Chen and Zhang carried out experiments in child psychology while gathering and analyzing teaching material from Western countries and Japan for reference. On the basis of the scientific research, they designed a curriculum for the kindergartens located near the Yangtze River; there, Western games and toys were adapted to Chinese children's use.

The Gulou Kindergarten's curriculum indicates these researchers' comprehensive understanding of modern education theories and their efforts to put them into practice. In their opinion, the essence of the theories of Pestalozzi, Froebel, Montessori, and Dewey was the child-centered approach, which regarded "observation by the senses" as the basis of human knowledge, and nature and its phenomena as the core of knowledge. Thus a child-centered curriculum was to focus on the growth of the child's intelligence rather than on a defined body of knowledge. In other words, the focus of early child education was not book learning but the surroundings of children, which they could see, touch, and smell. Consequently, Froebel's organized play—seen as an imitation of the natural life and the highest level of child development—represented both the content and method for teaching in kindergarten. Equipped with these theories, Chen Heqin, Zhang Zonglin, and other Chinese researchers put forward their principles in the making of the curriculum, which stressed that education should be contained in play and encouraged children to maintain the connection with nature, to develop individually and to obtain knowledge from their own experience (Zhang 1985, 137–38). Table 3 is a curriculum framework for the January courses in the Gulou Kindergarten, showing that nature and daily life were the main focus of learning, and children were urged to observe and discover their surroundings and to extend their narrow world (Zhang 1985, 140).

An outline concerning what children should learn in kindergarten, drafted by Chen Heqin and Zhang Zonglin, elaborated the content, which included seven categories: healthy habits, personal behaviour, manners in society, life skills, playing skills, language skills, and common knowledge. These seven cat-

Table 3. Framework for January Courses in the Gulou Kindergarten

Month	Festival	Weather	Animals	Plants	Farming	Games	Customs	Health
January	New Year	Ice, snow, northwest wind	Goldfish, pigeons	Sprouts, plum blossoms	Onions, chives, carrots, etc.	Drums	Gifts for the new year	Chilblain and colds

egories were grouped into three parts. First, "healthy habits" and "life skills" referred to physical development, including exercises for children to learn how to dress and wash themselves, and how to avoid biting fingernails, drooling, and spitting on the street. Second, "personal behavior" and "manners in society" were concerned with personal attributes of good citizenship. Instead of emphasizing Confucian virtues such as filial piety and loyalty as traditional education did, the outline centered on training in good habits and the development of individuality—such as how to get along with people (including family members and playmates in kindergarten), and how to get rid of bad habits. "Bad habits" referred to lying, crying easily, being short-tempered, being jealous of other people, mocking other people, snatching toys or food from other children, and picking flowers and plants in public parks. Third, "language skills" (conversation, recognition of Chinese characters, singing songs, telling stories) and play were a part of children's everyday lives; children were to acquire "common knowledge" (colors, common plants and animals, numbers, directions, national holidays) through their own observation and exploration of the world (Zhang 1985, 146–52).

Like his contemporaries in Nanjing, Zhang Xuemen in Beijing designed a Chinese curriculum on the basis of his understanding of Froebel's kindergarten. Zhang Xuemen knew of Froebel's kindergarten by chance. In 1920 he found incomplete lecture notes of Froebel's ideas about kindergarten when he visited the Boshi Kindergarten (Beijing). The papers had been used to wrap peanuts, but to Zhang Xuemen they were an invaluable treasure. From these incomplete lecture notes, Zhang planned his journey in the study of modern education: one year for Froebel's ideas about education, another year for Montessori's works, and the third year for world education. Based on his knowledge of modern education, Zhang was devoted to early childhood education (Zhang 1969, 5). After undertaking research on Japanese and Western kindergarten curricula, Zhang Xuemen (like Chen Heqin and Zhang Zonglin) realized that the Chinese kindergarten curriculum should be adapted to Chinese children's physical, spiritual, and social development. His proposed curriculum was based on his investigation and observation of ordinary people's daily life and customs in Beijing and Northern China (Zhang 1985, 139).

Apart from these intellectual efforts to reform the kindergarten curriculum, "people's education" and "village education," initiated by Tao Xingzhi in the 1920s, significantly marked the development of the kindergarten movement in this period. Tao Xingzhi was a promoter of Dewey's educational ideas in China. However, upon his return to China from the United States, Tao recognized the problems of superficial borrowing from the West which characterized the late Qing education reform. In addition, despite the 1922 regulations, education, especially on the kindergarten level, was not accessible to poor people. Tao Xingzhi was dissatisfied with this situation and advocated the diffusion of basic education and kindergarten at the village or factory level. He asked pointedly: "Where is there a desperate demand for kindergartens? Where are kindergartens mostly welcomed by people? Is there any 'new continent' to be discovered for setting up kindergartens?" (Tao 1983, 1:625) His answer was that the areas near factories and villages needed kindergartens badly, for children from the families of workers and peasants required care and education while their mothers were working. To meet the needs of the working class, the existing kindergartens had to be changed, for they superficially imitated foreign models, cost too much money, and served the needs only of rich families. In Tao Xingzhi's opinion, the way to change these kindergartens was to break away from blind imitation of foreign models. The kindergarten needed to be adapted to Chinese society, to be equipped with Chinese teachers, instruments, and toys while using only selected foreign materials. Tao believed that this kind of kindergarten, *pingmin youzhiyuan* (people's kindergarten), would be well received by ordinary people (Tao 1983, 1:619–25).

Tao's commitment to *pingmin jiaoyu* (people's education) and *xiangcun jiaoyu* (village education) was based on his philosophy of education, which transformed Dewey's model to conform with China's social conditions—and turned many of Dewey's principles upside down. The most drastic reformulation of Dewey's educational philosophy was Tao's proposal that "life is education," a reversal of Dewey's "education is life."[11] Other education reformers responded positively to Tao's proposals and actively participated in the experiment of "village education" and "people's education."

The establishment of village kindergartens was one of the most important programs in the movement. In 1927, Tao Xingzhi founded Xiaozhunang Shiyan Xiangcun Shifan Xuexiao (Xiaozhunang Experimental Village Normal School) outside Nanjing. In the same year, Tao with Zhang Zonglin and Xu Shibi founded the first village kindergarten in China—Nanjing Yanziji Kindergarten, where thirty children of peasants enrolled and three trainees from Nanjing Gulou Kindergarten undertook teaching. The curriculum of the Yanziji Kindergarten was similar to that of the Gulou Kindergarten, centering on seasons, weather, animals, plants, farming, games, customs, and children's health, and encouraging teachers to use the objects they found in the country as the focus of their teaching. The methods of teaching and administration were also flexible to the environment of the country, where children were required to engage in more outdoor activities than those in city kindergartens. In addition, the creators of the curriculum were fully aware of the fact that most children from peasant families would be forced to quit school and to undertake housework or to work in the fields as soon as they reached the age of seven or eight. In attempting to give these children more education, they designed the curriculum to teach children to read, and to train them in good habits, such as washing their hands before eating (He 1990, 161–62).

Obviously, the content and teaching methods in this kind of village kindergarten presented modern ideas in education, but institutionally they represented nonformal education. Because of the continuing problems of military obstruction and political intervention in the 1920s, it was very difficult for Tao Xingzhi and other educators to implement modern education practices within the national school system. For the purpose of creating a modern China by promoting modern education throughout the nation, Tao and his colleagues therefore gradually dedicated their energies to nonformal education, within which they carried out their education experiments. Meanwhile, these researchers exchanged their research findings and new ideas through the National Federation of Education Associations and scholarly journals, such as *Youzhi jiaoyu* (Early child education), founded by Chen Heqin in 1927, which later became *Ertong jiaoyu* (Education for children). These professional organizations and journals characterized this period of the kindergarten movement, indicating the mature integration of modern theories and Chinese practice in pre-school education.

CONCLUSION

By modern standards, China institutionally did not have a pre-school education system before the modern school system was announced in 1903. Kindergarten, as a new entity for early childhood education, became known to the Chinese education authorities later than other information about Western education. In the 1903 system, *mengyangyuan* was a substitute for kindergarten, and its curriculum represented the Chinese modification of Froebel's model. Confucian values, not Froebel's ideas, dominated its curriculum. For example, filial piety, one of the primary focuses in traditional education, remained a key subject in the *mengyangyuan* curriculum.

The Confucian feature of the *mengyangyuan* originated in the information on the kindergarten that came from Japan. Although mission kindergartens arrived in China before the kindergartens from Japan, both private practitioners and the education authorities obtained knowledge of the kindergarten from Japanese sources through either personal encounters or translated works. The Japanese version of the kindergarten, which already combined Confucian tradition with Froebel's design, was easily accepted by Chinese authorities. More important, the adoption of the Japanese model reflected the widespread idea of "Western learning for practical use and Confucianism for substance," which circulated among the late Qing court and the educated elite. It was not until the May Fourth Movement of 1919 that a drastic attack on Confucianism—along with other factors, such as anti-Japanese feelings and the changes in the direction of study abroad, as well as a campaign for promoting the Dewey Experiment in China—induced an intellectual and social demand for a more liberal education. Under these circumstances, the shift in the adoption of kindergarten models suggests that China was struggling for modernization and faced problems of cultural imitation.

Mission kindergartens did not play a significant role in the initial stage of the kindergarten movement, because religious practice conflicted with the interests of both the government authorities and the majority of the educated elite. Yet the rejection of the Japanese model and the change of attitudes toward Confucianism after 1919, to a certain extent, assisted in the growth of a number of mission kindergartens and the dissemination of Christian ideas. Then the fashion turned in favor of mission kindergartens, which attracted many rich people who sent their children not only for the pleasant environment, advanced equipment, and a better education, but also to announce their social position. However, the 1920s anti-Christianity movement reflected national attitudes toward foreign countries from another perspective. In regard to kindergartens, the new generation of education reformers criticized the blind imitation of Japanese and Western models and responded to the widespread push to "retrieve educational rights" from missionary schools in 1924 and 1925. In particular, in response to the dominant influence of missionary education on the training of kindergarten teachers, some reformers vigorously called for the closure of all mission normal schools in China, and believed that the action would encourage the development of Chinese kindergartens (Zhang 1985, 764).

However, compared to the reformers in the late Qing, these reformers represented a more mature attitude toward the Japanese and Western models, as well as toward mission education. They endeavored to avoid the two extremes of complete imitation and total rejection of other cultures. Fresh Western ideas— such as the child-centered curriculum, the individual's development, education in accordance with children's needs and natural instincts, and emphasis on games and play—were all included in their education experiments. Because of the political instability of the 1920s, Tao Xingzhi and other educators launched the movement of people's education outside the formal education system, and "village kindergartens" were part of that movement. In their opinion, the superficial adoption of Froebel's and Montessori's ideas concentrated only on the use of Western teaching material, toys, and equipment and ignored the essence of modern education theories which encouraged educators to create a type of kindergarten adapted to a particular culture and society. Their work in village kindergartens manifested their understanding of Froebel's kindergarten model. The curricula of the village kindergartens, as well as of those pioneering institutions like the Gulou Kindergarten, were designed on the basis of the Chinese society, customs, and daily life. "Ethical education" centered on behavioral attitudes of good citizenship rather than on filial piety and loyalty, and young children were taught through play and daily experience rather than through classroom instruction.

The reformers' experiments laid the foundation for the establishment of Chinese kindergartens. The curricula they designed were largely incorporated into the 1932 Standard Kindergarten Curriculum, which was further amended in 1936. This curriculum framework signaled the Chinese acceptance and demand for pre-school education on the one hand, and on the other it undermined what Tao Xingzhi and other pioneers did for modern pre-school education, as such priorities as loyalty to the government and religious practice were inserted into the kindergarten curriculum. Nevertheless, Tao Xingzhi and his colleagues significantly contributed to the transformation of the kindergarten, which was no longer simply an imported package from Japan and Western nations. As a new institution for pre-school education, the kindergarten was accepted as the first stage in a universal education, and the notion of the kindergarten was well-integrated with the scholarly research and intellectual movement of the time.

NOTES

I thank Mrs. Sheila Davies for reading a draft of this chapter.

1. In their memorandum to the throne in 1872, Zeng Guogan and Li Hongzhang advocated sending young children to America to study. The term *youtong* was used to refer to youths from thirteen to twenty years old, but primarily to those under fifteen. The memorandum said that after fifteen years of studying in America, those students would be only about thirty years old—the golden age to serve China. See Shu Xinchen, 1985, vol. 1, pp. 162–63.
2. In Japanese documents, the use of *baomu* is often related to the term *baoyu: bao* means to

protect; *yu,* to nourish. So, to protect and nourish young children were the objectives of the kindergarten. See Kuroda Shigejirou, 1969, p. 181.

3. Reynolds correctly points to the significant role of "Japanese terminology" in the introduction of new ideas and other modern elements into China (Reynolds, 1993). However, as well as this major Chinese intellectual debt to Japan, there was a strong foundation for China's preservation of Confucianism.

4. For the introduction and discussion of Wang Yangming's ideas about elementary education and the trends in education theories from the late Ming and early Qing onward, see Bai Limin, *Primers and Paradigms,* Ph.D. dissertation, 1993, chaps. 1 and 2.

5. In traditional China, primers for pre-school children were usually presented in rhymed form; also, popular poetry (such as the Tang poems) was often selected as teaching material. See Bai Limin, Ph.D. dissertation, pp. 17–32.

6. This theory was first presented in Zhang Zhidong's writing and was later crystallized as a slogan: "Chinese learning for the foundation, Western learning for application" (Zhang Zhidong, 1963, vol. 6, p. 3747).

7. In her *The Education of Women in China,* Burton translates the prospectus of the school and quotes missionary documents (Burton, 1911, pp 100–111). For Chinese documents concerning the school, see Zhu Youxian, 1986, vol. 1(B), pp. 885–907; and Zhu Jineng, 1935, pp. 129–31.

8. Allen's work was translated into Chinese by Ren Baoluo and published by the Society for the Diffusion of Christian and General Knowledge (S.D.K, Guangxue hui) in 1903. The information concerning mission kindergartens was recorded in vol. 10 (B), p. 42. With the exception of this information, no statistical report of mission kindergartens appeared in Chinese writings before 1920.

9. These numbers are based on Allen, *Wudazhou nüshu tongkao,* vol. 10(B), p. 35; China Education Commission report, *Christian Education in China,* New York, 1922; and the investigation conducted by the first Nanjing national school in 1924.

10. In 1921, Nanjing Higher Normal School was upgraded to a national university—National Southeastern University.

11. Barry Keenan (1977) discusses Tao Xingzhi's ideas on education and Dewey's education philosophy.

REFERENCES

Ayers, William. 1971. *Chang Chi-tung and Educational Reform in China.* Cambridge, Mass.: Harvard University Press.

Bai, Limin. 1993. *Primers and Paradigms: A Comparative Approach to Understanding Elementary Education as a Pre-condition for Industrialization.* Ph.D. dissertation. Melbourne: La Trobe University.

Burton, Margaret E. 1911. *The Education of Women in China.* Fleming H. Revell Company.

Chan, Wing-tsit. 1963. trans. *Instructions for Practical Living and Other Neo-Confucian Writings by Wang Yangming.* New York: Columbia University Press.

Chen, Baoxuan. 1971. *Zhongguo jindai xuezhi bianqian shi* [The evolution of the Chinese modern school system]. Beijing wenhua xueshe.

Chen, Hongbi. 1927. "Youzhi jiaoyu zhi lishi" [A history of early child education]. In *Jiaoyu zazhi* 19, No. 2.

Chen, Jerome. 1979. *China and The West, Society and Culture, 1815–1937*. London: Hutchinson of London.

Cihai. 1980. Reprint. Taiwan: Zhonghua shuju.

Diyici zhongguo jiaoyu nianjian (cited as DZJN). 1934. Zongqing tushu gongsi.

Fairbank, John K, and Liu Kwang-ching, eds. 1980. *Late Ch'ing, 1800–1911*, Part 2, Vol. 11. *The Cambridge History of China,* eds. Denis Twitchett and John Fairbank. New York: Cambridge University Press.

Gao, Mingkai, and Liu, Zhengtan. 1958. *Xiandai hanyu wailaici yanjiu* [A study of the borrowed words from other languages in modern Chinese]. Beijing: Wenzi gaige chubanshe.

He, Xiaoxia. 1990. *Jianming zhongguo xueqian jiaoyushi.* [A concise history of early child education in China]. Beijing: Normal University Press.

Jian, Bozhan, et al., eds. 1953. *Wuxu bianfa* [Wuxu reform]. Beijing: Shenzhou guoguang she.

Keenan, Barry. 1977. *The Dewey Experiment in China: Educational Reform and Political Power in the Early Republic.* Council on East Asian Studies, Harvard University. Cambridge, Mass.: Harvard University Press.

Kuroda, Shigejirou. 1969. *Meiji gakusei enkakushi.* Rinkawa shoten.

Lewis, Ida Belle. 1974. *The Education of Girls in China.* San Francisco: Chinese Materials Center.

Liang, Qichao. 1941. *Yinbinshi wenji* [Collected works of Liang Qichao]. Shanghai: Zhonghua shuju.

Lilley, Irene M. 1967. *Friedrich Froebel, A Selection from His Writings.* New York: Cambridge University Press.

Liu, Yusheng. 1960. *Shizaitang zayi.* [Miscellanies of Shizai Hall]. Zhonghua shuju.

Lutz, Jessie Gregory. 1971. *China and the Christian Colleges, 1850–1950.* Ithaca: Cornell University.

Reynolds, Douglas R. 1993. *China, 1898–1912, The Xingzhen Revolution and Japan.* Cambridge, Mass.: Harvard University Press.

Shapiro, Michael Steven. 1983. *Child's Garden.* University Park: Pennsylvania State University Press.

Shisan jing zhushu (cited as SSJZS). 1979. 2 vols. Reprint. Beijing: Zhonghua shuju.

Shu, Xinchen. 1927. "Zhongguo youzhi jiaoyu xiaoshi" [A short history of Chinese kindergarten]. In *Jiaoyu zazhi* 19, No. 2.

———. 1981. *Zhongguo jindai jiaoyushi ziliao* [Reference material of Chinese modern education]. 2d ed. 3 vols. Beijing: Renmin jiaoyu chubanshe.

Soothill, William E. 1924. *Timothy Richard of China.* London: Seeley, Service & Co. Limited.

Tao, Xingzhi. 1983. *Tao Xingzhi quanji* [The completed works of Tao Xingzhi]. 6 vols. Hunan: jiaoyu chubanshe.

Wang, Shuhuai. 1965. *Wairen yu wuxu bianfa* [Foreigners and the reform movement of 1898]. Niangang: Zhongyang yanjiuyuan jindaishi yanjiusuo.

Whitbread, Nanette. 1972. *The Evolution of the Nursery-Infant School.* Boston: Routledge & Kegan Paul.

Xu, Shen. 1977. *Shuowen jiezi* (100–130 A.D?). [The explanations of characters and words]. Beijing: Zhonghua shuju.

Yuan, Xitao. 1968. "Wushinian lai Zhongguo zhi chudeng jiaoyu, 1872–1921" [Chinese elementary education between 1872 and 1921]. In Liang Qichao et al., *Wanqing wushinian lai zhi zhongguo, 1872–1921* [China between 1872 and 1921]. Hong Kong: Longmen shudian.

Zhang, Xuemen. 1969. *Youzhi jiaoyu wushinian* [Fifty years of early child education]. Taiwan: Shudian.

Zhang, Zhidong. 1963. *Zhang Wenxianggong quanji* [The complete works of Zhang Zhidong]. 6 vols. Beijing: Chuxue jinglu, 1937; reprint, Taibei: Wenhai.

Zhang, Zonglin. 1985. *Zhang Zonglin youer jiaoyu lunwen ji* [Zhang Zonglin on early child education]. Hunan: Jiaoyu chubanshe.

Zhu, Jineng. 1935. "Diyici ziban nüxuetang" [The first time to establish a female school]. In *Dongfang zazhi* 32, No. 3: 129–31.

Zhu, Youxian. 1986. *Zhongguo jindai xuezhi shiliao* [Reference material of modern Chinese school]. Shanghai: East China Normal University Press.

Chapter 7 Preschool Education in Poland

Bogna Lorence-Kot and Adam Winiarz

Three political partitions, the last of which ended independence in 1795, shaped Polish pre-school education and fashioned Polish entry into the modern world. Poles began theorizing about pre-school education prior to their loss of independence and continued to do so more fervently after the shock of the First Partition in 1772. Fear of losing independence caused progressive Poles to focus and act upon innovations which prior to 1772 had been of interest to only a handful of individuals. Soon, all Polish leaders agreed that they had to protect their nation against further dismemberment but disagreed on how to do that. The conservative majority believed that the best defense was in retrenching tradition. In contrast, an influential progressive minority (which included the last king of Poland) believed that the nation could survive if its young were instilled with a spirit of intense national loyalty according to Enlightenment precepts emanating from France.

Division between native style and foreign innovation as formulas for national identity has had a long history in Poland: it preceded the First Partition and remained active throughout the period of foreign domination. The First Partition illustrated Poland's internal weakness, suggesting its lack of resilience in a rapidly changing world. Yet those who opted for the adoption of foreign models found it extremely difficult to inculcate novel child-rearing and educative models into Polish society because they had to contend with two conflicting factions. On one side were the occupying powers who sought to absorb, not advance, the Poles; on the other side was a society which lagged behind western European developments in every way, including liberal ideology (Szacki, 1994). At the beginning of the nineteenth century, Poles were barely on the threshold of economic modernization. Yet politically they clung, for a long time, to their native identity, which was that of the eighteenth-century system known as the Noble Commonwealth. Control by foreign governments further complicated the tension between native and foreign culture; Poles could never assume that their rulers were acting in Polish best interests (although they might have been, intentionally or not). Regardless of the specific reasons for Polish acceptance or distrust of foreign models in any given period, Polish historians of education are quick to acknowledge their country's connection to western European theory and method. They also want it known, however, that Poles have never been blind followers—they have adopted only that which has suited their purpose.

THEORIES AND SOURCES

European Enlightenment theories on natural education formed the genesis of Polish thought about children and pre-school. Imported by those rare individuals who had traveled or studied abroad, these theories did not easily propagate among the bulk of nobles who believed they were already living in the best of possible worlds. Still, the fact that such knowledge was sought suggests a viable audience for innovations, although there was disagreement about which ideas to adopt.[1] Prior to discussions about change, education in Poland applied almost exclusively to noble boys over the age of seven. These students learned by rote, because children were viewed as passive vessels whose task was to receive knowledge from wise and powerful adults.[2] Allusions to pre-school education at home appeared as early as the second half of the eighteenth century and, under the label of *elementary education,* were touted as the necessary first step to all schooling.

In 1773, the National Commission on Education, Poland's first ministry, stressed the connection between upbringing at home and successful schoolwork. Establishment of the commission resulted from the First Partition, and in that context it represents a politically motivated campaign to alter Polish society before it succumbed to further dismemberment. Its activity was terminated by the Second Partition, in 1793. The commission's public effort to reform and nationalize education was matched in the private sphere by an intense education campaign directed at parents, and specifically at mothers. Women were identified as primary caretakers of children, à la Rousseau, and were called upon to serve their own best interests as well as those of their families and the nation— by rearing children affectionately and tendentiously toward civic responsibility and patriotism (Lorence-Kot, 1985). Antoni Popławski, who won the commission's competition in 1774 for a plan to reform Polish schooling, said "public education builds on an existing foundation. The seed of bad and good is to be found in home care" (Popławski, 1957, 137).

Popławski had impressive credentials as a member of that small group of Poles who tried to reform education according to Enlightenment principles. In 1740 Stefan Konarski, a Piarist priest, introduced Polish educational reform by opening the Collegium Nobilium, a modern school intended to educate an elite noble group which, he hoped, would in turn reform Polish society. Popławski was later appointed professor at the collegium, which aimed to attract the sons of the most powerful nobles, known as magnates. This group tended toward cosmopolitanism which left it open to influences from abroad, unlike the more numerous, lesser nobles whose nativism resisted innovation.[3] However, that simple equation was changing during the eighteenth century because ideology began replacing estate as the determinant of allegiance. "His (Konarski's) tactic was to make the college exclusive, thereby establishing it as the arbiter of Polish education. . . . He did not permit corporal punishment and forbade punishment undertaken in anger, citing Locke as his authority" (Lorence-Kot, 1985, 83).

Within the faction which sought to nationalize education, the influx of new pedagogical ideas from the West forced discussion about Poland's existing education system and called for decisions about what children ought to be taught and when education should begin. Debate revealed that one group, which included Adam Kazimierz Czartoryski and Ignacy Massalski, wanted education to begin as early as the age of four, while another, which included Antoni Popławski and Grzegorz Piramowicz, favored natural and unhampered play along with cognitive development for pre-schoolers. Prince Adam Czartoryski was a pillar of the patriotic reform party, a member of the National Commission on education, and so progressive as to advocate education for girls (*Polski Słownik Biograficzny*, Krakow, 1938, vol. 4). Ignacy Massalski, bishop of Wilno, was a Russian agent and opposed political reforms. He was the first president of

the National Commission on Education, but was removed from office for steal-
ing educational funds. He was hanged by a Warsaw mob during anti-Russian
agitation in 1794 (*Słownik Historii Polski* Warszawa, 1969). Grzegorz Piramowicz, Ph.D., who was a member of the National Commission on education,
served as secretary of the Society for Elementary Textbooks and edited the texts.
His primary interest was in educating small children, particularly peasant children (*Polski* Słownik Biograficzny, Wrocław, 1981, vol. 26). Popławski's insistence on children as primary actors in their own education prescribed a process
driven by children's curiosity about their surroundings. He believed that sensory investigation by children led to experiences which developed their intellect,
naturally.

The first methodological tract on the subject of pre-school education, *A New
and Easy Method for Teaching Writing and Reading to Girls along with Instructions
for Teachers* (*Sposób nowy, najłatwiejszy* . . .), by Maksymilian Propkowicz, appeared in 1790. This guide stressed the natural and psychological need of children to play and move; however, the author did recommend that children be
systematically instructed to read and write before the age of six. Most Poles
thought the very idea of educating girls preposterous, even though the National
Commission on Education was formulating plans to include girls in its national
agenda. But the commission did not represent the will of the majority; it had
been founded by the king and his progressive party. The majority was content
with the status quo, which consisted of religiously controlled education for noble boys, and the conviction that parents were solely responsible for pre-school
care. This meant that specialists were to concentrate on advising parents (Propkowicz, 1790).[4]

Dymitr Michał Krajewski supported Popławski's combination of work and
play. He derived his ideas in the course of home teaching the sons of wealthy nobles. In *Games for Teaching Children* . . . (*Gry nauk dla dzieci* . . .), published in
1777, he postulated a child psychology based on children's movement, their desire to manipulate concrete objects, and their natural need to play. He warned
adults against any form of coercion and urged them to adopt a posture of indifference toward children's games, reasoning that the intrusion of adult influence
on children's spontaneous activities would be disastrous. Noting the short attention span of his charges, Krajewski also warned adults not to force children
to continue to play after they had lost interest.[5] Krajewski challenged Rousseau's
proposal to remove children from parents and isolate them from social influe-
ences. In 1784 he countered *Emile* with his own novel, *Podolian Girl Raised in
the State of Nature* . . . (*Podolanka wychowana w stanie natury* . . .), which urged

close contact between parents and children. Krajewski saw that relationship as primary in fostering education and intellectual as well as moral development. He expected parents to act according to conscious design intended to stimulate their children's most valuable traits of character, mind, and heart.

The link Krajewski made between children's early years and subsequent educational success represented the thinking of most late eighteenth-century Polish pedagogues who, despite ideological differences, agreed on the importance of the parental role in producing successful individuals, committed to their nation. That meant that with respect to civic education children would be led instead of leading. In 1771, on the eve of the First Partition, Rousseau pointed out that although the Poles could never match their neighbors militarily, they could maintain their identity. He wrote, "Children can be inspired to love their nation and its laws through play and through institutions which while appearing inconsequential to unthinking people, shape the heart into forming indissoluble bonds" (Rousseau, 1771, 188).

Rousseau's advice was realized during the nineteenth century when Polish educators, while remaining open to pedagogical innovation, focused on national goals. It was not possible during this period for Poles to view education apart from the national agenda because independent evolution of Polish pre-school education had ended with the Third Partition of Poland in 1795. The groundwork which had been laid during the eighteenth century had prepared Poles to cope with the loss.

PRE-SCHOOL EDUCATION IN PARTITIONED POLAND (1795–1918)

The Poles continued developing pre-school education during Poland's 123 years as the frontier regions of three great states. Until 1863 they did so against the backdrop of armed struggle. First they rose up against the Russians in 1830, and were defeated. In 1846 they took up arms in the free city of Kracow and western Galicia and were crushed by the Austrian army and its allies, the Polish peasants. In 1848 Prussian authorities squelched unrest in the Grand Duchy of Posen. The final insurrection of 1863 was put down by the Russians with great difficulty. This was the last resort to arms, because the Poles changed direction following the insurrection (Leslie, 1983). They relinquished armed struggle in favor of "organic" work meant to improve society, despite the presence of occupiers. To maintain their national culture, the Poles placed a high priority on education and developed systems of secret learning to augment, or possibly nullify, their children's Prussian and Russian schooling. Pre-schools provided the first layer of that national education, but they served only a small number of children. According to calculations by Adam Winiarz, derived from a survey of printed and archival sources, about 5 percent of all Polish children were pre-schooled in the first half of the nineteenth century and approximately 20 percent in the second half.[6]

The politics of a country under such completely segmented domination were necessarily limited, and any latitude that existed was complicated by the fact that Polish propertied classes, along with the Catholic Church, often found common cause with the occupiers in trying to stave off radicalism (Leslie, 1983). Nonetheless, regardless of their internal ideological and economic divisions, Poles continued to think of themselves as a nation and fought attempts at acclimation to Prussian or Russian culture by covertly educating their children in Polish culture. The Catholic Church provided the screen behind which national culture was fostered through the combination of Polish language, history, and Catholic symbols which were alien enough to elude Protestant and Orthodox bureaucrats. Throughout the struggle, class differences were clearly delineated, so that it was inconceivable that the child of even a déclassé noble living in urban poverty could attend the same school as a poor or orphaned child. For the most part, children of the poor received charitable physical care, while children of the "better" people were educated (M.G., 1881).

Prussians viewed assertions of Polish identity as a challenge to what they believed to be a permanent conquest. Consequently, having begun with a brief period of non-interference, they soon embarked on a campaign to strip Poles of their identity, a process which included numerous political and legal obstacles to pre-school education (Leslie, 1983). In a sea of restrictions, religious orders enjoyed the widest latitude; therefore, it fell to them to organize that pre-school care. The Sisters of Mercy opened day-nurseries in Poznań, Bydgoszcz, Środzie, Kościanie, Kórnik, and Zduny. Until the middle of the nineteenth century, private entities found it almost impossible to operate child-care centers, despite the 1839 ministerial order which encouraged their establishment. Practical implementation was nullified by stringent requirements which allowed only married women and widows of irreproachable character to care for children. Potential caretakers had to provide sufficient physical space which had to also meet health criteria. Next followed an extremely lengthy process of obtaining permission from the Prussian school authorities (Karwowski, 1918; Truchim, 1967).[7]

Child care provided by the Sisters of Mercy accommodated between twenty and one hundred children of the poor. Although the details of their program remain unknown owing to the paucity of sources, it is assumed that learning was religiously based and therefore probably limited to prayers, psalms, and catechism (*Przegląd Katolicki*, 1871). There are many unknowns with respect to preschool care in partitioned Poland. Terminology is the most problematic, because similar activities did not necessarily have similar or uniform labels across the three occupied areas. In general, the fact that the Poles were reluctant to send their children to Prussian or Russian pre-schools, for fear of endangering their national identity, led them to establish their own despite bureaucratic impediments and paucity of funds. It is said, for example, that Prussian pedagogues seldom missed an opportunity to prove Polish cultural inferiority to their Polish pupils (Trzeciakowski, 1970). Pre-school sites served practical needs but were, perhaps more important in the eyes of patriots, the first organized opportunity to inculcate native social identity. The charitably run Lublin day-nursery, which during the 1880s held clandestine classes for six-year-olds, is but one example of many (Kancelaria Gubernatora Lubelskiego, call #28). A Warsaw diarist recalled his secret schooling: "I remember the small room to which my mother took me each day early in the morning. We were taught to read in secret. Through a fog I remember the sight of police searching and finding hidden elementary books" (Poliński, 1939).

Most Poles supported and financed the child-care movement by raising funds through special drives, charity balls, and donations on the part of the wealthy (WAPL call #44). The term *day-nursery* was the first to be used, and it represented physical care of a philanthropic nature for lower-class children and orphans. That name lasted until the 1930s and was also used from the mid-nineteenth century onward to refer to Froebelian child gardens, which represented much more but, for numerous reasons, never received popular support among Poles. Pedagogically, they were viewed as too structured and potentially monotonous. Practically, they were costly and required trained personnel. But their biggest liability, particularly in Prussian Poland, was that they were German, and that officials utilized them in attempts to rid children of their Polish identity. It is difficult to delineate boundaries between various types of pre-schooling because so much depended on the training and methodology of personnel who might not have used accurate labels—for political or other reasons (Dawid, 1892a, 1892b). The term *przedszkole,* which literally means "pre-school," appeared in the 1930s and is used currently to represent the care and education of children between the ages of three and six within the context of the national education system.

Despite the unhelpful climate created by the Prussians, some Poles, like August Cieszowski, pushed for proliferation of pre-school care. His influential

About Village Day-Care (*O ochronach wiejskich*) proposed a network of rural day-nurseries to be financed by the state and, in addition, state training of child-care workers in order to ensure quality (Hellwig, 1978).[8]

Rural schooling took on political overtones in all partitioned areas. In 1836 the Polish Democratic Society issued a manifesto proposing that peasants be won over to the national cause by giving them freeholds to their farms. The Poles did not act, but the Austrians did in 1848, when they granted freeholds by imperial decree. In 1864 the Russians similarly outmaneuvered the Poles (Leslie, 1983). Another proponent of rural child care, Edmund Wojciech Bojanowski, preferred action to words and founded the Order of the Handmaidens of the Immaculate Mother of God in 1850, for the purpose of forming a network of day-care centers (Trentowski, 1970). Soon, the network extended operations to the other occupied Polish areas. Day-care centers satisfied several social concerns by undertaking the care of peasant children in a religiously nationalistic atmosphere, even as they relieved Polish landowners of financial responsibility for children of their employees (Wójcik, 1978). But Bojanowski wanted the nuns to provide much more than religious and moral training; he recommended games, physical exercise, and attention to intellectual development (Karwowski, 1918; Truchim, 1967).

Almost simultaneous with the emergence of the Order of the Handmaidens came a ban on Froebelian kindergartens because Prussians judged Froebel's insistence on the equality of all children to be conducive to forces destructive to politics and religion (von Meysenburg, 1960). The result was that the entire care of Polish children, under the Prussians, was left to the Catholic Orders of Mercy and the Handmaidens.

That situation changed in the 1860s when Prussians decided not only that Froebel's system was not inimical to Prussian interests, but that it could serve them. They relaxed their hold for a while, which meant that the Poles, who had been restricted in all activities, could build their own national network of pre-school sites (Truchim, 1967). Three Froebelian kindergartens had opened in Poznań by 1869, but child care took on political overtones again when Prussians embarked on an anti-Polish campaign whose apogee came shortly after German unification in 1871. Known as the *Kulturkampf,* the movement excluded religious orders from managing educational institutions (Karwowski, 1918). In addition, privately run sites were subjected to rising levels of qualifications which prescribed graduation from the Institute for Pre-School Education in Berlin and mandated testing in German language proficiency.

Despite continued obstacles and periodic attempts to germanize the Poles, pre-school education kept growing and evolving. By 1905, in Poznań alone there were ten day-nurseries and pre-schools, while in the countryside the conservative Landowning Women's Society funded covert day-nurseries situated on their estates or in Catholic parishes (Truchim, 1967). The society was registered with the Prussian authorities but was limited by them to activities pertaining to social and economic matters. The group violated that mandate by infusing peasant children with a brand of patriotism which served its own class interests (Zjednoczone Stowarzyszenie Ziemianek, call #232, book #2, 1906; Walewska, 1909). In 1911 the society initiated a one-year course for nursery-school teachers in Toruń. The quality of programs in the day-nurseries varied and their facilities were poor. S. Małecki described one site in his memoirs: "The nursery was in a large room adjoining the garden. Two thirds of the room were occupied by wide stairs which almost reached the ceiling and upon them sat the children listening to stories. When it came time for their nap, instead of lying down they put pillows on the higher stairs and thus slept sitting. They brought their own pillows" (Malecki, 1959, 42).

Although the Poles living under Austrian authority faced similar difficulties until 1867, when official control slackened, they had other problems. In 1846 Polish peasants murdered over one thousand of their landlords, and in 1848 they assisted Austrian authorities against Polish insurrectionists. Subsequently, landlords decided that the antidote to peasant discontent lay in active assistance through educational programs. Beyond serving immediate class interests, the programs purportedly served to advance the national cause (Sandler, 1959). Unlike the Prussians, the Austrians viewed Galicia as a province whose loss would not be critical to the empire; for that reason, the use of the Polish language, along with other emblems of national identity, were not seen as inimical to essential "Germanness" (Leslie, 1983). In 1848 the Kraków Charitable Society established a separate section for pre-school care and formulated a project for its first proposed site. Two years passed before the authorities gave permission, and only a handful of sites opened in the next few years (Łętowski, 1952). They were run by religious orders who provided physical care and inculcated piety and obedience along with habituation to work.

Polish activism quickened after 1867 when the Austrians allowed the Poles some autonomy in education. By the following year an article in the journal *School* (*Szkoła*) was promoting Froebelian kindergartens as vehicles for the active development of children (Beczalski, 1868). Austrian authorities, having been influenced by fervent Froebelians, enfolded existing pre-school sites into the elementary education system and proposed their spread to the countryside, claiming that society needed "institutions for the propagation, care and education of children who were not yet required to attend school"(Buzek, 1904, 53). A ministerial directive made clear the distinction between day-care, whose task was to promote good hygiene and work habits in poor children, and kindergartens, where the creative and intellectual capabilities of children were developed through play, song, and the study of objects (Buzek, 1904).

The first Froebelian kindergartens in Austrian territory opened in conjunction with newly established teacher seminaries for women, whose graduates ran the kindergartens after completing a ten-month Froebelian course in Kufstein (Kostecki, 1875). By 1875 Lwów, Przemyśl, and Kraków each had a kindergarten as well as year-long courses for kindergarten teachers. Because kindergartens had not proliferated, however, candidates from these teacher training schools faced poor job prospects. Polish preference was to support day-nurseries run by religious orders and philanthropic societies, which guaranteed twelve-hour care, one meal, catechism lessons, and handwork (Sandler, 1959; C.K., 1897). When the Kraków Nursery School Society and the Lwów Society for Christian Nurseries tried to modernize their systems in the 1880s they failed. Instead of accomplishing their goal, they provoked a public outcry that nurseries, especially kindergartens, loosened family ties (*Reforma*, 1884; B.a., 1895).

What did the accusers mean when they spoke of loosening family ties? Did they associate modern, child-oriented, government-sponsored institutional development of children's capabilities with alienation from Polish identity? Perhaps so, because families sustained and inculcated that identity in all those generations living under foreign rule in Poland. It has been said that during the nineteenth century Poles began overprotecting their children, and that they cocooned them into an educative formula which consisted of Catholic nationalism and preoccupation with the past (Archiwum Zamoyskich, call #108, no. 18, 1801–1823; Kowecka, 1989).

The advance of pre-school education in Austrian Poland was engineered by women's work as teachers and consciousness-raising activists. These designations of women's work were also observed in the other partitions. The first day-care employees were male; women did not appear on the scene until the 1840s, at which time they totally displaced the men, who were drawn to easier and better paid work in developing industries. Day-care work was hard and often involved twelve-hour days, but it was the only available work for women (Okszyc, 1877; Łagowski, 1884). This period coincides with the first phase of the Polish women's movement, whose roots are in the loss of political independence. The policy makers continued to be male until the 1870s, when women took over and kept the field vital through contacts with western Europe. That change coincides with the second phase of the women's movement. Adrift from their traditional role, numerous women were forced to fend for themselves because their men had lost their mooring, or were engaged in the struggle for independence, or had left the country. The absence of men in public and private roles accounts, in part, for the entry of Polish women into public life. For example, early on in the struggle against Russian occupation, over 9,000 men emigrated following the failure of the 1830 uprising. Later in the century, emancipation of peasants in Austrian and Russian Poland led to confiscations and loss of property among the gentry, which, in turn, set the foundation for industrialization and urbanization of Polish society. As a result women of the aristocracy were thrust out of their sheltered country estates when families lost land and men were exiled to Siberia. Raised only for marriage, these women had to find ways to support themselves and migrated to towns in droves, seeking employment (Lorence-Kot & Winiarz, unpublished).

Many women—including Barbara Żulinska, Natalia Cicimirska, Maria Jaworska, Helena Czaporowska-Wójcik, Frederyka Grotowa, Maria Pogorzelska, Aleksandra Gustowiczówna, and Maria Ida Schatzel—advanced Polish Education in Galicia by practical and theoretical contributions (Wróbel, 1967). They maintained contact with western Europe by sending scouts. In 1905, Żulinska visited kindergartens in Berlin, Prague, Leipzig, Dresden, Paris, Lausanne, Vienna, and Warsaw, and later Cicimirska traveled to reconnoiter kindergartens in Belgium, France, Switzerland, and Germany (Wróbel, 1939). When compared to western European accomplishments in the area of pre-school education, Polish accomplishments were substantive both with respect to theory and practical implementation. On the eve of World War I, 32 kindergartens and 194 day-nurseries using Froebel's method were operating in Austrian Poland. Interest in Maria Montessori and Gustowiczówna's trip to Rome to learn the method indicates Polish openness to innovations in this field (Gustowiczówna, no date).

Russians controlled the largest number of Poles through an entity called the Kingdom of Poland. It may be surprising to learn that in contrast to Austrian and Prussian areas, Russian Poland was socially and economically far more dynamic. Polish activism was due, in part, to Russian political and economic backwardness (Staszynski, no date). Early development of pre-school education stemmed from initial Russian inattention to it. That inattention changed when secret schooling developed and Russians understood that pre-schooling was part of the battle over identity. Prussians had grasped this at the outset. Poles under Russian rule were also more committed to armed struggle, which meant that the kingdom's social climate correlated child-care and education with national ser-vice—leading to intense involvement by laypersons. In contrast to Prussian Poland, the kingdom's religious organizations played a minimal role in pre-schooling. Poorly educated, the kingdom's clergy were subject to greater repres-sion; unlike the Prussians, who wanted to maintain relations with the Vatican and who valued European opinion, Russians had no such scruples. They sent priests to Siberia for engaging in any kind of nationalistic activity. After sup-pressing the 1863 uprising, Russians deported over 1,000 clergy members to Tunka, in eastern Siberia (Urban, 1966; Dylągowa, 1983; Olszewski, 1984).

Institutional child-care emerged out of the Warsaw Welfare Society which was founded in 1814. In 1838, the Society created a section for the Protection of Small Children. The following year the section opened its first day-care, which accommodated 120 children (Moliere, 1965; *Wiadomośći Handlowe,* 1838). Te-ofil Nowosielski, who had earlier traveled abroad to study day-care in Austria, Bohemia, and Germany, ran the facility. Nowosielski knew Froebel's method and respected it, but he chose to run the Warsaw site according to Jan Swoboda and Leopold Chimanie because he thought that their methods better suited Polish needs (Moliere, 1968; Sandler, 1968). Public interest and the volume of applicants led to the opening of more sites, which in the next five years were accommodating 450 children (*Tygodnik Ilustrowany,* 1889). Nowosielski had hoped to organize systematic teacher training but was unable to do so; even among his own workers there were few potential child-care specialists. Warsaw day-cares accepted children of working parents, who were required to pay for the cost of meals. The children spent ten hours playing, talking, singing, en-gaging in physical activity, and doing some practical work (Sandler, 1968).

Many cities followed the Warsaw example. Kalisz opened a day-care in 1844 and in Lublin, the Child Welfare Society opened two by 1853. In the next two years Płock, Biała Podlaska, and Kielce all joined in (Kępski, 1990; *Zdanie sprawy z czynnosci . . . za rok 1857,* 1858; *Zdanie sprawy z czynnosci . . . za rok 1858,* 1859).

By 1857, the proliferation of day-cares prompted the overview board for philanthropic organizations to issue the first set of Polish instructions for ad-ministrators and staff involved in day-care (Wydział Spraw Wewnêtrznych i Duchownych, part 3, vol. I, 1866). The instructions prescribed a religious and moral atmosphere, along with the need to condition children to their future of hard physical work, discipline, and obedience. Swoboda and Chimanie's influ-ence was pronounced in this format, which was quickly judged as outmoded by a public who had read recent translations of Froebel and Marie Pape-Carpentier. These developments prompted Ksawera Kuwiczyńska and Lucyna Mieroszewska to compile new texts.[9]

In the countryside child-care connected to efforts of Polish landowners to modernize the economy and intensify agricultural productivity. Cieszkowski's work was particularly influential in that context and was used as a handbook by Andrzej Zamoyski, Ludwik Górski, and Adam Golz, activist members of the Agrarian Society, which established the first village day-cares between 1858 and 1861 (*Rocznik Gospodarstwa Krajowego,* vol. 38, 1860). The Agrarian Society had formed a special day-care school committee, which, in cooperation with the Benedictine nuns, put together a course for child-care workers in Łomża. Candidates were young women at least twenty-four years old, single, healthy, and sound in their knowledge of Catholic tenets. They had to be able to read, write, count, have general knowledge equal to that resulting from an elementary education, and be able to teach all those household skills expected of women (*Rocznik Gospodarstwa Krajowego,* 1860). The course never materialized because the authorities dissolved the Agrarian Society in 1861, accusing it of propagating Polish patriotism—which, undoubtedly, it did.

Failure of the 1863 uprising against Russia halted development of village day-cares because their patrons, who had always been landowners, suffered repression and, more important, because tsarist emancipation of Polish peasants loosened and attenuated former bonds between manor and village. Landowners chose non-intervention with respect to villages and became indifferent to the needs of peasant children. Between 1864 and 1867 the number of day-cares fell from twenty-two to a handful (Sandler, 1959).

In the period of severe tsarist repression following the failed uprising of 1863, the one positive development was the growth of Froebelian ideas promoted by such publications as *Opiekun Domowy, Przegląd Pedagogiczny,* and, in particular, the positivist *Przegląd Tygodniowy* (Moliere, 1965). Adam Wiślicki, the latter's energetic editor and Froebelian activist, in 1868 pushed through a Froebelian section at a Warsaw day-care. Its success encouraged him to further action, and he managed to persuade Teresa Pruszak-Mleczkowa to open the first Froebelian kindergarten in Russian Poland (Moliere, 1965). She ran the school from 1870 until her death in 1885. Although the press described her school as "quite similar to that of Froebel's kindergartens," she in fact operated on a much broader level. In addition to the Froebelian agenda, she offered dancing lessons, horse-riding, and swimming for children up to the age of fifteen. Mleczkowa continually revised her method according to new trends in the field. Although she continued to rely on Froebel, she drew on Pape-Carpentier and other pedagogical literature (*Kronika Rodzinna,* 1881; *Kłosy,* vol. 1, 1885; Moliere, 1965). Despite frequent financial problems and difficulties from the authorities, she also opened a section for handicapped children and trained pre-school teachers. In all her activities she promoted Polish patriotism.

Inspired by Mleczkowa's example, other women took up similar work in Warsaw, Lublin, Radom, and other towns, opening kindergartens and organizing courses for nannies and child-care workers. By 1896, Warsaw alone had several hundred Froebelian kindergartens (Osterloff, 1896; Wiślicki, 1868a; 1868b; Miaskowski, 1868; Wernic, 1873; Nowosielski, 1877). Most of these catered to two age groups of children: those aged four to five and the older children aged six to seven. Their daily program included cleanliness control, prayers, religious stories, physical education, singing, games, and other activities involving movement, talk, and simple hand work (Wróbel, 1967).

The women's movement to open Froebelian kindergartens was paralleled by day-cares for children of workers in the newly developing industrial areas of Russian Poland. These sites were "occupation-specific," meaning that railroad workers had their own day-nurseries, as did other trade occupations. Their conditions are said to have been better than day-nurseries run by charity organizations (*Przegląd Pedagogiczny,* 1900; Sandler, 1959).

At the beginning of the twentieth century the proliferation of urban daynurseries was being matched by similar developments in the countryside. Much of this rural activity was due to the work of Maria Kretowska, an activist member of the Federation of Landowning Women, which evolved in 1905 out of the fusion of the Association of Working Women and the Association of Rural Housewives (Walewska, 1909). The association's conservative social and pedagogical focus led it to adopt the outdated 1840s Cieszowski model, which defined day-cares as places where working parents left their children to be inculcated with moral and religious values which stressed duty toward God and employer. The obvious intent of village day-nurseries to perpetuate the existing social order was criticized by progressives such as the highly credentialed Maria Weryho, who had completed an advanced pedagogical program of study for women in St. Petersburg, a two-year Froebelian course, and a course in the newly developing field of physical education under the pioneering Dr. Peter Lesgafta. Weryho had observed Froebelian sites in Germany and Switzerland and in 1885 opened a Froebelian kindergarten in Warsaw. She began training teachers and in 1885 began editing *Games and Activities for Pre-school Children* (*Zabawy i zajęcia dla dzieci w wieku przedszkolnym)* as a supplement to a pedagogical magazine (Merzan, 1955; Górska, 1956).[10] She gave advice and information about new pedagogical publications along with examples of games and activities for children. She published stories and reading units, and she discussed the methodologies of story-telling, and artistic and technical skills (Wroczyński, 1965).[11] In many instances the supplement served as an instructional manual for pre-school education primarily because Weryho excluded some of Froebel's abstract and mystical allusions. Her work was extremely popular in Russian Poland as well as Austrian Poland—so much so, that in time her ideas about organization, programs, and methodology filtered into the field of pre-school education.

Weryho was active in overt as well as covert organizations. She lectured in a Sunday classes series, taught secret purportedly "vacation" courses for teachers, and held membership in the Women's Association for Peasant Education and the Polish and Lithuanian Women's Association. In 1903 she founded the underground Association for Pre-School Education with considerable help from her former pupil Jadwiga Dziubińska, who was already a prominent organizer of rural education programs (Weryho-Radziwiłłowiczowa, 1930). That same year she married Dr. Rafal Radziwiłł, a Polish Socialist Party sympathizer whose support and involvement in her work attracted additional activists like Stefania Sempolowska, Irena Kosmowska, Aniela Szycówna, Helena Orsza-Radlińska, and Maria Młodowska, all of whom conducted clandestine courses for pre-school teachers (*Dziecko*, 1913). In 1907, Weryho (who took the name Radziwiłłowiczowa when she married) managed to legalize the training of pre-school workers under the rubric of the Society for Pre-School Education. Henceforth she organized open training of pre-school teachers, and after independence her two-year course was transformed into the first National Seminary for Nursery-School Teachers. She was not alone in her activity, for similar courses were also conducted by Radziwiłłowiczowa's former pupils, Stefania Marciszewska-Posadzkowa and Celina Bronowska (*Dziecko*, no. 1, 1913).

Growing interest in the training of pre-school teachers was paralleled by initiatives to reform the entire system. In the Children's House (*Dom Dziecięcy*) opened by Stanisław Karpowicz in 1911, children planned and supervised their own activities and corrected their own errors (Michalski, 1968). Karpowicz used games to develop children's thinking and creativity, and by ensuring the natural flow of one activity into the next he guaranteed a continual supply of new concepts, information, and skills as well as experience in various social situations. Playing with blocks, drawing, and singing were not simply ways to fill time; they formed a logical sequence according to plans formulated by the children themselves. In addition to stimulating autonomy, the program instilled socialization principles by emphasizing the spirit of fraternity and justice. World War I halted Karpowicz's work, and after its conclusion he lacked the strength to continue his efforts. He never swerved from insisting on respect toward the child's personality and from demanding that children be treated as members of a specific social group (Wroczyński, 1965).

The Poles under Russian rule outdid the other territories with respect to preschool education because, as Norman Davies points out, they could not reconcile Polish patriotism with loyalty to an alien government as could the Poles under Austrian and Prussian rule prior to 1871. In Russian Poland, "If a person continued to speak Polish, to practice the Catholic religion, and to cultivate Polish friends, he was automatically suspect in the eyes of the political authorities. In order to prove an acceptable degree of reliability and to qualify for a responsible position, a Pole had to abandon his native language, even in his home, to reject Catholicism or Judaism for Orthodoxy, and to shun his relatives and friends. . . . [Poles] were condemned by circumstances to love their country, and to hate their rulers" (Davies, 1982, 108).

Despite severe repression, the Poles under Russian rule developed networks of child-care and education for pre-schoolers and initiated systematic training of personnel. They also created organizations and professional associations which popularized the newest developments in the field.

PRE-SCHOOL EDUCATION IN INDEPENDENT
POLAND, 1918–1939

In addition to sharing Europe's post-war problems, Poland had to integrate three societies whose structural and cultural separation precluded an easy shift to one organic whole. In the meantime, new difficulties arose—such as the Bolshevik menace from the east.

Despite the plethora of problems, both society and state authority focused on pre-school education through the new Ministry of Denominations and Public Education, whose first task was to remove existing pre-schools from their previous jurisdictions. The new, uniform system was headed by Maria Radziwiłłowiczowa, who enlisted her former pupils Stanisława Okołowiczówna and Lucyna Mołedzieńska-Wernerowa as school inspectors (Konarski, 1923).

It was decreed that all pre-school facilities would henceforth be called "nursery-schools," thereby eliminating the jumble of terms inherent in the pre-independence period. In 1921 Radziwiłłowiczowa published *Instructions for People*

Organizing and Running Nursery-Schools (*Wskazówki dla osób zakłądających i prowadzących ochrony)*, which covered all pre-school issues including hygiene and health-care services for children (Weryho-Radziwiłłowiczowa, 1930). The ministry organized special courses to upgrade the training and education of existing child-care workers, and it initiated teacher seminaries for new workers (Wróbel, 1967). Between 1923 and 1926 the ministry took over and transformed seven of the existing teacher training sites, the best of which, the Warsaw Seminary of the Friends of Pre-School Education, had already been nationalized in 1919. It was run by Helena Czerwińska, whom Radziwiłłowiczowa had recommended for the post (Wróbel, 1967). Czerwińska was appointed ministerial instructor for all Polish seminaries.

Because the new system lacked regulatory statutes, it was run by improvised ministerial directives which impeded development of pre-school networks. In 1926 formal supervision over day-nurseries was turned over to the Department of Elementary Schools within the Ministry of Religions and Public Education. This shift in control was unfortunate, because the department treated pre-school education as a subsidiary matter (Wróbel, 1967).

The nursery-schools which opened in the 1920s did so because of initiatives by territorial self-governments and by social or religious organizations. The impetus for rural day-nurseries came from the Associations of Village Housewives, the Rural Youth Association, and in some instances the Women's Civic Association. Old pre-independence sites which had been managed by the manorial class for the children of its servants were replaced by Mother and Child Hearths (*Ogniska Matki i Dziecka)*, which served all village mothers and children by providing child care and medical attention as well as dispensing dietary supplements (Woźnicka, 1972). Accompanying outreach staff taught basic hygiene to village families.

The Friends of Children Society opened day-nurseries in urban areas with a special focus on large industrial centers. That society had emerged in 1926 from the fusion of the Workers' Department for Child-rearing and Child-care with others of similar nature in southern Polish towns (Winiarz, 1988). Tomasz Arciszewski, the society's chairman, proclaimed its goals: "We want to educate children of workers to become conscious and creative members of society. We wish to stimulate them to solidarity with the working class and imbue them with respect for work, love of freedom, and willingness to sacrifice on behalf of the working class and the nation. We are shaping contemporary workers who will become national leaders, but first and foremost—free men" (*Społeczne wychowanie dziecka robotniczego w Polsce 1919–1928,* Warszawa, 1929, p. 9). Of the eleven day-nurseries which the society opened in two years, six were located in Lodz, whose textile industry was dominated by women.

The 1932 Diet passed a statute which placed day-nurseries within the education system but failed to explain their connection to elementary education (*Dziennik Ustaw Rzeczypospolitej Polskiej,* no. 38, entry 389, 1932). It said nothing beyond the fact that three-year-olds were to attend until they began their elementary education. Failure to mention who was responsible for the creation of day-nurseries was rectified five months later, when the Minister for Religious Denominations and Public Education issued a directive allowing private persons as well as various organizations to open pre-school sites throughout Poland (*Dziennik Ustaw Rzeczypospolitej Polskiej,* no. 38, entry 389, 1932). With respect to personnel, the statute proposed two-tiered training consisting of either four-year seminaries or two-year lycees but made future provisions for university education in an attempt to raise the level of the profession. In the meantime, higher education correspondence courses were organized for the academic year 1936–1937 (Woźnicka, 1972).

Despite the increasing organization of the system, pre-school education sites decreased even as the number of children grew. By this time, pre-schools run by churches and religious associations were something like charitable institutions, dedicated to poor children from the lowest classes. Those who could afford it sent their children to public pre-schools, financed by the national budget or territorial budgets, or to private pre-schools. The charitable pre-schools took care of basic needs, meaning that intellectual and emotional development was secondary. Public and territorial pre-schools had better-trained personnel and a full program which accentuated intellectual development. Between 1932 and 1939 the number of sites dropped from 1,920 to 1,659 as a result of the world-wide economic crisis (Sledziewska and Stołowski, 1953; *Mały Rocznik Statystyczny,* 1939). The number of autonomous sites declined, while charitable and religious day-care increased and changed character to become nothing more than physical care for the poorest of children, particularly those of the unemployed.

Pre-school education between the two world wars was shaped mainly by Western pedagogical thought, specifically that of Maria Montessori, Orvid Decroly, and the House of Children in Geneva (Żukiewiczowa, 1934; Merzan, 1955; Woźnicka, 1972). The Poles selected only some elements of Western ideas because they had to meet local needs but primarily because they were unwilling to relinquish those elements which reinforced the Polish aspects of education.

Failure to produce a final and binding document on pre-school education meant that the ministerial advice manual, issued in 1933, continued to serve as the official document (*Rady i wskazówki dla wychowaczyń w przedszkolach [ochronkach]*, 1933). The document had been prepared by experienced pedagogical activists who emphasized the need to shape emotions and develop children's curiosity. More specifically, the authors spoke of developing children's senses, cognitive abilities, and aesthetic sensibilities. They defined school activities as based on the various natural inclinations of children, and they addressed hygiene, physical education, manual activities—and gardening!

POLISH CHILDREN UNDER GERMAN AND
SOVIET OCCUPATION (1939–1945)

The Nazi-Soviet Pact of August 23, 1939, was the preamble to the occupation of Poland by its two aggressive neighbors, who cooperated until June 22, 1941, when Germany attacked the Soviet Union. Both invaders closed and destroyed schools in premeditated fashion. The Soviets soon began massive deportations of Poles to Siberia and Kazakhtstan. Statistical analysis of how many Polish children were sent to Russia and of how many died on the way from cold, hunger, and exhaustion is not possible. But estimates calculate that over 380,000 Polish children were deported, burned alive, poisoned with gas, killed with lethal injections, hanged, smashed in the head, torn apart, battered with rifles, and dowsed with icy water in winter (Królikowski, 1960; Bugaj, 1986). Newborns were drowned in buckets of water and killed in mothers' wombs. Infants and others incapable of work were treated as unproductive elements (Wnuk, 1961). Rudolf Hess, the former commandant of Auschwitz, said after the war, "young children were killed regularly because they were too young to work (Pilichowski, 1982, 27). Over 2 million Polish children under the age of eighteen perished. Two hundred thousand children were sent to Germany for the purposes of Germanization, and only 20 percent of them ever returned (Hrabar, 1969; Pilichowski, 1982). Under both occupations, Poland lost approximately 2.6 million children, that is, about 38 percent of all Polish human losses during the war. Also lost were educators. About 1,800 women pre-school workers were killed by Germans and 274 by the Soviets. Two-thirds of all classrooms were damaged, and 20 percent were totally destroyed.

These statistics reveal the scale of human and material losses sustained among the Polish pre-school population during World War II. Beyond the statistics, the immeasurable pain and suffering of children remains.

PRE-SCHOOL EDUCATION IN POLAND AFTER
WORLD WAR II

At the conclusion of World War II, the great powers concluded agreements which placed Poland under Soviet control until 1989. Pre-schools were reactivated in the midst of great physical destruction and psychological devastation. Just as had happened after World War I, it was territorial self-governments, social groups, institutions of work, and parents who got the system moving. In 1945, 1,423 pre-schools were already functioning, accommodating 74,000 children (Woźnicka, 1972).

In July 1946 the Ministry of Education affirmed the pre-war decree which had made pre-schools part of the overall education system. The decree defined the main goal to be "the creation of optimal conditions for the multi-faceted personal development of children, and their preparation for social life which serves as the foundation for all future schooling" (*Dziennik Urzêdowy Ministerstwa Oświaty*, 1947). Implementation of those goals was to be overseen by the pre-school section of the Ministry of Education. It was the section's experienced women, headed by Dr. Antonina Jurewicz, who rebuilt the pre-school education system (*Dziennik Urzędowy Ministerstwa Oświaty*, no. 7, entry 221, 1947).

Only about half of the 3,750 pre-school workers had proper credentials in 1945. Eight-week courses for new workers were begun in June 1945. Candidates were to be between eighteen and thirty years old and had to have completed seven grades. Courses for existing workers who lacked full qualifications followed, as did reinstitution of the seminary system which accepted girls between the ages of fourteen and eighteen who had completed elementary school (Woźnicka, 1972). Initially the seminaries followed the pre-war curriculum, but by the end of 1945 the program was cropped from four to three years in order to speed up completion at the cost of quality (*Dziennik Urzędowy Ministerstwa Oświaty*, no. 4, entry 176, 1945).

Content and methodology operated according to their pre-war mode. Because of the absence of a mandatory program, some teachers used the 1939 advice manual. The resulting mix contained principles and methods from Froebel to Montessori and Decroly and, at the other end of the spectrum, politically motivated importation of systems from the Soviet Union (Woźnicka, 1972). That mélange of tradition and the growing influence of Soviet trends was mirrored in the first project for a program prepared by the Ministry of Education in 1949.[12]

An eclectic system containing ideas from the West had no chance in a society increasingly shaped by communism, because it was contrary to Stalinist totalitarianism. Communist authorities understood the need to shape children as early as possible and did so through meetings, slogans, and various social activities which conveyed a dualistic world in which there was the party of good, consisting of socialist nations, and the other, consisting of evil capitalist societies. Of course, a cadre of educators was needed to implement these goals. Many of them did not hesitate to rip crosses and medallions from children's necks (Radziwiłł, 1992).

In the early 1950s the Ministry of Education created the National Center for Pedagogical Studies, which was to prepare a program for pre-schools (*Program tymczasowy "Zajęcia w przedszkolu,"* 1950). Political pressure ensured that the program was produced and published within a few months and that it reflected a soviet model. Educational materials became highly politicized and suffused with new terminology tailored to the goals of socialist upbringing. The leading role of the teacher as purveyor of socialist goals was greatly expanded, and children were to acquire their experience through work and play and the formation of appropriate concepts. Pre-schools were to serve as the foundation for children's integration into the socio-economic life of the nation.

Soviet pressure to sever native traditions was also evident in the handbooks given to child-care workers; Polish texts were replaced with texts by Soviet authors such as J. Kairow, B. Jesipow, H. Gonczarow, and T. Tieplow (*Dziennik Urzędowy Ministerstwa Oświaty,* no. 18, entry 248, 1950).

Domination of Soviet models diminished after the October 1956 civil disorders. But the following period of liberalization was too brief to allow for reconnection to Western pedagogy. More important, an entire generation of pre-communist educators retired during the Stalinist period. Many highly qualified women retired or passed on in the first decade following the war (Moliere, 1964). Temporary democratization provoked critical scrutiny of the pre-school system, most notably at the National Teachers' Conference held in November 1956. Clamor to remove communist indoctrination and replace it with pedagogical goals led the authorities, however reluctantly, to modify the tone of their political propaganda. A directive was issued in June 1958 which permitted a broadening of school networks (*Dziennik Urzędowy Ministerstwa Oświaty,* no. 10, entry 127, 1958). Day-care centers began to appear, as did kindergartens, which were open two to three times a week in the afternoons alongside elementary school. The Friends of Children Society, reactivated in 1957, initially limited itself to organizing and running day-care centers. The Rural Housewives Society did something similar in the villages (*Ogniska Przedszkolne,* 1967).

The political events of October 1956 facilitated the reform of pre-schools. Three-year secondary schools for training child-care workers were transformed into five-year pedagogical schools which to all intents and purposes were professional schools offering three groups of subjects: general educational, artistic/technical, and pedagogical (*Program przedmiotów pedagogicznych,* 1958). There was also a less ambitious program for pre-school workers instituted in Poznań in 1957 (*Wychowanie w przedszkolu,* 1958).

The 1961 *Decree About the Development of Education and Child Care* defined pre-school as the first step in the education system which began when children turned three years old. The decree obligated the authorities to speedily prepare a new program, which they did by 1963 (*Ustawa o rozwoju oświaty i wychowania w Polsce Ludowej,* 1961). It was accepted positively by child-care workers as a thorough and comprehensive document, although some complained that it was not sufficiently instructive (Woźnicka, 1972). The program remained in force for the next eleven years.

The climate of political liberalization promoted by Edward Gierek in the early 1970s opened the door to further criticism of pre-schools. An expert diagnosis appeared in the *Report on the State of Education in People's Poland,* which criticized content, method, and the over-emphasis on physical health and child-care worker functions and the relegation of intellectual development to mere satisfaction of children's curiosity (*Raport o stanie oświaty w PRL,* 1973). A new program in 1973 which introduced elements of teaching basics and new responsibilities for child-care workers appeared under the title *School Readiness and Preparation of Children for School Work.* It involved reading based on the grasp of at least twenty-two letters of the alphabet, which provoked strong reaction from parents and child-care workers who feared that emphasis on reading might end up dominating the child's primary occupation—which was play (*Program pracy wychowawczo-dydaktycznej z dziećmi 6-letnimi,* 1977).

A new program in 1981 proposed no fundamental changes, because it was a combination of the two documents issued in 1973 and 1977 (*Program wychowania w przedszkolu,* 1981). It survived the fall of communism by remaining in effect until 1992. Annulled in April 1992, it was replaced by three new programs. Independent programs have also begun to appear, but they must be approved by school authorities.

Unfortunately, political change has provoked an economic crisis, which has diminished the number of pre-schools because their previous sponsors can no longer afford to support them. In contrast to the school year 1986–1987, when over 51 percent of children aged three to six attended pre-school (in the villages the statistic was 39 percent), only 10 to 15 percent were attending in 1994 (Lewowicki, 1994). The drop which followed the fall of communism is unacceptable to Polish society, which assumes that economic improvement will lead to regrouping for pre-school education.

Viewed from a general historical perspective, Polish education theory and practice was drastically transformed by the force of Enlightenment thinking. In the course of analyzing children's nature, this school of thought gave children active and sometimes leading roles in their own educational process. Throughout the development of the pre-school, the novelty of giving children an active role was limited to children of the privileged. The children of the powerless continued to be treated as vessels whose content was to serve socially defined hierarchical needs. In the future, the appeal of Froebel's ideas, which included the equality of all children, was countered by traditional beliefs that equality of opportunity for all was unimaginable. The tension was not exclusively one of class, however, for even with respect to the children of the powerful it was difficult for adults to forgo the input and control which allowed them to mold children to their design. Allowing children to set the pace seemed to go against the grain of even the best-intentioned adults. The free flow of that tension between control and its withdrawal, which was articulated at the end of the eighteenth century in Poland, was interrupted by the partitions. These upheavals collapsed the forging of modern secular education, which focused on the individual, but in service to the Polish nation.

Henceforth, all theorizing and action bent to the will of the occupation forces, which the Poles countered with their determination to shape their children into good Poles. The need to influence the children obviated the possibility of giving them educative free rein. National needs superseded individual development. The power of the Catholic Church, which had been muted by the National Commission on Education in 1773, was harnessed to maintain Polish identity.

Direction of pre-school care did not differ dramatically among the partitions of Poland, except that it was most dynamic in Russian Poland. In all three areas, the will of the ruling governments—and, for Poles, political and class concerns—intruded on pedagogical concepts, even as economics shaped what was possible to implement. The occupiers, above all, wanted to maintain social stability, which in traditional fashion was seen as inherent in the forces of religion and social hierarchy. Most Poles did not quarrel with that, except they wanted to define for themselves the nature and place of religion, and of hierarchy. Not until after World War I, during Poland's brief sojourn with independence, did

Arciszewski articulate something resembling developmental human rights for the masses.

Polish pre-school education developed in three separate societies which evolved while boxed in by foreign control. The process which began in a free Poland managed to continue, despite the domination of foreign governments and the inherent conservatism of Polish society, because of those rare individuals who saw and acted beyond their own private horizons. Men initiated pre-school teaching and theorizing; women replaced them as teachers in the 1840s and became theorists in the 1870s. Poorly paid, they frequently lived in dire circumstance, but it was they who, by shaping numerous oppressed generations, maintained national identity. Throughout the period of foreign domination, Polish pedagogical thought never separated from its Western roots. Yet the Poles selected only those elements which suited their conditions, for pedagogical merit was always balanced by their conscious intent to raise Polish children in a national style despite opposition, which came first from the partitioners and subsequently from the Soviets. The Stalinist era discarded Polish pedagogical traditions but could not sever contact with the West. This contact currently continues without any politicized opposition, for in 1989 the Poles won the freedom to chart their own course. What will that bring? There are some in Poland who welcome reattachment to western Europe. Yet some fear that the highly touted European common home, which promises to be warm and comfortable, will prove to be that only for the rich—while the poor are left out in the cold.

NOTES

1. The Poles translated several foreign texts on pre-schoolers and produced two original ones. A translation of Jacob Ballxard's *A Parental Guide for the Physical Care of Their Children* was published in Warsaw in 1774 and eleven years later was followed by his *Dissertation on the Question of What Are the Leading Causes of Such Large Numbers of Children and What Are the Best and Simplest Means for Keeping Them Alive*. Theodor Wichardt's *Advice for Mothers* came out in 1782, and Cracow published Samuel de Meza's *Care of Body and Soul*, in 1790. Polish originals consist of Andrej Badurski's very long title, which refers to the maintenance of health, particularly in children, *Mowa rostrząsająca skutki powietrza stosowane albo niestosowane dla zachowania zdrowia i życia czlowieka w ogólnośći, a w szczególnośći dzieci z przedłoženiem przyzwoitego zaradzenia i ratunku*, Kraków, 1782, and Antoni Popławski's book on civic education entitled *O rozporządzeniu i wydoskonaleniu edukacji obywatelskiej*, Warszawa, 1775.

2. Until the Enlightenment, Polish parochial schooling was under the control of Catholic clergy who seldom did the teaching. Instead it was organists, many of whom had had to interrupt their own studies, who taught and kept standards low. The Church had no rival

in controlling minds and bodies since it had crushed the Reformation movement. The number of parochial schools declined in the seventeenth century as a result of wars with the Turks, Cossacks, Swedes, and Muscovites. This number increased during the Enlightenment, but the Second and Third Partitions interrupted that growth. Urban schooling was much more impressive, especially in towns like Thorn, Danzig, and Elblong, which had substantive Protestant elements. In the 1660s academic "gymnasiums," secondary schools with extra courses, began appearing in towns. Until 1773 most Polish middle schools were run by the Jesuit Order, with Piarists, Benedictines, and Communis Vitae managing the remaining schools. The Kracòw Academy ran ten lay secondary schools. Stanislaw Kot, *Szkolnictwo parafialne w Malopolsce XVI–XVIII w.* Lwow, 1912; S.K. Olczak, *Szkolnictwo parafialne w Wielkopolsce w XVI–XVIII w. (w świetle wizytacji kościelnych)*, Lublin, 1978.

3. Konarski was the first, in the series of reformers, who sought to westernize Polish education by revising the Piarist Order's curriculum and education philosophy. In vain, he waited for change, which began one year after his death in 1773. At this time the Jesuits were expelled from Poland and their wealth was used to create the National Commission on Education. The commission organized 2 universities, 74 secondary schools, and 1,600 parish schools. It sought to replace moribund and fragmented Catholic schools with a coherent state system imbued with secular, national ideals. The commission replaced Latin with Polish as the language of instruction, and promoted subjects such as modern languages and natural science in order to meet the practical needs of individuals and state goals. Girls were to be educated as well as boys. Hygiene and physical activity, art, and midwifery were encouraged no less than book learning. National holidays and national occasions were to be observed in addition to the traditional church festivals. Teachers were to be trained in state colleges and paid in accordance with a national salary scale. The Society for Elementary Books set to work in 1775 to provide a full range of textbooks for all grades, prepared by specialists at home and abroad (Davies, 1982).

4. Propkowicz (1738–1807) intended this text for the Order of Presentation, which taught girls in Kracòw. The school was established through private funds and intended for poor and orphaned girls above the age of three. Propkowicz came from a noble family and became a Piarist priest, and it was his order which spearheaded school reforms. He held various pedagogical positions and also worked as a governor. He has been referred to as theologian to His Majesty the King.

5. Krajewski (1746–1817) taught at the Warsaw Piarist College in 1763. He later worked as governor to several wealthy noble families and in 1782 became a prefect at the Collegium Nobilium in Warsaw and its rector in 1784. He was a member of the Warsaw Association for the Promotion of Education.

6. Adam Winiarz specializes in the history of education.

7. Child-care sites in Prussian Poland were called either *kinder-garten* or *warte-schulen.*

8. Cieszowski came from a wealthy noble family. He studied at the Jagiellognian and Berlin Universities, received a Ph.D. at Heidelberg, and then spent time in Paris, England, and Italy. Between 1848 and 1862 he was a delegate to the Prussian Diet. In 1867 he founded an agricultural college in Żabikòw, which the Prussian government closed ten years later.

9. The new texts were: *Dziecinne ogrody Frederyka Froebla,* Warszawa, 1856, and *Rady Praktyczne o poczatkowym wychowaniu dzieci, epoka od 1 do 5 roku,* Warszawa, 1856.

10. Three years later the publication changed its name to *Ogrodek Dziecięcy,* meaning "children's garden."

11. She wrote *Gimnastyka dla dzieci w wieku od lat 4 do 9, Podręcznik do użytku rodziców i wychowawców,* Warszawa, 1887; *Wychowanie przedszkolne,* Warszawa 1895; *Jak zając dzieci w wieku przedszkolnym,* Warszawa, 1900; *Nauka o rzeczach. Materiały do pogadanek z dziecmi dla użytku nauczycieli wychowawców,* Warszawa, 1906; *Wskazówki dla osob zakładających i prowadzących ochrony (z planami budynków),* Warszawa, 1921.

12. This project never appeared in print but is referred to in Woźnicka's *Wychowanie w Polsce Ludowej,* Warszawa, 1972.

REFERENCES

English terms translate as follows: call no. = sygnatura (sygn.); no. = nr.; entry = pozycja (poz.).

Archiwum Zamoyskich, sygn. 108, nr. 18. Akta tyczące sie wychowania i nauki synow Stanisława Zamoyskiego, 1801–1823, Archiwum Głowne Akt Dawnych w Warszawie (AGAD).

B.a. 1895. *Szkice pedagogiczne przez "Starego Pedagoga."* Lwów.

Bęczalski, E. 1868. "Ogródki wychowawcze Froebla." In *Szkoła.*

Bugaj, T. 1986. *Dzieci polskie w ZSRR i ich repatriacja 1939–1952.* Jelenia Góra.

Buzek, J. 1904. *Studia z administracji wychowania publicznego.* Lwów.

Cieszowski, A. 1922. *O ochronach wiejskich.* 4th edition. Poznań.

C.K. 1897. *Seminaria nauczycielskie męskie i zenskie Królestwa Galicji i Wielkiego Królestwa Krakowskiego w okresie 1871–1896.* Lwów.

Davies, N. 1982. *God's Playground: A History of Poland.* vol. 2. New York: Columbia University Press.

Dawid, J. W. 1892a. "Potrzeba bon Polek," in *Przegląd Pedagogiczny,* nr. 18.

———. 1892b. "W sprawie zakładow freblowskich," in *Przegląd Pedagogiczny,* nr. 21.

Dylągowa, H. 1983. *Duchowieństwo katolickie wobec sprawy narodowej (1764–1864).* Lublin.

Dziecko. 1913. Nr. 1.

Dziennik Urzêdowy Ministerstwa Oświaty. 1945. Nr. 4, poz. 176.

Dziennik Urzêdowy Ministerstwa Oświaty. 1947. Nr. 7, poz. 221.

Dziennik Urzêdowy Ministerstwa Oświaty. 1950. Nr. 18, poz. 248.

Dziennik Urzêdowy Ministerstwa Oświaty. 1958. Nr. 10, poz. 127.

Dziennik Ustaw Rzeczypospolitej Polskiej. 1932. Nr. 38, poz. 389.

Górska, P. 1956. *Paleta i pióro (wspomnienia).* Kraków.

Gustowiczówna, A. (no date). "System wychowawczy Marii Montessori," in *Czasopismo Pedagogiczne.*

Hellwig, J. 1978. *Działalność pedagogiczna Augusta Cieszowskiego.*

Hrabar, J. 1969. "Dziecko w hitlerowkim systemie zagłady," in *Zbrodnie hitlerowskie na dzieciach i młodzieży polskiej.* Warszawa.

Jachowicz, E. 1882. "Ochrony: Zakłady Sierot Warszawskiego Towarzystwn Doloroczyn-

ności," in Niedole Dziecięce, published by Friends of Children (Wydane Staraniem Mi-
tośnikow Dziecięceço Wieku), Warszawa, pp. 119–121.

Kancelaria Gubernatora Lubelskiego. 1907. Sygn. 28. Gubiernskij Policijmejster Lublin-
skomu Gubiernatoru ot 20 XI 1907 goda. Wojewódzkie Archiwum Państwowe w Lubline
(WAPL).

Karwowski, S. 1918. *Historia Wielkiego Księstwa Poznańskiego*, vol. 2, Poznań.

Kępski, Cz. 1990. *Lubelskie Towarzystwo Dobroczynnośći za rok 1858*. Lublin.

Kłosy, vol. 1, 1885.

Konarski, K. 1923. *Dzieje Szkolnictwa w byłym Królestwie Kongresowym 1915–1918*. Kraków.

Kostecki, A., ed. 1875. *Status tymczasowy dla seminariów nauczycielskich*. Kraków.

Kot, S. 1912. *Szkolnictwo parafialne w Małopolsce XVI–XVIII*. Lwów.

Kowecka, E. 1989. *W salonie i w kuchni*. Warszawa.

Krajewski, D. M. 1777. *Gry nauk dla dzieci służące do ułatwienia ich edukacji, przez które latwo
nauczyç sie mogą: poznawania liter, sylabizowania, czytania w polskim i francuskim języku,
formowania charakteru pisania, języków ze zwyczaju, historii, geografii i początkow artyt-
metyki*. Kraków.

———. 1784. *Podolanka wychowana w stanie natury, życie i przypadki swoje opisująca*.

Królikowski, L. Z. 1960. *Skradzione dzieciństwo*. London.

Kronika Rodzinna, 1881.

Łagowski, F. 1884. "Kobiety nasze wobec pedagogiki," in *Bluszcz*, nr. 37, 293; nr. 38, 303.

Leslie, R. F. 1983. *The History of Poland since 1863*. Cambridge: Cambridge University Press.

Łętowski, L. 1952. *Wspomnienia pamiętnikarskie*. Wrocław.

Lewowicki, T. 1994. *Przemiany oświaty*. Warszawa.

Lorence-Kot, B. 1985. *Child-Rearing and Reform: A Study of the Polish Nobility in Eighteenth-
Century Poland*. Westport, Conn.: Greenwood Press.

Lorence-Kot, B., and A. Winiarz. 1995. "The Polish Women's Movement until 1914," in
Women's Movements in Europe in the 19th Century: A Comparative Perspective. Unpublished.

Lubelskie Towarzystwo Dobroczynnośći. 1990. Sygn. 44. Wydział dochodów niestałych. Wojewódzkie Archiwum Państwowe w Lublinie (WAPL).

Małecki, S. 1959. *Wspomnienia z mojego życia*. Kórnik.

Mały Rocznik Statystyczny. 1939, Warszawa, p. 329.

Merzan, I. 1955. "Metoda Decroly'ego w polskich przedszkolach," in *Wychowanie w przedszkolu*, nr. 3.

M.G. 1881. "Zakład frebelowski," in *Kronika Rodzinna*, vol. 9.

Miaskowski, S. 1868. "Kwestia ogródków frebelowskich u nas," in *Bluszcz*, nr. 17.

Michalski, S. 1968. *Stanislawa Karpowicza myśl społeczna i pedagogiczna*. Warszawa.

Moliere, S. 1964. "Poglądy i działalność Marii Weryho na tle współczesnego stanu wychowania fizycznego małych dzieci," in *Roczniki Naukowe Akademii Wychowania Fizycznego*, vol.
3. Warszawa.

———. 1965. "Poczatki warszawskich placówek przedszkolnych (1838–1905)," in *Wychowanie w Przedszkolu*, nr. 7.

Nowosielski, T. 1877. *Pokój dziecinny. Podręcznik w duchu frebelowskim do użytku matek*.
Lublin.

Ogniska Przedszkolne. 1967. Warszawa.

Okszyc, J. 1877. "Proletariat kobiecy," in *Kronika Rodzinna*, nr. 18.

Olczak, S. K. 1978. *Szkolnictwo parafialne w Wielkopolsce w XVI–XVIII w. (w świetle wizytacji kościelnych)*. Lublin.

Olszewski, D. 1984. *Przeminany społeczno-religijne w Królestwie Polskim w pierwszej połowie XIX wieku*. Lublin.

Osterloff, W. 1896. "O kształceniu umysłowym dzieci w okresie przedszkolnym," in *Przegląd Pedagogiczny*, nr. 18, 19.

Pilichowski, Cz., ed. 1982. *Dzieci i młodzież w latach drugiej wojny światowej*. Warszawa.

Poliński, Jozef. 1939. *Z walk o szkołę polską. Wspomnienia*. Warszawa.

Polski Słownik Biograficzny. 1938. Vol. 4, Kraków.

———. 1981. Vol. 26, Wrocław-Warszawa-Kraków-Gdańsk-Lódz.

Popławski, A. 1957. *Pisma pedagogiczne*. Wrocław.

Program pracy wychowawczo-dydaktycznej z dziećmi 6-letnimi. 1977. Warszawa.

Program przedmiotów pedagogicznyc. 1958. Warszawa.

Program tymczasowy, "Zajęcie w przedszkolu." 1950. Warszawa.

Program wychowania w przedszkolu. 1981. Warszawa.

Propkowicz, M. 1790. *Sposób nowy, najlatwiejszy pisania i czytania panienen, razem z przypisami dla nauczycielek*. Kraków.

———. 1791. "O potrzebie i środkach zniesienia żebraniny w Polsce," in *Pamiętnik Historyczno-Polityczno-Ekonomiczny*.

Przegląd Katolicki. 1871.

Przegląd Pedagogiczny. 1900. Nr. 12.

Rady i wskazówki dla wychowawczyń w przedszkolach (ochronkach). 1933. Warszawa.

Radziwiłł, A. 1992. *O szkole, wychowaniu, i politice*. Warszawa.

Raport o stanie oświaty w PRL. 1973. Warszawa.

Reforma. 1884.

Rocznik Gospodarstwa Krajowego. 1860. Vol. 38.

Rousseau, J. J. 1771 [reprint 1966]. "Uwagi o rządzkie polskim," *Umowa społeczna*, ed. B. Baczko, Warszawa.

Sandler, B. 1959. "System Froebla w Galicji," in *Rozprawy z dziejów Oświaty*, vol. 12.

———. 1965. "Wychowanie przedszkolne i kształcenie wychowawczyń placówek przedszkolnych (1838–1905)," *Wychowanie w Przedszkolu*, nr. 7.

Śledziewska, I., and W. Stołowski. 1953. "Wychowanie przedszkolne w Polsce w latach 1918–1939," in *Materiały pomocnicze dla czynnych niewykwalifikowanych wychowawczyń przedszkoli*. Warszawa, file #2.

Słownik historii Polski. 1969. Warszawa.

Społeczne wychowanie dziecka robotniczego w Polsce 1919–1928. 1968. Warszawa.

Staszynski, E. 1929. *Polityka oswiatowa caratu w Krolestwie Polskim (od powstania styczniowego do I wojny swia ıwej)*.

Szacki, J. 1994. *Lib. ʼalizm po komunizmie*. Warszawa: Społeczny Instytut Wydawniczy Znak, Fundacja im. Stefana Batorego.

Trentowski, B. F. 1842 [reprint 1970]. *Chowanna czyli system pedagogiki narodowej jako umiejętności wychowania, nauki i oświaty, słowem wykształcenia naszej młodzierzy*, vols. 1 and 2. Wrocław.

Truchim, S. 1967. *Historia szkolnictwa i oświaty polskiej w Wielkim Księstwie Poznańskim 1815 – 1915*, vol. 1, Lódz.

Ustawa o rozwoju oświaty i wychowania w Polsce Ludowej. 1961. Warszawa.

Trzeciakowski, L. 1970. *Kulturkampf w zaborze pruskim.* Poznań.

Tygodnik Ilustrowany. 1889. Nr. 347.

Urban, W. 1966. *Ostatni etap dziejów Kościoła w Polsce przed nowym tysiącleciem (1815 – 1965).* Rzym.

von Meysenburg, M. 1960. *Pamiętnik idealistk.* Warszawa.

Walewska, C. 1909. *Ruch kobiecy w Polsce,* part 2. Warszawa.

Wawrzykowska-Wierciochowa, D. 1965. "Jadwiga Dźiubinska 1874–1937," in *Rocznik Dziejów Ruchu Ludowego,* nr. 7.

Wernic, H. 1873. "Froebel i ogródki dziecinne," in *Opiekun Domowy,* nr. 36–38.

Weryho-Radziwiłłowiczowa, Maria. 1930. *Zarys Wychowania Przedszkolnego.* Warszawa.

Wiadomości Handlowe i Przemysłowe. 1838.

Wieniec. 1858. vol. 3.

Winiarz, A. 1988. "Dzialalnosc opiekunczo-wychowawcza Lubelskiego Oddzialu Robot-niczego Towarzystwa Przyjaciol Dzieci w latach 1925–1929," in *Geneza i rozwój ruchu przy-jaciól dzieci na Lubelszczyźnie w latach 1918–1975.* Lublin.

———. 1991. "Dzialanosc opiekunczo-wychowawcza Robotniczego Towarzystwa Przyjaciół Dzieci w Drugiej Rzeczypospolitej," in *Oświata, szkolnictwo i wychowanie w latach II Rzeczypospolitej.* Lublin.

Wiślicki, A. W. 1868. "O metodzie Froebla wprowadzonej do ochronki I," in *Kłosy,* nr. 79 – 85.

———. 1869. "W sprawie ochron warszawskich," in *Przegląd Tygodniowy,* nr. 39.

Wnuk, J. 1961. *Dzieci polskie oskarzaja.* Warszawa.

Wójcik, M. 1978. *Zgromadzenie Siostr NMP Niepokalanej.* Mariowka.

Woźnicka, Z. 1972. *Wychowanie przedszkolne w Polsce Ludowej.* Warszawa.

Wróbel, M. 1967. *Wychowanie przedszkolne w Polsce w latach 1918 –1939.* Wrocław.

Wroczyński, R. 1965. Introduction to *Stanisława Karpowicza myśl społeczna i pedagogiczna.* Warszawa.

Wychowanie w Przedszkolu. 1955. Nr. 12.

———. 1957. nr. 7/8.

"Wydzial Spraw Wewnetrznych i Duchownych." 1866. In Zbiór Przepisów Administra-cyjnych Królestwa Polskiego, vol. 1, part 3.

Zdanie sprawy z czynnosci Rady Glównej Opiekuńczej Instytutów Dobroczynnych za rok 1857. 1858. Warszawa.

Zdanie sprawy z czynnosci Rady Głównej Opiekunczej Instytutów Dobroczynnych za rok 1858. 1959. Warszawa.

Zjednoczone Stowarzyszenie Ziemianek, sygn. 232/1906, k2. Urząd Gubernialny do Spraw Stowarzyszeń, Archiwum Główne Akt Dawnych w Warszawie (AGAD).

Żukiewiczowa, Z. 1934, "Dydaktyka Przedszkolna," in *Encyklopedia Wychowania.* Warszawa.

Chapter 8 The Kindergarten

and the Revolutionary Tradition

in Russia

Lisa Kirschenbaum

From its first appearance in Russia in the early 1860s, the kindergarten was associated with opposition to authoritarianism—in the family, the school, and the state. The linkage of pedagogical and political radicalism was not unique to Russia; the Prussian government had seen Froebel's kindergartens as an arm of the socialist movement. But whereas Froebel had rejected such connections, Russian proponents of the kindergarten embraced them. What most clearly distinguished Russian kindergartens from those in Western Europe or the United States was the insistence on the radical cultural and social role of preschool institutions.

As understood by its Russian proponents, the kindergarten constituted a means of liberating children from the habit of slavish obedience, and of freeing women to pursue work outside the home. Appropriated by radicals, the kindergarten held no appeal for the tsarist state. By contrast, the Bolsheviks took up the task of organizing kindergartens almost immediately after coming to power in 1917. The Soviet institutions offer a case study in how radical visions were transformed when finally instituted and institutionalized.

THE RISING GENERATION

The radicals who emerged in Russia in the years following the Crimean War hoped to remake society, and not necessarily by means of political action. Russia's stunning 1855 defeat coupled with the government's relaxation of the rigid censorship that had existed under Nicholas I produced a rare period of optimism and heated debate on how to remedy the empire's manifest ills. The openness lasted until the unsuccessful attempt on the life of Alexander II in 1866. The radicals, or "nihilists," of this period were cultural rebels, apostles of physical science and materialism, asserting their independence by means of the rejection of all accepted standards.

Nihilists often defined themselves and were defined by contemporary observers in generational terms. Ivan Turgenev's novel *Fathers and Children* (1861) provides the classic, if not altogether flattering, representation of the nihilist in Bazarov, who dissects frogs and attempts to deflate what he regards as the romantic illusions of the "fathers." From another part of the ideological spectrum, Nikolai Chernyshevskii's novel *What Is to Be Done?* (1863), which was still widely known in radical circles when Lenin wrote his own "What Is to Be Done?" in 1902, similarly represented radical social transformation as the work of a growing number of "new people" struggling to reject artificial and oppressive social relationships and to reconstruct society. Historians have often co-opted such rhetoric, finding in the emphasis on generations a convenient means of conceptualizing the emergence of a new radical spirit grounded in realism, reason, and natural science.[1]

On one level, the generational approach simply underlines the degree to which the radicalism of the 1860s and 1870s was a youth movement. Chernyshevskii, thirty-five years old when he wrote *What Is to Be Done?*, was among the oldest of the "sons," and one of the few with whom the older generation felt some intellectual kinship.[2] His influential colleagues Nikolai Dobroliubov and Dmitrii Pisarev both died in their twenties. Nihilist habits and attitudes were most often adopted by university students and recent graduates. Young men took up science and cultivated a studied slovenliness; women signaled their rejection of traditional roles by cutting their hair short and donning simple dark dresses. At least one author has explicitly compared the unrest in Russian universities in the 1860s to the upheavals on American campuses a century later.[3]

The generational imagery also evokes the degree to which the young people of the post–Crimean War period understood themselves to be coming of age in a profoundly changed and, they hoped, changing nation. The emancipation of the serfs together with the easing of censorship and the reform of both local government and the legal system marked a deep divide between the experiences of university students and their parents; a "generation gap" of enormous proportions was perhaps inevitable.

The nihilists' predilection for representing themselves as the rising generation may also be understood as vital to their conception of cultural rebellion. More than a metaphor for social transformation, the displacement of the older generation came to be seen as the surest method of achieving it. A student activist looking back on 1861 recalled that many of his peers shared the "belief that we—namely the 'younger generation'—were destined to make the 'good word' into living reality."[4]

The older generation's continuing efforts to inculcate its own romantic morals and ideals—"prejudices and delusions," from the radicals' point of view—constituted the chief obstacle to the fulfillment of youth's glorious destiny. Dobroliubov, in a well-known essay "On the meaning of authoritarianism in education" (1857), condemned the arrogant assumption that the teacher stands "above an entire generation" and can therefore demand unquestioning obedience from his pupils. Indeed, Dobroliubov doubted the possibility of learning anything of value from the older generation because "in general, the teacher can't foresee or even understand the demands of a new age and considers them absurd."[5] The older generation and, by extension, the old order could be fully overcome only when children were raised in new ways.

Equating the struggle for social change with generational conflict, the radicals of the 1860s endowed debates about education and pedagogy with broad significance. Educators and non-educators alike framed criticisms of authoritarian structures in the language of school reform. It does not take a tremendous amount of imagination to see in Dobroliubov's condemnation of teachers who "consider the pupil their property, their thing, with which they may do as they please" a more general attack on all oppressive social relationships.[6] Elizaveta Vodovozova, a pioneer in the field of early-childhood education, noted in her memoir of the 1860s a widespread realization that "as practiced in pre-reform Russia, upbringing by means of fear, punishment, threats, and the rod produced only slaves."[7] The rejection of rote learning and strict discipline in the school was understood as the precondition and prefiguration of change beyond the classroom.

The radicals proposed to replace the system of education that required, in

Dobroliubov's phrase, "absolute obedience" (*bezuslovnoe povinovenie*) with a program of freedom in education. Petr Kapterev, who taught pedagogy and psychology at the Petersburg Froebelist Courses from 1874 to 1898, characterized the 1860s as an "epoch of liberation" that called forth a generation of "teacher-radicals," who viewed the child's lack of freedom in the classroom as the "root evil" in current educational systems.[8]

The school Leo Tolstoi created for peasant children at his country estate, Iasnaia Poliana, epitomized the reform era's preoccupation with freedom for children. Tolstoi envisioned the school as a "pedagogical laboratory." It operated from 1859 to 1862, and the journal *Iasnaia Poliana,* published in the last year of the school's existence, brought the novelist's experiments wide publicity. Viewing any systematic educational theory as an artificial imposition on students, Tolstoi organized his program around the observed interests of the children themselves. His permissiveness extended even to allowing students the freedom to skip class when they desired. The mischievousness and "external disorder" that might result from granting complete freedom for creative improvisation Tolstoi deemed "useful and necessary, however uncomfortable for the teacher."[9] The true enemy, according to Tolstoi, was not disorder but compulsion, authoritarianism, and externally imposed discipline. Tolstoi's maxim that "the only criteria of pedagogy is freedom" did indeed seem to capture the spirit of the age.

The conviction that freedom in education could serve as the germ of freedoms beyond the classroom informed Russian pedagogical literature into the twentieth century. In 1883, Vasilii Vodovozov (Vodovozova's husband) and Konstantin Ushinskii, by then the deans of Russian educators, warned parents and teachers to avoid "repressing children." "To upset or prohibit children's games without good cause" they deemed "brutality" (*zhestokost'*), rather strong language that suggests an aversion to more than just authoritarian parenting.[10] Konstantin Venttsel', a proponent of what was known as "free upbringing" (*svobodnoe vospitanie*), stressed the importance of equality within the family. He argued that free upbringing required that the "principle of the absolute power of the current over the future generation . . . be shaken." Calling parents "slave-masters," Venttsel' nonetheless hoped that once they understood that the "natural basis of the family union must be mutual love and respect" they would renounce their power, allowing their children to express their feelings, "even when parents do not like that expression," and to share in family decisions.[11]

While not explicit, the parallels between the family and the state are clear. It was not only parents who stifled dissent and refused to share power. Venttsel' predicted that schools and families based on equality and freedom would some-how catalyze broader social change.[12] Echoing the mid-century radicals, edu-cators continued to endow childrearing with vast social significance.

THE RADICAL CRITIQUE
OF THE KINDERGARTEN

The connection of educational reform to a larger social agenda profoundly in-fluenced the introduction of the kindergarten in Russia. Not surprisingly, the chief criticism leveled against the Froebelian system was the limits it placed on the independent activity of children. In an 1874 essay, Tolstoi called the kinder-garten "one of the most monstrous excrescences of the new pedagogy."[13] Most educators were not quite so ready to dismiss Froebel, but the kindergarten was initially tainted by its association with what was understood to be a specifically German and inordinately disciplined approach to children.

Educators envisioned the process of transplanting the kindergarten to Rus-sian soil in terms of disentangling it from its roots in German romanticism.[14] In her widely influential book on early childhood education, published in seven editions between 1871 and 1913, Vodovozova focused on practical means of adapting the kindergarten to a Russian context. She dismissed Froebel's "cloy-ing sentimentalism" and "mysticism" as nonessential artifacts of his social and intellectual milieu, and suggested that such attitudes had no place in Russian kindergartens. Noting that many mothers found Froebel's games and gifts "unsuitable for Russian children" as they required too much "patience and as-siduity," Vodovozova provided detailed descriptions of appropriate toys and ac-tivities.[15] She also included Russian folk stories as well as words and music for Russian folk songs to replace awkward translations from the German. Russian advocates of the kindergarten rejected any effort to imitate a program they viewed as best suited to another time and place.

Further shaping early kindergarten programs was the desire to bridge the per-ceived abyss between the peasant masses—the *narod*—and the thin stratum of educated society. Efforts to reach out to the people constituted a chief preoccu-pation of Russian radicals in general, and of reform-minded teachers in partic-ular. That many educated Russians felt more at home speaking French than Rus-sian marked one of the clearest divides between the people and the gentry; educators emphasized the importance of teaching children Russian before hav-ing them take up a foreign language.[16] The yearning for a connection with the people also helps to explain Vodovozova's advocacy of Russian folktales and songs. Some teachers translated the desire to go to the people into more literal terms. In accord with the "opinion of the times," makeshift kindergartens organized by female radicals in the early 1860s emphasized natural science and "acquaintance with the *narod* and working people in general," by means of visits to tinsmiths', blacksmiths', and cobblers' workshops or, for the older children, to factories.[17]

The early kindergartens, it should be noted, did not reach out to the people. The neighborhood associations described by Vodovozova were organized by educated daughters of the gentry. The small number of more formal institutions organized in the 1860s and 1870s usually charged tuition and were, therefore, closed to all but the intelligentsia.[18] The emphasis was less on raising cultural levels among the people than on inculcating respect among the children of the gentry for the simple and "truly" Russian life of the *narod*. The kindergarten aimed to encourage a strong sense of social responsibility.

THE KINDERGARTEN PROGRAM

The high value placed on the absolute freedom and independence of the child produced suspicion of any systematic kindergarten program. In a review of German kindergartens published in the journal of the ministry of education in 1857, Vodovozov granted that the "fundamental idea" of the Froebelist kindergarten was "excellent," but criticized a "much too strict system of children's games."[19] Thirty years later, Vodovozov and Ushinskii still found the Froebelian system too rigid. Even the Froebelist societies organized in St. Petersburg, Kiev, and other cities in the 1870s harbored factions hostile to a strict application of Froebel's program.[20] Later in the century, advocates of free upbringing denied the possibility of formulating any set schedule for the kindergarten; Venttsel' and his followers claimed that in order to respond to the needs of individual pupils, curricula had to be as varied as children themselves.[21]

Russian educators embraced not a specific kindergarten program but the conviction that education had to engage children's imaginations, and had to connect them to the life of the people. In Froebel's uncomplicated and age-appropriate materials, Russian teacher-radicals found a "natural" means of developing the child's curiosity, creativity, and independence, and of breaking down artificial barriers of class. Vodovozov and Ushinksii advised parents that "worthless" objects, which a child's imagination could transform into any number of things, made the best toys.[22] Vodovozova concluded that Froebel's primary achievement was his demonstration of the pedagogical potential of everyday objects that were accessible to rich and poor alike; she viewed expensive, elaborate toys as awakening only "envy, vanity, and arrogance."[23] The location of profound pedagogical power in the crudest of toys appealed to educators, who hoped to endow the rising generation with a spirit of independence and an understanding of the struggles and virtues of the Russian people.

In practice, it turned out that the desire to impress upon children the power of science as well as their duty to the community limited efforts to foster freedom of thought, action, and movement. A note of didacticism often crept into calls for complete independence from constraints imposed by the older generation. Vodovozova recounted with approval a friend's effort to ground her daughter Zina in natural science. The seven-year-old had boxes filled with natural objects—stones, leaves, oats, shells—that she had learned to name and explain. The apparently rote memorization of dry facts Vodovozova took as an indication of the new and improved nature of the child's education; Zina's appreciation of nature compared favorably to Vodovozova's own childhood envy of the toys of wealthier peers.[24] By contrast, she concluded that ardent efforts to acquaint children with the plight of working people often did more harm than good. Determining how much teaching it was appropriate to impose on children proved difficult.

At the turn of the century, proponents of free upbringing faced the same conundrum: how to reconcile the encouragement of individual self-expression with the teacher's desire to inculcate what she deemed necessary values and habits. More involved in theory than practice, Venttsel' recommended that a large portion of the kindergartner's day be devoted to "socially necessary work" such as housekeeping, preparing breakfast, washing dishes, and making items for use in the kindergarten, like toys or chairs. However, he avoided any detailed explanation of how such tasks could be squared with his insistence on full freedom for children; Venttsel' apparently counted on the children's "social instincts" to interest them in labor activities, even when they did not promise to be fun.[25]

For teachers trying to put his ideas into operation, the problem often came down to how to maintain some modicum of order. The harshest criticisms of free upbringing came from educators who found the level of primordial chaos advocated by Tolstoi and Venttsel' unacceptable in practice.[26] Even those who supported Venttsel' usually tempered his insistence on absolute noninterference in children's activities and devised at least tentative weekly schedules.[27] Yet despite the practical difficulties, most Russian kindergarten teachers remained committed to the fullest possible freedom for children.

THE KINDERGARTEN AND THE
"WOMAN QUESTION"

The radicals understood children's emancipation and women's liberation in much the same terms. In both cases they connected educational reform with efforts to end the "tyranny of the family." The debate over what was known as the "woman question" had, in fact, begun as a discussion of the need to reform women's education. In a signal essay published in 1856, Nikolai Pirogov, a doctor and educator who had trained female nurses for the Crimean War and who had been favorably impressed by their service on the front lines, argued the need to improve women's education. He charged that girls' schools turned out dolls, gracious housewives competent in French and music and little else. The conviction that new methods of education could emancipate women remained central to the evolving and expanding debate on the woman question.[28]

The question of how "new women" might be raised from earliest childhood, while not at the forefront of discussions of women's emancipation, did engage women involved in the kindergarten movement. Vodovozova describes the efforts of two sisters to raise a child to be science-minded, socially conscious, and unhampered by gender stereotypes that confined women to the home. The child's Aunt Vera, the more radical of the two sisters, feared that playing with dolls would foster coquetry and an empty-headed love of clothes. However, neither sister wished to thwart what she viewed as the girl's natural desire to care for something, so they decided to give the child a wooden village doll that she could nurture but not dress up. Vera pointedly rejected Vodovozova's mother's assertion that "to doll yourself up" is female nature; "if woman's nature is so empty and insignificant," Vera responded, "if her thoughts are primarily directed toward frivolity, then this nature needs to be changed for the better."[29] Perhaps nothing better sums up the radicals' faith in education as a tool of liberation than Vera's conviction that it could alter "nature."

A wholesale challenge to traditional gender roles rarely materialized. Instead, Froebel's insistence on the importance of mother love resonated even among the most radical Russians. It was the "frivolous," not the nurturing, aspects of women's "nature" that the radical Vera rejected. Despite male radicals' vocal commitment to equal rights for women, they continued to put woman on a moral pedestal, lauding her maternal instincts and natural capacity for loving self-sacrifice. In an 1861 article, Pisarev suggested that women, when liberated, would possess a "freshness and strength" that men could never match. He located the source of women's "future rich development" in the "love of mothers, sisters, lovers, and wives [that] pours on our grey lives bright rays of happiness and poetry" and in women's "lack of moral economy and reasonableness."[30] Similarly, Dobroliubov could find no male peer for the morally activated new woman.[31]

Such sentiments appeared in pedagogical literature in the form of paeans to the mother's role in early-childhood education and in scientific demonstrations of woman's unique virtues. Ushinskii and Vodovozov began their advice manual for teachers and parents with the aphorism, "the first education of the child is naturally the mother's responsibility." They found fathers "always by nature too harsh, too impatient" to care for young children.[32] Educators tended to propose purely biological explanations of gender differences. Kapterev provided detailed analysis of scientific experiments that he concluded demonstrated unequivocally the dangers of intensive mental activity for women and the suitability of a maternal role.[33]

At the same time, the women who ran the first kindergartens in Russia recognized that the institution served the interests of mothers as well as children. The women who organized neighborhood kindergartens did so not only in order to raise their children in new ways, but also to allow themselves free time to pursue interests outside the home. But while female practitioners immediately valued the kindergarten's childcare role, male theorists did not. It was not until the 1890s that the theoretical focus shifted away from reforming women's education and toward efforts to lighten the burden of childcare for mothers. The rapid growth of industry and the recruitment of women into the factory labor force spurred the organization of charitable kindergartens in the working-class districts of Russia's cities. Additionally, the dislocations of the First World War further justified attention to the kindergarten's caretaking role.[34] Charitable societies were most active in Moscow, where for the 1916–1917 school year they supported a total of forty kindergartens serving 2,000 children out of a total preschool age population of 103,000.[35] As the small number of private kindergartens established in St. Petersburg and Moscow in the 1860s and 1870s were joined by a growing number of free kindergartens in the next three decades, the assumption that childcare constituted a vital function of the kindergarten became more pronounced.

Although the philanthropic institutions had more in common with daycare centers than with Froebelian kindergartens, they were often regarded as more or less legitimate extensions of the German prototype. Among teachers accustomed to understanding schools in social context, full stomachs and decent hygiene were at least as important to the "harmonious development of the human personality" as correct toys. In many charitable kindergartens, the educational component was almost nonexistent. Children spent from six to eight hours per day in classrooms that often lacked materials and trained personnel—one teacher might be responsible for up to fifty pupils.[36] That such all-day caretaking institutions were considered kindergartens by their organizers suggests a tendency to value the kindergarten's social role over its educational role, a tendency that owed much to the roots of the Russian kindergarten in radical movements.

It was the Russian Marxists of the 1890s who saw the revolutionary potential in the all-day kindergartens. While organizations like the Society for the Care of Children attempted to provide food and adequate supervision for the children of working mothers, socialists who gave the matter any thought promoted the caretaking kindergarten as a critical step toward the emancipation of women and the "withering away" of the family.[37] Lenin valued the kindergarten primarily as a means of freeing women to work outside the home. His wife, Nadezhda Krupskaia, who wrote extensively on educational issues both before and after the Revolution, likewise viewed the socialization of childrearing chores as an integral component of the revolutionary agenda.

The desire to relieve working mothers of childcare responsibilities pushed pedagogical concerns into the background. In the socialist future, kindergartens grounded in scientific principles and run by professionals would supplant the family.[38] From the socialist point of view, the institution itself, more than any specific program it might implement, would facilitate social change.

Russian proponents of the kindergarten, from nihilists in the 1860s to Marxists at the turn of the century, Russified the Froebelian kindergarten by radicalizing it. By the time the Bolsheviks came to power, the Venttsel' concept of free upbringing shaped the programs of the majority of private kindergartens in Russia. Believing that only children accustomed to independence could successfully reform a state system grounded in compulsion, proponents of free upbringing took Froebel's insistence on child-centered pedagogy to extremes and renounced, at least in theory, all but the most essential interventions in children's activities. In practice, "freedom" for children often went hand in hand with the inculcation of new values. The all-day "kindergartens" organized in working-class districts were a long way from the ideals of both Froebel and Venttsel'. Yet purely caretaking institutions could be considered kindergartens in Russia, where the kindergarten had long been associated with, if not defined by, efforts to resolve the woman question.

Given the radicals' appropriation of the kindergarten idea, it comes as no great surprise that the tsarist state never established any public kindergartens. Indeed, in the late 1860s, the ministry of education emerged as one of the most consistently reactionary centers in the government. Apparently suspecting that educational reform might in fact have effects beyond the classroom, the ministry opposed innovations at all levels. In the primary and secondary schools, the state implemented curricula that emphasized religion and ancient languages; it simply ignored kindergartens.[39] Liberal-minded educators bemoaned their lack of influence on educational policy. "The participation of society in the organization of popular education," Kapterev declared, "is both unavoidable and necessary."[40] However, their pleas were never heeded, and in 1917, the newly minted bureaucrats charged with organizing Soviet kindergartens found not even a scrap of paper relating to preschool education in the old tsarist ministry.[41]

SOVIET KINDERGARTENS

Only when the Bolsheviks began to organize a system of public kindergartens did the contradictions and complications of the radical legacy become evident. Reconciling efforts to liberate children with the desire to inculcate new values proved far more difficult in practice than in theory. Likewise, the Bolsheviks had trouble squaring a commitment to the emancipation of mothers from the burdens of childcare with the assumption that women were natural nurturers. The dramatic shifts that occurred in Soviet preschool policy between the October Revolution and Stalin's first Five Year Plan reflect the Bolsheviks' eventual decision to curtail creative and independent self-expression in the name of building a productive new order.

Both ideological and practical concerns shaped Bolshevik approaches to the kindergarten. The social dislocations of the civil war period (1918–1921) made some sort of state care for children imperative. The compound crises of World War and civil war proved catastrophic for children, who were orphaned and abandoned in large numbers, and who suffered disproportionately from chronic urban food shortages.[42] Paradoxically, the leadership tended to perceive the crisis less as a threat to the survival of the Soviet state than as evidence of the dawning of a new age, as an opportunity. Socialists had long maintained that the oppressive bourgeois family would disappear after the workers' revolution, and in the early years of Soviet power the prophecy seemed on the verge of fulfillment.[43] The kindergarten offered a revolutionary substitute for families that appeared to be rapidly withering away.

Socialized childcare was supposed to benefit parents, children, and the Soviet state. The Bolsheviks equated the creation of "conditions necessary for the normal development of children" with the elimination of the individual family.[44] The Soviet leadership hoped that the very act of socializing childcare would communicate "socialist values" to children. Commissar of Social Welfare Aleksandra Kollontai voiced a widely held belief when she declared, "If we can raise [children] in our spirit, no enemy is terrifying. The future is ours."[45]

Preoccupied with efforts to replace the family, the Bolsheviks at first tolerated a broad range of kindergarten programs, regardless of their potential incompatibility with Soviet socialism.[46] Educators trained before the Revolution shaped Soviet preschool curricula into the early twenties, and free upbringing remained the dominant program. For their part, kindergarten teachers worked to persuade policymakers that free upbringing constituted an appropriately Soviet program. They distinguished preschool programs from the prerevolutionary school curricula that the Bolsheviks had immediately rejected as incompatible with socialism. Here the tsarist state's failure to establish public kindergartens proved advantageous. Teachers argued that since prerevolutionary kindergartens were untouched by the corrupting influence of the tsarist Ministry of Education, they could be conserved by the Soviet state.[47]

Additionally, teachers emphasized the degree to which free upbringing meshed with the Bolshevik's desire to liberate children. What better way to realize Marx's vision of a future where a person could hunt in the morning, fish in the afternoon, and criticize after dinner than allowing children the freedom to explore and develop their various interests? The complete autonomy of the child in the kindergarten and the faith that "social instincts" would make adult-imposed discipline unnecessary was presented as the necessary corollary of the Revolution's program of liberation. Moreover, even at the height of free upbringing's influence, most teachers recognized that the kindergarten had a duty to inculcate proper health habits and respect for labor—goals shared by the Soviet state.[48]

Only when the Bolsheviks abandoned the dream of an immediate socialization of childcare responsibilities did they attack free upbringing and turn their attention to devising uniquely "socialist" kindergarten programs. The economic disaster and political opposition that confronted the Bolsheviks as they emerged victorious from the civil war prompted the establishment of the New Economic Policy in 1921. A tactical retreat, NEP allowed the revival of private trade and mandated limits on government spending. The new policy's emphasis on restoring productivity, discipline, and order made the dream of socialized child rearing impractical in the short term and suspect as an ideal. Budget cuts effectively returned responsibility for child care to mothers. Kindergartens established during the civil war that managed to stay open typically came to rely on parents to supply what the state no longer provided. The withering away of the family came to be viewed as a threat to the state's stability.[49] Under these circumstances, the kindergarten *curriculum* took on new significance as a means of raising children capable of building the socialist future.[50]

The new socialist curriculum introduced in 1924 privileged the inculcation of "revolutionary" ideas over the liberation of the rising generation. However, it did so without abandoning child-centered pedagogy; in the Russian kindergarten movement, calls to honor children's present interests and desires had long coexisted with efforts to transform children into "new people." The premise that the legacies of the past could be overcome through education held particular appeal for the Bolsheviks, who aimed to root out the "backward" childcare practices of a largely illiterate peasant population and to raise a generation committed to Soviet socialism. Nevertheless, proponents of the "socialist" program took care to emphasize that while the curriculum valued useful labor above unstructured play, and introduced kindergartners to the history of socialism, it did so in the context of activities that appealed to preschoolers.[51] Without such assurances, the program would never have won the support of the core of kindergarten teachers trained in progressive methods before the Revolution.

The early twenties witnessed the abandonment of the kindergarten's role in facilitating the demise of the family, and the weakening of the link between the kindergarten and women's emancipation. The Women's Department of the Communist Party (the Zhenotdel) encouraged women to get involved in kindergarten work as much to lighten childcare burdens as to accustom mothers to public work.[52] Kindergartens offered lectures designed to persuade mothers to abandon notoriously "backward" practices, such as failing to provide each child with his or her own bed.[53] The recognition that a system of socialized childcare could not be implemented immediately went hand in hand with the hope that mothers would be transformed by the preschool institutions they helped establish.

The day-to-day work in the kindergarten remained overwhelmingly in female hands. With regard to women, the kindergarten's "revolutionary" potential was increasingly located in its ability to draw women into mothering work outside the home and to transform mothers into "rational" caregivers capable of raising their children in the spirit of socialism. The final emancipation of women from childcare responsibilities receded into the Communist future.

By the mid-thirties, the dual image of women as both workers and mothers that had been justified as a short-term expedient in the twenties took on the character of a permanent feature of Soviet life. Although the collectivization of agriculture and the breakneck industrialization of the first Five Year Plan spurred renewed state interest in the preschool as a means of freeing women to work outside the home, the new kindergartens could not—and did not aim to—relieve working women of all childcare chores.[54] The world would be transformed not by creating institutional substitutes for the family but by reeducating it. If mothers would raise their children as the state directed, there would be little need to replace them. The new utopia not only tolerated women's double shift, it required it.

The official kindergarten curriculum of the early thirties was built on the desire to inculcate the "socialist" values of discipline and hard work at a most impressionable age. Froebel's program, once criticized as too German and too disciplined, was ostensibly rejected in the thirties as incurably bourgeois. By the end of the first Five Year Plan, rigidly ideological statements of the purpose and practice of the kindergarten prevailed. The "chief task of the kindergarten" was "to arm the child with the temper of Soviet communism, to kindle his love for and devotion to our factories, machine tools, machines, our fields, our Red Army men."[55] Froebel was labeled "reactionary"; free upbringing was accused of producing "fops and dandies" rather than hardworking proletarians.[56] However, kindergarten teachers utilized the familiar array of child-centered activities even as they attempted to mold preschoolers into productive socialists.[57] Froebel's most basic lesson—the need to respect the interests and capacities of children—was never abandoned.

A decade after the Bolsheviks came to power, the Soviet kindergarten stood as a dim reflection of the efforts of nineteenth-century radicals to adapt Froebel to Russia. Like the radicals who first embraced the kindergarten idea, the Bolsheviks originally envisioned the kindergarten as a means of emancipating both children and mothers from presumedly despotic families, and of inculcating new and "revolutionary" values. For the small number of teacher-radicals hostile to the authoritarian tsarist state, reconciling these goals had presented few problems; the very notion of the free and unhampered development of the rising generation was revolutionary. However, for radicals in power, commitments to guaranteeing the future of the Soviet state and to insuring the liberation of the individual from oppressive relationships often came into conflict.

By the late twenties, the revolutionary optimism that had led officials during the civil war to view homeless children as the harbingers of the future communist society had all but vanished. The liberationist ethos that had animated at least a segment of the Bolshevik party before and immediately after it had seized power fell victim to dismal realities, to the state's interest in reinvigorating the economy, and to the desire to restore social order. Calls for antiauthoritarian education and women's emancipation ultimately fared little better in the Soviet state than in tsarist Russia.

NOTES

1. See for example Nicholas Riasanovsky, *A History of Russia,* 4th ed. (New York, 1984), 381.
2. Alexander Herzen, *My Past and Thoughts,* trans. Constance Garnett (Berkeley, 1973), 553, 619–39; Andrzej Walicki, *A History of Russian Thought from the Enlightenment to Marxism* (Stanford, 1979), 203.
3. Abbott Gleason, *Young Russia: The Genesis of Russian Radicalism in the 1860s* (Chicago, 1980).
4. Quoted in ibid., 159.
5. N. Dobroliubov, "O znachenii avtoriteta v vospitanii" [On the meaning of authority in education], in *stat'i, Reetsenzii, iunosheskie raboty aprel' 1853–iiul' 1857* [Articles, reviews, and youthful works, April 1853–July 1857] (Moscow, 1961), 498.
6. Ibid., 495.
7. E. Vodovozova, *Na zare zhizni: memuarnye ocherki i portrety* [At the dawn of life: autobiographical essays and portraits] (Moscow, 1964), 2: 87.
8. P. Kapterev, *Novai russkaia pedagogika, ee glavneishhie idei, napravleniia i deiateli* [The new Russian pedagogy: its chief ideas, directions, and figures] (St. Petersburg, 1897), 53–54.
9. Quoted in Nicholas Hans, *The Russian Tradition in Education* (London: Routledge and Kegan Paul, 1963), 97.
10. K. D. Ushinskii and V. I. Vodovozov, *Domashnoe vospitanie: rukovodstvo dlia roditelei i vospitatelei k vospitaniiu i obucheniiu detei s prilozheniem rukovodstovo k Frebelskim obrazovatel'nym igram* [Upbringing at home: a guidebook for parents and teachers on the upbringing and instruction of children with a supplement on Froebelist educational games] (St. Petersburg, 1883), 66.
11. K. N. Venttsel', *Teoriia svobodnogo vospitaniia i ideal'nyi detskii sad* [The theory of free upbringing and the ideal kindergarten] (Moscow, 1915), 22.
12. Ibid., 4.
13. L. N. Tolstoi, "On popular education," in *The Complete Works of Count Tolstoy,* trans. Leo Wiener (Boston, 1904), 272.
14. The conviction that all educational programs grew out of specific social contexts constituted a key feature of Russian pedagogical thought. Kapterev, 28–30, 53–54; V. I. Vodovozov, "Detskie sady v Germanii" [Kindergartens in Germany], *Zhurnal ministerstvo narodnogo prosveshcheniia* [Journal of the Ministry of Popular Education}, 96 (1857): 111.

15. E. N. Vodovozova, *Umstvennoe razvitie detei pervogo proiavleneiia soznaniia do vos̓milet-niago vozrasta: kniga dlia vospitateli* [The intellectual development of children from the first signs of consciousness to eight years old: a book for teachers], 3d ed. (St. Petersburg, 1876), 45–48.

16. Kapterev, 41–42.

17. Vodovozova, *Na zare zhizni*, 2: 85.

18. L. N. Litvina, ed. *Istoriia doshkol'noi pedagogiki* [The history of preschool pedagogy] (Moscow, 1989), 155–58.

19. Vodovozov, 103, 107.

20. Litvina, 155.

21. Venttsel', *Teoriia*, 5. R. H. Hayashida, "The pedagogy of protest: Russian progressive education on the eve of the revolution," *Slavic and East European Education Review* 2 (1978): 11–30.

22. Vodovozov, 105; Ushinskii and Vodovozov, 67.

23. Vodovozova, *Umstvennoe razvitie*, 49.

24. Vodovozova, *Na zare zhizni*, 2: 88.

25. Venttsel', "K voprosu o prakticheskom osushchestvlenii 'doma svobodnogo rebenka'" [On the question of the practical realization of 'the home of the free child'] (1908), Nauchnyi Arkhiv Akademii Pedagogicheskikh Nauk SSSR (APN SSSR) [The Scientific Archive of the Academy of Pedagogical Sources, USSR]. f.. 23, op. 1, d. 73, 1. 8; *Teoriia*, 18.

26. Hayashida, 16. M. Ia. Morozova and E. I. Tikheeva, *Sovremennyi detskii sad: ego znachenie i oborudovanie* [The contemporary kindergarten: its meaning and equipment] (St. Petersburg, 1914), 47–48.

27. M. Kh. Sventitskaia, *Detskii sad: kratkiia svedenii i plany zaniatii* [The kindergarten: short reports and plans of activities] (Moscow, 1912).

28. Richard Stites, *The Women's Liberation Movement in Russia: Feminism, Nihilism, and Bolshevism, 1860–1930* (Princeton, 1978), 29–49.

29. Vodovozova, *Na zare zhizni*, 2: 32, 88–89.

30. D. I. Pisarev, "Zhenskie tipy v romanakh i povestiakh Pisemskogo, Turgeneva, i Goncharova," in *Sochineniia* (Moscow, 1955), 238.

31. Dobroliubov, "Kogda zhe pridet nastoiashchii den'?" in *Izbrannoe* (Moscow, 1961), 212.

32. Ushinskii and Vodovozov, 3.

33. Kapterev, *Pedagogicheskii protsess* (St. Petersburg, 1905), 114–25.

34. Venttsel', *Detskii dom*, i.

35. L. Skatkin, "Vneshkol'naia rabota s det'mi v g. Moskve," *Pedagogicheskie izvestiia* (1917): 40.

36. Litvina, pp. 196–99.

37. However, socialists seem not to have opened a single day-care center. Soviet historians, who might be expected to play up such efforts, make no mention of socialist-run kindergartens. M. F. Shabaevaia, ed. *Istoriia doshkol'noi pedagogiki v Rossii* (Moscow, 1976); Litvina, 199–200.

38. N. Krupskaia, *Pedagogicheskie sochineniia v shesti tomakh* (Moscow, 1979), 1: 9–14, 105–13, 152–54, 277.

39. James McClelland, *Autocrats and Academics: Education, Culture, and Society in Tsarist*

Russia (Chciago: University of Chicago Press, 1979), Allen Sinel, *The Classroom and the Chancellery: State Educational Reforms in Russia under Count Dmitry Tolstoi* (Cambridge: Harvard University Press, 1973).

40. Kapterev, *Novaia russkaia,* 33.

41. D. A. Lazurkina, "V svete Otdel'a Doshkol'nogo Vospitaniia," *Narodnoe prosveshchenie* (hereafter, *NP*), 19 (1918): 11.

42. In 1912 in Moscow, nearly 29 of every 100 children died within the first year of life. During the civil war, statistics grew even grimmer. According to one count, half of all babies born in 1918 died within the first year of life. *Detskaia smertnost' i sotsial'naie uslovia* (Petrograd, 1916); Tsentral'nyi Gosudarstvennyi Arkhiv RSFSR (TsGA RSFSR) f. 2306, op. 12, d. 136, l. 56.

43. Barbara Evans Clements, "The Effects of the Civil War on Women and Family Relations," in *Party, State, and Society in the Russian Civil War: Explorations in Social History,* Diane Koenker et al., eds. (Bloomington, 1989), 105; Wendy Z. Goldman, *Women, the State, and Revolution: Soviet Family Policy and Social Life, 1917–1936* (Cambridge, England, 1993), 60–63.

44. APN SSR, f. 18, op. 2, d. 208, l. 4.

45. APN SSSR f. 18, op. 2, d. 198, l. 5. See also *Pervyi Vserossiiskii S"ezd po doshkol'nomu vospitaniiu: doklady, protokoly, rezoliutsii* (Moscow, 1921): TsGA RSFSR f. 2306, op. 13, d. 39, l. 2.

46. Narkompros, *Spravochnik po doshkol'nomu vospitaniiu* (Moscow, 1919); *Pervyi S"ezd.*

47. *Pervyi S"ezd,* 17.

48. V. Iakovoleva, "Organizatsiia dela doshkol'nogo vospitaniia," *NP,* 19 (1918): 5; "Podgotovka rabotnikov prosveshcheniia," *NP,* 18–20 (1920): 13.

49. Clements, 112–19.

50. L. Kirschenbaum, "Socialism in the Soviet Kindergarten, 1921–28," *East/West Education* 13 (Fall 1993): 126–38.

51. M. Vilenskaia, S. S. Molozhavyi, and R. I. Prushitskaia, eds. *Tretii Vserossiiskii S"ezd po doshkol'nomu vospitaniiu* (Moscow, 1925); M. Markovich, *Pervoe maia v doshkol'nykh uchrezhdeniiakh* (Moscow, 1924).

52. Carol Eubanks Hayden, "The Zhenotdel and the Bolshevik Party," *Russian History* 3 (1976): 150–73; Vilenskaia, Molozhavyi, and Prushitskaia, 10–18.

53. M. Vilenskaia "Doshkol'naia rabota v derevne," *NP,* 2 (1926): 100–101.

54. Goldman, 296–97; Z. I. Lilina, *Roditeli, uchites' vospityvat svoikh detei* (Moscow, 1929); M. M. Pistraka and R. E. Orlova, eds. *Doshkol'nyi pokhod* (Moscow, 1929–30).

55. Ia. A Perel', ed., *Doshkol'noe vospitanie* (Moscow-Leningrad, 1932), 28–30.

56. M. E. Maklinaia, N. A. Tumin-Al'medingen, and O. V. Shirokogorova, eds. *Doshkol'noe vospitanie v. Leningrade za 15 let. 1917–32* (Moscow-Leningrad, 1932), 14–15.

57. Lilina, *Roditeli;* Pistraka and Orlova.

REFERENCES

Clements, Barbara Evans. 1989. The effects of the Civil War on women and family relations. in *Party, state, and society in the Russian Civil War: Explorations in social history,* ed. Diane Koenker et al. Bloomington: Indiana University Press.

Detskai smertnost' i sotsial'naie usloviia. 8 diagramm s prilozheniem obiasnitel'nago teksta. 1916. Petrograd.

Dobroliubov, N. A. 1860 [reprint 1961]. Kogda zhe pridet nastoiashchii den'? In *Izbrannoe.* Moscow.

———. 1857 [reprint 1961]. O znachenii avtoriteta v vospitanii. In *Sobranie sochinenii.* Vol. 1, *Stat'i, retsenzii, iunosheskie raboty aprel' 1853–iiul' 1857.* Moscow.

Gleason, Abbott. 1980. *Young Russia: The genesis of Russian radicalism in the 1860s.* Chicago: University of Chicago Press.

Goldman, W. Z. 1993. *Women, the state, and revolution: Soviet family policy and social life, 1917–36.* Cambridge: Cambridge University Press.

Hans, Nicholas. 1963. *The Russian Tradition in Education.* London: Routledge and Kegan Paul.

Hayashida, R. H. 1978. The pedagogy of protest: Russian progressive education on the eve of the Revolution. *Slavic and European Education Review* 2: 11–30.

Hayden, C. E. 1976. The Zhenotdel and the Bolshevik party. *Russian History* 3: 150–73.

Holmes, Larry. 1991. *The Kremlin and the Schoolhouse: Reforming Education in Soviet Russia, 1917–31.* Bloomington: Indiana University Press.

Iakovleva, V. 1918. Organizatsiia dela doshkol'nogo vospitaniia. *Narodnoe prosveshchenie* 19: 5.

Kanel', V. Ia. 1918. *Vopros vospitaniia v svete sotsial'noi gigieny.* Moscow.

Kapterev, P. F. 1897. *Novaia russkaia pedagogika, ee glavneishie idei, napravleniia i deiateli.* St. Petersburg.

———. 1905. *Pedagogicheskii protsess.* St. Petersburg.

Kirschenbaum, L. A. 1993. Socialism in the Soviet kindergarten, 1921–28. *East/West Education* 14 (Fall): 126–38.

Krupskaia, N. 1978. *Pedagogicheskie sochineniia v shesti tomakh.* 6 vols. Moscow.

Lazurkina, D. A. 1918. V svete Otdel'a Doshkol'nogo Vospitaniia. *Narodnoe prosveshchenie* 19: 11.

Lilina, Z. I. 1921. *Pervoe maia: prazdnik truda—prazdnik detei.* St. Petersburg.

———. 1929. *Roditeli, uchites' vopityvat svoikh detei.* Moscow.

Litvina, L. N., ed. 1989. *Istoriia doshkol'noi pedagogiki.* Moscow.

Makhlinaia, M. E., N. A. Tumin-Al'medingen, and O. V. Shirokogorova, ed. 1932. *Doshkol'-noe vospitanie v Leningrade za 15 let, 1917–32.* Moscow-Leningrad.

Markovich, M. 1924. *Pervoe maia v doshkol'nykh uchrezhdeniiakh.* Moscow.

McClelland, J. C. 1979. *Autocrats and Academics: Education, Culture, and Society in Tsarist Russia.* Chicago: University of Chicago Press.

Morozova, M. Ia., and E. I. Tikheeva. 1914. *Sovremennyi detskii sad: ego znachenie i oboru-dovanie.* St. Petersburg.

Narkompros. 1919. *Spravochnik po doshkol'nomu vospitaniiu.* Moscow.

Nauchnyi Arkhiv Akademii Pedagogicheskikh Nauk SSSR (NAAPN). 1918. Arkhivnye mate-rialy gosudarsvennykh uchrezhdenii, obshchestvennykh organizatsii i chastnykh lits, f. 18, op. 2, d. 198.

Perel', Ia. A., ed. 1932. *Doshkol'noe vospitanie.* Moscow-Leningrad.

Pervyi Vserossiiskii S"ezd po doshkol'nomu vospitaniiu: doklady, protokoly, rezoliutsii. 1921. Moscow.

Pisarev, D. I. 1861 [reprint 1955]. Zhenskie tipy v romanakh i povestiakh Pisemskogo, Turgeneva i Goncharova. In *Sochineniia.* Moscow.

Pistraka, M. M., and R. E. Orlova, eds. 1929–30. *Doshkol'nyi pokhod.* Moscow.

Podgotovka rabotnikov prosveshcheniia. 1920. *Narodnoe prosveshchenie* 18–20: 13.

Riasanovsky, N. V. 1984. *A History of Russia.* 4th ed. New York: Oxford University Press.

Shabaevaia, M. F., ed. 1976. *Istoriia doshkol'noi pedagogiki v Rossii.* Moscow.

Sinel, Allen. 1973. *The classroom and the Chancellery: State Educational Reform in Russia under Count Dmitry Tolstoi.* Cambridge, Mass.: Harvard University Press.

Skatkin, L. 1917. Vneshkol'naia rabota s det'mi v g. Moskve. *Pedagogicheskie izvestiia* 1: 40.

Stites, Richard. 1978. *The women's liberation movement in Russia: Feminism, nihilism, and Bolshevism, 1860–1930.* Princeton: Princeton University Press.

———. 1989. *Revolutionary dreams: Utopian vision and experimental life in the Russian Revolution.* New York: Oxford University Press.

Sventitskaia, M. Kh. 1912. *Detskii sad: kratkiia svedeniia i plany zaniatii.* Moscow.

———. 1924. *Nash detskii sad (iz opyta doshkol'noi raboty Detskogo Gorodka imeni III Internatsionala pri Narkomprose v Moskve).* Moscow.

Tolstoi, L. N. 1904. On popular education. In *The Complete Works of Count Tolstoy,* trans. Leo Wiener, 251–323. Boston: Dana Estes & Co.

Tsentral'nyi Gosudarstvennyi Arkhiv RSFSR (TsGA RSFSR). 1918–20. Ministerstvo prosveshcheniia RSFSR. Otdel doshkol'nogo vospitaniia, f. 2306, op. 12, d. 136.

———. Otdel okhrany detsva, f. 2306, op. 13, d. 39.

Ushinskii, K. D., and V. I. Vodovozov. 1883. *Domashnoe vospitanie: rukovodstvo dlia roditelei i vospitatelei k vospitaniiu i obucheniiu detei s prilozheniem rukovodstva k Frebeleskim obrazovatel'nym igram.* St. Petersburg.

Venttsel', K. N. 1915a. *Detskii dom.* Moscow.

———. 1915b. *Teoriia svobodnogo vospitaniia i ideal'nyi detskii sad.* Moscow.

Vilenskaia, M. 1926. Doshkol'naia rabota v derevne. *Narodnoe prosveshchenie* 2: 100–101.

Vilenskaia, M., S. S. Molozhavyi, and R. I. Prushitskaia, eds. 1925. *Tretii Vserossiiski S"ezd po doshkol'nomu vospitaniiu.* Moscow.

Vodovozov, V. I. 1857. Detskie sady v Germanii. *Zhurnal ministerstvo narodnogo prosveshcheniia* 96: 93–114.

Vodovozova, E. N. 1876. *Umstvennoe razvitie detei pervogo proiavleniia soznaniia do vos'miletniago vozrasta: kniga dlia vospitatelei.* 3d ed. St. Petersburg.

———. 1964. *Na zare zhizni: memuarnye ocherki i portrety.* 2 vols. Moscow.

Chapter 9 Managing the Young Anarchists: Kindergartens and National Culture in Postcolonial Vietnam

Thaveeporn Vasavakul

The kindergarten as an organized educational space reserved for preschool-age children between three and five years old was a new institution in postcolonial Vietnam.[1] Under French colonialism, only a small number of preschool classes were attached to French schools and a weeklong kindergarten operated by a Vietnamese in Hanoi (VKHGDVN, 1991). After 1945, however, the Ministry of Education of the Democratic Republic of Vietnam worked to expand the kindergarten as an educational space. The status of the administrative agency responsible for kindergarten education was elevated from an office (*phong*) in 1948 to a department (*vu*) in the 1960s. Called *tre mau giao* (kindergarten children), the Vietnamese from three to five years old were officially treated as a separate group of children entitled to a separate educational space and training. According to the 1989 census, 1,607,940 (28.8 percent) of children between three and five years of age reportedly attended kindergartens. The percentage increased from 33 percent in 1990 to 37 percent in 1994.[2] These developments were indeed novel, given that during the precolonial and colonial periods no attention was given to this group of children, let alone attempts to create a separate formal educational space for them.[3]

In this chapter, I examine the development of the kindergarten in the Democratic Republic of Vietnam (DRV), or North Vietnam, between 1945 and
1975, and the Socialist Republic of Vietnam (SRV), or reunified Vietnam, after
1975. I examine the process by which the kindergarten was expanded and transformed, focusing on the process of borrowing and nationalization of this foreign concept. I highlight the peculiar coexistence of the modern concepts of
child development and child psychology and the Vietnamese concept of growing up. While child psychology and child development consider children as
physically and psychologically different from adults, the Vietnamese concept of
growing up downplays these differences. While child development considers
"growing up" as a step-by-step physical and psychological process, to the Vietnamese way of thinking "growing up" means the maturity of political consciousness and work habits which could develop any time, regardless of age. I
argue that while the institution of kindergarten that developed in Vietnam separated children from three to five years old from other groups of children and
adults, the content of Vietnamese kindergarten education taught preschool children the ethics of adults *cum* citizens.

I divide this chapter into four parts. In the first part, I examine the factors that
precipitated the expansion of the kindergarten in postcolonial Vietnam. I argue
that the Ministry of Education's philosophy changed over time, from regarding
the kindergarten as a mechanism which helped free women for social and economic tasks and prepare children to become citizens to one which guaranteed
children's rights to personal safety and intellectual development. In the second
part, I discuss the way in which the concepts of child development and child
psychology, both of which entered Vietnam primarily through the translation
of French, Chinese, and Russian writings, contributed to the development of
the kindergarten. Vietnamese educators invoked these concepts in the process
of separating preschool children from other groups of children and adults, organizing a different type of class, designing a different type of study program,
and developing a different teaching method. In examining this process, I focus
on the 1977–78 study programs and the 1994 revised study programs. In the
third part, I examine the content of the kindergarten study programs, high-
lighting the teaching of adult *cum* citizen ethics. I focus in particular on the
teaching of national time and space; the notions of friends, family, and nation;
and the meaning of growing up. In the fourth and final part of this chapter, I
discuss the role of the kindergarten teacher as a link between family teaching
and state-sponsored preschool education. To legitimize kindergarten education
as an alternative to, if not replacement of, family education of preschool chil-

dren, Vietnamese educators, from the beginning, advocated that kindergarten teachers be female, arguing that women possess innate child-rearing capabilities. They equated kindergarten education with "mother's teaching," the idea being reflected in the Vietnamese term for kindergarten education, *mau giao*. In the process, however, Vietnamese educators put forth a new model of mother's teaching, molding the image of civilized mothers and using state-trained mothers to teach biological mothers the appropriate ways of mother's teaching.

THE STATE AND THE KINDERGARTEN
IN POSTCOLONIAL VIETNAM: AN OVERVIEW

Although the general uprisings of August 1945 enabled the transfer of state power to the DRV under the leadership of Ho Chi Minh, the new government's claim to authority was challenged by the French, who, with British assistance, returned to Indochina in September. In 1946, the war between the French and the DRV government broke out and lasted until 1954, when the DRV's victory at Dien Bien Phu forced the French to negotiate a political settlement.[4]

During the postcolonial period, the Ministry of Education of the DRV both retained and modified the concept of the kindergarten. In a decree issued in August 1946 to outline the DRV's basic education principles, it endorsed the existence of an infant education level (*bac hoc au tri*) reserved for children under seven (Nguyen Trong Hoang, 1982); in 1948, it officially designated policy implementation tasks to the Office for Infant's Education. Yet, in response to wartime imperatives and with a commitment to socialist ideology, Vietnamese educators moved to redefine the role of the kindergarten and its education objectives. In an article entitled "Mau giao" (Mother's teaching) written in 1949, Nguyen Khanh Toan, party member *cum* Deputy Minister of Education, criticized kindergartens that developed in capitalist countries for serving the parochial interests of religious establishments, private entrepreneurs, middle-class women, and large families.[5] He contended that the objectives of Vietnamese kindergartens differed from those in capitalist countries; they would facilitate the emancipation of women, allowing mothers to participate in economic and social tasks and sisters to engage in school work, and would help prepare children to enter the first grade and to become good citizens of the new democratic republic regime.

To reach these objectives, Toan called for the opening of kindergarten classes to accommodate the children of workers, peasants, the urban poor, government officials, and petty traders. Their organization and content had to suit Vietnam's socioeconomic and political development. The teaching methods had to be age-appropriate to the children, the most suitable forms being fable telling and games. During the war of resistance, teachers had to both tell children about the war and organize them to play war-related games such as the digging of security tunnels, or to perform plays dealing with citizenship duties such as the election of people's committees and the emulation of patriotic actions (Nguyen Khanh Toan, 1991).

Toan suggested that kindergarten teachers be female as women had innate motherly virtues or were able to acquire such virtues. These included motherly love for children, endurance (*nhan nai*), and resourcefulness (*thao vat*).[6] Toan pointed out that mothers were traditionally considered home educators and children of kindergarten age remained under their mother's influence. That was why, according to him, the term used for kindergarten was *mau giao,* "mother's teaching."[7]

Because first and foremost the kindergarten served to help free Vietnamese women from home, Toan classified the kindergarten movement as a mass movement. As a result, he called for teachers also to develop the necessary qualities possessed by mobilization cadres (citizens working for the Communist Party and the government), that is, organizational capabilities and organizational initiatives. Teachers would mobilize support from production units (economic units engaged in different areas of agricultural and industrial activities) and mothers, while working with units of the Women's Union, work-exchange teams, literacy classes for adults, and health units, to provide mothers with a basic knowledge of child rearing (Nguyen Khanh Toan, 1991).

Although Nguyen Khanh Toan set down a policy outline for the development of kindergartens in 1949, the expansion of kindergartens did not gain momentum until almost a decade later. In 1950, the ministry designated to the Central Commission for Kindergartens the task of building an experimental kindergarten model, preparing study programs and teaching methods, training teachers and administrative cadres, and spreading information on child rearing to parents (VKHGDVN, 1991, 68–69). However, at the end of 1951, the ministry shelved its projects on security grounds after a kindergarten class in Yen Dinh village, Thai Nguyen province, had been bombed, a child killed, and the teacher wounded. In the three years between the end of the war in 1954 and 1957, the number of kindergarten classes only reached 29 and accommodated 826 children of communist cadres who had moved north of the seventeenth parallel after 1954 and the children of cadres whose parents had died during the war (VKHGDVN, 1991).

The dissolution of the commission resulted not only from the nature of guerrilla warfare, which made it difficult to organize permanent schools, but also from a shift in emphasis from children under six to children between six and twelve. After 1945, the Ministry of Education noted within its jurisdiction a large pool of children between six and twelve who had yet to enter the first grade. As children over six they were considered too old for kindergarten, and as children under twelve they were too young for adult literacy classes. The solution was to create an intermediary class called *vo long*, literally "clearing the heart," to prepare this group of children for the first grade. In 1952, the ministry set up the Office of Kindergartens, which was attached to the Department of General Education, to expand the *vo long* movement by turning existing kindergarten classes into *vo long* classes.[8] After 1954, *vo long* classes were retained to accommodate children between eight and eleven years old. The study program comprised reading, writing, arithmetic, hygiene, and example setting, with additional sessions on storytelling, singing, and games on Saturdays. The study period lasted for nine moths, following the general school calendar ("Chan chinh phong trao vo long," 1956; "Tai lieu huan luyen," 1956).[9]

The first turning point in the development of educational space for children under six years was between 1958 and 1960, the major factor precipitating the expansion being socioeconomic. In 1958, the Vietnam Lao Dong Party began its campaigns for cooperative agriculture. Women in rural areas were encouraged to join cooperatives and worked to earn work points. In September 1960, the Third National Party Congress of the Vietnam Lao Dong Party met to endorse the first Five-Year Plan which sanctioned socialist industrialization. At the end of 1960, the number of female workers in urban areas reportedly totaled 120,000 and formed over 20 percent of the work force, approximately a twentyfold increase since 1954. Women formed the main work force in many state factories: 48.68 percent in the Hai Phong wool factory, 57.71 percent in the Thong Nhat match factory in Hanoi, 70.9 percent in the Hanoi knitwear factory, and 75 percent in the Cau Duong wood factory. In the education, health, culture, and science sectors 15,000 women were reportedly employed (VKHGDVN, 1991, 76, 81). Beginning in 1958, the ministry issued a series of decrees to promote the organization of kindergartens in both rural and urban areas, and in 1962 it separated the administration of the kindergarten from that of general education. In 1964, the first school for training kindergarten staff was established in Phu Li, Ha Nam Ninh province, to train provincial and district administrators and teachers for provincial training schools (Do Xuan Hoa and Le Bich Ngoc, 1995, 9). As a result of these campaigns, the number of classes in rural areas increased from 609 during the 1959–60 school year to 4,601 during the 1964–65 school year, while the number of children increased from 20,266 to 127,682 during the same period (VKHGDVN, 1991, 76, 81). In urban centers, the number of classes reached 1,399 and the number of children reached 43,494 during the 1963–64 school year (VKHGDVN, 1991, 80). An estimated national average of 7.5 percent of children of kindergarten age attended kindergarten classes during the 1963–64 school year (VKHGDVN, 1991, 77).

The second turning point for the development of kindergartens came between 1965 and 1968, the period of the American bombing in Vietnam. The expansion of the kindergarten movement was aimed at further freeing women for economic and social work outside the home, replacing men who were sent to the front. During the 1968–69 school year, the percentage of children of kindergarten age attending schools reached 27.3 (VKHGDVN, 1991, 85).

In response to this expansion, the ministry elevated the status of the Office of Kindergarten to the Department of Kindergarten in 1966. It was then considered an administrative unit as important as the three other existing units managing complementary education for adults, teacher training, and general education. In 1967, 27 ministerial cadres were responsible for the administration of the kindergarten; 3 to 7 cadres in each province, and 1 to 2 cadres in each district (VKHGDVN, 1991). Between 1968 and 1970, the Department of Kindergarten, relying on researchers and cadres from the University of Pedagogy, worked to improve the quality of the kindergarten, the main task being the standardization of schools for training teachers at central and provincial levels. In 1969, the department began to circulate *Tap San Mau Giao* (Kindergarten Review) to guide school principals and teachers in the areas of administration and teaching (VKHGDVN, 1991, 83–89).

During this period, the kindergarten system began to assume a specific shape. In 1965, the ministry united the *vo long* with kindergarten classes to form a combined kindergarten system (VKHGDVN, 1991). It turned the *vo long* class into the senior class of the kindergarten level (*mau giao lon*). In 1966, it called for each village to set up a kindergarten consisting of a class for juniors (*be*), a class for intermediates (*nho*), and a class for seniors (*lon*). The first two classes served children between three and five years, while the last one served six- and seven-year-olds. Priority was given to the *vo long* class, the kindergarten class for the older children, which taught children the rudiments of reading and writing necessary for the first grade.

The third turning point in the development of kindergartens followed the reunification of Vietnam in 1975. The education system that had been developed in the DRV was extended to the former Republic of Vietnam, or South Vietnam, a process completed by the end of 1977 (VKHGDVN, 1991, 96–118).[10] This move was coupled with the setting up of schools in Da Nang and Ho Chi Minh City in 1976 for the training of kindergarten teachers for the southern provinces (Do Xuan Hoa and Le Bich Ngoc, 1995, 10). To facilitate the reorganization of kindergarten education for a reunified Vietnam, the Ministry of Education set up a Committee for Research on the Reform of Kindergarten Education in 1978, working on child psychology, appropriate programs for preschool-age children, teaching materials, and instruction manuals (VKHGDVN, 1991).[11]

In 1977, the Department of Kindergarten issued a draft regulation on kindergartens to serve as an administrative fiat for reunified socialist Vietnam. Modified and officially endorsed in 1980, the regulation confirmed that the kindergarten system was the basic unit of the national education system responsible for children from three to five years old (thirty-six to seventy-two months old). Kindergartens could be attached to communes, precincts, state enterprises, state factories, state farms, and government organizations. They would serve to prepare children to enter the first grade by nurturing their health, sentiment, morality, aesthetics, intellectual development, and good working habits. They would also serve as units which provided advice to parents on matters related to child development. Each kindergarten offered three classes: the junior class for the three-year-old, the intermediate class for the four-year-old, and the senior class for the five-year-old. If the number of children was small, teachers could organize combined classes. There were three types of kindergartens: two-shift-a-day kindergartens; full-day kindergartens; and week-long kindergartens.

Kindergartens would follow the general school calendar, beginning in September and ending in May. If there was a demand from parents, they would also operate between June and August. Each kindergarten was staffed by a principal, a vice-principal, teachers, health cadres, an accountant, a treasurer, a janitor, and a cook. Teachers were required to have earned certificates from schools for training kindergarten teachers ("Vu Mau Giao," 1977; "Dieu le truong," 1980). The central budget and local resources would combine to finance the building of the infrastructure, while the local budget, derived primarily from the social funds of production units and the collection of school fees, would finance the teachers' salaries and day-to-day expenses. The central government agreed to provide a subsidy if these local education offices and production units were unable to fully finance their kindergartens (Dang Dinh Luong, 1980).

The last turning point for the development of the Vietnamese kindergarten came after 1986 when the Sixth National Party Congress of the Vietnamese

Communist Party officially endorsed the policy of socialist reform, one aspect of which was the abolition of the central planning and state subsidizing system.[12] As a result, a major part of the financial responsibility for kindergarten education was transferred to parents, many of whom preferred to keep their children at home for economic reasons. Statistics indicate that between 1987 and 1991, the number of preschool children attending kindergarten decreased substantially (Do Xuan Hoa and Le Bich Ngoc, 1995, 11). In order to sustain the kindergarten movement and to stimulate parents to send their children to kindergarten, the Ministry of Education replaced the rhetoric of women's liberation and preschool education as the precondition for entering the first grade with the notion of "children's rights" (*quyen tre em*). Legal documents often invoked to sustain the kindergarten movement included the Covenant on the Rights of Vietnamese Children, promulgated in 1990 and the Law for the Protection and Caring of Children, promulgated in 1991. According to these documents, the state recognized the rights of children to personal safety and intellectual development and would join forces with parents to see that these rights were protected.[13]

The period after 1986 witnessed not only the rise of the new rhetoric but also the expansion of the administrative agency responsible for preschool children. In 1987, the administration of preschool children under the age of three and that of preschool children between three and five were merged. Prior to this, the Department of Kindergarten managed only preschool-age children between the ages of three and six. The Ministry of Health, between 1945 and 1971, and the Central Commission for the Protection of Mothers and Children, between 1971 and 1987, oversaw creches (*nha tre*) reserved for children between infancy and three years old.[14] In 1987, when the Central Commission for the Protection of Mothers and Children was placed under the Ministry of Education, its creche system was linked with the kindergarten, creating a combined educational space for children from infancy to six years of age under the administration of the Department of Preschool Education. In 1990, the Ministry of Education and the Ministry of Higher Education and Secondary Specialized Education, previously two separate entities, were merged to form the Ministry of Education and Training; as a result, the Department for Preschool Education became the basic education unit in the newly organized national education administration (Pham Mai Chi, 1991). The administrative network for preschool education consisted of the Ministerial Department (*cuc*) for the Protection and Education of Preschool Age Children under the jurisdiction of the Ministry of Education, Offices (*phong*) of Preschool Education under the jurisdiction of Municipal and

Provincial Education Offices, and Guidance Units (*to*) under the jurisdiction of District and Precinct Education Offices (Pham Mai Chi, 1991). The administrative merger was followed by the merger of research institutions responsible for preschool children. In 1995 the Committee for Research on Preschool Education, founded in 1978, was merged with the Center for Child Rearing, founded in 1984, to become the Institute for Research on Preschool Children (Do Xuan Hoa and Le Bich Ngoc, 1995, 10).

In summary, during the Franco-Vietnam war (1946–54) and the American war in Vietnam (1965–72), Vietnamese educators considered the kindergarten as serving Vietnam's need to release women from home in response to both wartime and economic development imperatives. After 1975, they highlighted kindergarten education as preparing Vietnamese children for the first grade. In 1990, they justified the expansion of the kindergarten through the concept of children's rights to personal safety and intellectual development.

The development of kindergarten education was a process of a mutually reinforcing expansion of the agency that administered kindergarten education and the kindergarten system. The administrative agency grew from an office into a department, with its own personnel and research organization. The institutionalization of the kindergarten for children between the ages of three to five years was gradual. In the 1950s and 1960s, Vietnamese educators were preoccupied primarily with preparing children from six to twelve years to enter the first grade; children in the kindergarten age bracket received more attention only after the number of kindergarten children over the age of six years declined. After 1975, Vietnamese children between three and five years old were separated from other groups of children and were entitled to an educational space of their own. The 1980s and the 1990s witnessed the further consolidation of the kindergarten as an educational unit, together with the strengthening of the administrative agency that oversaw it.

CREATING THE KINDERGARTEN SPACE:
ROLE OF CHILD PSYCHOLOGY
AND DEVELOPMENT

Awareness of child psychology and child development shaped the organization of the Vietnamese kindergarten. These came to Vietnam primarily through the translation of written texts. As early as 1946, the Office of Infant Education attached to the Ministry of Education received Nguyen Khac Vien's and Hoang Xuan Nhi's translation of Alica Descoecudrss's "The Intellectual Development of Children from Two to Seven Years Old" sent from Paris. After intellectual ties with France were severed during the war between the French and the DRV (1946–54), Vietnamese educators turned to written materials from China and the Soviet Union. In the 1960s, short writings in Chinese and Russian were translated into Vietnamese either as reference materials or as documents supplementary to certain policy debates. Major translations of writings from the Soviet Union appeared in the early 1970s. In 1973 and 1974, the Education Publishing House published *Giao duc hoc mau giao* (Science of Kindergarten Education) translated from the Russian by Pham Minh Hac, who had received a Ph.D. in psychology from the Soviet Union and who would serve as the Minister of Education in the 1980s before the ministry was merged with the Ministry of Higher Education in 1990. In 1974, Nguyen Khac Vien, a French-trained intellectual-turned-communist, published *Ngay tho* (Innocence), which discussed child psychology. In 1988, Nguyen Anh Tuyet, who became director of the Department of Preschool Education in the 1990s, edited a book entitled *Tam ly hoc tre em truoc tuoi hoc* (Psychology of Preschool Children). In 1993, Nguyen Khac Vien's Center for Research on Child Psychology, the first nongovernment research organization in Vietnam, published *Noi kho cua con em* (The Misery of Our Children) and *Tim hieu tam ly con em* (Understanding the Psychology of Our Children). The concepts of child psychology and child development served to justify Vietnamese educators' move to create a separate educational space for children between the ages of three and five.

Preschool Children

Vietnamese writings on child development and child psychology first appeared in the late 1950s. They distinguished children from adults, arguing that children's physical and mental strength developed in different stages. One article published during the 1956–57 school year divided child development into five stages: the infant period (0–3), the preschool period (3–7), the early school years period (7–12), the teenage period (12–16), and the youth period (15–25) (Nguyen Kim Anh, 1956–57). Cumulatively, a number of writings on children established that children between three and thirteen years of age were physically, mentally, and morally unstable. For example, one article argued that children between the ages of seven and twelve years differed from older youth in that they were unable to concentrate for a long time, and that their learning ability was undeveloped (Nguyen Kim Anh, 1956–57). Another article characterized children between six and eleven years old as being incapable of handling the abstract, overly sentimental, hyperactive, imitative, and outgoing ("Tai lieu huyen luyen," 1956). Another article emphasized the need for expertise in dealing with children between the ages of three and six, a population that totaled 1,781,155 in the early 1960s. This group of children was young, had different personalities, and did not know how to take care of themselves (Phuong Hoa, 1960–61).

The notion that children are different from adults gave rise to the conception of what was appropriate and inappropriate behavior for children. One article published in 1961 voiced concern over children's precocity, complaining that children between three and five years of age were receptive to inappropriate songs: songs for adults, songs for older children, romantic and courting songs, and songs with inappropriate wording (V.A., 1961–62). These songs were unsuitable not only because they were too difficult for young children to sing but also because they contained inappropriate content.

> There were adults' songs whose content was idealistic, whose wording was difficult to understand, whose rhythm was too complicated, whose pitches were too high or too low, and whose content was tangled and lengthy. I heard three or four year old children in a class singing " . . . we are teachers of the masses, . . . the vanguard soldiers who bring culture [to the people] . . . who train the youth" . . . etc.
>
> How absurd and inappropriate! Even worse, children at the kindergartens also sang songs for children of 12 and 13 years. It is possible to list the following titles: "Having fun during the mid-Autumn Festival," "The light of Mr. Star," "I go to visit South Viet Nam," "South Viet Nam belongs to me," "I am completing small work targets," etc. . . .
>
> There were kindergartens where teachers allowed children to sing lyric songs without trying to modify the songs. Teachers even recited these songs in front of children, and they remembered. Although they were only four or five years old, they sang these sweet tones:
>
> " . . . We love each other, we undress for each other . . .
>
> " . . . The pristine water reflects the shadows of you and me. . . ." (V.A., 1961–62, 13)

The article lamented that kindergarten children enjoyed such songs more than the songs taught in their classes.

> The children often listened to adults and older children sing and imitated. In fact, they liked singing lengthy songs, difficult songs, and nonsensical songs rather than ones taught in class. Teachers should have told them that those songs were uninteresting, were not good, and should have directed them to sing other songs which were both appropriate for them and would please them. On the contrary, teachers had implicitly "legalized" those songs by teaching them to the entire class.
>
> Letting children sing unselected songs will limit the effectiveness of the singing

class. It ruins children's voices and creates a habit of singing voraciously; it creates a bad effect on children's morality and destroys children's aesthetic minds. (V.A., 1961–62, 14)

The article called for the use of easy songs whose content dealt mainly with children's daily life activities and Ho Chi Minh's teachings (V.A., 1961–62).

Yet, in the 1950s and 1960s, the boundary of the kindergarten age bracket vacillated from three to seven years to three to six years and to three to five years. There was also disagreement over how to organize the kindergarten—whether it was a baby-sitting institution or an educational institution. There were also divergent opinions as to what the appropriate study program and teaching methods would be.

It was in the 1970s when state educators moved to adopt the Soviet model, which considered children between three and five years of age as kindergarten children. Articles published in the 1980s evoked images of the three-year-old having an amorphous personality. In the process of forming personality, three-year-olds expressed their desire "to separate themselves from adults, do all things by themselves, and have jurisdiction over all things around them" (Nguyen Anh Tuyet, 1983, 5). These articles emphasized the need to employ educational means suitable to the age of the child and to help children build their personalities. They criticized those who advocated the treatment of kindergarten children as general school students. For preschool-age children, moral instruction and aesthetics served best to promote well-rounded development. Playing had the same meaning for them as studying had for older children and as labor activities had for adults. However, the articles cautioned, while Vietnamese kindergartens advocated playing, they did not promote "free education" similar to that existing in capitalist countries. Vietnamese kindergarten educators did not entertain the notion that children were entitled to a separate world of their own. Although they relied on soft, flexible, and nonimposing teaching measures, Vietnamese kindergartens were aimed at planting the first seeds of the new socialist person (*con nguoi moi xa hoi chu nghia*) in young Vietnamese.[15]

The postreunification period witnessed the crystallization of the notion that children in different age groups have different psychological and physical needs and therefore deserve separate attention. This line of thought affected the development of the organizational structure of the kindergarten, particularly the components of the study program, methods of studying, the relationship between ages and classes, and the evaluation of preschool children's performance, all of which were reflected in the 1977–78 and revised 1994 study programs.

Components of the Study Programs

After 1945, the kindergarten study programs were revised and rewritten several times. Between 1945 and 1954, the study program included playing, hygiene, physical exercise, excursions, outside class visits, drawing, singing, kneading, handicraft, observation, practice talking, and storytelling. Drawing was considered one of the most important educational components (VKHGDVN, 1991, 73). Various materials indicate that in 1958, Vietnamese educators modified the study program along the structure applied in the Soviet Union. In 1966, it was revised to highlight the five components of education: physical, intellectual, moral, aesthetic, and labor education. Physical and hygienic aspects received the highest priority (Thai Thi Hoa, 1961–62). The 1966 program was further simplified to respond to the wartime situation in the areas under heavy bombing. The number of subjects was reduced from twelve to six to include practical hygiene, games, physical exercise, singing and dancing, poetry reading, and storytelling (VKHGDVN, 1991, 86).

Beginning in 1974, Vietnamese researchers worked to develop a new program for the kindergarten. Those working on the reform of the study program criticized the 1966 study program for being too demanding for preschool children, for lacking coordination among different aspects of education, and for emphasizing in-class study over playing activity (BGD, 1977). After applying the new program to a number of schools on an experimental basis, in 1978, the department officially promulgated study programs for kindergarten classes throughout Vietnam. Subjects retained from previous programs were grouped into four categories: "playing," "studying," "labor activities," and "other educational activities" (VMG, 1977b). "Playing" referred to sessions for different types of games. "Studying" referred to sessions reserved for learning about the environment, practice speaking, counting, drawing and handicrafts, physical exercise, and singing and dancing. Labor activities referred to learning about adult occupations, self-servicing labor, cleaning chores, animal and plant tending, and handicrafts. "Other educational activities" consisted of hygiene, morning and evening meetings, excursions, national/religious holidays, sleeping and eating, and daily and weekly learning by examples (VMG, 1977b; BGD, 1979a, b, c).

The 1978 study programs were later revised. The new study programs, officially promulgated in 1994, reflected an adherence to the concepts of child psychology and child development and served both to nurture children's health and to promote their intellectual growth. Child rearing covered the nutritional care of children and attention to their sleeping time, hygiene, and personal safety.

Minimum requirements for children's physical development and maximum expectations were given. For example, the instruction manual for the junior kindergarten class, that is, the class for the three- to four-year-olds, states that by the end of the school year the boy's weight should be between 12.9 and 16.7 kilos, while the girl's weight should be between 12.6 and 16 kilos, and that their height should be between 94.4 and 102.9 cm and between 93.5 and 101.6 cm, respectively (BGDDT, 1994a).

As with the 1978 program, the new study programs emphasized all aspects of education, while relating them to each other. They consisted of the following components: playing, studying, labor activities, and festival and holiday activities. The study sessions included physical education, kneading, music, literature, learning about the social environment, and preliminary counting. Differing from the previous programs, the 1994 programs also offered special classes in dancing, painting, foreign languages, and organ playing for all three levels. All the model schools in Hanoi offered these special classes, and other kindergartens could offer them if they had enough financial resources to hire teachers. Finally, because a large number of children did not attend kindergarten, the Department of Preschool Education prepared a twenty-six-week abridged version of the existing kindergarten programs containing similar basic components for five-year-olds who had not attended the first two kindergarten years (BGDDT, 1993).

Ages and Classes

The development of the kindergarten in Vietnam witnessed a move to create three separate classes and an attempt to keep children of the same age in the same class. For example, in 1966, state educators called for the spread of the three-year kindergarten, consisting of a junior class, an intermediate class, and a senior class. The first two classes accommodated children between three and five years of age. In 1977, the Department of Kindergarten issued a draft regulation on kindergartens which confirmed that the kindergarten system was responsible for serving children between the ages of three to five years (thirty-six to seventy-two months) and encouraged the placement of children of specific ages in specific classes: a junior class for the three-year-old, an intermediate class for the four-year-old, and a senior class for the five-year-old.

The 1994 study programs reflected a further move to match ages and classes. While the three kindergarten study programs shared certain similar structures, they offered programs with different degrees of difficulty and different amounts of time needed. The first two classes did not contain any strong components of cultural knowledge, while the class for the five-year-olds had an additional component of knowledge that would prepare them for the first grade. The 1994 study programs also differentiated the time allotted to different classes. While all three classes consisted of nine sessions per day, those for the junior class were shorter than those for the other two classes. Junior and intermediate classes studied only in the morning, playing and reviewing in the afternoon. The senior class studied all day. The length of the study session for each class was also reduced. In the 1978 study programs, the time allotted to study sessions had been twenty to thirty minutes each day for the junior class and forty-five to seventy-five minutes each day for the intermediate and senior classes (VMG, 1977b; BGD, 1979a, b, c). The 1994 study program reduced the study time for the junior class to two ten- to fifteen-minute sessions per day, and two twenty-five- to thirty-minute sessions per day for the intermediate and senior classes (BGDDT, 1994a, b, c).

Studying versus Playing

In the 1950s, storytelling (*ke chuyen*), toys, and games were the main teaching mechanisms in the kindergarten.[16] In 1966, emphasis was given to playing as the major teaching and learning method, which resulted in a reduction in the amount of time reserved for studying and an increase in the amount of time for play, general activities, and light labor (Thai Thi Hoa, 1961–62).

It was not until after 1975 that "playing" was emphasized as the main kindergarten methodology. The Department of Kindergarten published an article in 1978 which justified playing as the primary mechanism for educating preschool-age children. First, playing allowed children to learn to become independent, because in real life they were dependents and passive actors. When they played, they acted as adults, tested their strength, and made decisions. Second, playing helped to promote well-rounded development, the main objective of kindergarten education. When children played, they learned general knowledge, social skills, methods of interaction, social exchanges, moral principles, observational methods, and comment-making. Finally, playing helped to organize children's society (*xa hoi tre em*). When children played, they developed two types of relationship: one with the role they played and the other, the real relationship, with their friends when they discussed what to play (VMG, 1978a, 9–10).

The 1994 study programs confirmed playing as the major pedagogical mechanism, focusing on studying and labor activities to a lesser degree. The kindergarten study programs differed from the general school programs in that the former did not stress the division of scientific knowledge into subjects, but stressed methods which would help to create children's personalities—to turn children into "persons" (*lam nguoi*) (BGDDT, 1994a, b, c).

Well-Behaved Children and Healthy Children

Kindergarten children are differentiated from one another according to their performance and physical health. The designations *be ngoan* (well-behaved child) and *be khoe* (healthy child) are used. These criteria enable the grouping of children into normal children, well-behaved children, and problem children.

The certification *be ngoan,* reserved for well-behaved children, has been in vogue for some time. According to the 1978 study program, for example, at the end of the day and at the end of the week, teachers evaluated children's performance against the Ministry of Education's yardstick for the well-behaved child. They praised children who followed all the regulations and those who could successfully rectify their shortcomings. Individuals who were praised would receive different forms of awards: public verbal praise and applause from their peers; a flag inscribed "well-behaved child"; a "well-behaved child" certificate for those receiving four flags in a week; a nomination "Uncle Ho's well-behaved child" for those receiving four certificates in a month; and a nomination "Uncle Ho's well-behaved child" plus a present for those receiving six out of nine nominations in a year. Units with children who had many "well-behaved" child certificates would also receive public praise (VMG, 1977b). According to the 1994 program, this would be done after the study session, the playing session, and the afternoon activity session. Emphasis was given more to individual children than to units, and children who were considered "well-behaved children" would be given a flower or a flag which they would place in a slot with their name on it.

The certification *be khoe,* "healthy child," appeared with the 1994 study program, which considered nutritional care as one major aspect of the kindergarten. As a result, the label has become another yardstick to differentiate one kindergarten child from another. On June 1, International Children's Day, there is a competition among children for the label "healthy child."

CREATING A WORLD OF MINIATURE
SOCIALIST CITIZENS

Although the organizational structure of the Vietnamese kindergarten has been based on the idea of child development as a step-by-step process and on the idea that preschool children differ from other children and adults, the different components of the study program—"playing," "studying," "labor activities," and "holiday and festive activities"—familiarized preschool children with the expectations of adults and their world view. This emphasis on the need to teach the political and economic ethics of Vietnamese adults *cum* citizens is not new. As early as 1949, at the first conference on kindergarten education, the Ministry of Education stated that kindergarten education served to prepare children to become good citizens of Vietnam (Do Xuan Hoa and Le Bich Ngoc, 1995). Introducing the 1994 study programs, Vietnamese educators explained that they were aimed at responding to children's need to develop an understanding of and participate in their environment in order to be part of the community. The content of the study programs would not merely reflect the world of children (*the gioi tre em*) but serve to lead them into the world of the adults (*the gioi nguoi lon*) in which family life, labor activities, and traditional cultures were of importance. The study programs would help instill in children positive attitudes that would expedite their assimilation into the adult environment.[17]

Available teaching materials, produced in the late 1970s and 1980s and revised in the 1990s, reflected certain themes related to the ethics of adults *cum* citizens. They included the concepts of time and space, the notion of family and friends, and the meaning of growing up.[18]

Time

The kindergarten study programs structured children's days and years, thus helping to shape their perception of time. Each day consisted of nine sessions: arriving and free playing; studying; outdoor activities; creative games; hygiene and lunch; afternoon nap; hygiene, light activities and snack time; afternoon activities (learning praiseworthy models on Saturday); and free play and returning home.

Each year, children participated in the organization of national and traditional festivals: School Opening Day (September), Mid-Autumn Festival, Teacher's Day (November), Army Day (December), Lunar New Year Festival, International Women's Day (March), Ho Chi Minh's Birthday (May), International Children's Day (June), and the birthdays of classmates (VMG, 1977b, 13; BGDDT, 1994a, b, c). The teachers discussed future events in class and organized relevant excursions in order to raise the children's enthusiasm and enhance their understanding. Teachers would allocate tasks to all children, making sure that each had a part to play. Activities included artistic performances, singing, dancing, poetry reading, games, and so forth. On the actual day of the event, all the children sang or read together to open their collective artistic presentation.[19]

Space

Kindergarten education taught children different types of spaces. Children were first taught to love their home and objects found in its surroundings ranging from gardens, ponds, and trees, to rice fields. For example, in "I love my home,"

No place equals my home
There are sparrows chirping on the verandah floor.
There are hens
Cackling and clucking over their eggs.
There are sweet bananas
and ears of corn with their silky pink hair.
. . . .
Although I have to go far away
I will find no place as joyful as my home. (BGDDT, 1994b, 57)

Children were taught to love their school and were reminded of what they could do there. In a song sung to preschool children, the kindergarten is described as follows: "My school has a red tile roof and is next to a grove of green trees. Everyday there is an echo of songs calling for peace. We compete with each other to write Uncle Ho's name beautifully. We compete with each other to draw a star on the flag" (BGDDT, 1994c, 47).

They were familiarized with places far beyond their home and school. Children in the intermediate class sang a song expressing their affinity with the capital city, Hanoi. "Ha Noi, I love Ha Noi. I love my parents, my familiar house roof, my nice friends, and my kind teacher. There are so many people I love here. I love the Lake of the Redeemed Sword with its beautiful pagoda. I love the West Lake where blue clouds move over blue water. I go to visit Uncle Ho's Mausoleum. I will always love Ha Noi" (BGDDT, 1994b, 36).

A poem entitled "Along the Hai Phong seaport" describes a child's experience in Hai Phong when he visited the port, met naval officers, and saw naval ships.

I go to visit the port
and the uncles of the naval forces.
When the sunlight breaks,
and the morning dew is melting.
Amidst the immense ocean
there are gigantic buildings
with green walls and red stripes on the edges
floating up and down.
Oh no, there are not buildings,

there are our naval ships
queuing, one after another
looking like a row of streets.
When the sun goes high,
the water turns pink,
the flags on the ships look like flames
brightening the surface of the river.
Today, the naval ships rest in the port,
tomorrow they depart,
showing the flag of the fatherland
to brighten the ocean and the sky. (*Bai soan,* 1984c, 47)

Finally, children were taught to love their natural environment. Affinity between children and nature was fostered through the linkage between concrete images found in the children's daily life and natural objects. In "Moon, where are you from?," the Moon is linked with the rice field, the ocean, and the playground. In this poem, the moon is domesticated.

Moon, where are you from?
From a faraway field?
You are as pink as a ripe fruit,
rising above the house.
Moon, where are you from?
From the marvelous sea?
You are as round as a fish eye,
and you never wink.
Moon, where are you from?
From a playing ground?
You fly like a ball
that one of our friends has kicked into the sky. (*Bai soan,* 1984d, 68;
BGDDT, 1994c, 67)

Unfamiliar and unknown places and objects were linked with places known to children and to objects found in their daily life. In this process, the home, school, and unfamiliar places and objects become connected.

Family Members

The kindergarten study programs taught children the notions of family and family members. Children learned first about their immediate family members: father, mother, grandparents, sisters, brothers, uncles, and aunts. They learned that it was important to love and help their family members, especially the grandmother, mother, and their siblings.[20]

Stories read to children enlarged the family space to include a number of "strangers." Selected groups of people outside the family circle were given quasi-familial nouns. The pronouns *chu* (younger paternal uncle), *bac* (older paternal uncle/older paternal aunt), and *co* (younger paternal aunt/older maternal aunt) were placed in front of generic nouns referring to occupations or social classes: *chu bo doi* (Uncle Soldier), *bac nong dan* (Uncle Peasant), *bac cong nhan* (Uncle Worker), *co y ta* (Aunt Nurse), *chu hai quan* (Uncle Naval Officer), and so forth. The quasi-familial term used for teachers was *co* (younger paternal aunt/older maternal aunt), and that for children was *chau* (nieces/nephews). These quasi-familial terms were used for the paternal side and thus tacitly pointed to the omnipresence of the father figure.

Strangers *cum* family members who often appeared in stories and games were soldiers, peasants, workers, and Ho Chi Minh. The study programs used in the 1980s heavily focused on soldiers' contribution to the defense of the country. For example, a poem entitled "Applaud to Uncle Soldiers" depicted American bombing of kindergartens and how "Uncle Soldiers" intelligently shot down American planes and in so doing helped save the kindergartens (*Bai soan,* 1984e, 56). The intimacy between the children and soldiers was reflected in the children's aspiration to join the army. To celebrate the founding of the People's Liberation Army in December, children sang a song entitled "Going with Uncle Soldiers." The song described soldiers with their backpacks marching through villages on their way to border areas and the children's desire to join the troops (Hoang Lan and Hoang Van Yen, 1985, 1984, 40). The 1994 study programs, however, downplayed the war with America. Their emphasis was on the portrayal of children's aspirations to become soldiers, a long-lasting affinity between children and soldiers, and their remembering "Uncle Soldiers" (*chu giai phong quan*) who liberated South Vietnam.[21]

Children were taught to appreciate labor. The study programs used in the 1980s contained a class-based element in favor of peasants and workers and focused on teaching children to value the labor of "Uncle Workers" and "Uncle Peasants." A poem entitled "A New Bridge," for example, praised the achievement of workers in completing a new bridge which people, trains, cars, and bicycles used to cross a river (*Bai soan,* 1984f, 45–46). The study programs revised in 1994 focused more on the general appreciation of labor without emphasizing the contribution of any specific social groups.

Uncle Ho was presented as a family member who loved and cared for his children's well-being. The emphases were on Uncle Ho's love for his nieces and nephews, on his hope that all children would try hard "to compete with each other in study and practice," and on his suggestion of "young children doing small works, depending on their own strength" (*Bai soan,* 1984e, 39).

> In my house hung Uncle Ho's portrait,
> Above it is a fresh red flag.
> Everyday, Uncle smiles
> Looking at his nieces and nephews playing in the house.
> Outside there are a few chickens,
> In the garden there are a few ripe custard-apples.
> I hear Uncle saying
> My nieces and nephews, do not wander around far.
> Plant vegetables, sweep the kitchen, and chase the chickens away
> And remember to run to the tunnel when seeing American planes.
> Uncle has to care for so many things
> But everyday, he still smiles freshly at me. (*Bai soan,* 1984d, 77; BGDDT, 1994b, 56)

Children commemorated Uncle Ho's birthday by singing "On May 19, we visit Uncle's Mausoleum." It was an occasion when children visited the mausoleum and Ho Chi Minh's Thai-style house and fishpond, which was located close to the mausoleum (Hoang Lan and Hoang Van Yen, 1985, 38). They also sang "Who will love Uncle Ho more than young Vietnamese?" (BGDDT, 1994a, 53–53).

The use of quasi-familial terms was extended to domesticated animals found in daily life such as the chicken, cat, dog, butterfly, duck, and buffalo, especially when these animals appeared in stories as heroic and courageous figures. Aggressive animals such as the wolf, fox, and bear were not called by quasi-familial terms. Courageous animals that confronted aggressors were referred to with the pronouns *may-tao,* a pair connoting unfriendliness for I and you/me and you. These quasi-familial terms were also used to name natural objects such as the sun, moon, and stars, for example, *ong giang* (Grandfather Moon), *ong sao* (Grandfather Star), and *ong mat troi* (Grandfather Sun) (BGDDT, 1994b, 53–54).

Friends

Children learned to develop relationships with "strangers" of their own age. This group of strangers were called *ban* (friends). A poem entitled "A new friend" taught children how to turn a stranger into a friend.

A new friend arrives at school
Still looked worried,
I teach my friend to sing
[I] ask my friend to play,
When my teacher sees us, she laughs
She praises us for being united. (*Bai soan,* 1984b, 32; BGDDT, 1994a, 51)

Emphasis was given to minority friends in the central highlands. Children sang "Dancing with friends in the central highland": "My hand holds a red flag with a yellow star, dancing and singing along the rhythm. I have fun with friends from the central highland. When we are apart, we will miss each other. Today is the day we sing and dance together. All are Uncle Ho's well-behaved nieces and nephews" (BGDDT, 1994c, 34).

Friendship meant being united (*doan ket*). The story "Two Uncle Butterflies" showed unity between two friends: in a big storm, each butterfly refused to accept an offer of refuge unless its friend was also allowed shelter (*Bai soan,* 1984a, 41–42).

Children were taught to be cautious and afraid of "real" strangers, that is, those outside their circles of family and friends. Dangers from these strangers always came when children refused to listen to adults' words and went off on their own. In "The story of a girl with a red scarf," the Vietnamese version of Little Red Riding Hood, the little girl who ignored her mother's words brought trouble to both her loved one (her grandmother) and herself (*Bai soan,* 1984b, 27–29). Had they not been rescued by a woodsman, they would have died in the wolf's stomach. Another story entitled "Uncle Grey Duck" described the danger a little duck faced after he ignored his mother's warning and went off by himself to look for fun (*Bai soan,* 1984a, 35–36).

The Meaning of Growing Up:
Courage and Industriousness

The meaning of adulthood was linked to moral awakening and the maturity of work habits. "The Story of Giong," a Vietnamese legend, told how a three-year-old boy grew into a man. In Phu Dong village, there was a mother who gave birth to a child whom she called Giong. Although Giong was three, he did not talk. This made his mother very unhappy. One day, the An troops invaded the country. A representative of the king came to the village to look for a volunteer to fight the enemy. Hearing that the king's representative was coming, Giong began to talk. He asked his mother to call the representative in and told him to report to the king that he would volunteer to save the country. He asked for an iron horse, an iron cane, and an iron hat as his weapons. After the representative left, Giong asked his mother for food. He devoured all the food given to him first by his mother and later by the entire village. He grew up into a healthy young man. After he received his weapons, he went to fight the enemy. He defeated the invading troops. After his victory, Giong disappeared into the mountain. Phu Dong Villagers set up a shrine to worship him (*Bai soan*, 1984f, 49–50; BGDDT, 1994b, 60–61).

Another story entitled "Three Angels" suggested that a six-year-old child became an adult when he realized that he had to bear certain adults' work responsibilities.

> *Summary:* Although six years old, the tiny tot was about the size of an adult's large toe. The family of the tiny tot was very poor; his parents tended buffaloes for a landlord. The tiny tot often asked to tend the buffaloes for his parents. At first they resisted, but later agreed. The tiny tot did a very good job of not letting the buffaloes damage rice fields; he also kept them well-fed. One day, when the tiny tot found that the village's grass was gone, he took the buffaloes up into the hill. There, he saw a rose as big as a conical hat blooming on a branch of a tree. He discovered three tiny angels living in the rose. They invited him in and presented him with candies. The tiny tot thanked them and told them that he would keep the candies for his parents. The three angels were overwhelmed; they promised to help him and his family. They went back to his place together; then they sent him to look for his parents. While he was away, the first angel drew a nice house, the second one drew a big rice field, and the third one drew nice clothes. All the drawings turned real. When the family came back, the angels presented them with a new house, a rice field, and new clothes. One angel gave the tiny tot a set of clothes. After wearing them, he grew into a man. The three angels became three white pigeons, flying away. Nobody saw them again. The tiny tot, now an adult, continued to work industriously and skillfully. (Hoang Nguyen, 1956–57, 22–23; *Bai soan*, 1984a, 51–53; BGDDT, 1994a, 58–59)

These two stories deal with the meaning of growing up. In both stories, the children grow into adults; that is, they gain muscles and weight after they are politically awakened and after they are aware of the need to perform adult tasks. From this perspective, children can become adults when they are three and six years old. The process of growing up for Giong, in the first story, comes after his patriotic awakening. The story teaches patriotism, the consciousness which turns a child into a man. The process of growing into an adult for the little tot comes after he shows that he has developed work consciousness and mature work habits.

These two strands or ethics, courage and industriousness, became themes of many stories read to preschool children. The story entitled "Uncle Black Goat" depicted little goats who were not afraid of the wolf and fought back (*Bai soan*, 1984b, 33–35; BGDDT, 1994c, 78). United courage also brought about triumphal results. A poem entitled "A Fox and a Group of Bees," composed by Ho Chi Minh himself, illustrated this outcome (*Bai soan*, 1984c, 68).

Many stories read to children taught basic desirable work ethics found in the adult world. "The Rabbits Move to a New House" told children about how four rabbit boys and one rabbit girl divided jobs among themselves to help their parents. The boys moved the table and the chairs, while the girl carried her mother's sewing basket. On their way to the new house, the rain poured down. The rabbit girl suggested that they put the chairs on the table and use the table to shield themselves from the rain.[22]

KINDERGARTEN TEACHERS: ON BEHALF
OF MOTHERS AND THE STATE

The role of the kindergarten teacher in Vietnam was succinctly summed up in the writing of Ha The Ngu, a prominent Vietnamese educator, in 1983. He wrote that the teacher-pupil relationship (*thay va tro*) in the kindergarten represented two sets of relationships. One was the relationship between mothers and children, between grandmother and niece/nephew, and between older sister and younger siblings. The other was the relationship between the working class and its socialist state on the one hand and on the other, the working Vietnamese (women), children (national youngsters and the future of the fatherland), and family (the basic unit of society) (Ha The Ngu, 1983, 2).

Teachers and Mothers

To legitimize the kindergarten as an educational institution and to give teachers pedagogical authority, the Ministry of Education equated teachers with mothers. As mentioned earlier, the quasi-familial terms *co* and *chau* were used in the teacher-pupil relationship. Children called teachers "younger paternal and maternal aunt," while teachers called their pupils "nieces/nephews." The two women, mother and teacher, were portrayed as the two bright lights for Vietnamese children.

> In the morning I leave my mother
> And run to embrace my teacher.

In the afternoon, I leave my teacher
And rush into the arms of my mother.
The sun rises and sets
On the two horizons
My two horizons
Are mother and teacher. (BGDDT, 1994b, 57)

But at school, the kindergarten teacher was equated with the mother. In a song sung by preschool children, "At school, my mother is my beloved teacher who loves me endlessly and teaches me always. She teaches me word by word, sentence by sentence, gesture by gesture, and step by step. She hopes to make me a good person, to become a well-behaved niece/nephew of Uncle. I love you so much, my school mother. At school, my teacher is my mother" (BGDDT, 1994a, 35).

The kindergarten was equated with home. "People ask which school I go to. I am a child who is both well-behaved and dances well. My teacher is my mother and I am the child. My school is a kindergarten. People ask whether there are schools which are fun, where there are a lot of friends but the classes are still tidy. When returning home I miss school. My school is a kindergarten" (BGDDT, 1994a, 28).

It was the teacher who taught the children to appreciate a mother's love. A poem entitled "Gluing Flowers for Mother" praised kindergarten teachers for teaching children to make flowers for their mothers on International Women's Day.

I paste a flower.
The teacher lets me bring it back home
Saying "You give it to your mother.
It is a present for Women's Day."
Caressing my hair, my mother asks:
"You can make a beautiful flower?"
She thanks my teacher
Who teaches me to give her a flower. (*Bai soan*, 1984b, 25; BGDDT, 1994a, 46)

The teacher thus was recognized as the mother at school who not only took care of the children's physical and intellectual well-being but also taught them to love and cherish the biological mother.

Teachers as State-Trained Mothers

Teachers differed from mothers, however, in that they were also representatives of the Vietnamese state, trained and employed by the state. In this sense, they were state-trained mothers. As representatives of the socialist state, they received certain privileges from the state and fulfilled certain functions. The Ministry of Education opened schools to train teachers. Prior to 1975 it allocated local production units and parents to take care of the teachers' salary, but after 1975 it paid the salary of school principals and subsidized that of other teachers when local resources were insufficient. As state cadres, teachers worked to solicit local support for the building of kindergartens.

Teachers' mobilizational tasks were not insignificant. This was especially the case in rural areas. In the 1960s and 1970s, the attitudes of provincial administrative units, production units, and parents toward kindergartens fluctuated over time. Ministerial reports often complained that provinces, more often than not, failed to see the need for developing the kindergarten movement. They neither advocated the universalization of kindergartens nor spent time to manage them. Often, they subcontracted kindergartens to local production units (*khoan trang*). Ministerial reports also complained that cooperatives did not fulfill their financial obligations toward teachers: they refused to pay a proper salary or subsidize teachers' expenses for additional training (VKHGDVN, 1991). The statute of the cooperatives put forth in the mid-1970 had no clause related to the remuneration of teachers (*tra cong diem*). Many writings discussed rural parents' ambivalent attitudes toward the kindergarten movement ("Kinh nghiem," 1954, 28). Parents viewed kindergartens as places which "kept children" (*giu tre*) or as places for children to play. From this perspective, sending children to the kindergarten was a luxury. While general school education was subsidized, the kindergarten was not. In the countryside, parents paid by work points and in the city they paid school fees. Keeping children at home not only eliminated extra expenses but also created more helping hands for secondary jobs done by the family.[23]

Kindergarten teachers therefore were the main agents who could promote the spread of the state-designed kindergarten. In the 1960s, educators, in discussing the building of kindergartens, pointed to two factors which contributed to success: a close cooperation between the provincial educational office and the provincial women's union, and teachers *cum* cadres' ability to lead the movement (Do Duc Trien, 1960–61). Many articles reported that parents, after knowing what kindergartens offered, praised them. A minority mother reportedly stated that she could go to work in the field without having to worry that her children were left unattended or that they might set the house on fire. A father in Lang Son province reportedly said that before going to the kindergarten, his child was dirty, stubborn, and disrespectful of adults. After going to the school, he learned how to keep clean and how to greet parents, and he stopped cursing (Phuong Hoa, 1960–61).

In order to gain local support for the kindergarten, teachers had to know how to deal with local constituencies and how to run the kindergarten, and their skills seemed to develop over time. An article written by a teacher in 1974 pointed out that the best method to persuade mothers to let their children attend kindergartens and to mobilize party cadres, members of women's unions, and parents to support kindergartens was to make sure that children who attended kindergarten classes were cleaner, happier, more innocent, and more polite than those who stayed home.

> We trained the children to wash their feet and hands . . . and warned them not to sit around on the street, not to use their shirt sleeves when they blew their nose, not to eat raw fruit and drink unboiled water. Most of them remembered what their teachers said and passed the words to their parents. The families were surprised because since the children had been going to class, they had learned how to keep their feet, hands, and clothes cleaner.
>
> We also taught them to be polite to everybody; after class, on the way home, when we met older people, I greeted them then the children greeted them. Gradually, greeting people on the street became part of the children's unconscious act. When they were alone without their teacher, they still greeted older people.
>
> In class, I taught the children to sing and dance happily. I tried to teach them to sing evenly and dance naturally. When local party congresses met, we took the children to greet the congresses and perform a number of artistic programs that they had practiced. (Nguyen Thi Tham, 1974, 17)

In 1974, the Department of Kindergarten published a series of articles on the work of Nguyen Thi Thao, a kindergarten teacher in Dui Bui commune, Ha Tinh province. The department praised her contribution during the war with America, considering it a heroic action (VMG, 1974b, c). It also considered her an example of a *me van minh* (civilized mother) (BGD, 1974, 4). Initially, the kindergarten movement in Dui Bui commune was weak: villagers did not support the movement and reportedly criticized the cooperative for assigning a young person like Thao to tend children, while sending older ones to work in the field. Considering kindergarten work as light work, they criticized Thao for doing nothing but having a good time. Although Thao received only a small remuneration from the cooperative, she, backed by some party cadres, ignored the criticism and unfair treatment and tried to improve the pupils' health, personal hygiene, and the condition of their clothing. She adapted her teaching to local conditions, using available materials to make toys. Children who had wanted to stay out of the group began to participate in group activities. She gradually won over the love and attention of the children. She also succeeded in establishing a close relationship with the children's families and in persuading parents to send their children to kindergarten classes. During the bombing period, Thao evacuated the children from the commune to a safer place. When the bombing was over, she returned to rebuild the kindergarten movement in her commune. Of the preschool-age children in the commune, 90–100 percent reportedly attended kindergarten classes (BGD, 1974; Nguyen Thi Thao, 1974).

One further responsibility of state-trained mothers was to follow the study programs closely. Vietnamese educators often complained that teachers in rural areas failed to observe the officially sanctioned timetable. An article written in the early 1960s criticized rural teachers for rearranging classes or leaving out certain sessions, a partial result of the fact that parents sent their children to kindergartens and took them back home according to their own needs, work schedules, and economic conditions. The article lamented that teachers did not realize the scientific character of the study timetable, which allocated time for playing, studying, and resting based on child psychology (Thai Thi Hoa, 1961–62).

Another article published in 1982 echoed the same problems, while emphasizing the need for both teachers and parents to respect the class timetable. It asserted that if all the activities in the daily and monthly schedule were regularly performed, that is, if they were repeated at determined times and followed the determined order, they would foster children's natural responses. This type of internalization was the basis for the development of volition, a requirement for adulthood. After these practices became an integral part of children's lives, they would feel uncomfortable when they failed to enact them (Ta Thi Ngoc Thanh, 1982).

Another responsibility of state-trained mothers was to organize play activities. In the kindergarten, children were free to design the content and pace of their activity. Because games were important, the Department of Kindergarten warned that it was the teachers' responsibility to "organize" game playing (VMG, 1978a). "In reality, many teachers know how to guide children's play in different ways ranging from guiding them directly to giving them advice if they do not know how to play. For example, when they have to play the game "excursion," they often do not know how to organize it and how to begin the game. They run around aimlessly and without direction. At this moment, the teacher should warn them: 'Pupils have to sit still and the one who plays the role of the teacher will have to direct the pupils before they go on an excursion!' When getting to the place, children often do not know what to do. The teacher should say: 'The one who acts as the guide has to introduce [the place] to visitors and invite them to see the paintings'" (VMG, 1978f, 10).

A kindergarten teacher in Hanoi wrote an article narrating her intervention in organized game playing. Complaining that children "did not know how to play," she suggested that teachers prepare toys and game materials in advance in order to attract the children's attention (Phi Van Khanh, 1978, 16). She wrote about intervening to organize a game related to the army which was scheduled for the month of December to commemorate the birthday of Vietnam's People's Liberation Army.

> This is a subject closely connected to children, and which will have a great educational impact. The objective of this game is to make children see how our Army fought hero-ically in protecting the people, and won gloriously defending the fatherland, and building the country, all of which will bring a happy life to the children. The game is also aimed at instilling in children love, respect, and gratitude toward our Army. At the same time, the game will make the children realize the discipline, the morality, and the civilized practice of our Army in order to educate them with these beautiful qualities. In order to create a condition which would allow children to play blithely, I organized as follows:
>
> First of all, I tried to attract their attention to this topic by telling them stories, read-ing poems, and teaching them to sing songs about the Army. I collected paintings and pictures of the Army in battles and in production. Then I organized children to play "Exhibition of the Images of the Army." Several mornings, I organized for them to play games "Seeing the Army off," and "The Army building the Thong Nhat Rail-road." To guide children to play these games, I had carefully prepared the content of the games, toys, and playing methods in advance. These games gave children a good impression and pure sentiments toward the Army. Fun and happiness showed clearly on their faces. When they finished building the railroad, they wanted to bring out a train to run on it, etc. (Phi Van Khanh, 1978, 16)

This teacher concluded that games also helped to improve the behavior of children who were stubborn and hyperactive. "For example, in my class, C. and T. were so restless: they could not sit still for more than five minutes. They teased their friends, knocked down the chairs, chatted between themselves, and even left the room in the middle of a session, etc. Persuading them to play games, I could gradually rectify their shortcomings. For example, I arranged for them to play 'Uncle Soldiers guarding Uncle Ho's mausoleum'" (Phi Van Khanh, 1978, 16).

Finally, state-trained mothers were responsible for propagating the correct child rearing methods and child education to the actual mothers. They exchanged views with parents or visited them from time to time in order to discuss the children's progress. In 1990, with assistance from the UNFPA (United Nations Family Planning Agency) and the UNICEF, the Ministry of Education and Training carried out projects to educate parents about child rearing. Topics under discussion dealt with both health-related matters and appropriate methods for teaching preschool children. The former included measures to prevent certain illnesses, signs of malnourishment, and the advantages of breastfeeding. The latter included methods for teaching children from three to six years old, toy making, and tips for teaching children to talk.[24]

During the decades after the August Revolution of 1945, the Ministry of Education moved to create a formal institutional space for children between three and five years of age in response to the need to liberate the female labor force for both national and social revolutionary tasks. Vietnamese educators also evoked pedagogical concepts related to child development and child psychology to justify the building of the kindergarten. By the 1990s, the kindergarten had become part of the Vietnamese educational landscape, and "kindergarten children" were differentiated from other types of children and from Vietnamese adults. While state educators worked to implant the form of kindergarten, they designed its content to conform with socialist Vietnam's national political and economic ethics. The study program created a world of miniature Vietnamese adults—a world in which national time, collective space, the notion of a big family of nation, patriotism, and work ethics were of prime importance.

While advocating that kindergarten teachers be female and equating kindergarten education as "mother's teaching," state educators redefined what mother's teaching should be. They trained teachers to be "civilized" mothers who in turn would tell the real mothers about mother's teaching. *Mau giao,* or "mother's teaching," thus not only refers to teaching Vietnamese children but also how to teach mothers the correct "mother's teaching," that is, teaching young Vietnamese to become patriotic and work-oriented. When women assumed the major role in preschool education, the father-centered quasi-familial terms used to personalize the relationship between the nation, the state, and children created vertical hierarchies based on age and sex.

That the coexistence of these contradictory elements was presented as natural indicates the successful process of the Vietnamization of the foreign concept of "kindergarten."

NOTES

This chapter is based on library research and interviews conducted in Hanoi in May and June 1994 and in May 1995. For the 1994 field research, I thank Thai Duy Tuyen at the National Institute of Educational Science, who facilitated my documentary research at the institute's library, and Nguyen Anh Tuyet, director of the Department of Preschool Children, Ministry of Education and Training, who arranged my visits to four kindergartens in and outside Hanoi: Mam Non Kindergarten, Mang Non Kindergarten, Tu Liem Kindergarten, and Quang An Kindergarten. For the 1995 field research, I thank Pham Mai Chi, Center for Research on Preschool Children, who arranged working sessions between myself and the center's researchers. I also thank the Mang Non Kindergarten for allowing me to conduct site observations. I thank Benedict Kerkvliet, Craig Reynolds, and Saya Shiraishi for their comments on an earlier draft of this chapter. I remain responsible for the arguments made in this chapter.

1. The Ministry of Education's 1980 Regulations on Kindergartens considered the 3–5 age bracket (36 to 72 months) as the kindergarten age bracket. Vietnamese educators in their writings, however, refer to the 3–5, 3–6, and 3–7 age groups as kindergarten ages. This is understandably because Vietnamese parents are late in sending their children to kindergartens and primary schools.

2. According to the 1989 census, children up to 14 years old totaled 25,118,100; 4,254,400 lived in urban areas, while 20,863,000 lived in the countryside. Of the 0–14 age group, 22.53% were between 3 and 6 years; 19.45% of this age group were under 3, and 649,758, or about 12.1%, of children between 0 and 2 years went to day nurseries. See *Thong Tin,* 1991, pp. 56 and 59. See also Do Xuan Hoa and Le Bich Ngoc, 1995, p. 11.

3. For a discussion of the development of Vietnamese education during the precolonial and colonial periods, see Vu Ngoc Khanh, *Tim hieu nen giao duc,* 1985.

4. For detailed information about the political development in Vietnam in and after 1945, see David Marr, *Viet Nam 1945: The Quest for Power* (Berkeley: University of California Press, 1995), and Ken Post, *Revolution, Socialism, and Nationalism in Viet Nam,* vols. 1–3 (Hants: Dartmouth, 1989).

5. "Mau giao" was reprinted in 1991 as part of a collection of selected writings on education by Toan (Nguyen Khanh Toan, 1991, 39–56).

6. In 1956, Toan recapitulated the points he had made in 1949. To succeed, teachers had to love the children in their classes as they would their own children. They had to pay close attention to them in order to understand their psychology and family environment. Only with this type of devoted love could teachers fulfill their educational responsibilities (VKHGDVN, 1991, 74).

7. The term *vuon tre,* meaning "children's garden" or "kindergarten" and connoting a space, is not in vogue.

8. Interzone Viet Bac's six provinces, the revolutionary base, reportedly opened 23 classes (4 of which were kindergartens) accommodating 630 children. Figures for other DRV-controlled areas were not available. Writings on this period emphasize the contribution of local people to the *vo long* movement. In Interzone 4, in particular in Thanh Hoa and Nghe Tinh provinces, local people opened *vo long* classes, while provincial authorities helped with specialized issues and cadre training. In Interzone III, which was under French control, Thai Binh province was the only one which could open *vo long* classes ("Lop vo long sau mot nam hoat dong," 1953).

9. By 1961, when they had become universal in the plains areas of North Vietnam, the age structure of these classes had changed substantially: children who attended *vo long* classes were between 6 and 8 years of age.

10. In 1976, in Dong Nai province, 102 out of 274 kindergarten classes were run by Catholic organizations. In Minh Hai province, 6 out of 11 were run by Catholic groups. Ho Chi Minh City had 84 such kindergartens (VKHGDVN, 1991, 100).

11. Between 1957 and 1978, there were 42 books on kindergartens. Between 1978 and 1986, there were 64 books: 33 for children, 31 for teachers, and 2 for administrators (VKHGDVN, 1991, 116).

12. For more information on the policy of renovation, see Turley and Selden (1993) and Ljunggren (1993).

13. See *Viet Nam voi cong uoc cua Lien hop quoc ve quen tre em,* 1991.

14. The only systematic treatment of the creche system in Vietnam after 1945 can be found in *40 nam xay dung va phat trien su nghiep giao duc mam non.*

15. Nguyen Anh Tuyet, 1983, 1986, 1992. See also Ha The Ngu, 1983, 2–4.

16. Nguyen Van San, 1956–57; Nhuoc Thuy, 1960–61; Bao Thang, 1961–62; Nhuoc Thuy, 1961–62; Cam Tam, 1961–62; and "So tay mau giao: Ai hieu noi?" 1961–62.

17. See the introduction of the study programs.

18. All the translations are mine. They are meant to convey the meaning of the pieces without trying to reflect their poetic quality.

19. VMG, 1978f; VMG, 1983; and Tran Thi Trong and Pham Thi Suu, 3 volumes: 1994A, 1994B, 1994C.

20. "Tich chu" (*Bai soan,* 1984e, 58–59); "Hai chu khi con" (*Bai soan,* 1984f, 42–43); "Ba co gai" (*Bai soan,* 1984d, 62–64); "Bay con qua" (*Bai soan,* 1984e, 71–73).

21. "Lam chu bo doi," Tran Thi Trong and Pham Thi Suu, 1994a, 3; "Chau thuong chu boi doi," Tran Thi Trong and Pham Thi Suu, 1994b, 35; "Chu giai phong quan," Tran Thi Trong and Pham Thi Suu, 1994b, 55.

22. *Bai soan,* 1984f, 37–38. See also "Pulling the Cabbage" (Nho cu cai) in Tran Thi Trong and Pham Thi Suu, 1994a, 5.

23. An article published in 1974 on Nam Na village, Tien Hai district, Thai Binh province explained the weak kindergarten movement as a result of parents' old beliefs and their need to have children stay home to help with secondary jobs such as making hats and weaving mats (Nguyen Thi Tham, 1974, 16).

24. See materials prepared by the Ministry of Education and Training entitled "Bo tranh cham soc, nuoi duong, giao duc tre em duoi 6 tuoi" (A collection of materials on child rearing and educational methods for children under six years old) and and "Sach huong dan bao cao vien chuong trinh giao duc cac bac cha me" (A manual on educational programs of parents), printed in 1990.

REFERENCES

Books

Bai soan lop mau giao be, tap I (Lessons, junior class, v. I). 1984a. Hanoi: Giao Duc.
Bai soan lop mau giao be, tap II (Lessons, junior class, v. II). 1984b. Hanoi: Giao Duc.

Bai soan lop mau giao lon, tap I (Lessons, senior class, v. I). 1984c. Hanoi: Giao Duc.

Bai soan lop mau giao lon, tap II (Lessons, senior class, v. II). 1984d. Hanoi: Giao Duc.

Bai soan lop mau giao nho, tap I (Lessons, intermediate, v. I). 1984e. Hanoi: Giao Duc.

Bai soan lop mau giao nho, tap II (Lessons, intermediate, v. II). 1984f. Hanoi: Giao Duc.

Bo Giao Duc va Dao Tao. 1993. *Chuong Trinh 26 tuan cho lop mau giao 5 tuoi (khong hoc qua lop mau giao 3–4 tuoi) va phan bien soan* (26-week study program for the five-year-olds who have not attended kindergarten classes). Third Edition. Hanoi: Giao Duc va Mam Non.

———. 1994a. *Chuong trinh cham soc giao duc mau giao va huong dan thuc hien (3–4 tuoi)* (Kindergarten programs—guidance and implementation, 3–4-year- olds). Hanoi: Giao Duc.

———. 1994b. *Chuong trinh cham soc giao duc mau giao va huong dan thuc hien (4–5 tuoi)* (Kindergarten programs—guidance and implementation, 4–5-year-olds). Hanoi: Giao Duc.

———. 1994c. *Chuong trinh cham soc giao duc mau giao va huong dan thuc hien (5–6 tuoi)* (Kindergarten programs—guidance and implementation, 5–6-year-olds). Hanoi: Giao Duc.

Bo Giao Duc. 1977. *Chuong trinh giao duc mau giao (cai tien)* (Kindergarten study programs—revised). Quang Nam-Da Nang: Ty Giao Duc Quang Nam-Da Nang.

———. 1979a. *Phan phoi chuong trinh cac mon hoc truong mau giao: Lop mau giao be (ap dung tu nam hoc 1978–1979)* (Timetable for junior kindergarten classes—applicable from the 1978–79 school year). Hanoi: Giao Duc.

———. 1979b. *Phan phoi chuong trinh cac mon hoc truong mau giao: Lop mau giao lon (ap dung tu nam hoc 1978–1979* (Timetable for senior kindergarten classes—applicable from the 1978–79 school year). Hanoi: Giao Duc.

———. 1979c. *Phan phoi chuong trinh cac mon hoc truong mau giao: Lop mau giao nho (ap dung tu nam hoc 1978–1979* (Timetable for intermediate kindergarten classes—applicable from the 1978–79 school year). Hanoi: Giao Duc.

Hoang Lan and Hoang Van Yen. 1985. *To chuc ngay hoi ngay le trong truong lop mau giao* (Organizing festivals in kindergarten classes). Hanoi: Giao Duc.

Ljunggren, Borje, ed. 1993. *The Challenge of Reform in Indochina.* Harvard Institute for International Development. Cambridge, Massachusetts.

Ministry of Education and Training. 1991. *Education in Vietnam 1945–1991.* Hanoi: N.p.

Nguyen Khac Vien. 1993. *Noi kho cua con em* (The misery of our children). Hanoi: The Gioi.

Nguyen Khanh Toan. 1991. "Mau giao." In *Nen giao duc Viet Nam: Li luan va thuc hanh* (Foundation for Vietnamese education: theory and practice). Hanoi: Giao Duc, 39–56.

Tran Thi Trong and Pham Thi Suu, eds. 1994a. *Tuyen tap tro choi bai hat tho truyen mau giao (3–4 tuoi)* (Games, songs, and stories for the 3–4-year-olds). Hanoi: Giao Duc.

———. 1994b. *Tuyen tap tro choi bai hat tho truyen mau giao (4–5 tuoi)* (Games, songs, and stories for the 4–5-year-olds). Hanoi: Giao Duc.

———. 1994c. *Tuyen tap tro choi bai hat tho truyen mau giao (5–6 tuoi)* (Games, songs, and stories for the 5–6-year-olds). Hanoi: Giao Duc.

Trung Tam Nghien Cuu Tre Em. 1993. *Tim hieu tam ly con em* (Understanding the psychology of our children). Hanoi: Kim Dong.

Turley, William and Mark Selden, eds. 1993. *Reinventing Vietnamese Socialism: Doi Moi in Comparative Perspective*. Boulder, CO: Westview.

Vien Khoa Hoc Giao Duc Viet Nam. 1991. *So thao 40 nam xay dung va phat trien su nghiep giao duc mam non* (A summary of 40 years' development of preschool education). Hanoi: Giao Duc.

Viet Nam voi cong uoc cua Lien hop quoc ve quyen tre em (Viet Nam and the United Nations' covenant on children's rights). 1991. Hanoi: Su That.

Vu Ngoc Khanh. 1985. *Tim hieu nen giao duc Viet Nam truoc 1945* (On Vietnamese education before 1945). Hanoi: Giao Duc.

Articles

Ban Bien Tap Trung Tam Nghien Cuu Tam Li Tre Em. 1991. "Tim hieu, nghien cuu, tam li tre em" (Understanding and researching child psychology). *Nghien Cuu Giao Duc*. 9: 22–30.

Ban Giao Duc Quan Dong Da Hanoi. 1981. "Cong tac to chuc quan ly va chi dao nganh hoc mau giao thuoc khu vuc kinh te toan dan o quan Dong Da" (Tasks of organizing and leading kindergarten work in the state sector in Dong Da Precinct). *Mau Giao*. 2: 7–12.

Ban Giao Duc Thi Xa Hon Gai. 1980. "Phat huy tiem nang cua dia phuong de xay dung co so vat chat cho mau giao" (Developing the local potentials in building the infrastructure for kindergartens). *Tap San Mau Giao*. 1: 5–7.

"Ban ve muc tieu-noi dung-phuong phap giao duc mau giao" (Discussing objectives, content, and methods of kindergarten education). 1977. *Mau Giao*. 2: 11–20.

Bao Thang. 1961–62. "Huong dan suu tam va su dung do choi" (Guidance on how to collect toys). *Chuyen San Cap Mot Giao Duc Pho Thong*. Special issue: 8–9.

Bo Giao Duc. 1974. "Hoc tap anh hung Nguyen Thi Thao boi duong pham chat cao dep cua nguoi giao vien xa hoi chu nghia Viet Nam" (Emulating Nguyen Thi Thao, supplementing the beautiful quality of Vietnamese socialist teachers). *Mau Giao*. 2: 4–19.

Cam Tam. 1961–62. "Dung giao cu truc quan trong cac lop mau giao" (Using educational instruments in kindergarten classes). *Chuyen San Cap Mot Giao Duc Pho Thong*. Special issue: 11–12, 21.

"Chan chinh phong trao vo long" (Rectifying the *vo long* movement). 1956. *Chuyen San Giao Duc Pho Thong Cap Mot*. Special issue: 4–5, 22.

Dang Dinh Luong. 1980. "Ve viec chi tieu cho truong lop mau giao" (On the finance of kindergarten classes). *Tap San Mau Giao*. 1: 19, 24.

Dang Van. 1961–62. "Truong pho thong co the giup do cac lop mau giao nhu the nao?" (How can general schools help kindergartens?). *Chuyen San Cap Mot Giao Duc Pho Thong*. 3: 24–25.

Dao Thanh Am. 1994. "Van de quyen giao duc cua tre em tu 'Ban an che do thuc dan Phap' den 'Nghi quyet trung uong Dang lan thu IV'" (From the question of children's education rights in 'French colonialism on trial' to 'Resolution of the Sixth Plenum of the Central Committee'). *Nghien Cuu Giao Duc*. 3: 4, 7.

"Dieu le truong mau giao" (Regulations for kindergartens). 1980. *Tap San Mau Giao*. 2: 1–5, 24.

"Di tham quan" (Excursion). 1978. *Tap San Mau Giao*. 2: 15–17.

Dinh Khac Nhi. 1961–62. "Tang cuong lanh dao thuc hien tot nhiem vu giao duc mau giao nam hoc 1961–1962" (Strengthening the leadership and implementing the kindergarten tasks during the 1961–1962 school year). *Chuyen San Cap Mot Giao Duc Pho Thong*. Special issue: 1–2.

Do Duc Trien. 1960–61."Tinh Hung Yen xay dung phong trao mau giao trong hop tac xa" (Hung Yen province built the kindergarten movement in the cooperative). *Chuyen San Cap Mot*. 4: 24–25.

Do Thi Xuan. 1960–61."Giao duc ky luat tu giac o lop mau giao" (Teaching self-discipline in kindergarten classes). *Chuyen San Cap Mot*. 3: 23–25.

Do Xuan Hoa and Le Bich Ngoc. 1995. "Giao duc mam non—50 nam phat trien va truong thanh" (Preschool education—fifty years of development and growth). *Nghien Cuu Giao Duc*. 9: 9–11.

Ha The Ngu. 1983. "Mot vai dac diem cua qua trinh giao duc tre mau giao" (Several features of the process of educating kindergarten children). *Nghien Cuu Giao Duc*. 3: 2–4.

Hoang Nguyen. 1956–57. "Ke chuyen cho tre em" (Telling stories to children). *Chuyen San Giao Duc Pho Thong Cap Mot*. 10: 22–23.

"Kinh nghiem tuyen truyen phong trao vo long trong nhan dan" (Propagandistic experiences in the popular *vo long* movement). 1954. *Giao Duc Nhan Dan*. 6: 28.

Le Thi Hong Phan. 1975. "May kinh nghiem chi dao phat trien vo long" (Experiences in the development of *vo long*). *Nghien Cuu Giao Duc*. 38: 25–26.

"Lop vo long sau mot nam hoat dong" (*Vo long* classes after an active year). 1953. *Giao Duc Nhan Dan*. 11: 27–28.

Luu Duc Moc. 1991. "Ket qua dieu tra ve phong tuc, tap quan cham soc va giao duc tre" (Results of the survey on customs and habits of child rearing). *Nghien Cuu Giao Duc*. 9: 11.

Nguyen Anh Tuyet. 1983. "Quan diem he thong doi voi viec nghien cuu tre mau giao" (The concept of systems in the research work on kindergarten children). *Nghien Cuu Giao Duc*. 3: 5–6, 14.

———. 1986. "Nhung quan diem co ban cua giao duc mau giao xa hoi chu nghia Viet Nam" (Basic concepts of socialist Vietnamese kindergarten education). *Tap San Mau Giao* 1: 3–6.

———. 1992. "Mot quan niem ve truong mau giao" (A view on kindergarten). *Nghien Cuu Giao Duc*. 6: 6–7.

Nguyen Duc Minh. 1991. "Cac quyen cua tre em va trach nhiem cua cha me" (Children's rights and parental responsibilities). *Thong Tin Khoa Hoc Giao Duc*. 24: 20–22.

Nguyen Khac Vien. 1991a. "Tam li tuoi be bong" (Psychology of the young). *Nghien Cuu Giao Duc*. 9: 31–33.

———. 1991b. "Tre em trong xa hoi ngay nay" (Children in contemporary society). *Thong Tin Khoa Hoc Giao Duc*. 24: 34–36.

Nguyen Kim Anh. 1956–57. "Mot vai net ve tam ly va dac diem nhi dong" (Several features of child psychology). *Chuyen San Giao Duc Pho Thong Cap Mot*. 9: 27–29.

Nguyen Thi Nhat and Nguyen Khac Vien. 1986. "Ban ve giao duc mau giao" (On kindergarten education). *Tap San Mau Giao*. 2: 3–22.

Nguyen Thi Nhut. 1960–61. "Vai net ve tinh hinh phong trao mau giao nam hoc 1961–1962" (Several features of the kindergarten movement, 1961–62). *Chuyen San Cap Mot Giao Duc Pho Thong*. Special issue: 3–4.

Nguyen Thi Tham. 1974. "Toi da van dong cac chau ra lop mau giao nhu the nao" (How did I mobilize children to attend school?). *Mau Giao.* 4: 16–17.

Nguyen Thi Thao. 1974. "Thanh tich anh hung Nguyen Thi Thao" (Achievements of Nguyen Thi Thao, the heroine). *Mau Giao.* 3: 11–20.

Nguyen Trong Hoang. 1982. "Ve cuoc cai cach giao duc 1946" (On the 1946 education reform). *Nghien Cuu Giao Duc.* 10: 16–25.

Nguyen Van San. 1956–57. "Tro choi" (Games). *Chuyen San Giao Duc Pho Thong Cap Mot.* 10: 21.

Nguyen Van Trieu. 1961–62. "Cac tinh da hoan thanh thang loi ke hoach 3 nam pho thong cap vo long" (All the provinces have completed the three-year plan on the universalization of *vo long*). *Chuyen San Giao Duc Pho Thong Cap Mot.* 1: 27–28.

Nhuoc Thuy. 1960–61. "Mot so y kien ve mon ke chuyen o lop mau giao" (Opinions in story telling in kindergarten classes). *Chuyen San Cap Mot.* 5: 21–22, 30.

———. 1961–62. "Tai sao can thay ten mot so mon hoc mau giao" (Why did we have to change the names of some kindergarten classes?). *Chuyen San Cap Mot Giao Duc Pho Thong.* Special issue: 10, 12.

Pham Hoang Gia. 1985. "Ve muc tieu dao tao cua mau giao" (On the objectives of kindergarten education). *Nghien Cuu Giao Duc.* 2: 19–21.

Pham Mai Chi. 1991. "Giao duc mam non: mot so doi moi va nhung thu thach moi" (Preschool education: changes and new challenges). *Thong Tin Khoa Hoc Giao Duc.* 24: 24–26.

Phi Van Khanh. 1978. "Kinh nghiem to chuc vui choi cho tre o truong mau giao" (Experiences in the organization of playing in kindergartens). *Nghien Cuu Giao Duc.* 8: 15–17.

Phuong Chi. 1980. "Kinh nghiem khai thac kha nang cua cha me de xay dung lop mau giao du tieu chuan ve co so vat chat" (Experiences in the capitalization of parental ability to build well-equipped kindergarten classes). *Tap San Mau Giao.* 1: 8–10, 22.

Phuong Hoa. 1960–61. "Cong tac mau giao la mot cong tac rat quang vinh" (Kindergarten tasks are glorious). *Chuyen San Giao Duc Pho Thong Cap Mot.* 2: 21–22.

"So tay mau giao: Ai hieu noi?" (Kindergarten kits: who understands?). 1961–62. *Chuyen San Cap Mot Giao Duc Pho Thong.* Special issue: 25.

"Tai lieu huan luyen" (Training materials). 1956. *Chuyen San Giao Duc Pho Thong Cap Mot.* Special issue: 10–17, 22.

Ta Thi Ngoc Thanh. 1982. "Mot so y kien ve ke hoach giao duc hang ngay trong truong mau giao" (Opinions about the daily schedule of kindergartens). *Tap San Mau Giao.* 3: 4–5.

Thai Thi Hoa. 1961–62. "Tai sao phai dieu chinh thoi khoa bieu cua lop mau giao o nong thon?" (Why did we need to rewrite the time table for kindergarten classes in the countryside?) *Chuyen San Cap Mot Giao Duc Pho Thong.* Special issue: 5–7.

Thong Tin Khoa Hoc Giao Duc (Information on Educational Sciences) 24: 56–59.

Tran Thi Thanh. 1993. "Tre em trong gia dinh va viec chuan bi cho tre vao truong pho thong" (Children in the family and their preparation for entering the general school). *Thong Tin Khoa Hoc Giao Duc.* 37: 31–33.

Tran Thi Tinh. 1973. "Mot so van de xung quanh cac dien hinh tien tien mau giao" (A number of problems surrounding progressive kindergartens). *Nghien Cuu Giao Duc.* 28: 10–20.

Tran Thi Trong. 1980. "Tim hieu nhung yeu cau dao tao cua giao duc mau giao" (Understanding training needs in kindergarten education). *Nghien Cuu Giao Duc.* 12: 12–14.

———. 1981. "Ve van de giao duc dao duc cho hoc sinh mau giao" (On moral education for kindergarten children). *Nghien Cuu Giao Duc.* 10: 11–14.

Tran Van Lan. 1971. "Cac truong pho thong can nghien cuu ky de thuc hien tot chi thi cua bo ve viec chuyen hoc sinh mau giao len lop mot" (General schools have to research carefully to implement the ministerial directive on transferring kindergarten children to the first grade). *Tap San Giao Duc Cap Mot* 4: 11–13.

Truong Mau Giao Tan Tien. 1976. "Toan dan tham gia nang chat luong giao duc mau giao" (Everybody participates in raising the quality of kindergarten education). *Mau Giao.* 1:18–25.

V.A. 1961–62. "Nen cho cac chau hat nhung bai nao" (Which songs should we let the children sing?). *Chuyen San Cap Mot Giao Duc Pho Thong.* Special issue: 13–14.

"Ve chi dao va xay dung truong diem o nong thon" (Guidance on the building of key schools in rural areas). 1983. *Nghien Cuu Giao Duc.* 3: 30.

Vu Mau Giao. 1974a. "Huong dan nhiem vu cong tac 2 nam (1974–1975) cua nganh hoc mau giao-vo long" (A guide to the two-year tasks (1974–75) for the kindergarten-*vo long* sector). *Mau Giao.* 3: 1–10.

———. 1974b. "Hoc tap anh hung Nguyen Thi Thao ra suc phan dau vuon len tro thanh nguoi giao vien mau giao toan dien" (Emulating Nguyen Thi Thao, the heroine: struggling to become well-rounded kindergarten teachers). *Mau Giao.* 2: 20–21, 23.

———. 1974c. "Ke hoach hoc tap anh hung Nguyen Thi Thao" (Plans for learning the model of Nguyen Thi Thao). *Mau Giao.* 2: 22–23.

———. 1977a. "Du thao dieu le truong mau giao" (Draft regulations on kindergarten). *Mau Giao.* 2: 1–10.

———. 1977b. "Ke hoach giao duc hang ngay o lop mau giao" (Daily timetable for kindergarten classes). *Mau Giao.* 1: 1–17.

———. 1977c. "Mot so quy dinh ve phong cach nen nep cua co va chau o lop mau giao" (Several rules on the manners of teachers and students in kindergarten classes). *Mau Giao.* 1: 18–21.

———. 1978a. "Ban ve vui choi o cac truong, lop mau giao" (On playing in kindergarten). *Tap San Mau Giao.* 1: 9–10, 14.

———. 1978b. "Cham soc, giao duc ve sinh cho tre o tuoi mau giao" (Caring and teaching hygiene to kindergarten children). *Tap San Mau Giao.* 2: 1–5.

———. 1978c. "Giao duc lao dong o truong, lop mau giao" (Labor education in kindergarten). *Tap San Mau Giao.* 1: 1–4, 8.

———. 1978d. "Hat mua mau giao" (Singing and dancing in kindergarten). *Tap San Mau Giao.* 2: 7–11.

———. 1978f. "To chuc ngay hoi, ngay le trong truong, lop mau giao" (Organizing festivals in kindergarten classes). *Tap San Mau Giao.* 1: 5–8.

———. 1979. "Huong dan thuc hien nhiem vu nam hoc 1979–1980 cua nganh hoc mau giao" (A guide to the implementation of the tasks for 1979–1980 in the kindergarten sector). *Tap San Mau Giao.* 2: 1–2, 8.

———. 1983. "To chuc ngay hoi, ngay le trong truong, lop mau giao" (Organizing festivals in kindergarten classes). *Tap San Mau Giao.* 1: 1–4.

Chapter 10 The Kindergarten

in the Ottoman Empire

and the Turkish Republic

Benjamin C. Fortna

The history of cultural and institutional borrowing in the Islamic world is a prickly subject, particularly given the "power relationship" inherent in the modern period. Recourse to Western institutions is, of course, a major feature of the history of the modern Middle East but one that has been magnified by a historiographical tendency to privilege change over continuity. The heavy emphasis placed on Western influence in the region—and the correspondingly high degree of scholarly attention such influence has garnered—has produced the impression that Western-derived institutions were critical to transforming "traditional" Middle Eastern society. The presumption is that these institutions continued to function in their transplanted environment as they had in their original contexts.

Educational institutions illustrate this historiographical trend. To be sure, the "new style" schools erected in the Middle East in the late nineteenth and twentieth centuries owed much to their Western exemplars. Nevertheless, the indigenous reasons for their selection and the specific local roles they played have frequently been overlooked. For example, it has been largely taken on faith that the new schools operated as "secular," "Western" institutions that automatically furthered the cause of "modernization." Closer examination of these schools, however, reveals the extent to which the institutions were adapted to suit policies and interests that were often diametrically opposed to their Western origins. Much of the impetus for the rapid expansion of government schooling in the late Ottoman Empire can be traced to the state's desire to counteract what it considered to be the deleterious effects of foreign influence among its subjects. Although consciously patterned after Western European models, the late Ottoman schools were nevertheless built in large part to thwart Western influence.

This chapter is concerned with this paradoxical development, namely adaptation of an originally Western institution—the kindergarten—largely to further an Ottoman and Turkish Republican policy of combating Western influence through increasingly indigenized versions of this form of schooling. The history of the kindergarten in this context is largely opaque. Anyone interested in the topic will look in vain for references to the kindergarten in either the standard reference works or the indexes of the major books on education. The modest intention of the present chapter is to discern the broad contours of the story of the kindergarten within the context of educational trends in the region.

Introduced in 1885 by Protestant missionaries from the United States, the kindergarten in Anatolia affected only a very small number of lives until roughly a century later, and even then only relatively modest enrollments were recorded. Because the diffusion of the kindergarten was so attenuated, its development offers the advantage of considerable historical scope. The Turkish Republic of the 1980s and 1990s is naturally far removed from its Ottoman predecessor of a century earlier. The changing circumstances facing the kindergarten therefore offer perspective on the changes of the past century. But any given institution can reflect a historical trajectory. The kindergarten is illuminating in its ability to reveal such transformations as the expansion of the role of the central government into the lives of its subjects and the simultaneous predilection for shaping that process of expansion along ostensibly Western lines, as well as the volatile relationship between the central government and foreign missionaries and diplomats.

The story of the kindergarten is that of the introduction of an alien institution and the adaptation of that institution into a specific historical context. First implemented by foreign missionaries very much in conflict with the Ottoman imperial and later Turkish Republican authorities, the kindergarten was eventually appropriated by these governments and made to conform to their own deeply held convictions concerning the utility of education in molding the future. The kindergarten proved extremely adaptable to indigenous exigencies. From missionary tool to nationalist mission, the kindergarten in Anatolia is an institution rich in both ideological commitment and practical problems.

For the purposes of this chapter, the term *kindergarten* denotes those pre-schools that trace their institutional lineage to the movement launched by the German Friedrich Froebel (1782–1852). In the Ottoman and Turkish context, kindergartens are almost invariably referred to by the term *mother school* (*ana okulu*). Some writers have included in that designation schools that existed prior to Froebel and the international kindergarten movement. For example, one historian of the subject has suggested that the schools operated by the members of the Ottoman Muslim religious establishment (*sibyan mektepleri*) since the fourteenth century ought to be included under this term.[1] Here, however, we shall only discuss schools which were specifically founded as kindergartens in the Froebelian sense, following the pattern established by Osman Nuri Ergin in his monumental work on Turkish education.[2] Geographically, the discussion here is limited to those core provinces of the Ottoman Empire that eventually were incorporated into the Turkish Republic, founded in 1923. It is hoped that what is lost by this limitation in geography will be offset by the advantages of historical continuity. Normally, the fallacious equation of the Republic of Turkey with the Ottoman Empire is to be avoided due to the massive reduction involved, a problem further exacerbated by the long-standing but erroneous Western tradition of using the term *Turkey* to represent the Ottoman realms. In this case, however, we seek geographical consistency by referring to Anatolia, in both its Ottoman and Republican periods.

A preliminary word on periodization is also in order. The historiography of the kindergarten in this part of the world is almost as illuminating as the specific information available about the schools themselves. On the face of it, the natural watershed in the history of the kindergarten in Anatolia would seem to be 1923, the year of the Republic's founding. Such a temporal division corresponds to the tendency to emphasize the discontinuities between the imperial and national periods so prevalent in most historical treatments. The story of the kindergarten—and the other educational institutions that span this period—shows, however, that numerous continuities prevailed in spite of the change in government. Both periods shared an educational topography that featured the aggressive presence of missionary activity and the attendant redoubling of central government efforts to reduce the population's desire for foreign schools by offering its own version of "new method" schooling.

In both periods the competition between rival education systems reflected larger tensions between East and West. Both the Ottoman and Turkish Republican governments placed a premium on the value of education as a meliorative agent that could be used to help redress the unequal relationship with the Western powers. To this end, both states devoted considerable amounts of scarce energy and financial resources to effecting a thoroughly centralized and vertically integrated state school system. The main official difference between the policies of the two governments was that whereas the Ottoman system was ostensibly designed to inculcate a shared sense of allegiance to the empire among the wide variety of ethnic and religious groups that constituted the population of a state that stretched from the Balkans to the Persian Gulf, the Republican agenda was directed at a much more homogeneous Turkish population. Nevertheless, when we look beyond the aim of the Ottoman schools as stipulated in official pronouncements and examine the ways in which the schools were understood to work on a practical level, a different picture emerges. Although the late Ottoman state schools opened their doors to members of the non-Muslim minority groups as well as to the Muslim majority, the schools were regarded as "Muslim schools" by many of the officials administering them, particularly those stationed at the local level. Moreover, the state schools' curriculum contained a number of specifically Islamic lessons, much in the same manner as the schools of the Republican period would emphasize the Turkish nature of the state despite the presence of a sizable non-Turkish population.

These similarities between the education policies of the Ottoman imperial and Turkish Republican periods indicate that an alternate periodization is necessary. The chronology of the kindergarten suggests that emphasizing the evolving nature of education policy across time is preferable to focusing on the need to proclaim a watershed date. The year 1913 could just as easily represent such a demarcation. In that year the Ottoman government published a law that marked the first official mention of the kindergarten as a state institution.[3] Prior to that date, the kindergartens extant in the empire were all run by foreigners or by members of indigenous minority groups who replicated the missionary institutions. In hindsight the state's incorporation of the kindergarten into its array of educational institutions represents a major shift. While the non-state kindergarten providers, both foreign and domestic, would continue to play a role in the kindergarten movement, loosely defined, it was the state's role that proved to be crucial. Thus 1913 makes perhaps as much sense as a turning point in the kindergarten's trajectory as 1923. Furthermore, locating the turning point within the Ottoman period has the added benefit of underscoring the frequently overlooked commonalities between the Ottoman and Republican periods.

While this chapter dwells primarily on the Ottoman period and early Republican periods (i.e., c. 1885–1930), it also draws selectively on the later Republican period in order to trace the kindergarten's trajectory into the better-documented recent past.

The first kindergarten in the Ottoman Empire appeared in Izmir in 1885. Its founder was an American Congregationalist named Cornelia Storrs Bartlett, who had gone to western Anatolia with her missionary parents in 1867.[4] After returning to the United States to attend college, she trained as a kindergarten teacher in Minneapolis. She returned to the Ottoman Empire in 1884 and founded the Huntington Kindergarten and Training School in the spring of the following year, with seven Armenian children as her first pupils. From this humble start Bartlett's school burgeoned, for although initially it consisted of a few rented rooms in 1894 Bartlett purchased a building to house the school after securing funds from a Connecticut philanthropist.[5] The institution was planned as a demonstration school; six local women entered as the first training class. Between its founding and its merger with the Collegiate Institute for Girls in 1904, the school trained forty-two women who went on to teach in twenty-seven kindergartens in various places in the empire.[6] Perhaps this pace was overly rigorous for Bartlett; in 1904 she returned to the United States with a "nervous condition."[7]

Bartlett's school was replicated both by the women it trained and by local imitators. One sympathetic contemporary account penned by an anonymous Protestant Armenian from Izmir speaks of the widespread impact of Bartlett's kindergarten: "The kindergarten had its unexpected influence over all similar institutions of this country. Step by step the people were enlightened to acknowledge their duties to the young folk. They appreciated the educational system of the Americans and Europeans and partly attained to the state of their neighbors; and finally they have followed Miss Bartlett's example and made easy the foundations of a large number of kindergartens in almost all the large cities of Turkey."[8]

The kindergartens that opened in Talas (outside Kayseri) in 1889 and in Kayseri (ancient Caesarea) in 1891 conform to this pattern of expansion based upon a model school.[9] Furthermore, in at least one instance, we hear of institutions founded by imitators of these missionary ventures, for example, one opened by the members of the Gregorian Christian community in Kayseri.[10]

Meanwhile, further anecdotal evidence points to parallel missionary activity resulting in the opening of other kindergartens in the empire around the turn of the twentieth century. The American-run Armenian College in Harput had

411 students in its kindergarten section in 1898.[11] Another missionary kindergarten serving the minority population was that of the Gedik Paşa quarter of Istanbul, which was in operation before 1908. This school offered separate kindergarten classes for Greek and Armenian children.[12] This trend was not limited to Christian missionaries operating in Anatolia; the first Hebrew kindergarten in Ottoman Palestine opened in 1898.[13]

Thus, the kindergarten was introduced into the Ottoman Empire by foreigners to serve the minority population, who constituted the chief target of missionary activity. If, as the other chapters in this book demonstrate, the key factor in the worldwide diffusion of the kindergarten was its adaptation to the local conditions, the Protestant missionaries appear not to have been at all concerned with adaptation. Indeed, their agenda revolved around a principle that was diametrically opposed to the adaptation symptomatic of the kindergarten's spread. Instead of conforming to local conditions, the missionary movement had as its inherent objective the aim of altering the indigenous population's religious affiliation, traditionally the bedrock of identification in the Ottoman Empire.

Except for the education supplied by the Ottoman palace institution, which affected an important but extremely small percentage of the population, the various religious establishments had traditionally supplied all schooling in the Ottoman Empire. Reliable figures for the percentage of the population that could claim functional literacy are scarce. Most assessments agree that such a number would have been well below 10 percent prior to the impact of the educational changes of the nineteenth century. What schooling did exist was essentially religious, focusing on the texts of the Qur'an and the Bible, depending on one's background, and their interpretation. Teachers were inevitably members of the Muslim learned group, the ulema, priests, or rabbis. The long-standing association between religion and learning thus reinforced confessional identity.

In hindsight the missionaries' ambitions appear unrealistic. Ottoman and Republican educators, in proposing that parents bequeath their children to the supra-confessional auspices of the state, were themselves proposing a radical innovation. By contrast, the missionaries, in attempting to induce individuals to change their religious affiliation, seem to have been asking the unthinkable. Instead of converting large segments of Ottoman society, the missionaries managed to convert only small numbers of the minority population, frequently setting them at odds with those members of their denomination that did not shift allegiance to Protestantism. Their lack of success among the Muslim population (most missionary enterprises took the legal strictures against proselytizing among the Muslim population seriously) in general helps explain the failure of the missionary kindergarten relative to the subsequent success of the Turkish Republican kindergarten. After the extensive redrawing of borders following the First World War, Turkish educators were able to target a much more homogeneous society. Similarly, after the secularizing reforms of Mustafa Kemal Atatürk in the 1920s and the 1930s had disassociated the Turkish state from Islam, the state could inculcate affinity to the nation unfettered by sectarian identification.

Undeterred by their lack of success, the missionaries forged ahead. A missionary pamphlet published shortly after the Young Turk Revolution of 1908 offers a glimpse of the motives and activities of one missionary kindergarten. Entitled "The Cesarea Kindergarten" and published by the Women's Board of Missions in Boston, Massachusetts, the pamphlet was clearly intended to raise funds from like-minded Americans for the kindergarten in Kayseri.[14] It frequently addresses its readers as prospective donors in the second person. Although the author, Fannie E. Burrage, does not identify her position at the school, it is clear from context that she was its director. In this role she was presumably the successor to a Mrs. Fowle, whom Burrage describes as having been a resident in Kayseri who, "seeing the possibilities of the kindergarten work for the children of Turkey, wished to open one in Cesarea. At that time she had a society of young ladies who met once a month for Bible Study and to make fancy articles. When Mrs. Fowle suggested to them that the proceeds from their work and the contents of their mite boxes be used for such work, they very eagerly responded."[15] Two points are worth mentioning here. First, Burrage's account underscores the importance of Bartlett's kindergarten in Izmir as a model for others. Burrage mentions the Bartletts (presumably parents and daughter) by name and confirms that one of the graduates of Bartlett's school, an Armenian woman named Vartoohee Kelugian, founded the kindergarten in Talas. When Kelugian married, an Armenian woman whom Kelugian had trained took her place. The replicating process had the potential to be self-sustaining. Second, the American women were not operating on their own but had recourse both to a committed group of local inhabitants, presumably converts to Protestantism, and to the spiritual and possibly material support of their coreligionists in the United States.

Burrage's pamphlet tells of a kindergarten that shared much with the normative form of that institution but that also was working to satisfy the missionary purpose for which it was built. The boys and girls in the kindergarten in Kayseri ranged from four to eight years of age, ate communally, had stories read aloud to them, and played games both indoors and out. Apart from the fact that "the buildings have been falling into ruin," a claim illustrated by a photograph showing a crude classroom the walls of which seem to rely on the support of rough wooden poles to keep them from falling down, the school seems to resemble any other kindergarten.[16] One passage in the pamphlet is remarkable for its contradictory reference to the universality of children at play, not to mention its command of the non sequitur: "Children everywhere are alike at play. You will find many dark-featured ones among our little boys and girls. Children in Turkey know so little about real play! It would make your heart glad to hear their nalins (wooden shoes) chumping around in our court-yard as they play 'blacksmith' or some other kindergarten game."[17] Embedded in the prosaic descriptions of daily life at the school, however, are several passages that reveal its evangelical intent. The stories read to the children were Biblical: "They are very fond of the Bible-story talk which they have each morning. So easily they compare the grass growing in the cracks between the stones in the court with the grain in the 'Parable of the Sower.' How eagerly the little hands go up to answer the teacher's question! The little eyes are rapidly taught accuracy and quickness."[18] Through their work the missionaries hoped to create little missionaries of their own who would take their message back with them to their friends and families. "When the day's lessons are at an end, they scamper clumsily off down the street toward their dirty, noisy homes to be real little missionaries to their weary mothers and the dirty little children with whom they play. They are such bright rays of sunshine in these dark homes and lives! It is a work that angels well might covet a share."[19]

The metaphor of the missionaries bringing light to an otherwise dark East is echoed in the local Armenian account. After discussing the backwardness of the preexisting schools available to young Armenians, complete with references to "tyrant teachers" and "torturing machines," the anonymous author informs his American readers, "you will be glad to hear also of the light which was brought unto us by Miss Bartlett, who organized the new kindergarten and set to work to carry her high purpose into execution."[20]

The Ottoman authorities were well aware of the extent and motivation of foreign educational activity in the empire. This activity was of two types: that undertaken by educators arriving from overseas and that originating in neighboring states such as Iran, Greece, and Bulgaria. The discussion here is confined to the overseas missions because they are the most relevant to the kindergarten question, but it is significant that the existence of neighboring missionaries, many of whom were operating as much out of nationalist zeal as religious fervor, contributed to the Ottoman government's siege mentality. Furthermore, the advanced state of the indigenous minorities' educational activity further exacerbated the situation. But of all the types of pedagogical competition the Ottomans faced, that supplied by Western missionaries was the most alarming. Foreign schools were the first "modern" schools in most Ottoman provinces and set the standard for all subsequent institutions. The demonstration effect of the foreign schools was first felt by the minorities, as in the case of the Izmir kindergarten, and only later by the Muslim majority.[21]

The missionary schools were threatening to the Ottoman officials for several reasons. First, their numbers were increasing rapidly. In many provinces foreign schools outnumbered by a wide margin the indigenous schools established according to the "new style." Second, government officials saw that they were being outspent by the foreigners. In provinces such as Beirut where missionary activity was particularly intense, the money spent by just one foreign power to support schools operated by its nationals nearly equaled the Ottoman government's budgetary allocation for that province.[22] This financial advantage frequently allowed the foreign schools to offer monetary incentives in the form of tuition waivers and free uniforms, which helped insure their popularity.

Even more important than the number of foreign schools being built and the financial edge they possessed was the perception that the foreigners were succeeding in their aim of attracting Ottoman subjects away from their traditional loyalty to the empire and toward identification with the religious and national agenda of the foreigners. Reports sent to Istanbul from across the empire during the late nineteenth and early twentieth centuries share a common lament, namely that the foreign schools were causing harm to Ottoman subjects by "seducing" them away from loyalty to the Ottoman state and its religious-political embodiment, the sultan. In Islamic and Ottoman tradition, the sultan bore the responsibility for maintaining the security of his subjects, both Muslim and non-Muslim. The children of traditionally loyal minority communities were described in these documents as becoming inclined toward foreign governments. Worse still, Ottoman officials felt that the empire's youth, like their Japanese counterparts, were becoming morally corrupt.[23] Muslim students emerged from non-Muslim schools "denuded of Islamic customs," their morals "broken" or "poisoned" by the contagion of foreign influence.[24] Ottoman officials were fearful that changes in their Muslim subjects' style of dress and customs were only the external manifestations of a more serious shift away from tradition. As for the non-Muslim children, they were described not only as bereft of a proper Ottoman upbringing but also as having become inclined toward the state from whose schools they had emerged.[25]

In many respects the first kindergartens were typical of missionary education in the Ottoman Empire. The location of Bartlett's kindergarten in Izmir conformed to a general pattern of missionary activity occurring along the empire's coastline, with the major exception of the schools opened in the areas of concentrated Armenian population in the interior. The Kayseri kindergarten, like that opened in Talas, exemplified a second wave of school openings in the interior. In attracting non-Muslim children, these schools were also typical. Most missionaries quickly saw that attempts to convert the Muslim population met with little success and therefore concentrated their efforts on the empire's Christian population, much to the consternation of the various partriarchates, the heads of the Orthodox Christian hierarchies that governed their affairs. As American Protestant institutions, moreover, the Izmir and Kayseri kindergartens represented the most energetic and fastest growing segment of missionary activity. By the last decade of the nineteenth century the Ottoman bureaucracy considered American activity such a threat that it singled out the Americans among all missionaries and began to maintain separate registers of all their institutions.[26]

Faced with the growing number of missionary schools in the late nineteenth century, the Ottoman government took steps to control their activities. The international disposition of power, however, severely hampered the Ottoman state in this endeavor. When, for example, the government attempted to close a particular school for violations of the regulation governing schools in the empire, it frequently resulted in forceful diplomatic pressure being brought to bear on the government. On the whole, the Ottoman state chose to avoid direct measures such as school closings in order to remove another thorny issue in the already strained relations with the Western powers. Such Ottoman forbearance occurred despite rampant infractions. For example, a register of Protestant and American schools drawn up in 1893 reveals that only 51 of 392 schools had obtained official permission to open, a requirement clearly spelled out in the Education Regulation of 1869.[27] Instead, official attempts to monitor the missionary schools were limited to recording their numbers in registers and the occasional inspection.

Ottoman officials recognized that the most effective way to counter the missionary schools was to build state-run alternatives. Although the secondary literature on the subject has tended to overlook the connection, educational competition during the last two decades of the nineteenth century played a major role in convincing the Ottoman authorities to redouble state efforts to realize the goal of establishing a single school system that would stretch across the empire and provide education from the primary to the university levels. After several incarnations in the earlier years of the century, the Education Regulation of 1869 served as the blueprint for the state's ambitious educational expansion. The task was all the more daunting for the fact that the Ottoman government had in the past entered the field of education only to train the small number of scribes that ran the imperial bureaucracy. The tremendous expansion of the Ottoman bureaucracy in the nineteenth century coupled with the widely held acceptance of the belief that the empire's salvation lay in educating as many of its subjects as possible caused the state to abandon its long-standing policy of leaving the task of popular education to the various religious establishments.[28] The ambitious 1869 regulation, the plan for a preeminent role for the state in the pedagogical life of the empire, remained largely unimplemented until the school building campaign of Sultan Abdülhamid II (r. 1879–1909) transferred most of its optimistic agenda into reality. Documents sent to the capital from throughout the empire reveal the extent to which the hostile presence of the missionary schools goaded the state into carrying out the 1869 plan as rapidly as possible. Given the tremendous fiscal problems of the empire in this period, this was no mean feat.[29] Abdülhamid II nevertheless made educational expansion a priority of his reign.

The kindergarten, however, did not yet figure in the state's plan. All of the official Ottoman attention in the field of education was devoted to effecting a system that ranged from the primary to the university level. Although the kindergarten embodied many aspects of Hamidian educational policy, material considerations prevented its adoption by the state until after the main educational infrastructure had been laid down. The only mention of the kindergarten in official correspondence during the Abdülhamid era appears in a memorandum drafted by Said Paşa, a major figure in late Ottoman attempts to bolster state-sponsored education.[30] Said Paşa's memorandum to the sultan, dated September 1888, recommended the adoption of several educational institutions and techniques then being practiced in western Europe.[31] Most of his suggestions argued for a more practical and developmental approach, in which context he advised the selective adoption of the German *realschule* (modern secondary school), the concept of "mutual instruction" (*enseignement mutuel*), and the kindergarten. On the subject of the kindergarten, he wrote: "It comes to mind that it is necessary that we also should found and establish the institutions that some time ago were adopted in Germany and also implemented in other countries, which are in accordance with the new method, which are designated for male and female children between the ages of four and seven or eight and who have not yet reached the age when they will continue on to the primary schools, which are known in Europe by the term 'child's garden' (*çocuk bahçesi*), and which really are worthy of the term 'source of instruction' (*mebde-i ta'lim*). The aim of these institutions consists of inculcating the simplest natural information in children by way of familiarizing them with contrasting and comparing, thereby opening the minds of small children in an enjoyable manner."[32] Said Paşa's vision of the kindergarten thus conforms to the normative definition of that institution. What is intriguing about his document is the clearly foreign association of that and other institutions. Although the German term *kindergarten* does not appear, the other foreign techniques and institutions recommended stand out in Said Paşa's memorandum because they are rendered in the left-to-right letters of the Latin alphabet in an otherwise uniformly right-to-left Arabic-Ottoman script. In highly symbolic fashion, these imported ideas appear novel and alien.

The adoption of the kindergarten as part of the state's educational arsenal would have to wait until after the Young Turk Revolution of 1908 had removed Sultan Abdülhamid II. In 1913 the Temporary Primary Education Law was promulgated, which mentioned the kindergarten (*ana mektebi*) for the first time in an official capacity. The first unofficial mention of the kindergarten occurred in a biography of Friedrich Froebel published in Istanbul in 1914. Its author was the educator and writer Nafi Atuf. The slim volume (twenty-four pages plus plates) describes Froebel's life and thought, paying particular attention to the kindergarten (*çocuk bahçesi*). Photographs of kindergartens in Germany and France show interior and exterior scenes, handiwork, and game playing. Although the extent to which Nafi Atuf's book on Froebel played a role in subsequent events is unclear, it is perhaps more than coincidental that the Ottoman government promulgated a regulation governing Ottoman kindergartens the following year.

When the kindergarten appeared in an official capacity, its name had changed. For reasons unclear, the "child's garden" of Said Paşa's memorandum and Nafi Atuf's book appeared as the "mother's school," or "mother school" (*ana mektebi*), in the regulations dedicated to that level of schooling.[33] The first official mention of the kindergarten appears in the Temporary Primary Instruction Law (*Tedrisat-i İbtidaiye Kanun-u Muvakkati*) of 1913. It declared primary instruction to be compulsory and free in public schools.[34] Closer to our interest, it listed kindergartens (*ana mektepleri*) as a specific class of school, mentioning them along with the "old style" primary schools (*sibyan mektepleri*) of much longer duration. It defined the kindergarten as an institution for children from four to seven years of age. The kindergarten was described, along with the "old style primaries," as "institutions that served the children's spiritual and physical growth through the use of games, excursions, handicrafts, hymns (*ilâhiler*), patriotic verses (*vatanî manzumeler*), and lessons appropriate to their ages."[35]

The Kindergarten Regulation (*Ana Mektepleri Nizamnamesi*) of 15 March 1915 further enumerated the regulatory, administrative, and pedagogical concerns of the Ottoman government.[36] Its stipulations were not excessively burdensome—not surprising, given the state's desire to see them proliferate. Kindergartens could be attached to a girls' school, or not, and could accept tuition fees or operate free of charge. Students of four, five, and six years of age were to be admitted; classes were to be segregated by age group but not by sex. The school buildings had to be suitable to school use and to have a garden (*bahçe*) of dimensions sufficient to accommodate the number of students enrolled.

Health concerns assumed a prominent role in the regulation. Kindergartens had to conform to all health rules (*kavaid-i sihhiye*). Enrolled students were required to pass a doctor's examination to determine that they were free from contagious disease and properly inoculated. Each school was obliged to submit to a medical inspection no less than once a week, a process that included examining each child. Likewise, teachers had to furnish a doctor's report certifying that they were free from contagion. The children were expected to engage in healthy games, organized marches, and exercise.

The regulation made a few, suggested stipulations on the subject of classroom content. Along with healthy games, moral games (*ahlâkî oyunlar*) were to be featured during the school day. Religious (*dinî*) and sectarian (*millî*) stories and lessons were to be taught. Although the use of these terms varied over time, it seems clear from the context that the state education policy of the Young Turks continued the Hamidian emphasis on moral and religious education. It was only later, in the Republican period, that official use of the term *millî*, rendered here as *sectarian*, would become synonymous with the term *national*, as in the Ministry of National Education (*Millî Eğitim Bakanliği*), a change that speaks volumes for the altered political climate of the Republic.[37]

All teachers were female and were to be selected based on their having graduated from the teacher training college (*Darülmuallimât*), possessing documents attesting to their previous good conduct as teachers at a kindergarten, or having demonstrated by written examination that they had the proper qualifications. Furthermore, all teachers had to be Ottoman subjects and to command fluency and sound pronunciation of the Turkish language. While these were hardly onerous requirements, they suggest the beginnings of the trend toward the Turkification policies begun in the Young Turk era and accelerated in the Republican period.

Perhaps the most striking feature of the state's treatment of the kindergarten is that it ignored its missionary predecessors. Given the adversarial nature of the educational competition between the late Ottoman state and the missionaries, it is not surprising that neither the official regulation governing the kindergartens nor their subsequent discussion before the Ottoman parliament makes mention of the missionary kindergartens. In a speech before the Ottoman parliament, then Minister of Education Ahmed Şükrü Bey defended his ministry in the following way: "Children from four to seven were brought together in schools in order that they be taught to obtain school training, become acquainted with school discipline, and their minds become familiar with instruction, such that we called them 'kindergartens' (*ana mektepleri*). While these had never been established before in our country (*memleket*), they began to be established four years ago. Thousands of children, whether in Istanbul or in the provinces, were taken into these schools and thereby rescued from the socialization of the street (*sokak terbiyesi*) and from the health and other dangers to which they would be exposed while with their families."[38] As in much of the subsequent historiography, the extant missionary kindergartens do not figure in this education minister's perceptions; those schools were deemed to be entirely devoted to the minority population.[39]

Late Ottoman policy was concerned with expanding state education in two directions: horizontally, to complete the schooling grid across the geographical extent of the empire, and vertically, to extend the possibility of state education to a wider chronological cross section of the population. In this effort the authorities were waging what was tantamount to their own educational mission. The new education had to be extended at the expense of what was, in their view, the unenlightened mode of the past. It is telling in this connection that Şükrü Bey referred to the family as a potential impediment to raising the educational standard of the empire. A textbook used to teach morals to students attending Ottoman state schools during the Hamidian period refers to the family in much the same way, as the bastion of ignorance from which the empire's children must be saved.[40] The text, composed in a question-and-answer format, defined the teacher's role explicitly in parental terms.

STUDENT—Why must we respect our teachers?

TEACHER—The rights of our teachers are every bit as great as those of our parents with respect to us. Because [while] our parents are the cause of our existence and our growth, our teachers rescue us from the world of ignorance by teaching us and instructing us in both upbringing (*terbiye*) and science and knowledge (*ulûm ü fünûn*). In this respect we come to be considered distinguished and respected by the people. We live with all repose, and, ultimately, we leave life with a lasting good name.[41]

As this passage demonstrates, the importance of the Ottoman state school teacher to students not only equaled but also exceeded that of their parents. By initiating the student into the world of *"terbiye"* and science and knowledge, the teacher provided an entrée into a world of ease where one can make one's mark. This was a world in which, by implication, parents did not belong. Their role in the child's life was reduced to birth and early childhood development. They were thus equated with the "world of ignorance." It is a telling aspect of the state's moralizing campaign that it was the teacher—in this context, clearly an extension of the Ottoman state—who could effect the student's rescue from the ignorant orbit of the family.

The kindergarten offered the state the opportunity to extend its reach into the life of the family, to act *in loco parentis*. Ali İrfan's suggestion that "everyone should send their children to school while they are young" hints at the downward trend in the age of school entry that lay ahead.[42] This textbook from the Hamidian period clearly points the way to the state's adoption of the kindergarten during the waning years of the Ottoman Empire and the more concerted effort to establish the institution in the Republican era.

Thus by the time of the First World War, the kindergarten had been introduced to the Ottoman Empire in relatively small numbers; the state perceived it to be a foreign institution intended for the minority population until it decided to adopt the institution as its own in 1915. The Young Turk effort to introduce the kindergarten as a state-sponsored institution, however, produced few lasting results due to the First World War and the ensuing War of Liberation, which gave birth to the Turkish Republic in 1923.[43] Far from ushering in new schools, wartime conditions resulted in an "epidemic" of school closings.[44]

When the young Republic gained the opportunity to focus more intently on education, its policies bore considerable resemblance to their late Ottoman predecessors. As was the case in the late Ottoman period, Republican educational administrators were understandably more interested in expanding the school system inherited from the empire at the primary level and above. The proto-Republican educational credo, formulated during the independence war by a new, breakaway Ministry of Education in Ankara, contained elements that shared much with the late Ottoman agenda. Religious as well as national concerns predominated, as did the desire to continue the general policy of borrowing "modern" pedagogical techniques and institutions from the West.[45] Still, the kindergarten received no attention. After the official founding of the Republic in 1923, Turkey commissioned several Western education experts to visit the country and prepare reports that would include recommendations for altering the pedagogical status quo. These reports, prepared by John Dewey (1924), a German named Kuhne (a stand-in for Kersensteiner, who was ill) (1926), and the American Kemerrer Group (1933), did not take up the question of pre-primary schooling.[46]

While the early preoccupations of the Republic lay elsewhere, several important changes had taken place or were being formulated, changes that would have a major impact on the development of the kindergarten in Turkey. First, the new country was much smaller than the old empire. Gone were the remaining Ottoman possessions in the Balkans, the Levant, and the Arabian Peninsula. The new country's borders were reduced to the Ottoman provinces in Anatolia and to the relatively small amount of territory in Europe proper, including parts of Thrace up to Edirne and the old capital of Istanbul. This reduced size allowed for the possibility of greater central government control. Second, the loss of many of the far-flung lands meant that the population remaining inside the Republic's new borders had a higher concentration of ethnic Turks, a situation that had been intensified by the stream of refugees that had been flowing into the core lands of the Ottoman Empire as its borders shrank in the course of the late nineteenth and early twentieth centuries. Third, the military victory won by the Republic against the Allies ensured the young state a much stronger bargaining position than the empire had been able to maintain with respect to the powers. A fourth factor likewise derived from the War of Independence: the disposition of the Allied forces on the side of the Greek invasion of Western Anatolia exacerbated the anti-foreign sentiment already present in the waning days of the empire.

Thus when Republican education policy emerged in the years following Turkish independence, it assumed a far more forceful character than that projected by the late Ottoman Empire. Two main trends may be discerned in this new policy: one worked to tighten restrictions on foreign educational activity in Turkey, and the other strove to nationalize the education project. These parallel trends directly affected the development of the kindergarten in the Republic of Turkey.

The government's increasingly energetic regulation of foreign educational institutions operating on Turkish soil played a major role in curtailing the leading role that the missionary kindergarten had previously played. The first evidence of this restrictive policy came as early as 1924. The promulgation of the Unity of

Instruction Law (*Tevhid-i Tedrisat Kanunu*) in March of that year stated that all educational institutions in Turkey would fall under the purview of the Ministry of National Education.[47] A circular published soon thereafter prohibited schools from disseminating religious propaganda or providing education with a religious basis of support, and from displaying religious symbols on their buildings. Crosses and pictures of Christian kings, generals, and saints were ordered removed. Some schools that failed to comply were closed in spite of the pressure brought to bear by the powers.[48] A regulation of February 1926 required that all teachers of Turkish history, geography, and language be recommended by the ministry. They also had to support the concept of a Turkish nation. School papers now had to be written in Turkish. All schools were likewise required to display a photograph of the Republic's founder and president, Mustafa Kemal Atatürk. The photograph, measuring a regulation eighty by sixty-six centimeters, was to be hung in the school's most distinguished location.[49] Inspection, that standby of the Ottoman system, was enhanced to ensure that these rules were followed. More detailed provisions devoted to regulating the foreign schools appeared in 1927. These prohibited the appearance in textbooks of pejorative references to the Turks and the discrediting of their history. Textbook publishers could not print errors in Turkish history and geography. Propaganda favorable to foreign countries was outlawed, as was the misrepresentation of the Republic's borders to the advantage of any foreign power. Five hours of class time per week were to be devoted to Turkish literature, geography, and literature, all taught by Turkish citizens.[50] By the 1980s virtually every aspect of foreign school life had fallen under the purview of the Ministry of National Education. Schools had to prove that their education principles were appropriate to the Basic Principles of Turkish National Education (*Türk Millî Eğitimin Temel İlkeleri*). These included such principles as secularism and the "Nationalism of Atatürk" (*Atatürk Milliyetciliği*).[51]

As early as 1939 the government's aggressive stance against the missionary schools was beginning to be reflected in their dwindling numbers. While other causes, such as the growing attractiveness of state-sponsored alternatives and the straitened fund-raising conditions in the United States in the years following the Depression, played a major role in the declining presence of American missionaries in Turkish education, increased governmental control undoubtedly hastened its demise.[52]

The contest between missionary and national versions of education in Turkey had strong parallels in neighboring Iran. Protestant missionary activity in Iran began in the final years of the Qajar dynasty (1779–1925), with the majority of schools being founded in the late nineteenth and early twentieth century.[53] The Qajars, like the late Ottomans, saw the necessity of creating a state school system. Although the Qajar educational effort was not as successful as its Ottoman counterpart, it provided the foundation upon which the more ideologically motivated and stridently nationalist regime of Reza Shah could build. The connection between missionary education and the state's program to advance its own pedagogical system was less overt in Iran than it was in the Ottoman Empire and Turkey, yet there seems to have been a causal relationship between the two phenomena. Evidence of the hostile reaction to the missionary schools began to appear in the Iranian press in the 1920s, the decade in which Reza Shah took power in a coup d'état (1921) and made himself king (1926).[54] The first mention of government-sponsored kindergartens in Iran appears in 1935 as part of Reza Shah's campaign to expand state schooling, giving particular attention to breaking down the barriers between male and female institutions.[55]

In subsequent decades the Turkish Ministry of National Education extended an increasing degree of control over foreign schools while simultaneously deploying its own national version of the kindergarten. Throughout the latter half of the twentieth century the ministry standardized the state-sponsored kindergarten, nationalized its content, and expanded its numbers. Major state-sponsored activity on the kindergarten front began in the late 1950s and continued to gather momentum through the following decades as more regulations and plans were promulgated and implemented.[56]

Official statistics reflect both the numerical expansion of Turkish kindergartens in this period and the simultaneous demise of foreign and minority analogs. The table below is based on kindergarten enrollments chosen at more or less decennial intervals from figures published by the State Statistical Institute.[57] Although the numbers are small, the pattern by which the state displaced foreign and minority counterparts in the role of primary provider of kindergartens in the Republic is clear.

Like all other schools in the Republic, the kindergartens were obliged to reflect the state's nationalist agenda. While the basic nature of the kindergarten

| School Year | Number of Students, by School Type | | | |
	State	Private Turkish	Minority	Foreign
1964–1965	165	1,092	1,644	240
1974–1975	912	2,990	917	124
1985–1986	9,870	3,623	172	84

curriculum precluded heavy-handed political indoctrination, the Turkish version of the institution, like its counterparts in other countries, could be counted on to begin the process of national acculturation. As in the final years of the Ottoman Empire, the Republican kindergarten accomplished this process through the use of songs and poetry and the celebration of national holidays. Unlike the education program of the late Ottoman period, however, the Republican nationalist program attempted to cement loyalty to the new state of Turkey. Schools inculcated in their students an intense patriotism for the recently founded Republic and the people, land, and culture it was meant to reflect. The following poem was recited by students at the Republic Kindergarten in the mid-1950s:

"Our Monument"	"Andimiz"
I am a small child	Ben çocuğum, küçüğüm,
But I am great of name	Fakat adi büyüğüm.
This then is my joyous song;	Budur benim şen türküm;
The Turk is great;	Türk büyüktür,
I am a Turk.	Ben Türküm![58]

The Republican emphasis marked a shift away from the multiethnic, multinational Ottoman concept and toward a more easily focused Turkish identity.

There was, however, much in the Republican kindergarten project that continued the work of its late Ottoman predecessor. For example, the Republican education hierarchy placed considerable emphasis on the ability of the kindergartens to play a corrective role in the lives of their young charges, instilling in them habits that were both healthy and morally sound. As the director of one Turkish kindergarten wrote in 1956, "Many parents have told me that their children who were hesitant eaters rid themselves of this bad habit and began to gain weight after enrolling in the Republic Kindergarten and they conveyed their indebtedness and thanks to the school authorities. Moreover, an officer's wife informed me with her thanks that her previously very foulmouthed child had abandoned this evil custom after going to kindergarten."[59] Once again, the government appreciated the kindergarten's potential to free students from the "upbringing of streets" and to extend a much more regimented and "modern" environment in its stead.

Thus the kindergarten appealed to the Ministry of National Education of the Turkish Republic, as it had to its Ottoman predecessor, as a logical extension of the policy of educational expansion. Although introduced by foreign missionaries whose proselytizing intentions directly contravened the patriotic agendas of the Ottoman and Republican states, the kindergarten was soon incorporated into their educational plans. The late Ottoman state was extremely wary of the missionaries' intentions but lacked the strategic leverage needed to take strong measures against the foreign schools. The strengthened international position of the Turkish Republic, however, allowed it to adopt much stricter measures against the missionary institutions. Meanwhile, the Republic undertook to realize the plans for establishing state kindergartens that had been in place since the final years of the Ottoman period but which had remained largely unrealized owing to the First World War. During the Republican period the Ministry of National Education adapted the kindergarten and made it conform to its staunchly nationalist agenda. The kindergarten became thoroughly "Turkified" while maintaining the universal components (e.g., outdoor play and story time) and age grouping characteristic of its international definition. Its ability to target a younger segment of the population was particularly attractive to the Ottoman and Turkish governments, which were interested in extending their influence to an ever broader segment of the population. The kindergarten in Turkey proved easily adaptable to the task of introducing the rudiments of the nationalist agenda to its young charges. In the final analysis, the source of the kindergarten idea mattered less than its utility to the state. The case of the kindergarten in Anatolia demonstrates the critical nature of the adaptive environment over and above that institution's origins.

NOTES

1. Feyzi Öz, "Okulöncesi Eğitim," in Millî Eğitim Bakanliği, *Cumhuriyet Döneminde Eğitim* (Istanbul: Millî Eğitim Basimevi, 1983), 237.
2. Osman Nuri Ergin, *İstanbul Mektepleri ve İlim, Terbiye ve San'at Müesseseleri Dolayisiyla Türkiye Maarif Tarihi*, 5 vols. (Istanbul: Osman Bey Matbaasi, 1939–1943): 1406.
3. For the details concerning this law, see note 34.
4. Frank Andrews Stone, *Academies for Anatolia: A Study of the Rationale, Program and Impact of the Educational Institutions Sponsored by the American Board in Turkey: 1830–1980* (Lanham, MD: University Press of America, 1984), 89–90.
5. Ibid., 90.
6. Although the claim that its trainees went on to serve in 27 other kindergartens cannot be confirmed by the information available, anecdotal evidence indicates that graduates of the Huntington School did found several similar institutions.
7. Stone, 90.
8. An Armenian, of Smyrna, "The First Kindergarten in Turkey," *Missionary Herald* 90 (12), December 1894, 512–13.
9. Necmettin Tozlu, *Kültür ve Eğitim Tarihimizde Yabanci Okullar* (Ankara: Akçağ, 1991), 139.

10. Fannie E. Burrage, *The Cesarea Kindergarten* (Boston: Woman's Board of Missions, n.d.), 6.

11. Tozlu, 86.

12. Stone, *Academies,* 77–79.

13. Yael Zerubavel, *Recovered Roots: Collective Memory and the Making of Israeli National Tradition* (Chicago: University of Chicago Press, 1995), 79.

14. Burrage, *Cesarea,* n.d. The pamphlet lists no date of publication, but internal evidence suggests that it was written after the Young Turk Revolution of 1908.

15. Ibid., 2–3.

16. Ibid., 1, 4.

17. Ibid., 4–5.

18. Ibid., 1, 4

19. Ibid., 4–5.

20. An Armenian, "The First Kindergarten in Turkey," 512–13.

21. On the demonstration effect of missionary education in Syria, see Donald J. Cioeta, "Islamic Benevolent Societies and Public Education in Ottoman Syria, 1875–1882," *The Islamic Quarterly* XXVI (1) 1986, 41.

22. BOA, İrâde Meclis-i Mahsus 4222; J. P. Spagnolo, "French Influence in Syria prior to World War I: The Functional Weakness of Imperialism," *Middle East Journal* 23 (1969): 58n.

23. Roberta Wollons, "The Black Forest . . . ," p. 3.

24. See, e.g., Çetin, "Yabanci," Yildiz Mütenevvi (hereafter, "Y Mtv.") 32/45; İrâde M 1310, 5. On the late Ottoman concern with moral decay and actions taken to remedy the situation, see Forna, "Morals," in my dissertation "Education for the Empire: Ottoman State Secondary Schools during the Reign of Sultan Abdülhamid II" (Chicago: University of Chicago, forthcoming).

25. Başbakanlik Osmanli Arşivi (BOA), Y Mtv. 32/45.

26. BOA, Yildiz Esas Evrâki (YEE) 35/232; Sadâret Resmî Mârûzat Evrâki (YA Res) 122/88; and YEE 5/109. See also, Atillâ Çetin, "Maarif Nâziri Ahmed Zühdü Paşa'nin Osmanli İmplaratorluğundaki Yabanci Okullar Hakkinda Raporu," *Güney-Doğu Avrupa Araştirmalari Dergisi* 10–11 (1981–1982): 189–219.

27. BOA, YEE 35/232.

28. On the transformation of the Ottoman bureaucracy beween the late eighteenth and early twentieth centuries, see Carter Vaughn Findley, *Bureaucratic Reform in the Ottoman Empire: The Sublime Porte, 1789–1922* (Princeton: Princeton University Press, 1980), and *Ottoman Civil Officialdom: A Social History* (Princeton: Princeton University Press, 1989).

29. Engin Deniz Akarli, "The Problems of External Pressures, Power Struggles, and Budgetary Deficits in Ottoman Politics under Abdülhamid II (1876–1909)" (Ph.D. diss., Princeton University, 1976).

30. On Mehmed "Küçük" Said Paşa, see *International Journal of Middle East Studies* (*IJMES*) article and his memoirs, *Said Paşa'nin Hâtirati,* 3 vols. (Istanbul: Sabah Matbaasi, 1910).

31. BOA, YEE 31/1937/45/82. 4 Muharrem 1306 (September 10, 1888).

32. Ibid.

33. The nomenclature assigned to the kindergarten in the Islamic world varies. In Arabic the term generally used is a direct translation of "kindergarten" (*rawdat al-atfāl*). Kinder-

gartens in Iran are referreed to by a Persian term which literally means "place for children" (küdakestān). In Turkish, the adoption of the term "mother school" (*ana Mektebi*) in place of the previously used "child's garden" (*çocuk bahçesi*) may be linked to the emerging nationalism of the Young Turk period. It is possible that there was some sort of link between the choice of the term *anaokulu* and the word for "motherland," *anavatan*, but such a connection is never explicitly made in the sources I have seen. In the 1960s the literal translation (*çocuk bahçesi*) made a limited comeback in reference to the upper of two kindergarten levels. The "child's nest" (*çocuk yuvasi*) appeared as the term for that part of the school designated for three- and four-year-olds, while the "child's garden" was reserved for five-year-olds. The terms *kreş* (Fr. *crêche*) and *gündüz bakimevleri* (day care centers) also appeared in reference to institutions that could not be included under the "kindergarten" rubric (Cicioğlu 1982, 25).

34. The text of the law may be found in *T. C. Millî Eğitim Vekâleti, Millî Eğitimle İlgili Kanunlar*, vol. 1 (Ankara: Millî Eğitim Basimevi, 1953), 931–52.

35. Ibid., 931–32.

36. The text of the regulation can be found in the collection of official decrees and proclamations known as *Düstûr*. Tertib-i Sani, vol. 7, pp. 514–15.

37. An earlier unofficial use of the term *millî* as "national," or perhaps "patriotic," appears in the subtitle of Mehmed (Mizanci) Murad's novel of 1890–1891, *Turfanda mi Yoksa Turfa mi* (Millî Roman) (Istanbul: Mahmud Bey Matbaasi, 1308 [1890–1891]). The title has been translated as "First Fruits or Forbidden Fruits?" and as "The Early or the Spoiled Seed?"

38. Cited in Ergin, *Türkiye Maarif Tarihi*, 1407. Şükrü Bey served as minister of education between 1913 and 1918. Although Ergin does not give the date of this speech, it seems likely that it was delivered in 1919. İbrahim Alâettin Gövsa, *Türk Meşhurlari Ansikolopedisi* (Istanbul: Yedigin, 194-) 371–72.

39. Examples of historical accounts from the Republican period that continue the trend of ignoring the missionary kindergarten in describing its historical development include İbrahim N. Özgür, *Bugünün Ana Okullari* (Ankara: Maarif Basimevi, 1956, 7–10); and Feyzi Öz, "Okulöncesi Eğitim," in Millî Eğitim Bakanliği, *Cumhuriyet Döneminde Eğitim* (Istanbul: Millî Eğitim Basimevi, 1983), 237–38. Özgür and Öz's treatments of the subject moves directly from Froebel and Maria Montessori to the 1913 Ottoman law, thereby bypassing the intervening missionary kindergartens.

40. Ali İrfan [Eğriboz], *Rehber-i Ahlak* (Istanbul: 1317 [1899–1900]), 49–50.

41. Ibid.

42. Ibid., 29.

43. Hasan Koçer states that the Temporary Primary Instruction Law (Tedrisat-i İbtidaiye Kanun-u Muvakkati) of 1913 resulted in many kindergartens being opened in Istanbul and the provinces—so many, in fact, that, in his view, the Kindergarten Regulation of 1915 had been promulgated in order to regulate all the schools. Koçer, however, does not provide any numbers. Hasan Ali Koçer, *Türkiye'de Modern Eğitim Doğuşu ve Gelişmesi (1773–1923)* Istanbul: Millî Eğitim Basimevi, 1970: 193–94.

44. İlhan Başgöz and Howard E. Wilson, *Educational Problems in Turkey, 1920–1940* (Bloomington: Indiana University Research Center for the Language Sciences, 1968), 39–41.

45. Ibid., 38.

46. Ibid., 64–72.

47. Hidayet Vahapoğlu, *Osmanli'dan Günümüze Azinlik ve Yabanci Okullari (Yönetimleri Açisindan)* (Ankara: Türk Kültürünü Araştirma Enstitüsü, 1990), 151.

48. Ibid., 151–52; Başgöz and Wilson, *Educational Problems,* 79–80.

49. Vahapoğlu, *Osmanli'dan Günümüze,* 154.

50. Başgöz and Wilson, *Educational Problems,* 80.

51. Vahapoğlu, *Osmanli'dan Günümüze,* 160.

52. Stone, *Academies,* 282.

53. Michael P. Zirinsky, "A Panacea for the Ills of the Country: American Presbyterian Education in Inter-War Iran," *Iranian Studies* 26 (1993), 119.

54. Camron Michael Amin, "The Attentions of the Great Father: Reza Shah, 'The Woman Question,' and the Iranian Press, 1890–1946" (Ph.D. diss., University of Chicago, 1996), 243.

55. I am grateful to Camron Michael Amin for providing several references to works on education in Iran and for his explanations of the Qajar and Pahlavi periods. The reference to the first mention of the kindergarten in the plans of the Iranian state appears in his dissertation in the form of a government memorandum he has translated from the Persian. See his "The Attentions of the Great Father: Reza Shah, 'The Woman Question,' and the Iranian Press, 1890–1946" (Ph.D. diss., University of Chicago, 1996), 271. On the general subject of education in Iran, see David Menashri, *Education and the Making of Modern Iran* (Ithaca: Cornell University Press, 1992).

56. Öz, "Okulöncesi Eğitim," 241–45.

57. Source: T. C. Başbakanlik, "Devlet İstatistik Enstitüsü, *Millî Egitimi İstatistikleri: İlköğretim, 1961/65,* (No. 530) (Ankara, 1967), *Millî Eğitimi İstatistikleri: İlköğretim, 1974–75* (No. 812) (Ankara, 1977), and *Millî Eğitimi İstatistikleri: İlköğretim, 1985–1986* (No. 1232) (Ankara, 1987).

58. Cited in Özgür, *Bugünün Ana Okullari,* 54. Attributed to the periodical entitled *Türk Çocuğu* (The Turkish Child).

59. Özgür, *Bugünün Ana Okullari,* 37.

Chapter 11 Education and Culture in Early Childhood: A Revolution in Jewish Schooling, 1899–1948

Shoshana Sitton

INTRODUCTION

The Hebrew-language kindergarten, created in 1899 to replace the *heder*, is a product of Zionist ideology and represents a revolution in early Jewish childhood education.[1] The *heder* was a Jewish early childhood educational institution developed in the Middle Ages and designed for male children only, three years old and up. Its purpose was to teach children to read Bible verses. The teaching method emphasized oral learning, and the pace of instruction was left to the discretion of the *melamed* (teacher). Students were not graded, there were no auxiliary readers or scholastic texts, and physical punishment was common practice. In many communities, the rabbi regularly tested all the children on the Sabbath.

The Hebrew-language kindergarten brought about three revolutions in early childhood education. First, since it was a secular institution with a Western orientation, it employed newly developed contents and methodology which gave rise to a new childhood culture. Second, it opened early childhood education to girls, who were not accepted in the *heder*. Third, it freed young children from education run by men and delivered it into the hands of female kindergarten teachers, educated, for the most part, in Germany.

This chapter concentrates on the first revolution, namely, the creation of a secular curriculum for kindergartens, designed as a new cultural repertoire which would reflect the ideals of the new society that Zionists wished to create. It also addresses the influence of this repertoire on the development of a new childhood culture.

The Zionist ideal was to create a modern, Western, secular society, unique in that it was based on a rich Jewish heritage. The image of the "New Jew," unlike the Eastern European stereotype, was based on the Jew of biblical times: a farmer and a fighter who lived according to the ethical standards set by the prophets. The creation of a new cultural code dictated the materials to be integrated into the kindergarten curriculum, including traditional Jewish materials as well as newly developed materials relating to Zionist ideology and to European culture.

The period between 1899 (when the first kindergarten was established) and 1948 (when the State of Israel was established) was fraught with conflict regarding the cultural repertoire of the Hebrew-language kindergarten. The outlooks which divided contemporary educators can be located on a continuum between ethnocentrism and universalism. There was general agreement regarding the components, but not the relationships between them. In essence, no set, comprehensive formula was adopted, and the lack of a unifying government framework allowed each kindergarten teacher to construct her own curriculum. Despite this, a comprehensive cultural repertoire was created.

BUILDING A NEW CULTURE

Culture and Nationalism

In developing its new culture, the Zionist movement was no different from many other national movements. Current research on modern nationalism which focuses on the cultural plane shows culture to be the link connecting the forces which play a part in the development of national movements: ideology on one hand and economic and social conditions on the other.

Benedict Anderson states that nationalism is a cultural product and that nations, which he calls "Imagined Communities," are created when a sufficiently large number of people imagine that they constitute a nation.[2] In his opinion, nationalism is a new religion rather than a political ideology. Like religion, nationalism deals with issues of death and human suffering, arouses excitement and deep passions, and is supported by uniting texts.

Anthony Smith describes ethnocentric nationalism, which existed in ancient times, and claims that in certain circumstances it undergoes transformation into political nationalism.[3] The historical continuity between the old and the new nationalism may also have a common cultural basis such as religion and history. At the beginning of the transformation, there is religious reform, then secularization, and in the next phase historic and social meaning is conferred upon the tradition. The case of Zionism fits this paradigm.

The Education System

The dominant presumption of the heads of the Zionist movement was that a national culture is not spontaneous but methodical and organized according to a guiding idea. Within this concept, various actors play the roles of ideologists and cultural agents. They determine the models and contents appropriate to the cultural experience and apply various means to create and disseminate such models and contents.

The consensus of the Zionist movement regarding the character of the new culture was that it would rest on three cultural characteristics: it would be established in the Land of Israel, dominated by the Hebrew language, and linked to Jewish history. Beyond this, there was no fully developed vision and no agreement as to the essence of the new culture. As a result, the cultural repertoire within the kindergartens was built by educators with views ranging from ethnocentrism to universalism.

Hebrew education developed into three streams: a religious (Mizrahi) stream, a "general" (secular) stream, and a socialist stream. In the religious stream, components relating to traditional Judaism were emphasized. In the general stream, emphasis was placed on European components borrowed mainly from German and Russian children's culture. In the socialist stream, the values of the workers' parties found expression. In the absence of an authoritative state or a ministry of education, no permanent and inclusive formula was determined for the different streams. It was this situation that made pluralism in education possible.

In the kindergartens, the development of tools for disseminating culture was an offshoot of the unique history of the development of the Hebrew kindergarten.

THE ASSOCIATION OF KINDERGARTEN
TEACHERS AS CULTURAL INITIATOR

The History of the Kindergarten

The first Hebrew-language kindergarten in Palestine was opened in 1899 by a group of schoolteachers. Faced with the fact that most Jewish children knew no Hebrew when they started school, the teachers' work was very difficult. They felt that a preparatory year in kindergarten would make the beginning of schooling easier for both pupils and teachers. The kindergarten's role was to instruct the children in Hebrew, reading, writing, and some arithmetic, and to teach them discipline, hygiene, and order prior to their entry into school. Successful teacher trainees who knew how to deal with young children but who had no formal training were appointed by the founding group of schoolteachers to serve as kindergarten teachers.

Beginning in 1906, kindergarten teachers who had studied in German educational institutions began arriving in Palestine under the auspices of the Berlin-based Jewish philanthropic organization Ezra, which dealt extensively with the promotion of Jewish education in Palestine prior to World War I. These teachers were graduates of the Pestalozzi-Froebel Haus kindergarten teachers' seminary in Berlin, and upon their arrival, a new chapter in the history of kindergartens began. With their high level of professionalism and the self-confidence which stemmed from their pedagogical training, these teachers opposed the existing order. They demanded the separation of the kindergarten from the larger school, the physical and mental removal of the children from the school environment, and their own release from supervision by the schoolteachers. In 1919, the kindergarten teachers created a separate division within the Teachers' Union. This marked the beginning of the struggle with schoolteachers to achieve independent status for kindergarten teachers, which was accomplished in 1923 with the establishment of the Association of Kindergarten Teachers.

The claim that the teachers had neither suitable training nor appropriate knowledge to work with young children acted as a boomerang. After the kindergarten teachers left the Teachers' Union, the union no longer considered itself responsible for either the kindergartens or the kindergarten teachers. As a result, the education establishment disregarded and neglected the Hebrew kindergarten. Although everyone paid lip service to the importance of the kindergarten to the quality of society and Hebrew education, the kindergarten did not receive the financial support it deserved. The kindergartens were financed by supportive parents, by the local authorities, or by voluntary women's organizations assisted by Hadassa, the Zionist women's organization in the United States. Thus, lacking a central policy-making body, the Association of Kindergarten Teachers took on the role of the Ministry of Education: it determined education policies, their implementation, and, in many cases, their financing.

The Role of the Association of Kindergarten Teachers

The Association of Kindergarten Teachers was actively involved as a cultural agent in developing the kindergarten curriculum. It maintained constant contact with the "Language Committee" (a committee composed of linguists, teachers, and writers who created written and oral modern Hebrew terms needed in all areas of life) and published the committee's decisions in *Hed Ha-Gan* (The Kindergarten Echo), a magazine published regularly by the association, which was the sole source of information for kindergarten teachers on this subject. Pedagogic information was transmitted through *Hed HaGan*. Each issue included a number of articles on pre-school education in Western countries, the important schools of thought of the period and their theories (some accompanied by authors' notes and opinions), as well as teachers' reports on visits to pre-school education institutions during trips abroad. The association also established mobile pedagogic libraries in different parts of the country which traveled to settlements and loaned out Hebrew and foreign pedagogic literature.

Study seminars for kindergarten teachers were organized by the association during summer vacations. The seminars in 1935, for example, included the following courses: "Music education in the kindergarten," "The Dalcroze method," "The story in the kindergarten," "The Montessori method," "Discipline in the kindergarten," "Hygiene in the kindergarten," "Nature studies in the kindergarten," and "Taking care of the garden in the kindergarten." These in-service training sessions were a way of communicating the new cultural repertoire.

Along with the activities initiated by the Association of Kindergarten Teachers, spontaneous activities by kindergarten teachers dealt with curriculum development and implementation. These personal initiatives were supported and encouraged by the association. The teachers recorded and reported on these initiatives in *Hed HaGan*.

Disseminating the New Culture

The creation of the new cultural repertoire necessitated the creation of new children's literature in Hebrew: stories, songs, and games. Traditional materials including biblical stories were adapted for young children, and new ways of cele-brating traditional Jewish holidays were devised. New areas of learning not pre-viously included in Jewish education, such as music and art education, a chil-dren's theater, a radio corner, and a children's newspaper, were developed. All these contributed to the creation of a new childhood culture. The Hebrew lan-guage was not the mother tongue of the majority of children during the settle-ment period. Teaching Hebrew was considered essential as the Hebrew language was a central component of the new culture, and the kindergarten was charged with the task of teaching it. The Hebrew kindergarten teachers undertook this task with the assistance of Dr. Yitzhak Epstein, a linguist who developed an orig-inal method for teaching Hebrew to pre-schoolers called "Hebrew in Hebrew." Their goal was to teach the children a living language encompassing all domains of life, in contrast to the literary and religious emphasis of *heder* studies.

Epstein's method was based on imitation of mother tongue acquisition. He determined that the children should first be taught oral language and only later reading and writing. The kindergarten teachers therefore stopped teaching read-ing and writing as they had originally intended, and concentrated on oral lan-guage. The topics were determined by the child's interests, needs, physical ac-tivity, and sensory stimulation. The curriculum took into consideration the child's environment (city or village) and the season of the year. Learning units were short, and each was repeated after a certain interval, on the same day, for reinforcement.

A wide range of songs and musical games were incorporated into the cur-riculum to enhance learning. Many folk stories and songs were translated, mainly from Russian and German into Hebrew, including adaptations of Grimm's fairy tales, Krilov's fables, and Hans Christian Anderson and Russian folk stories. These translations were adapted to the local culture and eventually became an integral part of the children's lives. Other stories were composed specifically for the Hebrew kindergarten. This contributed to the enrichment of modern Hebrew with new terms and expressions.

Bible stories and traditional Jewish practices were another important cultural component connecting the children to the ancient heritage of the Jewish peo-ple. These practices were adapted to suit the secular Zionist ideology and were integrated into the new culture, giving it an authentic and original dimension which distinguished it from all other cultures.

The Zionist ideology viewed teaching the Bible as the Jewish people's most important cultural work, as opposed to teaching the Talmud, which was the most important book for the Jews of the diaspora. According to Zionist ideology, the Bible represents classical Jewish literature in the same way that Homer's works represent classical Greek literature. But the question of incorporating Bible stories into the kindergarten curriculum was a disputed issue. During the 1930s and 1940s recurring arguments on the subject appeared in the pages of *Hed HaGan* and other publications. Some kindergarten teachers claimed that Bible stories had no place in the secular kindergarten, as the Bible is connected to religious concepts and leads children to ask complex questions about God and his actions. Others felt that the introduction of Bible stories into the kindergarten was crucial. In the end, it was decided that these stories were appropriate to the kindergarten class but that they had to be selected and adapted for children, in terms of language and content. The choice of subject matter and biblical heroes accentuated the agricultural life in biblical times, in accordance with Zionist ideology. Bible stories were presented in simple language, and songs and verses on Bible-related subjects were composed in order to appeal to children. Children did not encounter the Bible itself in the kindergarten class.

Holidays were an effective way to transfer the new cultural code to children. Celebrations were considered important as a means of experientially-emotionally transmitting ideological messages. Such an indirect method especially suited the young children who could not be convinced by cognitive means or through ideological arguments. In accordance with the curriculum, new celebrations were designed to commemorate traditional Jewish festivals, new festivals of the Zionist movement, and birthday celebrations for each child. On Fridays, a "Kabalat Shabbat" (welcoming of the Sabbath) accentuated the celebration of the social aspect of the Sabbath—the worker's day of rest. All these were at the center of the cultural–educational activities in the kindergarten. Ceremonies incorporated skits, plays, songs, recitals, and dances through which the story of the holiday was presented.[4] As a part of the construction of the new cultural style, appropriate decorations for the celebrations and characteristic foods (eating local seasonal fruit at celebrations) and games (for example, the spinning top, a traditional Hanukah game which in its original form had the initials of the words "a great miracle happened *there*," was changed to "a great miracle happened *here*") were all emphasized.

Traditional holiday items and celebrations were modified to accentuate secular, nationalist messages and agricultural elements such as the sowing, reaping, and picking of fruits connected to the season; religious elements were obscured. Nationalistic elements typical of Western culture, such as flag-waving and torchlight processions, were also incorporated into the celebrations. Decorations displayed indigenous flora and fauna along with seasonal fruits and vegetables. Thus, religious holidays were transformed into national ones expressing the new Zionist-Jewish identity. Through the elements of the celebration (the ceremony, the performance, and the backdrop), the children learned the story of the holiday with an emphasis on nationalist motifs. For example, Hanukah is celebrated in memory of the Jewish victory over the Greeks, the liberation of Jerusalem, and the establishment of the Kingdom of Israel, at which time all the Greek statues were removed from the Temple. Traditional Hanukah celebrations of the holiday emphasized the miracle of the oil, when a small can of oil sufficed to light the Temple for eight days. The Zionist celebrations also told of the miracle, but especially emphasized the story of the Jews' military victory. The celebration enacts the victory of the small number of Jews, who have few arms but are brave and clever, to teach the children to identify with cultural heroes who are courageous and successful fighters. New holidays and memorial days connected to the history of the Zionist movement and the settlement of Palestine were added to traditional holidays—for example, the commemoration of the death of Theodor Herzl, the founder of the Zionist movement, and Tel-Hai Day, commemorating a bitter battle in the Galilee, which later became Jewish Heroism Day.

Kindergarten children learned about holidays long before the actual celebrations. They decorated their classrooms, rehearsed texts, and learned new songs and dances. Teachers provided them with explanations about the holidays, emphasizing their ideological values and messages.

Holidays were considered an important element in the development of the child. The educational goal of holiday celebrations was to nurture the individual child's artistic expression at that age. The kindergarten was expected to enable children to develop and express their creativity through various artistic means such as dramatic play, recitation, singing, playing musical instruments, and dancing. Moreover, through holiday celebrations, children learned that there is a certain order and arrangement in the world. The week was arranged around celebrating the Sabbath, and the cyclical aspect of the holidays gave order to the year.

New Hebrew literature was written specifically for these kindergarten celebrations in the spirit of Zionist ideology. Over the years a variety of plays, skits, songs, and dances were composed, some of which became new classics. Along with these, folk stories and songs were translated, mainly from Russian and German, into Hebrew, including adaptations of Grimm's fairy tales, Krilov's fables, Hans Christian Andersen, and Russian folk stories. These translations were adapted to the local culture and eventually became an integral part of the children's life.

The Hebrew Children's Theater was established in 1928 by a kindergarten teacher who had come to Palestine from Moscow. Her ambition was to establish a theater similar to that founded in Moscow in 1918 by Natalia Schatz, a theater which presented plays written for children. The Moscow theater operated as a collective with approximately 50 members: actors, composers, set designers, and stage hands. It was housed in a beautiful building in Moscow and had an 800-seat auditorium. The theater in Palestine was much more modest. It was a traveling theater established under the patronage of the Association of Kindergarten Teachers. Part of the kindergarten curriculum, it traveled to settlements throughout the country. Its purpose was to offer children an aesthetic-artistic education. Audiences were familiarized with the story and music in advance and took an active part in the performance itself. They talked and sang with the actors. During intermissions, the orchestra would play music familiar to the children so they would not become bored. After each play, teachers would discuss the play with the children, who would draw and paint pictures which they sent to the actors.

The theater was funded by contributions from the Tel Aviv municipality, the Central Parents' Committee, and various private individuals as well as by the sale of tickets. It was constantly short of funds, which seriously hindered its development. It had a fixed repertoire of about ten plays which were presented time after time. No new works were introduced and nothing was altered. The fact that the audience—children—constantly changed enabled it to continue functioning for many years. Only following the establishment of the State of Israel in 1948, when conditions changed, did the circumstances of the theater change.

The repertoire of the Children's Theater reflected the desired cultural synthesis. Two plays represented the Jewish tradition: "Grandpa and Grandma Tell the Story of the Creation," the story of the seven days of creation, and "Hanale and the Sabbath Dress," a four-act play with a moral and a happy ending which became part of Hebrew classical children's literature. Two plays reflected agricultural life: "Adventures of the Nanny-Goat," a lighthearted musical comedy about a little mischievous goat, and "The Scarecrow," a three-act play about Grandma's garden, birds, and a scarecrow. The Zionist version of the Jewish holidays was presented in plays for Chanukah and Purim, and the European stories of Pinocchio and Goldilocks and the Three Bears were adapted for the stage.

In December 1944, the Voice of Israel, the radio station of the Jewish settlement in Palestine, began to broadcast a daily half-hour children's show between 5:30 and 6:00 p.m. The program targeted kindergarten-age children and was supervised by the Association of Kindergarten Teachers. Programs dealt with seasons of the year, holidays, nature, music, and personalities (telling of Zionist cultural heroes such as Yosef Trumpeldor, a legendary Jewish fighter killed in battle in the Galilee, whose last words were "It is good to die for our country," or the life story of H. N. Bialik, a children's poet). The program was constructed around a short story, a well-known song (sometimes teaching a new one), a recitation, a quiz, and a selection of classical music, usually explained first. In the kindergartens, the teachers would discuss the previous day's program with the children. Through the program, children were exposed to European children's music and literature, mainly from Germany and Russia, which was translated and adapted into Hebrew and became part of the new Hebrew culture. To enable the kindergarten teachers to become familiar with the songs and stories, the contents of the programs were published in the kindergarten teachers' magazine. The program encouraged parents to send their reactions, comments, and suggestions to the Association of Kindergarten Teachers.

The nature of the radio program demanded that its creators work virtually nonstop to prepare new material. In contrast to the children's theater, the program constantly changed and greatly contributed to the development of Jewish children's culture.

The Jewish National Fund Curriculum

By the end of the 1920s, education in most of the kindergartens had begun to take on a clear ideological direction—education in the values of Zionist socialism. According to these values, the pioneer, the fighting farmer, was the cultural and educational ideal—the manifestation of the Jew willing to waive his personal comfort, well-being, desire for self-realization, and financial stability for the good of the country, the person willing to be a farmer or fighter in order to turn Palestine into a country where the Jewish nation might rehabilitate itself. The core values of this ideal were contentment with little, and personal sacrifice for the benefit of the community. The cultural expression of this ideal was to adopt the way of life of the Hebrew farmer in biblical times as opposed to the urban culture of Jews in the diaspora.

The educational manifestation of the Zionist ideal was the implementation of a curriculum designed by a group of teachers called The Teachers' Council for the JNF. The JNF (Jewish National Fund), a financial body established in 1904 to raise funds from Jews around the world for the purchase of land in Palestine, served as a symbol and an educational framework. The curriculum created by the JNF provided for the explicit transmission of nationalistic and cultural values. One of the stated aims of the teachers' council was "Education stressing

Zionist Socialism," defined as "Establishing new secular folklore and culture to replace the traditional (religious) Jewish culture." This aim was carried out through the creation of new versions of traditional celebrations and festivals in which agricultural elements were emphasized; through the renewal of the ancient agricultural festivals celebrated in biblical times; through the development of new festivals and memorial days associated with the Zionist movement; and through the production and dissemination of new children's songs, plays, games, and stories.

This curriculum was designed primarily for children from the fourth grade of primary school and up, as its developers thought that only older children would be able to comprehend the ideological messages of the JNF. However, the Association of Kindergarten Teachers wanted to implement the curriculum with younger children for two reasons, one organizational and one personal. The organizational reason relates to the struggle between the schoolteachers and the kindergarten teachers. Kindergarten teachers sought recognition of their independent status and to demonstrate that the kindergarten had an important role within the national education system. The second reason stems from the personality of Tova Haskin, who headed the Association of Kindergarten Teachers. She immigrated to Palestine at the end of World War I from Russia, where she had managed the first Hebrew kindergarten in Petersburg. She was ideologically committed to Zionist socialism. In Tel Aviv she managed a kindergarten which later became the pedagogical center for the implementation of the kindergarten curriculum. Intensely involved in the development of teaching methods and ideas, she encouraged other kindergarten teachers to become involved. She instructed kindergarten teachers in the afternoons and encouraged them to take the initiative.

Under the leadership of Tova Haskin, the kindergarten teachers took up the challenge of fitting the JNF curriculum to the capabilities and needs of young children. They also held regular discussions to clarify working methods in the kindergartens in general, which gave them the opportunity to apply personal initiative in the development of new kindergarten teaching methods and ideas.

A standard component of all the ceremonies and celebrations was the children's contribution to the JNF. The concept of the JNF was explained to the children by way of the notion of deficiency. The children were taught that when the people of Israel were scattered throughout the world they had no land, and just as it is possible to purchase things lacking in the home such as milk and bread, the JNF purchases the land which is lacking. The term *diaspora* was familiar to most children because, during that period, many of them had families abroad—in the diaspora. The JNF was personified as a man buying land. The children wove stories around these pictures and, in one example, described how one of the characters went to purchase land just as their parents would go to a store.

Children regularly contributed to the JNF by bringing a penny each week. This was deposited in a blue contribution box, which became the symbol of the JNF. The purpose was not primarily to collect money, however, but to teach children to give of themselves for national needs. The assumption was that when children become accustomed to contributing, it is easier to educate them later in pioneer values, which stress giving of oneself.

In the kindergartens the children learned to celebrate birthdays—a practice unknown in traditional Jewish culture. This personal celebration was also given a national touch: the child made a donation to the JNF and received a gift from that organization. When the practice was first instituted, the gift was a birthday greeting card. Eventually, the gift consisted of a pamphlet describing the season and festivals occurring during the Jewish month in which the child's birthday fell. In this manner the JNF's gift became an additional medium of ideological education.

Additional means for complying with the new cultural priority on educating children in the area of agriculture were the garden and outdoor excursions. Soil was used creatively in free play and gardening activities, which were part of the Zionist consensus and therefore emphasized even in urban kindergartens. It was one of the Froebelian principles which the Zionist kindergarten teachers adopted. However, in addition to all the reasons for gardening documented by Froebel, gardening also advanced Zionist aims: The garden served as a means for bringing children closer to agriculture and to nature in Palestine. Through these activities, kindergarten children were taught subjects connected to the seasons of the year, the produce of the land, and the life cycle of plants. In addition, local flora and fauna were permanent elements of the curriculum. Kindergarten teachers viewed outdoor excursions as educational in nationalistic terms and in terms of intellectual development. Children learned to observe, to understand processes in nature, to identify plants and animals, and to develop their senses of sight and smell and their imaginations.

Educating Parents

In addition to educating the children in the spirit of the new culture, the Hebrew kindergarten educated parents and thus contributed to the spread of the new Hebrew culture. In turn, this helped to establish a common, stable, and uniform basis for educating children in the kindergarten and in the home.

Kindergarten teachers believed that the education of young children required the full cooperation of parents and kindergarten teachers. Typically, parents were involved in their children's kindergarten education to a greater degree than they were involved in primary school activities, and their participation in the educational process was encouraged. In addition, for ideological education to be effective at this age, continuity and reinforcement had to be provided in the home. If parents did not repeat the songs and recitations or the fairy tales and stories their children heard in the kindergarten, the children would not recall and retain the material.

Involvement in the kindergarten also served the parents. Because the majority of parents were immigrants who were unfamiliar with the new culture and way of life, the kindergarten helped them become acclimated to their adopted society and enhanced their relationship with their children. Parents were invited to parent-teacher meetings before each holiday and celebration, where they received explanations of the holidays, their ideological messages, and the related songs, recitations, dances, and games. In addition, the kindergarten teachers handed out song books and taught the parents the songs. Many teachers noted that these meetings prepared parents for what to expect and how to behave at each celebration. This preparation was important because the kindergarten itself was an institution unfamiliar to most of these parents.

An additional aspect of parental participation was related to the blue JNF collection boxes. Parents were the ones who emptied the blue boxes and transferred the money to the JNF. This ceremonial role developed from a combination of psychological, pedagogic, and Zionist ideas. Kindergarten teachers claimed that the children expected somebody they knew to empty the box during a festive ceremony. Therefore, the idea of a JNF clerk coming to collect the money was dismissed. The kindergarten teachers recognized that this parental involvement was a suitable opportunity both to convey educational messages to the parents and to strengthen the bond with them. Another factor was the importance of the event for the child, who enjoyed great attention on the particular Friday when one parent arrived for the ceremony, emptied the box, counted the money, and took it in order to transfer it to the JNF. Parents also recognized the pride and happiness which filled their children during such an event, and willingly performed their part.

By recognizing the importance of parents' participation in the educational activities at the kindergarten, the Hebrew kindergarten became an important agent not only in the building of the new Hebrew children's culture but also in the dissemination of this culture among the wider public.

DEVELOPING NEW EDUCATIONAL AREAS
AND TEACHING METHODS

The development of the new cultural repertoire reflected the strong connection between early Hebrew education and Western education. This connection was expressed in the adoption of the Western cultural repertoire together with Western educational concepts and teaching methods. The Hebrew kindergarten was greatly influenced by the German Pestalozzi-Froebel Haus—the institution at which the first qualified kindergarten teachers in Palestine were trained. These teachers brought with them the spirit of the institution at which they had studied, its teaching methods, and its materials. Games, songs, dances, and other activities were translated from German into Hebrew and served as the kindergarten's educational base, together with Jewish and Zionist materials. The heritage of the German kindergarten was transmitted to later generations of kindergarten teachers after 1913 by these early teachers.

Over the years, the Hebrew kindergarten was influenced by other schools of thought, thanks to teachers educated in other countries, especially in Eastern Europe and Russia, who immigrated to Palestine and brought new methods with them. Teachers were also exposed to new knowledge and ideas in various courses taken overseas, often funded by Zionist organizations.

Influenced by these educational and psychological theories, teachers emphasized children's games and creative activities. The nature of activities such as handicrafts and painting was dictated by the reality of sparse funds and a lack of toys and suitable tools. According to Froebel and Montessori, the kindergarten teacher had to improvise. The combination of the belief in children's freedom to express themselves and the lack of funding fitted in well with accepted educational concepts and became a teaching method. Teachers used various easily obtained raw materials such as wood shavings from the local carpenter, old newspapers, magazines and paper from the printer, home-made glue from flour and scraps of materials.

Music and Physical Education

Musical education in the kindergarten consisted of songs, games accompanied by music, children's orchestras, music appreciation, rhythmic games, dances, and processions. Song was not only considered an excellent way to learn the Hebrew language but also to train the children to control their voices; therefore singing accompanied most kindergarten games. Musical games were used to develop memory, vision, hearing, and balance. Music appreciation lessons were designed to acquaint the children with light classical works suited to their age.

Musical education in the kindergarten was greatly influenced by the Montessori method. Montessori claimed that in order to develop the sense of hearing the kindergarten teacher should use whispering, silence, and give the children a musical education. The purpose was to teach the children to distinguish between sounds, and to awaken in them a sensitivity to rhythm and harmony.

The Dalcroze method, based upon the association of music and movement, was also enthusiastically adopted in the Hebrew kindergarten and became an important part of the kindergarten's activities. This theory served as the basis for rhythmic exercises and for the development of many games. In most kindergartens, music lessons were held five mornings a week for half an hour. The children played in the orchestra twice a week, played rhythmic games and danced twice a week, and once a week they had music appreciation. The repertoire of musical education was intended to contribute to the development of the Zionist child's identity as part of modern, Western culture. Physical education aimed at developing children's awareness of physical fitness. Traditional European Jewry, in contrast to the Helenistic culture, advocated nurturing the human spirit rather than the body. The Zionists believed that body and spirit are equally important; the slogan was "A healthy spirit in a healthy body." This attitude was naturally related to the image of the pioneer, strong in mind and body, who would be capable of building an independent country.

SUMMARY

The kindergarten as an educational concept reflected the clearly defined status of the child and the place of childhood in society and was accepted with great enthusiasm by the public. The new secular Jewish society which had begun to develop in Palestine adopted the concept of the kindergarten to replace the "heder"—the traditional Jewish educational establishment for pre-school children. The Hebrew kindergarten became a cultural initiator within which the new Hebrew children's culture was planned, implemented and spread in order to establish a modern Western society. The cultural uniqueness of this society would be expressed in the use of the Hebrew language and the values and contents of biblical culture transformed into a modern nation with a rural character.

Under the special conditions which existed prior to the establishment of the State of Israel, the Association of Kindergarten Teachers operated as the body which determined educational policies and designed the curriculum. The leaders of the Association were the agents who gave Zionist education its ideological character. The result was that the Hebrew Kindergarten adopted European education and teaching methods and also defined its cultural content. The new cultural system which developed exposed the children to European literature and music, along with adapted Jewish contents and new holidays celebrating the Zionist movement.

NOTES

1. Zionism is a Jewish national movement whose goal was the establishment of a homeland for Jews scattered throughout the diaspora.
2. Benedict Anderson, *Imagined Communities: Reflections on the Origin and Spread of Nationalism,* London, 1983.
3. Anthony D. Smith, *Nationalism in the Twentieth Century,* Oxford, 1979.
4. For more about the holidays, see Shoshana Sitton, "School festivals and ceremonies: Transmitting a new cultural code in Israeli schools," *Journal of Jewish Education,* 62 (3): 1996, 54–62.

Contributors

Ann Taylor Allen is professor of history at the University of Louisville and has served as coordinator of the Women's Studies Program.

Limin Bai is assistant professor in the Department of Asian Languages at Victoria University in Wellington, New Zealand.

Barbara Beatty is associate professor in the Department of Education at Wellesley College.

Kevin J. Brehony is a professor in the School of Education at the University of Reading, in Reading, England.

Margaret Clyde is an early childhood educator and director of Pythagoras Enterprises in Balwyn, Australia.

Benjamin C. Fortna is a lecturer in the history of the modern Middle East at the School of Oriental and African Studies, University of London.

Bogna Lorence-Kot is a professor in the humanities and sciences at the California College of Arts and Crafts, in Oakland, California.

Lisa Kirschenbaum is assistant professor in the Department of History at West Chester University, in West Chester, Pennsylvania.

Shoshana Sitton is a lecturer at the School of Cultural Studies at Tel Aviv University, in Israel.

Thaveeporn Vasavakul is a professor in the Department of Political and
   Social Change at the Australian National University in Canberra,
   Australia, and a researcher at the Council of International Educa-
   tion Exchange in Hanoi, Vietnam.

Adam Winiarz is a lecturer in the Department of Psychology and Pedagogy at the Marie Curie–Sklodowska University in Lublin, Poland.

Roberta Wollons is associate professor of history and director of the
   Women's Studies Program at Indiana University Northwest.

Index